NEW MEXICO
POLITICAL HISTORY
1967–2015

Trudie,

We have a good time together at Rock Steady Boxing. I hope you enjoy the book.

Jamie

NEW MEXICO
POLITICAL HISTORY
1967–2015

CONVERSATIONS WITH THOSE
DIRECTLY INVOLVED

JAMIE KOCH

SUNSTONE
PRESS

SANTA FE

Note: All information current as of the date of the publication of this book.

Sunstone books may be purchased for educational, business, or sales promotional use. For information please write: Special Markets Department, Sunstone Press, P.O. Box 2321, Santa Fe, New Mexico 87504-2321.

Book and cover design › Vicki Ahl
Body typeface › Goudy Old Style
Printed on acid-free paper
∞
eBook 978-1-61139-541-9

Library of Congress Cataloging-in-Publication Data

Names: Koch, Jamie, 1935- author.
Title: New Mexico political history, 1967-2015 : conversations with those directly involved / by Jamie Koch.
Description: Santa Fe : Sunstone Press, 2018.
Identifiers: LCCN 2017058480 (print) | LCCN 2017059184 (ebook) | ISBN 9781611395419 | ISBN 9781632932167 (softcover : alk. paper) | ISBN 9781632932174 (hardcover : alk. paper)
Subjects: LCSH: New Mexico--Politics and government--1951-
Classification: LCC F801.2 (ebook) | LCC F801.2 .K63 2018 (print) | DDC 978.9/053--dc23
LC record available at https://lccn.loc.gov/2017058480

WWW.SUNSTONEPRESS.COM
SUNSTONE PRESS / POST OFFICE BOX 2321 / SANTA FE, NM 87504-2321 /USA
(505) 988-4418 / ORDERS ONLY (800) 243-5644 / FAX (505) 988-1025

DEDICATION

I wish to dedicate this book to my loving wife Nene, to whom I have been married since 1959, the love of my life and my best friend. I couldn't have done this book (or much else) without you. Also, to Amy and Julie, my incredible daughters, and Eric, my son-in –law. You all make me so very proud to be your father and father-in-law.

CONTENTS

4 / 155

Carry the battle to them. Don't let them bring it to you. Put them on the defensive and don't ever apologize for anything.
—President Harry S. Truman

5 / 179

Intense feeling too often obscures the truth.
—President Harry S. Truman

6 / 227

Men make history and not the other way around. In periods where there is no leadership, society stands still. Progress occurs when courageous, skillful leaders seize the opportunity to change things for the better.
—Harry S. Truman

7 / 249

If you can't stand the heat, get out of the kitchen.
—Harry S. Truman

The buck stops here.
—Harry S. Truman

*A pessimist is one who makes difficulties of his opportunities and
an optimist is one who makes opportunities of his difficulties.*
—Harry S. Truman

I never gave anybody hell! I just told the truth and they thought it was hell.
—Harry S. Truman

PREFACE

It's amazing what you can accomplish if you do
not care who gets the credit.
—Harry S. Truman

A few years ago, I started gathering information about a number of different projects I had worked on throughout the years. I wanted to be able to document all of the efforts I have been involved in that meant something to me. I had always kind of shied away from the idea of writing memoirs; mostly because, I always felt like there was more to do. I wasn't ready to look backwards. Also because I'd read other people's memoirs and I would think, well, "It didn't exactly happen quite like that."

I still feel that there is a whole lot more to do. I was lucky to work with some pretty remarkable people and I gained a lot from those experiences. After eighty plus years, I realized I have learned a thing or two and I want to share these stories with you. So this volume isn't your traditional memoirs. This is not a recounting of what I, Jamie Koch, did. This is not a chronological history of my professional life.

Instead, I want to give credit to the people I have collaborated with over the years to get important things done in New Mexico. Some of these people worked with me on one project. Others were collaborators over the course of many years on several different projects. What follows is a collection of conversations with people that helped me bring about important changes in this beautiful state of New Mexico. This is a story of New Mexico political history from 1967 to 2015 through conversations with those directly involved. Some of these folks are well known names that you will know and recognize. Others are the unsung heroes that I am pleased to introduce you to.

As I mentioned before, accuracy is very important to me. I don't want you to take my word for it. I wanted to be sure that everything I share with you be backed up and validated by someone else that also can remember these important projects. So I decided the best way to share this history was by sitting down and talking with people. I really enjoyed listening to their memories of our times together. It felt like it was the right way to do this, because after all, relationships are really the key to getting things done. That's one of the themes in this book. You have got to build relationships by listening to people and addressing their needs and concerns.

Since anyone that knows me knows I love to visit with friends, I thought I better have a way to keep this project focused. I figured it would be helpful to have a standard set of questions that I used in each interview. So you will see that every time we sat down, I'd ask the person to tell a bit about him or herself. Then we would talk about the things we did together and finally we wrapped up the interview by talking about the future and what the person being interviewed thought would be necessary for the future. I wanted this forward-looking part of the interview because these people I interviewed are really smart people. They all have managed to move the needle on big ideas.

Between 2010 and 2016 according to the *Albuquerque Journal*, 37,780 more people left the state than moved in. Brian Sanderoff, President of Research and Polling, Inc., analyzed the census numbers for a recent *Albuquerque Journal* story published on Sunday January 29th, 2017. Sanderoff stated, "We've had steady and consistent growth in New Mexico since statehood, but from 2010 until 2016 we've been flat. Sanderoff said, "That is historic." So it is in this unfortunate stagnant context that I share these tales of the implementation of some big ideas. I am hoping by sharing these stories you, the reader, will be inspired in your own life to think big and achieve your own goals. I also hope these interviews offer a road map for getting things done in New Mexico.

I guess I am telling you it is worthwhile to listen to what these people have to say. The individuals interviewed in this book were all big picture people. They saw problems. But they didn't ignore the problems and they didn't complain about the problems. Instead they found ways to make things better and they quickly got down to business. Once they embarked on a project with me we didn't quit until we saw the desired outcome.

I have always admired President Harry Truman. I have a simple philosophy of life based in part on many of the sayings/practices of our former President Harry Truman, a man who inherited a job from the legend and made it his own. I want to impart some of his wisdom to you, the reader, so I have titled the chapters of this book as well as the over-all title of the book using President Truman's pithy sayings, which I compiled into a list that I refer to as my "philosophy for a life in public service."

For me, Truman was a great leader because he was a president that personally took the blame or got the praise for the failure or success of his policies. He did not blame events, which were out of his control, global market conditions, his advisors, his friends or his enemies, for in the end, it was his responsibility to improve the lives of Americans and he knew there were no excuses: only actions and reactions, only results.

I believe once we each take full responsibility for our own actions and for their results, we will always seek what is best; we will always stand up when we fail and we will always try our hardest. The title of this book is the flip side of that idea, i.e., often politicians are entirely too concerned with who will get the credit rather than focusing on what needs to be done. As you will see in the interviews, to get things done, the key is collaboration, give and take.

In this book I deliberately interviewed some people that didn't always agree with me. But we always shared a common desire to improve the lives of all New Mexicans. Together we were able to get a lot done for New Mexico. So, finally I am giving credit where credit is due. To that end, I started this book with a chapter about my father and my grandfather and their influence on my career.

In chapter one I explain how circumstances affecting our family's business led me to carry the Open Meetings Act when I was elected to the legislature. Shortly thereafter, another very important development was the creation of the Tort Claims and the creation of the Risk Management Division.

In the second chapter, I deal with my time in the legislature from 1968 to 1974. It was a very interesting time in New Mexico history and in US history. It was actually quite similar to the times we are currently going through. I discuss the rise of the Mama Lucy's and some of the massive fights I went through in the legislature to get bills passed. I admit I have often caused a ruckus. Autumn Gray wrote an article about me in 2010 in the *Albuquerque Journal*. She said, "Jamie Koch admits he's one public servant some people love to dislike. He's a scrappy competitor, both in sports and politics." It's true. The situation is when you're in politics; you've got to have a thick skin. I mean, I sleep every night. You're gonna make people upset, and when you make changes you're going to make people upset. I've introduced legislation that's made people very upset. But you grow used to that. When you're doing stuff, you're going to make some people very happy and some people will be mad.

In the third chapter the interviews focus on environmental stewardship: protecting the water, cleaning up the environment after toxic spills (Terrero Mine site cleanup), ensuring that gaming licenses were handled in an equitable and fair way and protecting Mountain Lions. In chapter three we also talk about the Game and Fish Commission and the establishment of the Office of the Natural Resources Trustee. In one interview we cover the Subdivision Act, which was probably the most controversial legislation I ever carried.

In chapter four, the interviews cover my transition from legislating to my involvement in the executive branch of New Mexican government by serving as the fundraising chair for two major gubernatorial races: Governor Bruce King's fundraising committee and Governor Bill Richardson's fundraising committee. In 1975 I was defeated in the legislature. By that time, I'd passed legislation that angered many different groups of people. At that point, I realized I could be much more impactful raising money for candidates than in the legislature. Plus Nene and I were raising Amy and Julie and the legislature is very hard on families.

In chapter five, I explore how oftentimes the things that we think are difficult are actually the experiences that mold us and shape us to be stronger and better. In this chapter I discuss the struggles I had growing up with dyslexia and how that affected my entire career, particularly as it relates to the founding of New Vistas Group Homes, the Success Center at the University of New Mexico and the establishment of Project SEARCH in New Mexico. I also cover the University of New Mexico Athletics Department and my efforts to engage the support of

14

Governor Richardson to get significant upgrades in place to support athletics and bring the University of New Mexico inline with the athletic programs available at other flagship universities.

In chapter six we talk about the creation of New Mexico Mutual Insurance Company, which happened when I (and others) had to confront a serious crisis affecting not just my livelihood, but also the entire insurance industry in New Mexico. Unlike every other endeavor discussed in this book, this was the one project I worked on where my professional life and my political life intersected. I discuss how I was acutely aware of the need to legislate changes to help avert a serious statewide economic crisis that was brewing if we did not reform workers compensation.

In chapter seven, I interview several people from my time serving as a member of the University of New Mexico Board of Regents. The interviews include former Regents, a former and current president, and former and current University of New Mexico Executive Staff. This chapter is dedicated to exploring how we were able to change the culture of the Regents and how important the new transparency was towards encouraging campus-wide participation on a broad range of issues. I unabashedly discuss some pretty sweeping changes I enacted when I became President of the Board of Regents in 2004. I also openly and candidly talk with Interim President, Chaouki Abdallah, about the vote of no confidence that happened in 2009.

In chapter eight, I interview more folks from the University of New Mexico including lobbyists and multiple key administrators from the main campus as well as have a discussion with Kim Murphy from the University of New Mexico Real Estate Office who was a key player in the land swap deals in which the university participated. These innovative land exchanges allowed us to ultimately build the University of New Mexico Sandoval Regional Medical Center and the University of New Mexico West Campus. In my interview with David Harris in this chapter, from 2003 to 2015, capital improvements in the amount of $1,092,069,902 were completed to support and strengthen the university. In this chapter I also interview Regis Pecos, former governor of Cochiti Pueblo, because Regis explains the return of over two hundred acres of land, Horn Mesa, which was returned in 2009 to Cochiti Pueblo. After centuries of getting the run-around from the state of New Mexico, the federal government and the University of New Mexico, the

Cochiti Pueblo finally got their land back. I've done a lot of things in my career, and returning that land was one of the most gratifying. What had happened to the Cochiti Pueblo was just wrong and I felt if there was a way I could correct that wrongdoing it was important and necessary to do whatever I could to ensure that their sacred land was returned.

In chapter nine, I interview several key members of the leadership team on the north campus of the University of New Mexico. We discuss the growth of the University of New Mexico Health Sciences Center in the last decade and the importance of creating the right system of governance for main campus and the Health Sciences Center to flourish. In this chapter, I discuss with the University of New Mexico Hospital CEO Steve McKernan the exciting opportunities that New Mexico has to be a nationwide leader in the "Knowledge Economy."

Finally, in the epilogue, I offer my own thoughts about the future after approximately sixty years of public service. I am very grateful to all the people that took the time to sit down and reminisce with me. This book encompasses thirty-nine actual interviews with people spending an average of one and a half hours each, and I also received letters from three additional contributors. This year I achieved fifty-eight years of perfect attendance at the Rotary Club. My dad also had fifty-eight years of perfect attendance. For more than a hundred and ten years, Rotary members have been addressing challenges around the world. Grassroots at the core, according to the Rotary website, Rotary links 1.2 million members to form an organization of international scope. Founded in 1905, the aim of Rotary was for professionals with diverse backgrounds to get together to exchange ideas, form meaningful, lifelong friendships, and give back to their communities. Rotary's name came from the group's early practice of rotating meetings among the offices of its members. In the epilogue I review the key lessons I learned over the years. It's been a lot of fun putting this book together. I hope you enjoy reading it and I hope it inspires you to get involved.

1

You can always amend a big plan, but you can never expand a little one.
I don't believe in little plans. I believe in plans big enough
to meet a situation which we can't foresee now.
—Harry S. Truman

No story about my insurance career and the projects I initiated as a public servant would be complete without first talking about my grandfather, Christian Adolph Koch (1873–1939), and my father, Ferdinand Adolph Koch (1898–1982). I think one of the reasons I was able to be successful was because I understood early on that there are no short cuts. If you are going to do something of value, chances are, it is going to take some time and you may have to take some risks. They both had an unbelievable work ethic. My grandfather came to New Mexico in 1912, the year of New Mexico's statehood. My grandfather had left Dunkirk, New York in the early 1880s to go west to Colorado to found a new laundry business in Pueblo, Colorado. Fred Harvey became aware of my grandfather and asked him to build a laundry for the new La Fonda Hotel Harvey which was opening in Santa Fe. When my grandfather finished building the laundry, Fred Harvey sold the business back to my grandfather and the Santa Fe Electric Laundry and Dry Cleaning was established in 1912. It was named the Santa Fe Electric Laundry and Dry Cleaning because all the machinery was run on electricity. Prior to that time, all laundry had been done manually. So my family was advertising the fact that the business utilized the most up-to-date technology.

Dad was born in Denver in 1898 and according to a short biography published in the *Santa Fe Mirror* in 1961, "he (Ferdinand) could remember driving a team of horses over the streets of Denver, collecting laundry bundles from the firm's smaller delivery vehicles, operating the shuttle service after school and during summer vacations. He delivered newspapers on foot, had a paying flock of laying hens and a constantly increasing hutch of rabbits. He also had the usual chores of splitting kindling wood, carrying out ashes, lugging in coal and doing sundry other jobs." All my life, people have talked about my energy and all that I can get done in a day. I just chuckle. For the most part, our lives today here in the United States are so much easier than what my parents and grandparents had to do to put in a day's work.

Dad was still in high school when the United States got involved in World War I. Dad enlisted right away and was made a part of the 5th Division and was shipped overseas to a combat role in France. When the war ended he was given the choice of training for a commission or taking his corporal's stripes and joining the Army of Occupation. He decided to join the Army of Occupation and he stayed on in Germany until 1919. When he returned home from the war he started working with my grandfather. He married my mother, Kathleen Long, in 1921. He went by the name "Ferd." My mom was the daughter of a prominent University of New Mexico biology professor and she put a lot of emphasis on education. Dad joined the Rotary Club, which had just been established in 1923.

Dad was instrumental in bringing skiing to Santa Fe. The Santa Fe Winter Sports Club elected my dad as the first president, and that was a position he held for many years. He thought skiing was a great sport and an important economic driver for Santa Fe. He loved skiing. As a result, we all grew up skiing quite a bit. Dad was very into sports. He played football, baseball, basketball, track and tennis. All of his passion for sports definitely got handed down to me! Heck, my parents even met at a track meet in 1914. They eventually married on October 1, 1921. I am the youngest of five boys and I was born in St. Vincent's hospital on June 4th, 1935.

As a little person, I was always in trouble. You know, very aggressive. I had four older brothers and played football all the time, as well as basketball, track, and field. I was very hyperactive. I think that's why I did so many sports. Schoolwork was very challenging. I have dyslexia which had an impact on my life and career. But, sports made me number one. In other words, if I hadn't had sports I think it would have affected my confidence. You know a lot of people look up to athletes and if you're the best, well, people look up to you. So sports is one way that I overcame dyslexia by participating in athletics.

I have continued being very athletic and physically fit throughout my adult life. When I was sixty years old I became aware of Senior Olympics. I found I could be competitive with the shot put and I practiced a lot. I built a shot put circle at home and I trained hard, and then winning the New Mexico Senior Olympics. At age sixty-five I won the National Senior Olympics. When I was sixty-nine, I won the World Games in Canada. I currently hold the Shot Put State record for competitor ages: sixty-five, seventy, and seventy-five. I've always believed that being physically fit helps you stay mentally sharp too.

I had a great childhood. I went to public schools and I had great friends. Santa Fe was a good place to grow up. In 1953 I got a full scholarship to Oklahoma State.

My dad was very close to the president of the University of New Mexico, Tom Popejoy. Pete McDavid was the athletic director. Pete had come to the University of New Mexico from Albuquerque High, and knew me from when I had played high school football against Albuquerque High, and thus he knew my ability. I transferred to the University of New Mexico and they gave me an athletic scholarship. I red-shirted the first year. The next year I played for Coach Chuck Clausen and the following two years for Coach Marv Levy.

While I was at the university, in 1957, I met a wonderful woman named Nene Ackerman. I sat in class behind her. One day I stole her books and a friend, Sam Pick, later introduced us at the University of New Mexico. Initially, she helped me with my homework if I had questions, but I knew quickly that I wanted to marry Nene. I am happy to say that she accepted my proposal and on August 22nd, 1959 my brother, Chris Koch, an Episcopal minister, married us in Albuquerque at St. Mark's Episcopal Church. One of the secrets to our long and happy marriage is that every Friday night we have "date night." Also, she is the kindest and most patient person I have ever met. We have two beautiful daughters: Amy and Julie. My daughter Julie has three children, so we have been blessed with three beautiful grandchildren. Just as my parents instilled a strong work ethic in me that was crucial for my professional advancement, my wife's presence in my life has been the bedrock of my success. She has been my most trusted advisor and my closest friend for the last sixty years.

After I graduated from the University of New Mexico in 1959, I went to work for my dad at the laundry. We had 120 employees and we were doing tons of laundry. At that time businesses like hotels didn't have their own laundries. The laundry got sent out. It was a really big, big business and I was there seven days a week in the summer.

I continued to work in the laundry for the next few years. In the mid 1960s there was a program that started up in Santa Fe called "Urban Renewal." The City of Santa Fe could go to the federal government to get funds to come in and renovate certain areas. The city councilors wanted to do an Urban Renewal project where the Hilton currently is. We owned the biggest parcel of land in the area where they were putting together the Urban Renewal. There was a group of different owners, but my dad had the most land. The City of Santa Fe knew all the rest of the owners would not go in on the deal unless my dad decided that he was going to accept the Urban Renewal.

The Urban Renewal people came to us, and the City came to us, and Jack Verhines with Scanlon Engineering talked to us. The organizers said they would come and give us an idea, in writing, potentially on how much we would get if we went with Urban Renewal and what the advantages would be, etc. So, my dad said "Okay." They came and told us that we would get close to $250,000. Plus they said we would be eligible for Small Business Administration (SBA) loans and discounts and additional incentives. When the information came, my dad looked at it. Dad, in addition to founding the laundry business, was also on the board of the New Mexico Building & Loan, which was a savings bank, so he was very strong financially. He studied the deal and he said he would agree to participate in the Urban Renewal project. He agreed to get bought out. So everybody went with the deal.

My dad hired Mack Resnick, a consultant on laundries, to do a market analysis and tell us whether there was enough business to support the size of the laundry dad wanted to build. He thought that there was enough business, so we built a huge laundry. Well, we hadn't gotten our final Urban Renewal offer yet, and dad asked me, because this is where I knew people, to check out how the deals had gone for the other Urban Renewal businesses that had joined the program. I went around and visited with everyone that had gone in on the deal. Most of them had gotten what the planners had said they were going to get.

Well, to make a long story short, we didn't get what they had estimated. Apparently, they decided that the ones that would take the big hit would be us, which we did. We didn't get the proposed $250,000. I think $150,000 is what they said they would do. We already had this big building being built back there on San Mateo. We already had been approved by SBA to have a loan to do that. Dad didn't agree on the $150,000 figure, so he hired an attorney. Our attorney thought we ought to have a jury. So, we got a jury. Jim Snead, my personal attorney, warned me that once we got a jury involved, we were going to have a problem. He was right.

In the end we got $95,000. And there was no way we could pay for the new building with $95,000. At that point, I took over the laundry. And I took over the liabilities. I decided that, first of all, I had to sell the business. We had this huge building and we had competition with a competitor. I went to the hospital and I gave them the cheapest price ever to do their laundry. So when prospective buyers walked into our laundry, we had bags and bags and bags of laundry to be washed—it was full.

I sold to a large commercial laundry in Albuquerque. I went to them and worked out a deal. I got them to agree to buy my business, but they were not going to buy the building or the equipment. I sold the building and I was able to sell all the equipment to laundries all across the country. Eventually, we broke even, but that's why we sold the laundry in 1972.

I will never know what happened on the Urban Renewal deal. The decisions had gone on behind closed doors. It was perfectly legal at that time. I was already in the legislature at that point, so I knew something had to be done legislatively to stop these closed door meetings. In 1974, I introduced HB 63, the Open Meetings Act. I also drafted the language for the Inspection of Public Records Act or "IPRA" but that didn't pass until 1978. The Open Meetings Act passed. In that legislative session, in 1974, there was a tremendous amount of resistance to the bill and it was greatly watered down by Franklin Jones, a legislative aide working in Governor King's office. According to an article which appeared on February 4, 1974 in the *Albuquerque Tribune*, "Representative James Koch, D-Santa Fe, was rudely awakened when Jones "butchered and weakened" his strong Open Meetings proposal. A pragmatist, Rep Koch decided that it would be wiser to try to re-strengthen his measure in the House rather than argue with Jones and the governor about the changes." Representative Don King, Governor King's brother and I sponsored the Open Meetings Act, HB 63. Even though this legislation passed in 1974, the Inspection of Public Records Act (IPRA) was not passed until 1978 and is on the books today. The importance of this law, for all New Mexicans, cannot be overstated. Openness and transparency are the cornerstones of a democratic society. During virtually every legislative session since these "sunshine laws" were passed there have been attempts to revise the legislation to create new exceptions to the law. As recent as March of 2016, the New Mexico Foundation for Open Government (FOG) put out a press release when a Court of Appeals ruled that committees appointed by public bodies must comply with the Open Meetings Acts, even when the meetings are closed due to the attorney-client privilege. The Court of Appeals held that the Security Investment Council had no authority to delegate settlement decisions to a litigation committee. In the release, Santa Fe attorney Daniel Yohalem, who represented FOG said, "The Open Meetings part of this decision is a great victory for transparency and for the people of New Mexico. The Court of Appeals has put a stop to a major ploy used by state boards and local governments to avoid taking action in the public's eye." I was very pleased to see this decision. The State Investment Council is not the first organization, nor will it be the last, to hold itself exempt from the Open Meetings Act. Safeguarding the Open Meetings Act and the Inspection of Public Records Act will be a very important task for the future.

When public bodies meet, how they conduct themselves and especially how they allocate taxpayer dollars, is of tremendous significance to all of us. The Open Meetings Act and the Inspection of Public Records Act, are the tools which allow citizens access to information that keep our public servants accountable to the public. Open Meetings Act requires public bodies to post their agendas at least seventy-two hours prior to the meeting, which guards against last minute official actions without public notice. The possibility for impropriety occurs when publicly elected officials or politically appointed officials think they can make decisions in a vacuum.

In 1974, I fought very hard and negotiated to ensure the passage of the Open Meetings Act. In 2004, thirty years later, I was awarded the William S. Dixon First Amendment Freedom Award from the New Mexico Foundation for Open Government. I was awarded it, not just for getting the laws passed initially, but also for my continued dedication to insuring the law was followed in countless public settings. I believe public officials can have a lasting effect long after they have left office because through their words and their actions they can remind us to adhere to the highest standards of conduct. The importance of keeping tabs on what public officials are up to is perhaps best summed up in Federalist Paper #51, where James Madison famously wrote,

> But what is government itself, but the greatest of all reflections on human nature? If men were angels, no government would be necessary. If angels were to govern men, neither external nor internal controls on government would be necessary. In framing a government which is to be administered by men over men, the great difficulty lies in this: you must first enable the government to control the governed; and in the next place oblige it to control itself.

An article by Autumn Gray appeared in the *Albuquerque Journal* on April 26, 2010 titled "One-on-One with Jamie Koch" which captures much of my life work as I express in the coming chapters of this book.

In 1974, after a lot of revisions and in-fighting, HB 63 made it to the governor's desk and was signed. The Open Records Act was passed in 1978 and tightened up some of the loopholes in the proposed bill from 1974. I knew the first bill wasn't perfect. But, I also valued the enormous leap forward we had taken to ensure that public bodies would be much more accountable to the public.

Kent Walz gives his thoughts below.

∾∾∾

Kent Walz, senior editor for the *Albuquerque Journal*

Kent Walz, Senior Editor for the *Albuquerque Journal*, at the time this book was published serves on the Board of the New Mexico Foundation for Open Government. I asked Kent if he would explain, from his perspective, the importance of the Open Meetings Act. Kent replied, "You cannot overstate the importance of the Open Meetings Act in New Mexico. It is a powerful tool to make sure government business is done in the open and not in the back room. I can't think of a stronger and more persistent advocate for open meetings and public records than Jamie Koch. His support and leadership on transparency issues has been of great value to New Mexicans. As we all know, this work isn't easy and ruffles powerful feathers, which never fazed Jamie one bit."

I was successful getting a lot of legislation passed in my life. I carried seventy bills that were chaptered into law. Over the course of my career, approximately forty-nine percent of the bills I introduced were passed. Compare that with the fact that according to the Sunlight Foundation, only four percent of bills in Congress become laws nationally. None of the bills I got passed would have passed without some sort of compromise in the final language of the bill. We had to be willing to listen to the other person's point of view.

So even though the Urban Renewal deal personally burned my family, I believe it's the best thing that ever happened to me. My family got the short end of the stick on that deal, but I saw a systemic problem and was able to work with others to create a long-term solution. That experience taught me that business and politics is a lot like athletics—you win and you lose. How do you come back after you lose? Do you give up? Or do you decide not to give up? So ultimately, even though it was rough and it was stressful for my family personally to sell the laundry business, it was actually a blessing in disguise.

When I got out of the laundry business, I didn't have a job. At that time I was in the legislature. I had already met some people before in my first term, when we were still in the laundry business. Anyway, I worked closely with Jack Daniels in the legislature and Jack Daniels was a good friend of Dave Norvell, Speaker of the House.

By 1972, I knew I was getting out of the laundry business and I had to figure out a new job. I asked Jack Daniels, (not knowing that I was going to work for Jack), about the insurance business. He said, "Why don't you go to work for me?" I said "Well, I don't want to move to Hobbs." He said, "No, why don't you work with me. We'll open an office in Santa Fe?" But he didn't offer me a job at that time. He wanted me to come down and meet with his nephew, Mike Tinley. I went to Hobbs and they offered me a job. I was in Hobbs for a full year learning the business. Then I opened the door of the Santa Fe office of Daniels Insurance Agency.

Jack Daniels and Mike Tinley are people I admire very much. There are certain people in your life that you know, by virtue of meeting them, that they changed the entire course and direction of your life. Jack Daniels and Mike Tinley were those people for me. Robert Daniels, the father of Jack Daniels, established Daniels Insurance in 1937. After World War II, Jack Daniels joined his dad in the business. After his dad died in 1948, Jack became president of the business and he continued until 1972. In 1972, Jack became chairman and Mike Tinley became president. In 1991, Tinley became vice-chairman and I became president. Daniels Insurance Agency is based out of Hobbs with branch offices in Santa Fe and Albuquerque. They represent approximately one hundred insurance carriers nationwide in the areas of commercial and personal property and casualty, workers compensation, life and group insurance. I could not have had two more formidable mentors than Jack and Mike.

Later in this book I will talk about revising workman's compensation and the founding of New Mexico Mutual Insurance Company. But, by the time those initiatives began I had already become quite successful as an insurance agent. In 1972, I didn't know anything about insurance but I studied hard and learned quickly. By 1982, less than ten years later, I was elected president of PACER out of three thousand agents for CNA Insurance. PACER stands for the Professional Agents Council for the Eastern Region and according to a Business Wire news release for the organization, "serves as the foundation for the global insurer's agency/ company relationship where agents' concerns are heard and addressed." First I was elected PACER panel chairman of New Mexico within the western region, later I was elected president of the Western Region. I ended up as the National PACER chairman. There were several times in my career as a public servant, and you will hear similar comments from others in this book, that I chose personally to lose business in order to avoid even the appearance of a conflict of interest. I always knew I could recoup those losses by developing other business opportunities elsewhere.

This issue of conflict of interest was in part dealt with at the state level by the passage of the Open Meetings Act in 1974 and Open Records Acts in 1978, but another very important development was the creation of the Tort Claims and the creation of the Risk Management division. Prior to July 1, 1976 you could not get a judgment against a public agency in the state of New Mexico, whether it was state or local. They could claim that they had immunity, because they did. Then the courts threw that out, and the legislature and the governor responded by passing the Tort Claims Act so that now you could get a judgment up to certain limits. Also, at that time, the way in which all insurance contracts were awarded was very political. Insurance contracts were not bid. There was no RFP system and the real losers were the various New Mexico political entities; the municipalities (cities and counties), schools and universities. On November 1, 2016 I sat down with Taylor Hendrickson, who really is the father of Risk Management for the state of New Mexico. He served as deputy director of Risk Management for twenty-three years.

Taylor Hendrickson / Interviewed November 1, 2016

Jamie: Tell me a little bit about your background, your total background in the insurance industry.

Taylor: I worked fifteen years for Hartford Insurance Company. I was in underwriting for a few years, then I went into marketing, and then I was promoted as a supervisor back into underwriting. Then, in my last job before I took the job with the state of New Mexico, I was the manager of the Property and Package Policies department for Hartford in Cincinnati, Ohio.

Jamie: What I knew was that you were a non-politician. You had a tremendous background in many types of insurance that would be valuable to be able to come in to set up the New Mexico Risk Management. We're very fortunate that you agreed for the state to hire you. I made sure that Governor Jerry Apodaca knew that the state would not be hiring some political person, because doing the risk management has to have a non-politician, and you never got involved in politics.

Taylor: I never did. In twenty-three years, I was never involved. Everybody knew that, and I never even contributed to a governor's campaign on either side of the fence, ever.

Jamie: They didn't have a Risk Management division, really. Am I correct, before you came?

Taylor: No, because it was just being set up when I came to New Mexico. So yeah, it was just brand new. See, what we did at first, not only worker's comp but everything else, also and we were just trying to audit everything to find out where everything was. On some of the property we found out that some of the smaller agencies didn't even have any coverage. We were also trying to get everything together so we could consolidate and get the best coverage we could for the lowest price.

Jamie: When Bruce (Governor King) got elected I went and told him all about what you had done with the Risk Management division. He made you in charge of it.

Taylor: Right.

Jamie: I advocated that on the worker's comp RFP it should say that you would negotiate with the top five carriers. Remember that? It was the top five carriers when you bid because you had all different kinds of parameters under the bids. So the Board ruled that it would deal only with the top five carriers. Could you explain what you found in your audit? Could you share what the problems were and stuff like that? Because you're really the "father" of the Risk Management, could you tell us what you found when you became the Risk Manager?

Taylor: When I first became the Risk Manager, the big emphasis was on liability insurance because the Tort Claims Act was brand new. And so actually, I had to immediately study all that. We had to have meetings with the state agencies, but also we had to have meetings with the local public bodies because this was new to them also. At the state for example, the state had not purchased what we call general liability insurance. They had purchased auto liability insurance and by doing that, they had basically waived their immunity on that, but on the general liability they proclaimed immunity saying that "nobody could collect from them." After the Tort Claims Act, as of the first of July in nineteen seventy-six now you could sue an agency and get a judgment up to a million fifty thousand dollars [$1,050,000] against these different agencies, so they all had to have coverage. So everybody was scrambling to get coverage. We were able to get coverage at that point but when Risk Management was put together they decided, and I think you were heavily involved in that, Jamie, they decided that they would bring all types of insurance in house, not just on liability, but all types of insurance.

Jamie: Everything.

Taylor: Liability, worker's compensation, property, bonds, all of the different coverages. Malpractice was added. They brought all of those coverages in house.

Jamie: Governor Jerry Apodaca started the Tort Claim but I believe it was during the first year of Governor Bruce King's administration when you started to develop an RFP system. Is that right?

Taylor: Yeah. We began asking for Request for Proposals (RFPs), to get proposals, and we put it out for bid, is basically what we did.

Jamie: That had not been done before?

Taylor: No. Agencies had pretty well just "done their own thing," or you got it together like worker's comp. You know that could be done but you may recall too, that we found out there was one agency that wasn't included somehow or another. Dick Cottrell.

Jamie: Keep going.

Taylor: Yeah, Dick Cottrell, we found out that he supposedly was insuring the Department of Labor for worker's comp but there was no policy. The company had no policy and so that was all turned over to attorney general, Toney Anaya.

Jamie: He was just taking the money?

Taylor: Cottrell was just taking the money. Anaya was the attorney general. Yeah, that was turned over to him, so that was resolved through the attorney general's office and the courts.

28

Jamie: Continue telling about your agency.

Taylor: Well, so anyway, initially our work was dedicated to finding out where everything was and getting it all consolidated, and then we would put out bids to cover all state agencies and universities in different areas. Eventually we went self-insured on a lot of things. As for the liability, we were insured for a while and we lost the coverage, as did most states because the market was really tight at that time. We self-insured the worker's comp, the liability. We insured the first million dollars of the property, as I recall.

Jamie: In other words, the whole thing we're talking about is why you were so important because it should have been self-insured, and you explained why it should have been self-insured.

Taylor: Well, we just felt with it self-insured and having some staff, we could get better control on the claims, and with us being a state agency and working with the other agencies, we felt we could get it somewhat more under control.

Jamie: Didn't you hire attorneys?

Taylor: Yeah, we hired attorneys, too.

Jamie: Explain all that.

Taylor: We had to bid that, too.

Jamie: Explain that we hadn't done that before in the past, had we?

Taylor: No. We hadn't.

Jamie: You explain that.

Taylor: We put out a bid for legal counsel.

Jamie: Before the bids for legal counsel, the hiring process was basically, "You're my friend. You get it."

Taylor: We had to create a board and our board was established to deal with that. We also had to have a Claims Committee. Now, I set up the Claims

Committee, and we always had at least the Claims Manager and two attorneys and myself as the director. We had the group health coverage, too. It's unusual. Most states do not put their group health coverage under the Risk Manager, but I liked it, so we had a group health plan.

Jamie: What was the size of Risk Management? How large was it?

Taylor: Well, of course it grew. It was just a small group of about half a dozen in the beginning, but by the time we went self-insured, on a lot of things we were up over thirty. We had around five attorneys on our own staff that handled cases, but couldn't handle all of them. We had five or six claims adjusters and we had insurance people, so over the years it got up to over thirty on staff.

Jamie: Why did we do all that? What was our reason for forming the Risk Management? In the past, it was not bid, but also, why did the governors want you to have a Risk Management department? Was the benefit to stabilize the cost or something?

Taylor: One thing, to make sure that everything was covered, because there were questions about some agencies, but also to get it all together because if you put things out on a blanket bid you can usually get a better price than just piecemeal. We created the new system to save money, basically.

Jamie: Who designed that system? You did, didn't you?

Taylor: Yeah because we gathered all the information. The new law required that we do it.

Jamie: That's right. I got the law changed. You had to do it, right?

Taylor: We had to do it.

Jamie: You had to develop an RFP, right?

Taylor: Right.

Jamie: And you required different entities to get bids. How often?

Taylor: I'm thinking that we usually would try to go out around four years.

I won't say that that was always the case but typically, it would be around four years.

Jamie: How long have you been the Risk Manager?

Taylor: Well, I was the director for twenty-three years. There were a few years there that I became the deputy. Governor Anaya wanted certain types of people, which he certainly had the right to, at the director's level. I was offered the job as deputy director and I stayed in that for several years. Then eventually at the very end, I went back to being the director.

Jamie: That's why I think it is so important for the running of Risk Management to be non-political.

Taylor: I will say this, that they had retirement with the National Risk Managers Meeting occasionally, and they had a retirement recognition for two of us because we were the only ones that had made it through Risk Management to retirement, because most of them were political and they got fired after a couple of years or something. They would get higher paying jobs in private industry. And so, like I said, out of thirty State Risk Managers, there were only two of us that made it to retirement.

Jamie: How many governors did you work under?

Taylor: I worked for five governors.

Jamie: You could see why the other governors recognized your ability. I mean, you wouldn't have been able to stay through that time, unless it was being run properly.

Taylor: When I was nominated for State Employee of the Year and didn't get it the first time, but did get it the second time, I was very pleased that I had letters of recommendation there from Governor King, (Democrat), and Gary Caruthers, (Republican). I was pleased at that.

Jamie: Did you help design some of the coverages?

Taylor: Oh, yeah, oh, yeah. I did. Particularly, when we got into local public body business. There for a long time we had little coverage for local public bodies because it said, "You may do it," and they were able to get coverage, and we didn't particularly want to get into that, but when everybody lost their coverage, just like that, we had to pick up cities, and counties, and school districts real quick if they came to us. I designed some policies very quickly.

Jamie: You see the situation, you can see why it was important that a person of your ability and non-political, was hired to do it because there's a lot of money involved. Did you get complaints from other independent agents against your department?

Taylor: Well, yeah. There would be some, but you know like when the real crisis came, we didn't really get much then because they had clients that they were desperate to get coverage for, and they were glad that we could get it. You know what? The law said that law enforcement and medical malpractice are mandatory. We had to do that—mandatory.

Jamie: Mandatory.

Taylor: But general liability and auto, we're only supposed to do that for what is available in the market. Actually, what I did, because I believed in the market, I actually pushed those entities to get back out with their insurance agents as quick as they could. We bent over backwards, and I think the agents appreciated that.

Jamie: That's why I asked you the question. Go on.

Taylor: We would get them back in the market just as quick as we could.

Jamie: Then you found out later on that it doesn't work. In other words, people weren't able to get back into the market again?

Taylor: No. Well, some of them got back in fairly soon, but some of them, we had a couple years before they could. Let me tell you another thing I did. The law enforcement was hard to deal with and we didn't have enough loss control people to really work that area.

Jamie: Can you explain what loss control's all about?

Taylor: Loss control is trying to prevent losses. Trying to go out and educate and tell police, "You got to be careful in your job." Some meetings I would tell law enforcement, "There's ten or fifteen percent of you that shouldn't even be law enforcement officers. You may know who you are." I didn't mind telling them.

Jamie: That's right. What do you think the important thing is in regards to the Risk Management in the future?

Taylor: Well, I'm glad that they have a board and also, there's a Group Health Committee that's separate, too. I'm glad for that and I hope they still have a Claims Committee because I think that's very important. I hope they still have that. That wasn't required. That's one of the best things because you get different ideas, and you have legal people there, but you have administrative people like the director and the deputy director and your claims manager. We didn't always agree, but that's a good thing. You talk about it, the claims and everything, and then you come to a decision on what you need to do. Sometimes it was, "Wait, we're not ready. Go back and let's look this thing over again." See, we'd always have, at least in the liability areas, we would always have at least three hundred fifty lawsuits going any day. They would ask for millions and millions and millions. You'd get rid of one or two and another new one would come along. Of course the agencies we were working with would try to prevent lawsuits, but in an organization as big as the state and the universities, you're just going to have them.

Jamie: Due to the state going self-insured on their worker's compensation, Daniels Insurance lost all of this insurance business, which was a substantial loss of income.

Taylor: You shot yourself in the foot.

Jamie: You know, it was right. It was the right thing to do.

Taylor: It was good for the state of New Mexico.

2

If you can't convince them, confuse them.
—President Harry S. Truman

In this chapter, I will discuss my time in the New Mexico legislature from 1968 to 1974. I will also get into some of the key initiatives of my career that happened as a result of connections I made while I was in the legislature. I will introduce you to people that I met during that time. The individuals I interviewed for this chapter became good friends and life-long collaborators and I wish to give them credit where credit is due.

I got elected to the legislature in 1968. I won the Santa Fe seat vacated by Bruce King when King ran for governor. My time in the legislature was a very interesting moment in New Mexico history. In the late 1960s the New Mexico legislature was pondering major constitutional changes. Following a legislative report, which came out in 1967, it became clear it was necessary to revise language that had been on the books since the 1930s. According to the New Mexico Legislative Council Service, "The 1967 legislature proposed a call of a constitutional convention to rewrite the constitution in 1967." About that same time, I decide to run for the legislature. Jim Snead was my campaign manager. Jim and I worked on many issues together over the years but our journey started in college at the University of New Mexico. Later, he managed my campaign for the legislature. In addition to being my personal attorney for the last 50 years, he has also been a very close friend for the last sixty years.

Jim and I sat down on November 15, 2016 to talk about the different projects we have worked on together. As I did with everyone I sat down with, I asked Jim to start by sharing a little bit about his life and I also asked him to talk about how we met.

Jim Snead, my personal attorney, campaign manager for my bid for legislation, legal counsel for New Mexico Mutual Casualty Company (NMMCC) for several years and served on Governor Bruce King's cabinet / Interviewed November 15, 2016

Jamie: How long have we known each other?

Jim: Well, you, Nene, Georgia and I have been friends for about fifty years, and we continue with our friendship, but you and I have known each other since we attended the University of New Mexico in the late nineteen fifties. In college we were not well acquainted. In fact the only recollection I have of you during that time was when I dated the girlfriend of your roommate, Mason Rose. You and Mason were in the Kappa Sig fraternity and I was a Sigma Chi. The Kappa Sigs were known for being trouble makers and the Sigma Chi's had very little to do with them. Mason Rose was a tough guy, with a physique like Joe Palooka. Someway I persuaded his girlfriend, nicknamed "Boo Fink" to go to a Sigma Chi beer bust. Mason took offense, and I spent about six months dodging him.

When I graduated from the University of New Mexico I went to George Washington University Law School, and was away from New Mexico for about three and a half years. During that time I married my college sweetheart, Georgia Phillips who was from Las Vegas, New Mexico. We met, then became "pinned," then got engaged while we were students at the University of New Mexico. Since we had both grown up in New Mexico we wanted to return to the state when I graduated from Law School in the winter of nineteen sixty-three. I got a job as a state assistant attorney general. The office was located in Santa Fe, so we moved to Santa Fe.

Jim: You and Nene were already living in Santa Fe, where you grew up.

Jamie: Yes, I was still working with my dad in the Santa Fe Electric Laundry.

Jim: Working as an assistant attorney general for the state of New Mexico brought me into close contact with state politics. About a year after Georgia and I arrived, our good friends Jerry and Mary Carole Wertheim moved across the street from us. Jerry had graduated from Georgetown Law School. He and I had been fraternity brothers at the University of New Mexico, and Mary Carole was a sorority sister of Georgia's. Not long after Jerry and Mary Carole arrived, we started getting active in local Democratic politics. You were also active. I think you had been raised as a Republican.

Jamie: That's right, but that party in Santa Fe did not suit me so I changed early on.

Jim: We started supporting candidates that we liked, and very rapidly found out that the county machine was corrupt. We decided to "clean up" the Democratic Party in Santa Fe. We became known as the "Young Turks." We would go to the party meetings and challenge the old leaders, such as former state Attorney General Fred Stanley, County Democratic Chairman Dicky "Chicken" Montoya and several of the Gonzales brothers. There were at least three lawyers in the "Young Turks": Jerry, Tom Donnelly and me. You and Nene, Jay and Janet Miller, Austin and Judy Basham and others rounded out the group. We called ourselves the "Chicken Hawks" in honor of our goal to unseat Dicky Montoya. We succeeded in that project, and that probably was the beginning of your rise as a power in the Democratic Party.

Jamie: Weren't we also involved in the Jaycees at that time?

Jim: That's right. At the same time you and I were actively involved in the Jaycees. The Jaycees were at that time a very active social service organization in New Mexico and nationwide. That enlarged our acquaintance of socially active men throughout the state of New Mexico. During our time the New Mexico Jaycees were number one in the nation two times, first under the leadership of Jerry Geist and then Jim Hill. I was state legal counsel for the organization both times.

Jamie: Could you talk a little about the Game and Fish stuff we did?

Jim: You and I were also active in what had been known as the Game Protection Association when we were growing up. By the time we settled in Santa Fe the name had changed to the New Mexico Wildlife Conservation Association. Georgia's great uncle, Elliott Barker, was "Mr. Conservation" in New Mexico and nationwide, and you were adopted by Elliott to help him in his projects. The result of that was the two of you drafted me into the organization. That organization eventually became the New Mexico Wildlife Association so as to conform its name to the National Wildlife Association.

I became president of the Santa Fe Chapter, and eventually was elected to the board of the State Association. You were very active in that organization.

Jamie: You helped me get my ducks in a row to run for the State House of Representatives didn't you?

Jim: Yes I did. At that time, you formed a local group of men and women for that project. I remember Jerry and Mary Carole Wertheim, Georgia and me, Clancy Rehorn, Sam Pick, Herman Weisenteimer, Austin and Judy Basham and several other Santa Fe residents were involved. I was the "erstwhile" campaign chair. I say "erstwhile" because, as always, you really were the leader and the chief motivator. We knocked on a lot of doors, and recruited our spouses and kids for the effort. The effort was successful because you became a member of the state legislature. You were very productive, although you served only a short time.

Jamie: Do you remember any of the bills I got passed?

Jim: You carried the legislation to start a kindergarten program in the public education system. I remember that.

You also created the New Mexico Environmental Agency, and passed a statewide Land Subdivision Act. You got Governor King to name me as the first chairman of the Environmental Improvement Board. We adopted the first Air Quality Improvement Act for the state that complied with the Federal Air Quality Act. You were a very successful legislator but your very success helped to cut your career short. You were the primary mover and shaker in the passing of the Open Meetings Act, the Land Subdivision Act and the Environmental Improvement Act. You stepped on the toes of quite a number of people and the result was that in the next go round you had a primary with several opponents: Chuck Atwell for the realtors, Greg Salinas for the school board, Julian Grace and another independent candidate. The independent got 40 votes, and that was the exact margin by which you lost the primary. Julian won the seat. His term was short, as well, because Frank Bond beat him, and I think you helped Frank Bond. Frank Bond ran for governor and Max Coll ran for his seat. Max ran as a Republican. I think you later were involved in getting Max to become a Democrat. Right?

Jamie: Yes I was involved. There are a lot of apocryphal versions of how that happened and we will discuss that famous party switch later in this book.

Jim: Max went on to serve many years and became a powerhouse in the legislature because he developed a reputation for integrity and a great deal of knowledge on state finances. You turned your considerable energy to helping others get elected, and I served on several of the gubernatorial campaign finance committees you chaired, particularly to help Bruce King to get re-elected.

You persuaded Governor King to name me as chairman of The Board of Regents of the Museum of New Mexico. That board controlled all of the Santa Fe State Museums, (as well as all State Monuments) and selected the director of those Museums. The Museums were having trouble with the legislature. The Board of Regents had gotten into a fight with the powerful chairman of the House Appropriations and Finance Committee, John Mershon, over creating an Indian Arts Museum, and with another powerful state Senator Martinez, who wanted the Museum to give him patronage over several jobs in the museum system so that Sen. Martinez could put his constituents into those jobs. The museum refused to do that. The result was that the legislature was threatening to abolish the budget for the whole museum system, and they had tasked the Legislative Finance Committee to find cause for doing just that. It was a mess, and Governor King asked me to do my best to straighten it out. The museum system also needed to hire a director. George Ewing had been the director, but when the Office of Cultural Affairs was created under Governor Apodaca's administration, George became Secretary of Cultural Affairs and was occupying both that position and the position of the director of the museum system. George was good at his job, and very good to work with, but doing both jobs was just too much.

Because you were so strong, and had a very good relationship with Governor King, I was able to get a free hand in my efforts to solve those problems. I had a devil of a time finding out just what was bothering John Mershon, but eventually I found out that he wanted to locate the new museum up on Museum Hill, and the Regents, led by my predecessor, Peach Mayer, had refused to listen to him. They were going to locate that museum in downtown Santa Fe. The result was that the funding for the project was held up in Mershon's committee, and Sen. Martinez was about to get the entire budget abolished. I made friends with the analyst assigned to the museum from the Legislative Finance Committee, Bobbie Gallegos, and we managed to round up the funds and to get some independent financial advice to straighten out the budget. We established a well-balanced search committee to recommend a new director for the museum system. That took some time, but the result was good—temporarily—because we were able to reorganize the entire state museum system and to get the Legislature off our back. We finally got the funds to build the Indian Museum after we concurred that it would be built on Museum Hill. The downside was that it took so much time that Governor King's term ran out and Governor Anaya was elected to replace him. The whole political system got turned on its head. I was fired from the Board of Regents and Governor Anaya started a campaign against the new director. Cleta Downey, who replaced me as chair, was a strong and loyal individual. The director we had hired left, but the board hired a new strong director, Tom Livesay, who served for an unbelievable fourteen-year term.

I got a lot of satisfaction, and hard work, out of handling problem agencies and commissions.

Jamie: And you were darn good at that work. I kept stumbling on situations, and I would think to myself, "I know just the guy that can fix that problem."

Jim: Well, that definitely seemed to be my lot as far as the state of New Mexico was concerned, and you got me appointed to a leadership position in many troubled state agencies and commissions.

The next one was the State Commission on Higher Education. The chair of the commission, Bob Taylor from Silver City, was an academic, and he had gotten crosswise with both the Executive and Legislative branches of state government. The commission had hired an out-of-state academic to run the commission, and she had no clue about New Mexico politics, and her staff was dysfunctional. The job of the Commission was to recommend a budget for state institutions of higher education. The executive branch recommended a budget, and the Legislative Finance Commission recommended a budget. The commission was supposed to be an independent agent to give the legislature straight facts on what funding was necessary.

At the time I was appointed, neither the executive nor the LFC paid any attention to recommendations of the commission. Based on your urging, Governor King asked me to take the chairmanship of the commission and see what could be done to get it functional. Since I replaced Bob Taylor, his input was no longer a problem. The next thing I did was to ask the executive director to resign. That was difficult. She was professional and a single woman making her way in a very difficult situation, but she just did not have the skill set that I believed was needed. Perry Toles, from Roswell, was vice-chair, and John Davidson from Raton was a member, and very engaged in the work of the commission. We needed someone on the Commission who had strong credentials in Finance, and we had a vacancy. I persuaded Governor King to appoint Irvin Diamond, a CPA with the accounting firm of Rogof, Diamond and Walker to fill that position.

Governor King was remarkably cooperative. I could meet with him if I needed to, and from time to time I would give him notes about something we were doing that he needed to know about. He actually read the notes and kept them as I found out later in the process. Again, your efforts made the job a lot easier than it otherwise would have been. It also helped greatly that Kay Marr was Secretary of Finance and Administration for the King administration. Kay and I had known each other since the sixth grade in Hobbs. She was a straight shooter and helpful in keeping me out of mine fields in the finance arena in both the museum position and the Commission on Higher Education. She was a very hard worker and didn't beat around the bush. That was a refreshing contrast from some of the politicians I dealt with who either would not give me a straight answer to a question, or told me that while I was right, they would be against my position because it would cost them votes.

This epistle is about you, Jamie Koch, not me, so I will just say that I spent six and a half years as the chairman of the Commission of Higher Education. When I left, the new director, Bruce Hamlett, had been executive director for several years, the staff was straightened out and doing a fine job, and the commission was established as the "go to" agency for accurate and honest information relating to higher education financing. Governor Richardson later abolished the commission. I have since had some staffers and higher education people tell me that the six and a half years of my term is referred to as the "golden years" of the CHE. Maybe it was, maybe not.

Jamie: Could you talk about the creation of New Mexico Mutual?

Jim: My next and ultimately last job with you was the creation of New Mexico Mutual Casualty Company. It was a state created quasi-public worker's compensation company. A task force created it, led by you, to solve a critical economic situation in the state. At that time, it was becoming impossible for small employers to get worker's compensation insurance at an affordable premium. I did not have anything to do with the law, but you had the taskforce hire my law firm, led by me, to create the company, handle the financing process and to be outside general counsel for the company once it was in business. It was a tremendous undertaking. Manuel Rodriguez, one of my law partners, and I did all of the legal work. You were the key in getting it all set up. The state financial officer, Phil Archibeque thought it was a bad idea and he opposed any funding despite the fact that law mandated it. When Archibeque would get hard to deal with, you would call a meeting in the governor's office, attended by the governor, to get us off of high center. One memorable meeting included the governor having to take a bathroom break. You followed him right into the bathroom, and when you both came out, the deal was sealed. Once the company was up and running and making lots of money, Phil made speeches from time to time declaring that he was responsible for its success. Who cares? It was a success.

I was outside general counsel for many years through many issues and problems, as well as successes. I resigned my association in around the year twenty-twelve when the company was doing very well, had its own in-house general counsel and I felt that it was time to move on.

Jamie: Could you touch on our time in Rotary Club together?

Jim: You were a very active member of the Santa Fe Rotary Club. You served a term as president. You felt strongly that I should be a member, but at that time the rules limited membership to males, and one member for each profession or business category. Billy Gilbert was the lawyer member, so that ruled me out. You were not the kind to give up, so when the opportunity arose to create sub categories we established the category of "intellectual property attorney." I was admitted shortly thereafter. I was indeed an "intellectual property attorney" since I had been a patent examiner, and included "intellectual property" in my law practice. That has generated some rye comments like: "intellectual" and "attorney" is an oxymoron. I have been a member of the Santa Fe Downtown Rotary Club since nineteen seventy-eight, and am happy to report that women have been admitted for many years. We have gone from "The Young Turks" in the nineteen sixties to the "Old Timers" now. If someone learns nothing else from this book, I hope they will understand that you have often stepped up to the plate and taken on a leadership role. I love the title of this book, because it's true: you really did not care who got credit as long as the job was done. The state of New Mexico has profited immensely by your efforts. Some appreciated those efforts and some took credit for what you did for them. It has been quite a run.

So you can see how Jim and I met in college, developed a friendship and we worked hard together to find solutions on many issues over the years.

But, let's go back to 1968 when the people approved the call for a constitutional convention. In November 1969, a completely new constitution was presented to the people for ratification. The new constitution was defeated statewide with a very low margin of defeat. Because the new constitution didn't pass but nearly did, in the early 1970s there was widespread recognition of the need for a broad revision of the existing constitution and it was accomplished through piecemeal amendments.

We got a lot done because of important coalitions that were formed that allowed us to push legislation through. *The Santa Fe New Mexican* reported in 1970 in an article entitled, "Koch Theatrics Aided Martinez" that I played a "pretty important role" in Speaker Walter Martinez' victory. Jack Sitton, the author wrote, "State politicos are still trying to assess the significance of Representative Walter Martinez' victory over Representative George Fettinger here last Friday for the speakership of the New Mexico House of Representatives." Walter Martinez succeeded David Norvell as Speaker of the House.

I want to tell you the story of what happened with Fettinger and Martinez.

Fettinger was going to run for Speaker of the House. I met with Walter Martinez at the Albuquerque Airport. We had coffee at the airport because he was going somewhere. Anyway, I made a proposition to him. I said, "Walter, here's the deal I'll make. If you get all the Hispanics to vote for you, I will get the votes from the progressive democrats with the help of David Salman, Gene Chianelli, Eddie Lopez and Bill O'Donnell, since they are already committed to you. Then you'd be elected Speaker." He decided he would run. So we had our democratic caucus to choose the leadership, and we're all sitting in the caucus and everything's by secret ballot, okay? The vote was counted and it was a tie vote. Sitting on my right was Cecil Cook, on my left John Tomlin. George Fettinger and Walter Martinez got up to leave the room to negotiate a deal. I knew I would really get it in the shorts, so I quickly jumped up, walked over and pulled George Fettinger aside and said "I have a vote change." But really nobody had changed his vote.

So, we re-voted. A number of people, including Cecil Cook and John Tomlin showed me their vote was for Walter. So now, who won the Speakership? Walter Martinez. That was the beginning of the group of legislators that would become known as the Mama Lucy's. The Mama Lucy's hadn't been formed yet. Mama Lucy's didn't get formed until after that first year with Walter Martinez as Speaker. But what did we do? We elected David Salman as the Majority Leader; Bill O'Donnell as Chairman of Appropriations and I became Chairman of Natural Resources. What we did is we created a situation where we were the ones in power.

In the Senate I became very good friends with Aubrey Dunn. When I introduced the first bill on the subdivision, it really created a lot of tension, so I said we needed to appoint a committee of legislators and non-legislators to meet, and we did over at Pendaries. We sat down for four days and worked out the language to get the subdivision passed. Many people don't do that any more—they just go ahead and they write the bill the way they want it and then they get into committee and then it gets tabled or they get into trouble. They get into hot water because now all of a sudden people are coming in and testifying against the bill in committee, because they didn't take the time to work with the other side when they were drafting their bill. Another bill that created a task force to draft legislation was for the workers' comp reform.

Marty Chavez introduced the worker's compensation reform legislation. What I admire about Marty Chavez is that he was a plaintiff workers' comp attorney, okay? He made his living on going after insurance companies for benefits. In the 1990s in New Mexico, workers comp was called the assigned risk pool and businesses were really having a hard time. So, Marty formed, after my suggestion to Speaker Raymond Sanchez, a subcommittee to work out the language for the worker's comp reform. Marty Chavez is the one that pushed it. We had labor unions there; we had business on there; and only one insurance guy was there and that person was me. No other attorney was there—just Marty. The task force many times that summer to discuss the proposed legislation.

In our discussions we came to an important decision that tells you something about Marty Chavez. Everybody was saying that there's got to be a limit that the attorneys can get on workers' comp. And so, we put into writing in the law that the most an attorney could get, plaintiff and defense, was $10,000. Now here's Marty Chavez, who makes his living on workers' comp and he does that. You know, stop and think. In other words, he knew what the situation was and he did that. That's why I've always had a special respect for Marty Chavez. I'll never forget because he gave up his business really to get that law passed. He sacrificed his own personal gain for what was good for New Mexico. So when a committee sits down and works together, that's the way it should be.

One person that I got to know from the Constitutional Convention in 1969 was former Speaker of the House, Raymond Sanchez. I sat down with Raymond on November 29, 2016 to discuss our nearly fifty years of friendship and his vast experience with the New Mexico legislature. I worked with him on many pieces of legislation. He ultimately became the longest serving Speaker of the House of Representatives in New Mexico serving sixteen years.

≈≈≈

Raymond Sanchez, speaker of the House of Representatives, a University of New Mexico Regent / Interviewed November 29, 2016

Raymond: I'm the son of Gil and Priscilla Sanchez from Belen, New Mexico. My father and my mother were instrumental in setting certain boundaries and creating an atmosphere within our family that never used the word hate. We were never taught to discriminate against anybody. We were never told that people, because of the color of their skin, didn't belong in our restaurant. We were brought up understanding something very simple: that the people who worked for us needed to be treated with dignity and respect. The people working for us were the ones that were putting us through school and helping us put clothes on our backs, bicycles to ride, cars to own later, and the money to go to college, and so we were always taught to respect those people who provided services to others.

So, my dad was very involved in politics. He served on the school board in Belen for, I think, forty some years, forty-two years. He was on the city council in Belen for probably fifteen years. He was the first elected magistrate when these guys changed the law back in nineteen sixty-nine, when they changed it from JPs to magistrates.

Jamie: Got rid of the JPs?

Raymond: Yes, and he was among the first elected magistrates, and he served in that position for another thirty years. That's who I am.

Jamie: Tell us about, Raymond, when you got in the Constitutional Convention, tell how all that worked.

Raymond: Well, I'd gone to law school at the University of New Mexico, gone to undergraduate and law school, both. I got married, just before I started law school, to a young lady who was interested in horses, and this has something to do with this, and when I graduated from law school, we had one son, and she was determined that she was going to train horses and she was going to train kids how to ride horses, so she went out looking for a place to live in the North Valley of Albuquerque. And she saw a sign on Rio Grande Boulevard, house for sale, owner. So she pulled into the driveway and she met this older couple. They were Swedes, just the nicest people in the world, and they fell in love with her. And so she calls me a couple days later and said, "I think I found a house." I said, "Really?" I was just out of law school. I was working under a Ford Foundation grant at the time. And she said, "Yep, on Rio Grande Boulevard where the Sims live." I said, "How much do they want for this property?" She paused for a minute and she says, "Twenty thousand dollars." For a house, two acres and a barn.

Jamie: Jesus, twenty thousand dollars for two acres?

Raymond: And I said, "Really?" I said, "Okay, how much do they want down?" Well, they want to finance it and I said, "Okay". So, I called a woman I knew, John Salazar's sister, who headed up one of the credit unions here in town. And I said, "Look, I want to buy a house." She says, "Okay, you're out of law school, where do you work?" I said, "For Ford Foundation." "What are you making?" I was making about forty thousand a year. And so they gave me credit, two and a half percent interest, and we bought the house.

So all of a sudden, the Constitutional Convention came along and my neighbor, a guy by the name of Alfredo Garcia, and his wife were both very active in politics. I was new to the North Valley, but he adopted me. I was in the middle of this Garcia clan. They owned the land all around me, all the Garcias, and I was stuck in the middle there. Not stuck. It was a great place to be. And they decided that maybe I should run for the Constitutional Convention. I said, "You know, I'm not interested," but they convinced me. So, there were about five of us in the race, nonpartisan, and I won.

Not by a whole lot of votes, but I won. And, served in that Constitutional Convention. It was the summer of nineteen sixty-nine.

Jamie: We haven't had a Constitutional Convention since then.

Raymond: No, we haven't.

Jamie: And that was under Governor Jerry Apodaca. He's the one that pushed that, the Constitutional Convention. It was his reorganization of state government. That was done when Bruce King was Speaker of the House.

Raymond: Right, Bruce King was Speaker of the House. Then the legislature authorized the convention for the summer of sixty-nine and we had no staff, because Clay Buchanan, who was head of the Legislative Council Service, was not real excited about the Constitutional Convention, or even staffing it, but he had to. So, we're there in the summer of sixty-nine and I went up there, there was a group of us, a lot of us Hispanics were elected, and Max Coll was actually a member of that Constitutional Convention.

Jamie: And he was a Republican and was in the legislature.

Raymond: He was conservative. The guy was a conservative, oil and gas family. Filo Sedillo decides he's going to run against Bruce King for president of the Constitutional Convention. He was the county chairman from Valencia County, the second strongest democrat stronghold in the state of New Mexico. Rio Arriba, Valencia and Santa Fe, were the three strongest democratic strongholds, and by strong, I mean amazing. So, Filo got us together and he said, "Look, we have got to hang together. I don't think I can win it, but at least we'll be able to pressure Bruce into recognizing the Hispanics and giving us good committee assignments, and we can force that and we can also stop merit selection of judges." He was absolutely against merit selection of judges. And there was a contingent, a former supreme court justice, who was adamant that we get merit selection on judges. That didn't happen.

Jamie: Weren't you chairman of one of the committees?

Raymond: Yeah, I was named chairman of Local Government Committee.

Jamie: Remember, you were a pretty young freshman at this time.

Raymond: I was twenty-seven years old. I was elected. We had a good run at it. I got a lot of publicity, good publicity, but the Constitution was defeated because we put some provisions in there to do away with some of the elected positions and made them appointed. You know, people didn't like that. They wanted to vote for everybody, and that was a problem.

When I came home, all of a sudden Bob Murray comes to me one day and he says, "Look, I'm not gonna run again, but I'm not telling anybody. Why don't you run?" and I said, "I'm really not interested." And I get a phone call from David Salman, who I happened to have met because the group I worked for was setting up businesses throughout rural New Mexico, especially in northern New Mexico. I was setting up co-ops under the auspices of a group called Home Education Livelihood Program which had the grant from Ford Foundation.

So, anyway after the Constitutional Convention he called me and he said, "Look, you really need to run for the legislature." I said, "I don't know." He says, "Well, we're planning something." I said, "Well, what are you planning?" He says, "Well, I think we're gonna be able to elect the next speaker, would you please run?" I said, "Well, I'm not committing to anything because I don't know that I can get elected, but yeah, I'll run." So, I ran.

Jamie: You won.

Raymond: And I won, barely, because I didn't campaign.

Jamie: When I heard about you it was from Bruce King and he told us how good you were. I think the first time I met you, you were in the Constitutional Convention, not a long visit, but that was the first time I met you. And the situation we had there, as I told you, is that Dave Norvell was running for the Speaker of the House when I went in and before he was elected, we had all a bunch of freshman, the biggest class of freshman, I guess ever. And we all went: David Salman, Eddie Lopez, myself, Gene Chianelli. We all sat down with Dave Norvell, and I said, "Dave, we'll make a deal with you. Because George Fettinger wanted to be Speaker, we'd make a deal. You put us on finance and taxation and we'll give you the votes" and that's how Norvell got elected.

When you got elected, what were some of the first things you did in helping organize the Mama Lucy's?

48

Raymond: Well, you know we didn't really, it wasn't quite like that. It was, you know before we got there, of course you tell the story about the caucus. George Fettinger had called me and wanted to meet with me, and so he flew his private plane to the airport and I went there to have a cup of coffee with him. And the first thing he tells me is, "Well, I want you to know that I'm gonna be Speaker and I want to get rid of Walter Martinez. He won't be Chairman of Judiciary and I'll make you Chairman of Judiciary." I said, "Well, what are you gonna do with Walter?" He said something to the effect you know "He'll be lucky if he has a place in the bathroom." And I looked at him and I said, "Give me that again?" And he said, "Yeah, you know all these guys running against me will lose their positions."

Jamie: Yeah, we were.

Raymond: I said, "I really appreciate that" and I called the waitress over and I said, "Miss, could you come over here?" I said, "I'd like to pay for my coffee" and I looked at George and...

Jamie: I didn't know that.

Raymond: I said, "George, I'm really sorry, but that's not the way I operate and if that's the way you're gonna be," because I hadn't made up my mind until I sat there. I had talked to Walter Martinez already. My dad knew Walter. They were friends for twenty years. I didn't know Walter, but I liked him and he wasn't mean spirited. And George actually was, and so I said, "I'm sorry, I'm out; you can't count me in."

Walter brought me in as a freshman, and of course, that was a larger class than your class that came in, because all these guys had run for the Constitutional Convention. Every one of them decided to run for the House of Representatives practically.

Jamie: Oh is that right, I didn't realize that.

Raymond: So, we had a bunch of new guys in there—Republicans and Democrats. And what was so interesting about it is once the vote was taken and we went to the floor, there were some rumblings about how they were going to create a coalition. Bruce King was elected governor, and they went to Bruce to see if Bruce would support some sort of initial coalition, and Bruce told them not only no, but hell no. He told them, "You know we're gonna get this thing off to the right start, I'm not gonna do it." But, they went up there and they tried.

Jamie: Oh, they tried it.

Raymond: And he refused, and so Walter brought me in as one of the freshman, together with all these other guys that had only been there two years longer than I had, Gene Cinelli.

Jamie: Eddie Lopez.

Raymond: Eddie Lopez, Bill O'Donnell, Bill Warren was another freshman.

Jamie: Oh, Warren, I forget yeah, Bill. Lenton Malry.

Raymond: Lenton was a freshman. Cecil was a freshman. And, we had a guy from Carlsbad. They defeated him two years later.

But, the thing is the Mama Lucy's weren't really the Mama Lucy's at that time. Nobody called us Mama Lucy's. We were the kids from up north and what happened is one day we were sitting at a place called The Bull Ring, across from the capitol. It was David, myself, Eddie Cinelli and the Boss. It wasn't even at night. It was mid-afternoon. Mark Acuff happened to be sitting at the bar.

Jamie: He's a reporter.

Raymond: He was a reporter and he had a small newspaper, *El Independiente* (*The Independent*). And we were sitting there and we were talking and we always called Walter "the Boss." I can't even remember what bill it was. He says, "Look, you guys, you don't need to vote for this thing, you know, if it puts you guys in jeopardy. Don't worry about it." And David Salman says, "Look, you're just like Mama Lucy. You're always trying to take care of us." He just used that term, "You're just like Mama," and I knew Mama Lucy from having spent a lot of time in Vegas. Mama Lucy had a hotel in Las Vegas and she was a wonderful chef. She made meals for people that came to the hotel. A group of us used to get together to eat at her restaurant.

So, Mark Acuff overhears that conversation. Two days later, in *The Independent*, he talks about the Mama Lucy Gang, and that's how the name started. There are a lot of other stories about how that happened, but that's exactly how that happened. Mark Acuff happened to say that.

With Walter Martinez, he had eight years. At that point he was the longest serving Speaker after eight years. And the legislation that we introduced, I mean we wrote the School Funding Act, oh my God, what we did. We put in incentives for businesses.

Jamie: What about the Permanent Fund?

Raymond: The Permanent Fund, Walter introduced, in nineteen seventy-three I believe it was—the Severance Tax Permanent Fund. That passed.

Jamie: I carried it, yeah that's the one where I carried it on the floor of the House for Walter. Per the *Albuquerque Journal* [February 20, 1973], Speaker Martinez says: "A severance tax investment fund, as proposed in House Bill 501, sponsored by Rep. James Koch, D-Santa Fe, along with Rep. William O'Donnell, D-Dona Ana, and Martinez would be a hedge against federal cutbacks in two ways."

Raymond: In nineteen seventy-five they passed a Constitutional Amendment to put it in the Constitution that you can't, you couldn't get to the corpus unless you had three quarters of the vote, which was stupid, but they passed it and of course, the public voted for it, and now it's the largest severance tax fund practically in the United States. But it was all Walter's idea. And he came from the uranium company and he foresaw what was going to happen. He said, "Look, eventually that's not gonna be here. We'd better start saving some money from it." The oil and gas industry was, they were opposed to it. It barely passed. Interestingly enough, Bruce King fought it. He finally signed it, and later on he took credit for it!

Jamie: You were in there when I introduced the Open Meetings Act?

Raymond: Yes, I was there when the Open Meetings Act was introduced.

Jamie: Remember the story that I had it locked—nobody could defeat it and then you guys, all the leadership came over to me, I'll never forget: David Salman, Eddie Lopez, you, Walter, people from the Senate, Aubrey Dunn and them, they said, "You know, Jamie, we're gonna vote for your Open Meetings bill, but you must get up and remove members of the legislature, exempt them from the bill." Remember that?

Raymond: Uh huh.

Jamie: And even the Republican leadership, and I said, "Okay, I'll take it out," and then I got up before the House and I amended the bill. I took the legislature out as they had requested and it just sailed through the House and the Senate. But I'll never forget. You came over. I remember David came over and Eddie came over and everyone said, "Now you know you really have got to take the legislature out of it."

Raymond: That's funny. Jamie, you also did a lot of environmental law, I remember.

Jamie: Subdivision Act.

Raymond: You had the Subdivision Act; they were going to kill that Act. They eventually killed it in the Senate, initially, didn't they?

Jamie: Yeah, then we formed a committee with Aubrey Dunn and myself, who met over at Pendaries.

Raymond: When I first was elected there was a University Investigative Committee because of a pornographic poem. There was a poem that was read on the campus and it was kind of a pornographic poem. Harold Reynolds, "Mudd" who was a state Senator at the time, got a hold of it and turned it into a major exposé against the university.

Jamie: They had more copies done on the copy machine.

Raymond: Oh, he printed out copies for everybody. So, they had this investigation and they started this investigative committee, the University Investigative Committee, and I went to Walter Martinez. (I was a freshman) and I said, "The first thing I want to do; I want that committee killed." He said, "Wait a minute, Raymond, wait a minute, just take it easy." He said, "Let's see what happens."

And so in the interim he appoints me as vice-chairman of this committee and I said, "Boss, what are you doing?" He says, "No, I'm telling you, just calm down a little bit." "Do you know that Ike Smalley drinks the same thing you do?" And I said, "No, CC and water?" He says, "Well, the first meeting is gonna be scheduled for Roswell, Sally Port Inn." He says, "Do you know he also like cigars?" I said, "No."

He says, "Well, you like them." I said, "Yes, I do." He says, "Do you have a couple good Cubans?" I said, "I can get them." So he says "I want you to follow him. You go down, you get a bottle of Canadian Club. You'll be in Roswell. Invite Ike Smalley for a drink in your room." Sally Port didn't have liquor down there in Roswell. Do you remember they couldn't serve liquor?

Jamie: Yeah.

Raymond: So, I go down there and the first night I get Ike Smalley and I say, "Smalley, I really want to learn. They tell me you're the impresario. You're the man who knows everything" and he says, just, "Really?" Flatter him as much as you can. So I do. We go up there and we start drinking CC, smoking cigars. It's two o'clock in the morning. I'm yelling, "I can go all night if I have to." We drink. We smoke. We laugh. We get to know one another. He starts telling me about his stories—he was prospecting for gold down in Mexico, right across from Deming, down in that area, and he knew a bunch of people I knew. The Salazars and all those people; so we got to like one another. The next morning we get up and he says, "Why don't we kind of make a recommendation that we change the name of this committee? Instead of "University Investigative Committee," what if one of our first bills we change the name. Let's call it "University Studies Committee." We talked a little bit about that, I said "Yeah, that's a good idea. Instead of being 'investigative,' let's do some 'studies.'" So, we changed the whole tenor to that committee, and as Walter told me, "This is how you handle the guy."

Jamie: Uh huh.

Raymond: Walter was brilliant with understanding people. In a different situation, Walter was having issues with Fettinger. He decided he had had enough of that stuff, so he removed George. Previously, he had put George Fettinger as Chairman of Judiciary, named him as chairman. So, two years later the Boss said, "Enough of that" and he took him off as Chairman of the Judiciary and installed me. It was my second term.

Jamie: Your second term, my last term.

Raymond: I'm the Chairman of Judiciary; I'm sitting there, youngest chairman, I'm sitting there saying, "Okay." Senator Ike Smalley comes to me one day and he says, "I need to teach you something, son," with the cigar. He said, "I'll sit in on a couple of your committee meetings. I'll give you ideas about how to handle a committee, how to run it." Sure as hell, man, he shows up, sits in the back of the committee, my first week as committee chair. Afterwards he'd come to me and give me advice and stuff and we became really close friends. After that, just about anything I wanted I could get through the senate.

Jamie: That's right.

Raymond: He was the most powerful man around. Nobody would challenge the old man.

Jamie: Raymond, do you remember when I brought the mountain lion?

Raymond: Yep, brought a little mountain lion in.

Jamie: David Salman and I sponsored the bill to protect the mountain lion and we ran it through our committee. I found a person that had a tamed mountain lion, and I had him bring it to the Natural Resources committee hearing, and had it sitting right in front of me. I invited all the kindergarten and first grade schools. The place was filled with kids, just filled with kids and also the lobbyist for the cattle industry.

We had a hearing in the committee and the bill passed unanimously. From there the bill went to the floor of the house and I had the mountain lion on the table in front of everybody. The legislation passed the house, then passed in the senate and eventually became law and was signed by the governor. Do you remember that?

Raymond: Yeah, we did a lot of stuff like that.

Jamie: Let's talk about Max, what we did with Max.

Raymond: Well with Max, I'll tell you exactly how that happened. How it really happened was this. Max got sick. He's in the hospital here in Albuquerque. And his wife, Sally Rodgers, and my then ex-wife, Liz, she trained Sally's horses, Arabians, and they were good friends. And Max is in the hospital and Liz calls me one day and she says, "You know, Max is in the hospital and nobody's come to see him. Why don't you go see him?" So, I said, "Yeah I'll go by and say hi to Max, see how he's doing." So, I call and I say, "How are you doing?" He says, "I'm doing okay." "Sally says you want to talk to me about something?" He says, "Yeah, I'd like to. You know, I'm pretty sick and nobody sees me. You're the only one that's ever called me."

So, I talked to Liz, I said, "Liz, what was that all about?" She says, "Well, we were sitting there, Sally and I, and Sally's trying to convince him to switch parties." I said, "Really?" She says, "Yeah, but if you go visit with him, it just may happen."

Jamie: I told him, I said look, "We've got a chance to get him over, but two things need to happen: one, you can't run anyone against him; it can't be a coalition, and two, he wants a chairmanship."
    I told Max: "You will have to change your party affiliation."

Raymond: He doesn't want to have opposition and he wants me to give him a chairmanship. And I said, "I can't make a commitment like a chairmanship, but we can make other commitments. I will do the best I can, Max, to be sure you get what you want."

Jamie: He was in my district. Max was in my district. I sat down with Max and told him I'd help him after he changed his party affiliation, and he said, "Well, you're gonna have somebody run against me." Raymond sets up a meeting with Governor Anaya, and we all went to see Governor Anaya. The governor said, "We won't run anybody against you," and Max changed his party affiliation and he was there as a Democrat until he died.

Raymond: He became a liberal. I mean, I actually met him at the Coyote Café. We put the final touches to the deal. Max and I sat there over red chili and biscuits and I told him: "Here's the deal." He says "Okay." That afternoon, we walked over to the courthouse, changed his affiliation. Our caucus was gonna be held about a week later. They came into the caucus and they gave up and they said, "Without Max we can't win it." And so, they didn't run against me. And I won it and so he stayed and I put him in as Chairman of Tax and Revenue.

Jamie: When did you move him to Chairman of Finance?

Raymond: Well, next, I got defeated, remember? And they took the Speaker back from me. I'd made Fred Luna chairman. Because Bill O'Donnell was gone, so it was just a lot of movement. And so, two years later, when I got the Speakership back, I went to Max. I said, "Max, the business community is really uptight with you as Chairman of Tax. I mean you're just making it really tough on everybody" and I said: "What if I made you Chairman of Appropriations?" And his eyes got about this big. He said, "What?" I said,

"Yeah, you like to control spending money. I'll put you on as chairman of the committee. I want you to go there and take care of the needs of the public" and he jumped at that, big time.

Jamie: Do you remember the election reform you did?

Raymond: Gosh, there was too much to that one, I can't remember everything about that.

Jamie: Well, what happened on that was we were trying to keep Bill Richardson from using his federal money to run for governor. So, you had Fred Nathan come down and Fred said: "Look at what I found in the regulations of congress. I told Richardson it came from Tom Udall. Boy did that raise a lot of hell."

Raymond: They got so upset.

Jamie: They sued me.

Raymond: Richardson was not happy, because he couldn't use his money.

Jamie: We didn't want Bill Richardson to run against you, Raymond.

Raymond: That was funny. There were a lot of things we did. Jamie, you helped me put a lot of projects together. We did the workers' comp stuff.

Jamie: Workers' comp reform.

Raymond: And I was told, you know workers' comp was in a crisis situation. Real crisis. And Caruthers was governor and Caruthers wanted to put together something and he put together a horrible group of people. Anyway, we sat down. I told Ben Alexander, "Look, this thing isn't gonna work, so I'll put together a group that will have business included, local businesses, labor, everybody included."

Jamie: Yeah, well the committee, Marty Chavez chaired.

Raymond: You know I made him chair. He didn't want a chair. So I sat with Ben Alexander and I said, "Ben, we need to do something for the people." And so I sat here, and I called Manny Aragon here, and I said, "Manny,

I'm gonna put this thing together," and Manny said, "I don't want to have anything to do with it." I said, "Okay" and I called Les Houston. Les said, "I don't want to have anything to do with it." I called Toby Michael—this is when Toby was running against me, he said: "I don't want to have anything to do with it." I said, "Okay, I'm going to do it. I'm Speaker of the House." Bob Desiderio was the moderator. He was the Dean of the Law School at the time. Stuart Bluestone and Paula Tackett were staff. We hired an independent guy from out of state and Governor Caruthers gave up his committee—disbanded his—once he saw who I had on mine. Marty didn't want to serve on it and I finally convinced him.

Jamie: He ended up chairman. Marty Chavez ended up chairman.

Raymond: I had finally convinced him, Marty, because Marty was a worker's comp lawyer, a good workers' comp lawyer. Anyway, that worked. It actually worked and we put it together. We made a commitment that what came out of the committee, Manny Aragon made a commitment also, that whatever came out of that committee is what we would pass and we would rush, run it through no matter what. And we kept our word and we didn't amend it, (a couple of minor little changes, just technical things), and now it became a model.

Jamie: New Mexico Mutual is the largest writer of workers' comp, as you know.

Raymond: And we created an insurance company out of it.

Jamie: New Mexico Mutual.

Raymond: New Mexico Mutual. So it was two things: one, we redid the Act and we created the mutual company, and that was you. You came in and said, "Well, you're gonna need a company."

Jamie: We couldn't get any insurance because the insurance companies raised a bunch of hell and so I asked a bunch of them: "Well, now when we change the law, will you provide coverage?" They said, "We'll have to wait and see." And so I realized we could have passed all this legislation and then nobody would write anything, so we did some research. There was a company in Minnesota, out of St. Paul, which is the mutual company that we patterned New Mexico Mutual after.

Raymond: This is all the history of what the Mama Lucy's did. Anyway, so we did a lot of that. Something else we did that was really interesting is I got tired of looking at what was happening at the University of New Mexico. This was before I was on the Board of Regents, and we were developing a lot of stuff and the labs were developing a bunch of stuff, and I had read an article, way back in sixty-nine, about technology transfer and defense conversion. So I passed legislation called Technology Transfer and Defense Conversion. In fact, I put a memorial together that memorialized Bruce King to do something in his first term, way back in seventy-one, and everybody lauded it. It was a great idea, but it just died. He never did anything with it. So, then I passed a bill called Technology Transfer and Defense Conversion.

Jamie: The Science Technology Committee

Raymond: And got that passed. That was somewhere around probably eight something, maybe even the nineties. Anyway, Bingham saw it and Gore, Al Gore, both saw my legislation. And they introduced a similar bill in congress and I remember going to testify in Washington DC, before the select committee. It was Jeff Bingaman's request that I testify.

Jamie: Then the university formed the Science Technology Committee.

Raymond: The university formed it and now you're finally starting to see the fruits of that. It was a precursor to what they're doing now with Innovate Albuquerque.

Jamie: Raymond, when you joined the Regents, tell us about some of the highlights, and you're the one that developed the new, formed the setup of Health Sciences Center, am I correct?

Raymond: Well, we did that. Yes, we did, and don't you forget it.

Jamie: I haven't forgotten. No, I haven't forgotten. That's why we're here doing this interview! However, before we get into that, when Governor Richardson appointed me to the Regents, with your leadership and Don Chalmers and Mel Eaves participation, we achieved the greatest amount of capital improvement in the history of the university, over one billion. What is your comment on that?

Raymond: Well, my involvement wasn't all that great. You were more involved with it because you were chairman of Finance and on the Facilities committee.

Jamie: At first, I was just chairman of the Facilities committee. Then most of it was approved when Mel was chairman of Finance and I was president of the Regents.

Raymond: Yeah, but what it had to do with is we were willing to take risks with bonding, and that's what we did. We bonded it against tuition. We bonded it against income that was coming in, and we were able to expand. One of the things that always worried us, however, was when we were gonna bond ourselves to the point that the indebtedness would eventually catch up to us, and fortunately, times were good, so we guessed right.

Jamie: And of course, the governor had a lot of money to put in capital improvements because Johnson was such a conservative.

Raymond: That's right, so we had money left over.

Jamie: I always said Bill Richardson should have kissed Johnson on the cheek, because when he came in he had a pot of gold.

Raymond: And so, we were able to do all those sorts of things. And interestingly enough, just as a matter of history, I was never once, ever, called by Bill Richardson and told to do anything.

Jamie: Neither was I.

Raymond: On the Board of Regents, I was never, even once, called. Not as a member, not as President of the Regents. The governor never said, "I need you to do the following." He trusted us. He allowed us to, you know, be the stewards of the university, unlike what's happening now.

Jamie: Tell us about Health Sciences and the amount of time you and Don Chalmers, and all of us spent working on Health Sciences, trying to set it up so that we would ensure its viability in the future.
    Because they generate almost two billion and the university's eight hundred million.

Raymond: Main campus always needed money. We'd look to the north campus. And, it was always a deal where people would work it out, but we wanted to be sure and insulate them from, you know, all of a sudden the chancellor not having any say over what was done on the north campus. It was important. And so, we set up a system where you would have a board that actually had members of the Board of Regents on it. But, the idea was to protect Health Sciences from main campus gobbling it up, gobbling up their funds. And there was never a time, in my memory anyway, that when main campus didn't need something that the north campus would help them that I remember.

Jamie: Do you think there's always going to be a problem and the way it's set up now because the Health Sciences area is always going to be larger, always be more profitable? The majority of their money is self-generated. They only get seven percent from the legislature. My thought is that they ought to be separated. There should be a separate board, appointed by the governor, to oversee the Health Sciences Center and then the university, the main campus work on an agreement where they work together on certain things. Because it seems to me, it's natural, when you have financial problems, everybody wants to look to the gold pot over there, and it's natural. What would your thought be on something like that?

Raymond: Well, that was pretty much the objective we had when we redid it, and we had this Health Sciences Board. Recently it ended up just the Board of Regents the way it was changed. The Board of Regents took over both boards, basically.

Jamie: You don't have a board any more. And that was done in one weekend.

Raymond: Yeah, and that was just done with nobody's input other than the governor and probably two other people, maybe three.

Jamie: Yeah, where I'm coming from, I understand...

Raymond: I understand what you're saying. You're saying a constitutional amendment to have a separate Board of Regents for the Health Sciences Center.

Jamie: Stop and look, just a minute. You got a two billion dollar operation that is very well run—Health Sciences. Then you have an eight hundred dollar million operation that is the main campus budget. Obviously it creates a problem between the two operations since the one with the least money has the most difficulty with its revenue. I feel the only way to properly handle this situation is to have a separate board, appointed by the governor. They've done this at the University of Oregon.

Raymond: I'd have to think about that.

Jamie: Well, that's why I'm asking you. Do you think it's worth looking at?

Raymond: Yeah, anything's worth looking at.

Jamie: Not now, but I was thinking this is something to be done two years from now.

Raymond: But to have a separate Board of Regents, constitutionally provided, I don't want to see what's happening on main campus with the Board being politicized, as it's been recently, to happen on the other side of campus. I'm not happy with what I see as a politicization of the Board of Regents. All the time I was on it, there was, it wasn't politicized in the sense that we had factions in it. We were always unanimous. I mean we were together, we knew where we were going, there were people who learned to talk to one another and accept other people's viewpoints. Right now, as far as I can tell, the university is being run from Santa Fe, the Board of Regents. Decisions are being made that nobody knows where the ideas came from. One Regent said she made, it was all her idea; another Regent says it was all his idea. One Regent says he doesn't know what's going on, and he's gonna try to help, but he can't do it because he wants to be reappointed.

Jamie: Well, and two years from now...

Raymond: And I'm not sure that a separate Board of Regents is gonna solve that problem because the problem is within the main campus right now.

Jamie: Well, I would like for you to think about that.

Raymond: I'll think about it, you know it may be something that could be done.

Jamie: But not now, I'm not saying now.

Raymond: I'm trying to figure out how that would help main campus, because main campus isn't supporting the north campus. It isn't supporting the hospital campus.

Jamie: Well, I just think it's something I wanted to run by you. But what I hear you saying is that we have a philosophical problem happening everywhere. It's not just in the politicization of the Board.

Raymond: Well, that's exactly what I'm saying.

Jamie: They don't talk to each other.

Raymond: You know interestingly enough, when I went to the Constitutional Convention, going back, let's go all the way back. I went up there and I was blind to partisanship, because we were nonpartisan. You'd see it spout up, but it was more a philosophical difference. It wasn't "I'm a Republican and therefore, I'm voting this way because other Republicans are voting this way. I'm a Democrat and I'm voting this way because the Democrats are voting this way." I mean, we tried to cross fertilize each other's brains with our own thoughts, and some people were amenable to some of the changes we suggested, other people weren't, because they were philosophically separated, okay? And that's okay with me, if you have one philosophy and I have another. I can accept that fact. I don't necessarily have to accept your philosophy, but what I don't do is tie myself to my party, under any set of circumstances, where my conscience says, "that's not right." And you saw that, just in this last election, where on the national level and even at the state and local levels, people were voting a way, on both sides, because that was the party. I mean prominent people refused to come out, even though they were disgusted. They were surprised, they were shocked, they wouldn't speak out against some of the things that were happening in the last election, and that goes all the way to the local level. What happened in many of the house races and the senate races, were people told outright lies. The people not telling the truth admitted it and said, "Yes, we do it. Why? Because we can."

And that's the type of trash we ended up having all over this nation, and in this state, and we let people get away with it because people didn't speak up. Yeah, there's a difference. There's a big difference and what I experienced in my formative years in politics, and living in my hometown of Belen, where the Democrats and Republicans used to come into my dad's restaurant and each of them had their table there. Whoever got there first got the bigger table. And it was fun and they laughed, they shared coffee. They shared opinions. When it was over, you go have a drink together. There were only really three bars in Santa Fe that people went to. You'd meet there. You'd have fun. It's different. I can remember George Buffett and I one time. We were talking. I looked at George and I says, "George, I don't know why you carry so much animus." He was a basic good guy. He and I got along really well. In fact, he used to come to me with ideas all the time about how we could do things. "Don't let anybody know it was my idea, Raymond." "Fine George, don't worry about it." So, I told him one time, I says: "George, you know I'd be willing to bet you that we vote together seventy-five percent of the time, at a minimum, seventy-five percent of the time." He says, "There's no way." I said, "Tell you what, a hundred bucks, we're gonna each ask Paula Tackett to do a search on our records, our voting." He says, "You got it." We voted together almost eighty percent of the time. It was just a few of those, you know right-to-work issues, things that were so far out to the right or the left that we didn't get along with. Actually, I think it was almost ninety percent of the time we voted together. Anyway, I won the bet.

Another time we were doing, another true story, this is another with George Buffett. We were trying to pass a bill. He came to me and said, "Look, I'm gonna introduce term limits." And I said, "Okay, George." He said, "You're gonna kill it, aren't you?" I said, "Yeah, George, I'm gonna kill it." He says, "Good, good, I have got to do this for my constituents, you know that, don't you?" I said, "Okay, George." So, one time he comes to me and he says: "We need to increase our per diem." I said, "Yeah, George, I know we do, so we're gonna introduce it." He says, "I have an excellent idea," he says, "Why don't we tie it to IRS?" I look at him and say, "Tie it to the IRS?" He said, "Yeah, while we are in Santa Fe during the session. God, if it goes, it'll almost triple our pay." And I look at him and say, "George." He said, "Everybody will vote on a constitutional amendment that says it's tied to the IRS limit, you watch." So, sure enough, we introduce a constitutional amendment and we frame it, "shall not be more than allowed by IRS," putting a negative tone on it, "shall not be more than that allowed by the IRS, for per diem." It was George's idea, not mine, so we co-sponsored it and it passes. But those were things that were fun and funny. Things that you pull together behind the scenes, where you get along with people. The last few years up there it has just been gut wrenching. John Dendahl really changed the tenor.

Jamie: Yeah, I went after Dendahl.

Raymond: He really changed the tenor of politics in New Mexico. And he brought Jay McCleskey.

Jamie: Oh yeah.

Raymond: He brought McCleskey here. And then it was just so, say what you want to say now, you can get away with it, destroy people's lives, destroy their reputations.

Jamie: So, as you look forward, for New Mexico, what do you hope for, what do you hope happens for our state?

Raymond: What do I see, or what do I hope for in the future?

Jamie: Yes.

Raymond: I would hope that people would start looking back to a lot of the stuff that was done to create economic initiatives in the state of New Mexico back in the eighties, early to, through about ninety-eight. Look at those tools that we put in place. Try to refine them. Find out what portions of them worked, which portions of them aren't working, and try to incentivize, not just businesses to come into New Mexico, but to incentivize many of our younger population to educate themselves, to improve their condition and their position in life. I'm worried about the divisiveness that's been created, not just in this last election. It's been latent. It's been sitting there just right beneath the surface. These last elections brought out what a lot of people were thinking, but wouldn't say, and it's unfortunate that they were thinking it. They found their voice and somebody else to say it for them.

I want a New Mexico where I can walk down the street. Let me put it this way. In New Mexico, better than most states, when you walk down the street if you see somebody of a different color, race or maybe expressing their religion, it doesn't raise some sort of fear factor. It doesn't; it really doesn't. I don't want to see that happen in this state. I'm worried that maybe it will and I think that will be truly unfortunate for us. We have an opportunity in this state. We have the natural resources. We have the climate. We have the expertise. We have some of the greatest universities. We just need to express what's good about our state, rather than focusing on what we think is bad about our state, and we need politicians who will be honest with the public; people who really care about the state of the state, rather than the state of their future. Too many are thinking about what they want to be rather than what they should be at the time, in terms of taking care of the needs we have. I suspect that we will survive the current downturn. If you look back in the early eighties, we survived it. But you need to have someone who's going to have the courage to say you need to invest if you want to grow and prosper. Right now the attitude is "look back," instead of "look forward," and that's unfortunate.

Jamie: Well, I appreciate it again, very much you taking some time with me.

Raymond: It's all relative Jamie. But for Walter Martinez, everything we talked about today would not have come to pass. Walter instilled in all of us, who were at one time called "the Young Turks," and later became known as the "Mama Lucy's." He helped us build that legacy by giving us the courage to do what we felt was right, rather than what we thought was politically expedient.

Jamie: When I sat down with you, we sure had fun remembering all the things we did in in the legislature to get legislation passed that we felt was in the best interest of all New Mexicans. You heard the lobbyists explain how it is just bad luck to leave the legislature before all the business is concluded for the day. Getting legislation passed does have a Darwinian component and the founding fathers designed the process with that "survival of the fittest" mentality. They knew that it is very hard to get laws through both houses and signed by the president, or at the state level, signed by the governor. Not all the time, of course, but most of the time, these three layers of accountability help ensure that what gets passed has undergone great scrutiny. I am proud of the fact Walter Martinez and I, in nineteen seventy-three, introduced the Severance Tax Permanent Fund Act. At the time, the legislation had a seven million dollar appropriation, now the fund is worth approximately eight billion. The great issue facing our state now, is how we can devise a plan to raise New Mexico out of its economic distress so that more New Mexicans can achieve their goals. I never introduced legislation with the idea that we would never touch the corpus, which has unfortunately become the prevailing viewpoint of many legislators. Obviously, if money is taken from the corpus, it must be repaid and there must be a solid plan in place to repay it. But problems are rarely solved without the influx of a little cash, and the founding of New Mexico Mutual is a good example of a situation where the state loaned money and there was a reasonable plan in place to have that money repaid. If the state had not been willing to fund that initiative, we would have had a serious economic crisis. I offer this reminder now when we find ourselves again at the bottom of so many lists and our state continues to be passed over as a contender for corporate expansion. I have often referred to the fund as a "rainy day fund." From that perspective, as one of the two people [Representative O'Donnell] who carried that legislation, let me say loudly and clearly, "it is raining." In the next several years the legislature needs to look to finds ways to work together and innovatively solve the state's problems. The idea that we are a "poor state" when we have resources we could leverage must be recognized. Again, I want to reiterate that spending that corpus is only a good idea when there is a plan in place to repay it, but such possibilities exist and must be explored.

I mentioned that I took Bruce King's seat when he ran for governor. Governor King assisted me on many important initiatives during my time in the legislature. On February 7, 2017, I sat down with Bruce King's son, Bill King to talk about some of the big bills that I got through while I was in the legislature and how important the governor's support was for me to get done what I was able to accomplish.

Bruce King's mentorship and his willingness to publicly show his support for the bills I carried were instrumental. Remember, all politics is local. I returned the favor by chairing Governor King's fundraising committee two times when he ran for governor.

Bill King, son of Governor Bruce King / Interviewed February 7, 2017

Bill: I was born in Albuquerque, New Mexico in nineteen fifty-one and grew up in Stanley. I've lived there all my life. I was always my dad's boy. He took me everywhere with him, so we were very close. And basically, he was just a cowboy and so I am still just a cowboy. I learned what he taught me about cows and I like doing all of that, but that's basically what he was. And then he got involved in taking care of political things in New Mexico, and so I kind of got dragged along with him. That's the reason I know about these things. He felt he could trust me in Santa Fe, which is sometimes a good thing. So, I've grown up in politics and understand politics and I was my dad's legislative lobbyist for part of his terms when he was the governor. He was governor three times. So I was privileged to be in a lot of meetings.

Jamie: Bill, could you tell us about the convention when we wanted to make sure Bruce was on the ballot in the primary?

Bill: The first time he ran for governor it was nineteen sixty-six. And back in those days, the way you got placed on the ballot was by how many votes you got at the Democratic convention. They had a nominating convention and they picked the candidates that got placed on the ballot. Since then we've had a court overturn that, and anybody can file if they get enough signatures. But at that time you had to get enough votes out of the convention. In nineteen sixty-six, my dad was only forty years old. He was a young guy to be running for governor. He'd been in the legislature a few years. He worked his way up to Speaker and that's what made him decide he could run for governor. I never knew why he decided he could do that, but he had a spirit about him that thought he could do anything. So that's why he did it.

So anyway, they were having the Democratic convention in the civic auditorium in Albuquerque. It's since been torn down. They had all the delegates sitting on the floor in chairs, supposedly and every county had a spot. It's just like you see the national presidential convention now—every county had a stake and a spot. They were going down through the votes alphabetically, by county, and my dad was just a little short in vote count to make the twenty percent needed to be on the ballot. They still had Valencia County to go. Filo Sedillo was the county chair. At that time I was like, you know I was fifteen years old. I was just sitting up in the crowd. You were probably more involved than me then because you were working in politics.

Jamie: Your dad said to me, I'll never forget, he said: "You go see Filo. You ask him to give us enough votes to get on the ballot. Tell him I sent you." I remember I went to see Filo and he said, "Okay, I think we can do it." I came back and then they started the count, but the first number they gave was not enough.

Bill: They counted 'em up again.

Jamie: Five or ten minutes went by while they tried to give us just the exact twenty percent. John Burroughs and Gene Lusk were running against your dad.

Bill: They didn't want dad to get on the ballot.

Jamie: So your dad got on the ballot with a little over twenty percent. And then later on, before we launched the campaign, your dad dropped out.

Bill: He helped Lusk.

Jamie: He helped Lusk.

Bill: Dave Cargo was an unknown representative from Albuquerque. Nobody thought he had a chance, and I remember he was a legislator up here in Santa Fe. Originally he was a guy from back east or somewhere, that got elected to the legislature out of Bernalillo County, and he was kind of a, he was a, really a quick guy, but he was a pain in the butt. I remember, you know in the legislature. My dad ran the legislature with an iron fist, you know he had...

Jamie: He had control.

Bill: He was the Speaker and he ran it the way he wanted. Well, a lot of times if he was getting something done, Cargo would jump up and want to speak, and my dad wouldn't even recognize him. He would just leave him out there sitting. And I also remember, and I wasn't very old, I was maybe eleven or twelve, Cargo brought a cowbell to the floor. Do you remember? He'd get up and ring that cowbell when he wanted to talk, so my dad would recognize him. But anyway, Mr. Lusk had been around a long time. He was from Carlsbad. In those days we didn't have as many high-powered campaign managers and pollsters and all that crap that you have now.

Jamie: We weren't that sophisticated.

Bill: No, so he just had these signs put up, saying that "Dan Blocker recommends Gene Lusk for governor," all around the state. Well, Cargo didn't have much backing. He didn't have much money and he needed it. And so, he had these little three by three signs that he put up all over the state that said "Hoss Cartwheel Endorses Dave Cargo." Remember those little signs? He had them put everywhere. And he was, in a way he was kind of like Trump. He didn't have any money, but he had the ear of the press and he was in the paper every day. I mean, he got lost once, his wife got lost, remember? Ida Jo got lost and they couldn't find her for a day. She was up in Las Vegas. Do you remember that? He was in the paper every day for something because he would say something.

Jamie: We think he had made sure that his wife was lost.

Bill: Outrageous, you know? And damned if he didn't beat Lusk, he did.

Jamie: That's right.

Bill: And that was a big upset at that time. But, then the next time, two years later,
in nineteen sixty-eight, my dad ran for governor again. He dropped out of the legislature that time.

Jamie: Yeah, that's right.

Bill: The other time he hadn't dropped out of the legislature; he was still Speaker. And so, he quit the legislature and he said "I want to run for governor and I'm not dropping out this time, no matter what." And they ended up with four Anglos and one Hispanic, and Fabian Chavez won by a little bit.

Jamie: That's right, that's right.

Bill: And that was, it was Calvin Horne, Harry Stowers and Bobby Mayfield, and they were all pretty strong candidates, you know.

Jamie: But then Hispanics usually voted with Hispanics, except in Bruce's case, not this time, but the Hispanics really liked Bruce.

Bill: But still just from the name ID, Fabian Chavez won that time. And then Cargo beat him again, so Cargo got to stay in four years.

Jamie: That's exactly right.

Bill: Yeah, in two year terms, yeah.

Jamie: Then in nineteen seventy-one is when your dad got elected governor.

Bill: Right. He was running against Pete Domenici.

Jamie: And Pete, Pete was the mayor of Albuquerque, appointed mayor, right?

Bill: Pro Tem. They had a council, but they made him the Mayor Pro Tem. Remember, he was the councilor and he was the chief. Yeah, he was a popular guy too, yeah. So was my dad. They used to make a lot of fun of him for wearing boots and all kinds of stuff in the paper back in those days.

Jamie: Bruce would go into a restaurant and he would head straight for the kitchen. He went to see the people in the kitchen. I mean I'll never forget; he'd go right in. There goes Bruce. And by God he'd work a table like you can't believe. I remember one day we were in the Palace Restaurant and Bruce came in, he was governor, and there was a guy sitting next to him and he said, "Well, you know I met this guy in Cimarron City; he says he's the governor. Who's this King guy?" Because he'd ask everybody for their vote, regardless if you were in New Mexico or whatever.

Bill: It didn't matter. He shook everybody's hand, every little kid, every old person, everybody, even when we went to Europe. But those county chairmen had a lot of power then. And the reason they had so much power, in my opinion, is that we didn't have a personnel system then. So, whoever got elected governor, they got to change a lot of jobs and they worked with those county chairmen and they had a lot of power about who got hired to work for the highway department, who got hired to work for all these positions. And now, the county chairman doesn't have any power over who gets hired for anything, so the party structure is pretty well gone.

Jamie: It's gone. Then when I got elected to legislature, Bruce signed the Open Meetings Act. Don King, your uncle, and I were the sponsor on that, and Franklin Jones worked in the office with Bruce. He was against that and he was also against the Open Records, but we had Don.

And when I went in nineteen sixty-eight. I took Bruce's place. Then in nineteen seventy-four, Julian Grace defeated me. That's when your dad appointed me to the Game and Fish Commission. That was the first time I went on the Game and Fish Commission. I remember sitting in Governor King's office and you were in there and a commissioner from Socorro had just resigned. Your dad looked at me and he says, "Do you want to be on the Game Department?" I said, "Yeah." He said "You're on." That was the start of that. And I believe, I remember you were in the room.

Bill: Oh, I used to sit around there a lot.

Jamie: Well every time I talked to your dad, ninety percent of the time you were there. You were there, and of course, the kind of campaign we ran, Jerry Apodaca came in later and Bruce comes in and we ran a typical campaign, not a big highfalutin campaign. Then, I didn't think Bruce would run again, I thought he was going to be through. I thought he was going to say "I'm not gonna run any more."

Bill: He never quit, did he? He just kept on.

Jamie: Paul Bardacke came to see me before I knew Bruce was going to run. We met in 1991 over at the La Posada, I'll never forget.

Bill: Oh, that was the last time he ran.

Jamie: I told Bardacke, "Yeah I'll support you, unless Bruce calls me." "Well," Bardacke says, "He's not gonna run, plus if Bruce runs we'll beat him because he doesn't know how to run a campaign. We know how to campaign." So Bruce runs. I call Paul and tell him, "I'm going to help Bruce. I'm gonna do everything to get him elected. I'm going to try and raise him money." He said, "We're not worried at all because we know you won't run a sophisticated campaign." That's when I went to your dad, if you remember. We hired a whole bunch of people. They were in Albuquerque at the hotel. We had Romero, we had Jack Daniels, we had Ben Alexander, Linda Kehoe, Judy Basham, and we were gonna interview people to run Bruce's campaign. Bruce talked to Senator Edward Kennedy. It is my understanding that Kennedy had given him some names of campaign managers. So that's what we did. Tom Hujar was the one we selected. We ran the most modern campaign. By the time Bardacke went up, we had it done. Do you remember those days?

Bill: Oh yeah, that was the only time he really had a campaign manager, I think, and everybody said he needed one. And Hujar and him worked together pretty well because in the end, my dad always did what he wanted anyway, you see.

Jamie: Well, and your mom.

Bill: My mom, he didn't cross my mom. We both knew he didn't cross my mom.

Jamie: So, the situation, what happened, we hired this Hujar and he put a hell of a campaign together. Bardacke was really well organized. But by the time Bardacke found that we had a really well organized campaign also, it was too late for him.

Bill: He had been AG, right?

Jamie: Yeah he was AG. And I remember that campaign. We started the Gold Boot, raising money, and that's when I started raising money to do that. Then again, when Bruce got elected, he calls me, he says, "You're going back on the Game and Fish," so I went back on the Game and Fish. But my start in all of this was with Bruce, and I followed him around all the time, too.

Bill: I was trying to think why I was thinking you were on the Appropriations Committee. Were you on the Appropriations Committee?

Jamie: Yes I was on the Appropriations.

Bill: That's what I thought.

Jamie: Yeah, I was on the Appropriation committee when your dad was governor, but I was not chairman. I was also chair of Natural Resources. Your uncle, Don King and I co-sponsored the Open Meetings Act which Franklin Jones was against.

Bill: I worked with Franklin too. He was a smart guy. He was a tax wizard you know. He's the one who structured New Mexico's taxes. My dad always listened to Franklin about taxes. But just about tax issues, because Franklin was very strident in his beliefs. He wasn't open to any changes, you know.

Jamie: But I'll never forget, I don't know if you know the story. We were riding the train from Belen or Las Cruces, whatever, right before the election, and Casey Luna (he was running for lieutenant governor) and his wife were there and they had a little box in the train. They called me down there to go see them and Casey said, "We owe forty thousand dollars. We want you to raise money to do our forty thousand." I said, "Oh, I have got to talk to Bruce first." So, I went and talked to Bruce, and Alice was sitting there and Alice said, "No damn way do we want you to raise the money." So I went back and said, "Well, we're just so busy I can't do that." And so, you know he was ticked off. Then, remember we had a party the night before at Gene Gallegos' house, before the inauguration, remember that? At that time we had the Gold Boot and we said that certain people with the Gold Boot would be able to have reserved seating in the Convention Center and would be able to come to Gene Gallegos' party the night before. Well, I got a call from Casey. Casey said "We want 40 tickets, front row seats" and, well, I was chairman, and I said, "Well, I've got to talk to Bruce." He said, "Well you tell Bruce what we want." I went to Bruce, and Alice was sitting there. She said, "No way we're gonna do that. You can give him fifteen tickets."

Bill: We had a tumultuous relationship with Casey Luna.

Bill: I told my dad that we probably shouldn't run. You know, he was getting older and he'd been around three terms and I said "We've done everything you need to do," but everybody who worked for my dad, all those people, all those years, they all said, "Run once more governor, and we can all retire while you're still governor." You know, I mean they would have their twenty-five years in, he'd been there that long.

Jamie: Well I remember sitting with your dad and your mom.

Bill: And my mom probably still had energy, but then, and we hired Tom again, Hujar, and we did, you know they ran a pretty good campaign. But Casey Luna ran against my dad in the primary. He was the lieutenant governor, so you had to run against your own lieutenant governor. And so that was, you know, that took money and energy and time. Then Roberto Mondragon, who had been his lieutenant governor the two terms before, got on the ballot as a Green Party candidate, and he ran in the general election and Gary Johnson didn't really get fifty percent. Roberto Mondragon got ten percent and Gary got forty-two. My dad got a couple of percent less.

Jamie: One of them, one that Gary Johnson got was from the Indians because Bruce was not going to sign that gaming compact. And he's totally, one hundred percent correct. He would not sign it.

Bill: He got, you know I think that, the first time my dad ran for governor and won, I think we only had a hundred thousand dollars, Jamie—a hundred-twenty thousand, something like that. It wasn't very much. And the last time I think it took about a million. But I remember that the gambling guys gave Gary Johnson four hundred fifty thousand of the million that he raised.

Jamie: And that's where Gary Johnson got it.

Bill: Yeah, and he had some money, and the Republicans had money too, I'm sure. But the big chunk was from the gambling guys who wanted him to sign the compact. The gambling guys had been trying to get my dad to sign the compact the last two years.

Jamie: And he wouldn't sign it.

Bill: He wouldn't sign it. You'd have to know how strict a Christian back ground my grandmother and other people were in my dad's life to know why he was so against the gambling. You know, I mean when I was a kid, I couldn't play any games that had a dice in them—you know like Monopoly. My grandmother would take the dice out and throw them away and get a big old square eraser and put dots on it and she'd say, "You can play with this."

Jamie: And Robert Mondragon—your dad asked me to go see him because he's on the Green ticket. I'll never forget that. I went to see Robert up in Espanola. I said, "Look you're not gonna win this race. Bruce is gonna win. Why don't you just drop out?" "No," Mondragon said. "I'm gonna stay in. I remember your mom and your dad sitting in the governor's office before the general campaign, and I believe it was your mom who said, "Look, they know how good a job Bruce has done. He has done a great job as governor that term, one of the best jobs he has done." She said, "You know if they don't recognize it, we're just not gonna spend the kind of money that we're doing. Because if they don't recognize how much Bruce has done for this state, then so be it." Do you remember that?

Bill: Yeah, but I mean I, it was time to be gone, that's what I say. We should have not even run, you know? Politics is all timing. If you're in the right place at the right time, anybody can get elected. And if you're in the wrong place at the wrong time, the best person in the world doesn't get elected, you know?

Jamie: Your father signed my Subdivision Bill. I had the subcommittee with Aubrey Dunn; he signed that bill. Do you remember? That bill was extraordinarily contentious, the Subdivision Act. Do you remember? There's plenty of newspaper clippings talking about what was going on.

Bill: You know, it's gotten progressively stricter since then. But you were kind of a progressive in those regards, on all those things, open meetings, all those things. I don't know as I remember how contentious it was, but I'm certain as much land as we owned and stuff, we looked at it very closely too, and made some compromises, right? It was probably good in the long term. I think at the time we had gone through those Deming Ranchettes and we'd gone through a lot of things that were pretty detrimental, you know—and Rio Rancho communities. We had a lot of people just coming out here and buying big ranches and drawing lines on a map and selling them back east. And that's what it was set out to correct. And I think we did that without hurting anybody otherwise.

There were a lot of things that most people don't know we passed including the Environment Department.

Jamie: That was my bill, which he signed.

Bill: But the Environment Department is certainly a huge department that got started under my dad. The Children, Youth and Families Department also got started under my dad. We did a lot of different things that had a far-reaching effect over time.

Jamie: Do you remember the Terrero Mine site Superfund cleanup? I was on the Game and Fish at that time. When I first went on the Game and Fish, Governor King had just gotten elected. They were going to get a Superfund cleanup. So I did some research on that. We needed to have a Natural Resource Trustee. New Mexico did not have a Trustee Officer. So, I went to the governor and told him that. He said "We'll make you the Natural

Resource Trustee Officer, but we better get an attorney general opinion because it said the Trustee had to be a state employee." The attorney general ruled since I was chairman of Game and Fish...

Bill: You were an employee.

Jamie: The AG said I was an employee. People forget that Bruce was governor and the legislature had to come up with five million dollars to do the Terrero Mine cleanup, plus the Highway Department was going to have to do the repaving, and if it hadn't been for Bruce, we wouldn't have gotten the funding to support that.

Bill: I remember one of the hardest things we did was when we passed some of those permanent funds and we put these extractive taxes on the oil and gas.

Jamie: I was a sponsor of that bill.

Bill: And that was a very difficult thing to get passed. But it's proven to be a good thing for New Mexico in the long run. We had Senator Aubrey Dunn involved.

Jamie: I remember.

Bill: That was a very difficult thing that passed that nobody paid much attention to at the time, but has had far reaching effects for New Mexico for the last fifty years. It's been fifty years.

I remember it was very difficult to get the votes for that. We had to come to a compromise with the gas producers and the Yates Family, who had just sold their holdings for two and a half billion. They were large New Mexico, independent natural gas producers. And we were trying to put a tax on all of these things: oil, uranium, natural gas that would go into a fund for the future to pay for things. The Yates family had a lot of swing down there in the south, you know. But anyway, we worked out a deal that first time and we got it passed, in part because of Clay Buchanan. He was from down there too, and he was a smart guy. And we figured out to pass that tax onto the people who were purchasing in California since the gas was going to California then, remember?

Jamie: Yeah.

Bill: That's how we got it passed the first time. We passed the tax onto the consumer instead of making the producers pay it. But that was, yeah a lot of things got done in those years that people didn't read about in the paper. You know, when I started, my dad had Fabian Chavez and Franklin Jones lobbying for him and I was just kind of up here; it was wintertime. It was slow at the ranch, and I grew up in the legislature. I think I was seven when dad first got elected in fifty-eight in the old Bataan Building, you know? So, I had been there all the time. I knew all about everything and knew most of the legislators, and so I remember my dad was having a little trouble communicating with some legislators because what he would tell Fabian wouldn't be exactly what they heard when they got the message.

Jamie: Fabian changed it?

Bill: Well, I don't know, but my dad said, "We'll cure this." He said, "You're just gonna tell them." He said, "I know you" and so that's when I started lobbying for him. And then I did do that. I mean I helped him do the budgets and I did all that stuff. It was fun. I enjoyed it. My dad always told the story, the first session he was in the legislature in nineteen fifty-eight, he introduced a bill to ban billboards. He didn't like the billboards or something. So, the sign guys were fighting it and stuff, and he says, "I got it out of the House and I got it over to the Senate and they sent it to Senator Smalley's committee, Senate Judiciary." And he said, "I'd go every day and ask him if we could hear my bill" and he'd say, "Yeah I'll get to it. I'll get to you when it's time." And he says, "I get up one morning and my bill's got a 'do not pass' and they've adopted it on the senate floor." And he says, "I went over there and I asked him, I said: Senator Smalley, what the heck happened?" And he said, "Well, we had a lot of bills left here last night and it was the last day" and he says, "We put 'em in piles and we threw 'em up and any of them that stuck to the ceiling got a 'do pass,' and any of them that fell to the floor, got a 'do not.'" And he says, "Yours didn't stick." And you know, that was the honest truth. You know that's the way they ran the senate back then. It wasn't a bad thing, I don't think. I mean there's always a lot of legislation that needs killed and somebody needs to kill it.

Jamie: But your dad, mainly the reason he was talking to the legislature was because he was a northern rancher, but he also had the southeast part of the state, and most of those down there were Democrats at that time.

Bill: They were all Democrats at that time.

Jamie: Coming out of Hobbs, they were all Democrats and that changed.

Bill: What did they call them, Roosevelt Democrats, those guys?

Jamie: Yep.

Bill: They were all conservative, fiscally conservative.

Jamie: That's right.

Bill: And pretty conservative over all. You know they were pretty much Bible belt guys, you know? I think in the U.S. Senate they call them "blue dog Democrats."

Jamie: Yeah, but your dad also bought a lot of cattle from some of the northern ranchers, am I correct on that?

Bill: Oh yeah, he bought cattle from all over up there, yep. They'd bring them to our ranch.

Jamie: Well, you know as I said earlier—I really appreciated your dad. I'll show you a picture I brought down. I wouldn't have gone where I did if he hadn't appointed me to the Game and Fish. I would never have been on there, and he appointed me three times to the Game and Fish—a total of fourteen years.

Bill: You always did a good job. I remember the other controversial bill that was hard. It was the introduction of the bill to protect the mountain lion, by you and David Salman.

Jamie: That was my bill. Let me tell you the story about that. I was reading in *Readers Digest*, Bill, and they were talking about the mountain lions going away. So, I went over to the legislature and I showed the article to David Salman. David says, "Draft that." So I'm going to draft a bill. When you sign the bill, you know the top signature is the sponsor, okay? So, I had the bill drawn up, took it to David, David put his name right above mine, but I'm the one who pushed the bill. I'm the one who brought the little mountain lion and I had him sitting on my desk.

Bill: I don't think we helped you much with that one, but you made it through anyway.

Jamie: You didn't help me, but David, I'll never forget, they put his name right above mine and I said "Okay."

Bill: I think the good thing about the legislature then, and this kind of goes to the future and what they're gonna have to do to get it back, is my dad ran for governor against Pete Domenici and won the first time. He ran against Joe Skeen and won the second time.

Jamie: That's right. Frank Bond was our third.

Bill: And Frank Bond, the third time. I think all of those people worked with my dad later and worked with him before, because they all had the interest of New Mexico at heart. They weren't trying to do presidential politics or vice-presidents or any of that. They all knew they were New Mexicans and they wanted to take care of New Mexico.

Jamie: So, as we wrap this up, is there anything that, in terms of this vast experience that you had watching your dad and being part of those conversations, and being involved, as you look to the future, what do you think is gonna be important for the future here in New Mexico?

Bill: Well, I think you know a couple of things that my dad would do, and is like when Intel came here, my dad would go to California and meet with the president of Intel and say, "You know, we'd really like to have you here," and then he would make it easier for them to come. But you know, I mean there were just a lot of things that you could do that way and I think that that's a personality thing, that you can't replicate. I think Bill Richardson got some of that done, for sure. He was good to go and meet with people and get things done. But you have got to have that kind of personality I think, and I think the other thing is you have to work with your Washington representatives, too. You know, I think right now we've got all this back and forth and everybody taking care of themselves and nobody looking out for New Mexico as well as they should. You know, because all of these guys have got campaign managers, they're all looking out for what they might do in the future. And those campaign managers—they don't answer to the people and they don't see the people and they don't think of things like that. They just think about taking care of what they're tasked to do, you know, which is a different task than what the actual politician has, I think. And so, if they listen to them too much I think that they lose sight of what's the best for New Mexico while they're trying to balance all these stones. But, you know I remember my dad at one time saying, "You know you have got to be positive about things" and he says, "I'm gonna go down and talk to the guy who owns the *Journal*—Lang. Tom Lang was his name. He says "And I'm gonna tell him we've got to emphasize the positive for New Mexico. You know, if we don't emphasize the positive all the time, this big *Journal* Center you got out here ain't never gonna fill up." That's what he told him. He said, "Don't just be running that negative crap every day, you know?" And you know, I think little things like that, that people don't think about, I think they make a difference, because you know, I noticed this year when they, when the Balloon Fiesta was in New Mexico, the headline articles in the *Albuquerque Journal* was, "What's Wrong with New Mexico?" That's all they wrote about that week. Well, hell, we don't want to do that when everybody in the world's here? We ought to be saying what's great about New Mexico that week. But you know, I don't know exactly how you cure it because it's a different age. I mean right now we're losing population because our young people, they want to go live in Austin or Denver, somewhere where there's a different kind of deal because it's what young people want to do. And so, maybe when a little time passes they'll decide to come back. The guy who does the cartoons for the *Albuquerque Journal*, John Trever, this week his cartoon showed a bunch of tall basketball players, you know, Texas, Colorado, Utah. And their population growth was around ten percent the last ten years, and New Mexico's was less than one percent. He had this little, short guy you know. Eventually we're gonna grow just because it's gonna fall in here. You know we're gonna be so low people are gonna say, "Oh let's go over there, we can go for half the cost."

Jamie: What do you think the cost of campaigns are, what do you think?

Bill: Oh, I know that's crazy too, I mean and I don't know how you cure it, but Susana spent six million beating my brother and he only had eight hundred thousand. I mean, that was overkill.

Jamie: How are we going to get away from this?

Bill: You know, as long as people, and I think that's the other thing that's wrong, you know is when all those people give that much money, they come to the legislature. You know they've got things that they need, you know. It's way worse in Washington, and that's why we end up with laws that maybe favor the drug companies, the hospitals. I don't know who makes all the money in healthcare. Somebody does. But it's whoever has the best lobbyists in Washington probably.

Jamie: That's right.

Bill: Maybe all of this new interest in politics that people are showing will help. Because that's the bottom line—people were not interested in politics. They didn't go vote. They didn't pay attention. The people that got elected were the name they heard on ads because that was familiar. If people don't pay attention to the people they are electing, it's their own fault, you know. That's the bottom line. When they get interested and feel like they can do something, then maybe it'll change.

Bill King mentioned in our interview the family's decision in 1990 to hire Tom Hujar after I suggested that they would need to hire a professional campaign manager to beat Paul Bardacke. I asked Tom Hujar of FDR Services out of Seattle, Washington to reflect on that campaign. He is still a very successful political consultant. He advises candidates across the country.

Tom Hujar, campaign consultant for Governor Bruce King / Written by Tom Hujar May 2017

Over the course of the last forty-four years, I have found that there are many variables to a winning campaign. Finances, a charismatic candidate, a great ground game, creative media are but a few of the ingredients that make up a winning campaign. Very rarely does one individual (other than the candidate) have a significant influence on the campaign. There is a story behind every successful campaign—many of these stories are never made public for obvious reasons.

FDR Services is a full service political consulting firm that has represented over 600 campaigns over the course of the last forty-four years. Founded in 1982, the company started in the Pacific Northwest and expanded to thirty-two states running state wide, initiative and congressional campaigns. FDR has also worked overseas providing strategic and campaign resources to political parties in eight different countries across the globe.

In the early part of 1990, I was invited to make a presentation to a steering committee on behalf of Bruce King. There were over a dozen participants who I later found out represented a broad cross section of the democratic political establishment in New Mexico. They wanted to select a political consultant who could lead their candidate to victory. The problem was that few, if any, of the participants had ever hired, much less worked with, a political consultant. They were all experienced campaign workers, but none of them had ever run a modern style campaign. All of them knew that they needed help while still wanting to keep control of the campaign.

At the same time, they represented a candidate that exemplified the term "old school". Bruce King was one of those rare individuals who loved campaigning. He could not go into a gasoline station, restaurant or public place without stopping and shaking the hand of every person nearby. He had already won two statewide governor races and believed he knew what it took to win the 1990 governor's race. His wife, Alice, was one of the most strong, opinionated women I had ever met. She was reluctant to bring in anyone who was not part of the inner circle. Bruce and Alice knew the state of New Mexico better than anyone else and did not see the value of bringing in an outsider to tell them how to run a campaign.

At the time of my presentation, I did not understand the dynamics of the campaign. I did not understand the infighting and the political agenda of the different participants. All that I knew was that it would be a tough campaign to win and that the nineteen ninety democratic primary would be as difficult as the general election. Four candidates including Paul Bardacke, Tony Scarborough, Bob Gold and Bruce King would contest the primary election. It was evident from the outset that Paul Bardacke would be the strongest candidate facing Bruce King. He was the former attorney general who had strong support within the progressive community and appeared to be well funded. On the

Republican side, Frank Bond was a state representative who had the support of both moderate and conservative party leaders. Although he had a contested primary, it was clear that Frank Bond would be the republican nominee. Both Paul Bardacke and Frank Bond were running on providing a "new generation" of political leadership to New Mexico, which was a perfect contrast to the old-style politics that most people associated with Bruce King.

I was one of a number of out-of-state political consultants who was invited to make presentations to the campaign. I spent over two and a half hours at the meeting and it was clear to me at the time that Bruce and Alice King were uncomfortable with the entire process. Rather than asking questions about what services I provided, they were more concerned with who would control the campaign. It was for that reason that I was surprised to receive a phone call a few weeks later from Jamie Koch who advised me that I was selected to be the consultant to the campaign. The next week I flew into Albuquerque to meet with Jamie Koch and then Bruce and Alice King. I quickly learned that the campaign was divided into two camps.

Jamie Koch was head of the steering committee. The committee had insisted that the Kings run a modern, professional style campaign. He was a well-known power broker in New Mexico who could raise a lot of money from special interests throughout the state. As a former state legislator, Jamie was assertive, strong willed and used to getting his way. He was a strong King supporter but he also wanted a winner. I later found out that Jamie Koch was the main reason that I was hired to run the campaign.

My first job was to draft a comprehensive strategy for the campaign. I interviewed everyone on the steering committee, completed a demographic analysis of the state and conducted a 600 sample survey of likely primary election voters. At a weekend retreat that included Bruce and Alice King and the entire steering committee, we pounded out the overall strategy of the campaign. Normally these meetings are pro forma since most of the strategy is defined by the polling and demographic data. Although the Kings agreed with much of the strategy, some of the recommendations were not well received. One issue in particular was divisive. Everyone agreed that we needed to project a "modern image" but buying Bruce a new wardrobe and hairstyle with this new image was a hard sell. Another difficult issue was whether we would run an aggressive, comparative campaign against our primary opponent, Paul Bardacke. The persuasive leadership of Jamie Koch resolved all of these issues. Most of the time Jamie used the logical soft-sell approach, but there were times when the debate became heated. We left the meeting with agreement on how the campaign would be won.

During the course of the campaign, many of the issues that we thought were resolved in the steering committee meeting were challenged. The Kings wanted to run a positive campaign and ignore our opponents. Jamie Koch and I believed that we needed to run a comparative campaign and deny our opponents the opportunity to gain momentum against us. Although we didn't win every fight, we won enough to carry the primary election with 52.9% of the democratic vote. The general election proved to be a difficult race. Frank Bond was a young telegenic candidate who was well funded. Three debates were scheduled and it was clear that they would be pivotal in the election. As silly as it might seem, the Kings were reluctant to have me hire a rhetorician to assist in debate prep. They also did not want to run any negative commercials or mailings against Frank Bond. It was only with the persuasive power of Jamie Koch that we were able to convince the Kings to hire a rhetorician and to run a comparative campaign. On election day Bruce King carried the state of New Mexico with 54.61% of the vote.

I have worked with many power brokers in many states and countries throughout the world. With all candor, Jamie Koch is one of a kind. He not only fulfilled the role of most power brokers by raising money and bringing in outside interests to the campaign. He also became deeply involved in the personal lives of the candidates and in the strategy of campaigns. This was not only evident in the 1990 New Mexico governor's race, but in many other races in the state.

Over the course of the last 25 years I have had the privilege of working with Jamie Koch in a variety of races. While he has promoted many establishment candidates such as Martin Chavez, Bill Richardson and Diane Denish, he has also promoted many new young candidates including Peter Wirth and Phil Maloof. In New Mexico, very few people know the story of Jamie Koch. Koch is a power broker, but also a brilliant strategist who unselfishly works behind the scenes to elect quality public officials.

~~~

As Tom Hujar discussed, I did insist that the Kings run a modern campaign. I think that desire to stay current is one aspect of my personality that has played out multiple times over the course of my career in politics and in the insurance business. I have always embraced new technology and new ways of thinking about things. I understand that in our lives, both publicly and privately, the one constant is change. How you adapt to that change is going to be the primary indicator of your success or failure in life.

3

It is understanding that gives us an ability to have peace.
When we understand the other fellow's viewpoint, and he understands ours,
then we can sit down and work out our differences.
—President Harry S. Truman

In this chapter we discuss my environmental stewardship: protecting the water, cleaning up the environment, ensuring that gaming licenses were handled in a fair and equitable way and protecting mountain lions. A lot of this work was accomplished while I served on the Game and Fish Commission from 1981 to 1995. I was chairman ten times out of the fourteen years I served on the commission. The last time I held the chairmanship, the New Mexico Game and Fish Department was an $18M state agency with 228 employees. But, even before I joined Game and Fish, I worked very hard on an extremely controversial piece of legislation I carried in 1972: the Subdivision Act. Some folks have hypothesized that carrying the bill ultimately led to the decision by Chuck Atwell, a realtor, to run against me in the democratic primary in 1974. In a book by Anthony Wolff, entitled *Unreal Estate*, published in 1973, in his chapter 'Showdown at Santa Fe' Wolff explained the massive power subdividers had in the late '60s and early '70s in New Mexico. Wolff stated, "The subdividers' political muscle in New Mexico has been strong enough to fight off determined attempts to pass unfriendly legislation. In 1972, the issue in dispute was the subdividers' beloved Section 75-11-1 which guarantees domestic well permits and allows the promoters to avoid the tiresome and expensive business of acquiring water rights for the entire subdivision at its inception...the bill specifically denied the subdividers recourse to Section 75-11-1." In another book entitled, *The Great Land Hustle* the author, Morton Paulson, quoted me as saying, "The subdividers' lobby is the strongest I've ever seen up here. It's stronger than the liquor lobby ever was. It's stronger than the truck lobby. These people (the subdividers) showed absolutely no willingness to work, to compromise...and the result of this is going to be in the very near future their representatives are going to run over them, and they'll deserve every bit of it." The Subdivision Act was defeated in 1972 but I refused to be daunted by this initial setback. I remain proud of the negotiation I did with a group of industry representatives to get that bill through in 1973. Over the course of three days, getting both sides to sit down and listen to each other and hammer out a draft at Pendaries was no easy task.

On December 8th, 2016 I sat down with Sally Rodgers, a long-time environmentalist in New Mexico, to discuss the work I did with Sally and others when I served as chairman of the House Natural Resources Committee as well as other times over the course of my career. As you will see, Sally thinks, perhaps I didn't do enough to guard against developers in the Subdivision bill we passed. But I wanted you to hear from Sally because she was instrumental in getting the word out through an organization called "The Central Clearing House." This federation of many different environmental groups developed a well-organized system for ensuring that people were properly briefed on the issues and showed up at the appropriate time and place to testify in committee. I owe Sally a big "thank you" for all that she did, not just on the Subdivision bill, but also for the mountain lions and the work that I did on the Terrero Mine site cleanup, and over the years many, many other environmental efforts. There are several factors that affect whether or not legislation gets passed, but what I admire about Sally is that she has never been afraid to talk to anybody and she knows how to roll up her sleeves and do the hard work. She learned a lot about the ins and outs of the legislature because she was married to famed legislator, Max Coll, for nearly thirty years. Sally Rodgers and others stood up for what they believed in and they took heat for it. She even received death threats and vandalism to her property. But, she and the other leaders of The Central Clearing House did not back down. They continued to peacefully and lawfully advocate for change. She mentored several individuals who have carried on the environmental fight today. I am very proud to have worked with Sally Rodgers on environmental issues and I am pleased to document her substantial contributions.

Sally Rodgers, leader of New Mexico environmental issues, Santa Fe Living Treasure / Interviewed December 8, 2016

Jamie: Do you remember where we first met?

Sally: I met you in your office at the state Capitol because I had a copy of the *New Mexican*, which publishes photographs, little bios of who the legislators are. And I knew that this Jamie Koch guy was my legislator. And so, what took me to the Capitol?

Jamie: Yes.

Sally: I came to Santa Fe in nineteen sixty-eight, the year that my daughter was born. And I was nursing my new baby, three weeks after I got here, watching the Johnny Carson show and this scientist came on for an interview. And he started talking about his book and dots started getting connected in my head. And so the next day, I went out and bought his book. Then, I read it. I read all the books in the bibliography and it's like oh, okay. I get it. As I say, dots were connected. And within a month, I organized the first chapter of Zero Population Growth in New Mexico, and then later I organized the first Earth Day in Santa Fe. Our group included Ken Bond and Pat French. We figured out very quickly that if we wanted to make a difference in the world, we had to get involved in the legislature. So it was like, does anybody know anything about it? No. Anybody want to volunteer? Okay, I will. And that's when it began. There were many firsts that year in nineteen seventy, and nineteen seventy-one was my first session. You were the very first politician that I met.

Jamie: You poor thing. And what were you going to talk to me about?

Sally: Population. Family planning information and you were, I believe you were that year, but correct me if I'm wrong, I think you were Chair of Resources.

Jamie: Yes, Chair of Natural Resources.

Sally: Right. And so, you said "Well, I'm kind of busy right now. But I'll tell you what. I recommend you go see this Max Coll guy." So, I went downstairs and met Max Coll.

Jamie: The Republican from Roswell.

Sally: Yes, who was then the House minority floor leader and we ended up getting married and were married for almost thirty years. And so Jamie, in a different kind of way, you introduced us.

Jamie: But then you organized an environmental group. Tell us about your environmental group.

Sally: Okay. Very soon after that, I wanted to know who the environmental people were in Santa Fe and in New Mexico. I met Bill Lumpkins, who I'm sure you knew. And the Garcias, Sam and the Isaacs, the whole group of folks. I also met Jack Loeffler who's a well-known oral historian. Jack and a fellow named Jim Hopper and a man named Harvey Mudd had just begun an organization they called The Central Clearing House and I was immediately involved in that organization.

Jamie: And what does The Clearing House do?

Sally: The Central Clearing, the organizing idea was that there were a few known environmental organizations in the state: Sierra Club, Audubon, a very infant, New Mexico Citizen for Clean Air and Water, Southwest Research Organization, etc. But there was no organization that was actively involved in the legislature, in politics, and in coordinating all the efforts of the groups. And we didn't want to be competitive with anyone. We wanted everyone to all work together. Harvey Mudd was one of the big founders as well as financial supporters of the organization. We quickly identified that the two major environmental issues as we saw it were number one: coal fired power plants, at that time was huge in the nation, and number two: unregulated development, subdivision development in New Mexico. So, our first foray in the legislature was an attempt to get a statewide land use plan. Over the course of the years in which I was involved in that issue, there were various bills to address subdividers.

Jamie: So, what did you want me to do when you came to see? Do you remember? First of all, the subdivision was born and raised here. You had El Dorado, which was just roughly starting. And you had some other places that were getting developed and they weren't in my district but also were happening. And you had Rio Rancho and there were no guidelines for them.

Sally: Rio Rancho came after the Subdivision Act.

Jamie: Yeah, I know. But they were already talking 'cause I knew the Kings had land down there.

Sally: 'Cause the Kings were selling the land.

Jamie: Huh?

Sally: 'Cause the Kings were the ones selling the land.

Jamie: Yeah, I knew that was coming.

Sally: And the Bonds.

Jamie: And the Bonds. So, tell us how we worked together? How your organization worked together with me?

Sally: It was in stages. The first effort was to have a comprehensive statewide land use-planning bill that would address residential development, subdivision development, as well as citing issues so that the state would be seen as a whole. So, where people lived? Where the power plants were going to go or the transmission lines would be? That would be part of a comprehensive bill. That got shot down. People weren't well educated enough and very quickly we learned from people like you and other old hands that with big, tough issues, sometimes you can't get what you want the first year. You have to educate the body, the legislative body. They have to have enough information number one: to understand it's a problem and number two: that there is something that we should do about it. And number three: how to do it and reach a solution that will get the job done. So, that was the first year. Then the second year was the Subdivision Act that The Clearing House was strongly behind, and you were as well.

Jamie: Yeah, that's the one where the committee was non-legislators but some legislators and senators; we met over at Pendaries for three days to try to come to an agreement on the legislation.

Sally: I think that was the third iteration because the first one, we went down in flames.

Jamie: Yeah, it did. The first version went down in flames. That was the lead into the committee. Because we couldn't get it passed, we put together a group of people who were involved. We had that conference. Can you tell us what you thought about the conference?

Sally: The big issue that became clear to those of us, at least on the environmental side and many of course elsewhere, was water. And we wanted there to be a uniform way statewide to address, to require subdividers to furnish water because all of this land was being sold back east. Big corporations involved were AMREP and they developed Rio Rancho and El Dorado, Horizon and there was a member of the legislature who represented Horizon. He was their attorney, if you remember. And there were several others who were involved—big, big, big money people. And they didn't want to do that. One of the ways that they were going around purchasing the water rights, dedicating them to development was a statute pertaining to domestic wells. We came to call it "75111" because that was the statute number. What we attempted to do was to prohibit developers from utilizing that statute because it was originally intended for ranchers who needed to have a well for their little house to be able to manage their five hundred acre ranch or whatever it was. Or people who lived out in the boonies but they were using it to create whole communities without making sure there was sufficient water supply available.

Jamie: That was the one I introduced on the floor. It passed out of the House but not in the Senate. That bill never did pass that session because Senator Ike Smalley killed it.

It was an issue that was around for all the time I was in the legislature until we passed it. And I'm sure what we passed wasn't what everybody wanted. But that's not what I'm concerned about now.

Sally: It took twenty-five years Jamie, before we could amend it. That was one of the reasons that we opposed it, was because we were fearful that people would say, "Oh we dealt with that so we don't have to deal with it any more."

Jamie: Conversely, I knew, if we did not get it passed, we would have had nothing. So, what would have happened is "Well, let's kill it and we'll get it next time." But on the magnitude of that, I knew that when we introduced it and passed it, that if we didn't do that, we wouldn't have a Subdivision Act today. And you just said what I was going to say: "Twenty-five years obviously before they could amend it shows you how controversial that bill was." Am I correct on that? This bill really demonstrated how correct President Truman was when he said that both sides have to be willing to understand the other's viewpoint so they can sit down and work out their differences.

Sally: Well, that is to me, this is an interesting part of my relationship with you, is because you and I and Harvey Mudd and Brant Caukins and a whole bunch of other people were really trying to prevent worse damage from happening. But from where I sat, I know how much effort it took to be able to raise it to a level where we could even make some progress at all, and there's a philosophical difference, and that's fine between people who work together. The philosophical difference created momentum to do something and the momentum would stop if something were done that didn't get the job done.

Jamie: I understand your position. But it's obvious to me; we had to get something passed. If we didn't get it passed then, I don't know if I'd been back. How the legislature would have continued with it? Hopefully by passing it, they'd eventually be changed to where some of the concerns you have would've been taken care of.

Sally: Well, sadly that didn't happen though. We would have continued with the momentum. We would have built it. I mean sometimes, outrage has to get so huge and so big that it's like an ocean current. You have to build it up to make it happen.

Jamie: We didn't anticipate it was that way.

Sally: Well, it created some problems back at the ranch. This is real history and this is what happened. Did you know about the threats the Montoyas made against Harvey and I?

Jamie: No, I don't remember.

Sally: There were attempts to plant drugs at The Clearing House so that we could get arrested and go out of business. My children were threatened and we traced it all back to some of the larger developers who were making this happen. We got personal pressure on us, on our families, the organization to back off. In fact, Montoya just flat out tried to bribe us.

Jamie: As you know, forty votes defeated me but that was all right. The fact is that because I passed the Subdivision Act I made a lot of people upset. If I hadn't passed the Subdivision Act, the realtors wouldn't have gone against me. They were one of the ones who did, as well as persons opposed to the Open Meetings Act. So, the situation is that the Subdivision Act wasn't perfect, but if it hadn't been done then, I don't know if it would ever have gotten done. 'Cause it would just depend on who got re-elected and stuff like that.

Sally: We don't know. We don't know.

Jamie: And a lot of times, environmental groups push something and they push it and they don't get any of it and it never gets done. And so, on the Subdivision Act, it was a difficult piece of legislation. Luckily nobody threatened me, but I had signs put near my house, phone calls, and all that sort of stuff. That's the nature of the beast. When we put that committee together, Brant was a good participant on the committee. He was very vocal. That committee was greatly influenced by Senator Aubrey Dunn. If it hadn't been for Aubrey, we wouldn't have passed anything. If Aubrey had not been on that committee, it wouldn't have passed. It would've been killed in the senate just as the water bill got killed in the senate. Domestic water rights still should be changed because it is still three acre feet.

Sally: Well, there has been one good change. There's been some reduction in the amount of the three acre feet in some circumstances. There have been attempts over the years to try and reduce it. I think Peter Wirth actually got something done when he was in the House.

Jamie: What about the Environment Improvement Agency? Remember, I sponsored that.

Sally: Yes, I do. I'm struggling for the right word to describe the importance of it. To elevate the issue by designating it, by recognizing its importance in state government was the greatest achievement. You started by just separating environmental work from restaurant inspection and things that were not particularly consequential to everyone.

Jamie: Yes, my bill was tagged as the Environment Improvement Agency and this ultimately became a cabinet position.

Sally: Yes. Yes, and that was just enormously important, symbolically. But symbolically is not the real word I want to use because it's not as big as I want. But it was, as I say, elevating the issue to that level was critical to making progress and providing more environmental protection.

Jamie: And then also, the Natural Resources Committee. How did that change when I became chairman?

Sally: How did it change? Well okay now, what was your first year in the legislature? I have to ask you a question or two.

Jamie: My first year was nineteen sixty-eight.

Sally: See, my first session was nineteen seventy-one.

Jamie: The Natural Resources, we normally handled all the ranchers and everything else. And when Walter Martinez became Speaker, I became chairman of that for the four years. That committee oversaw all environmental legislation.

Sally: Right. You set the tone because to this day, it is critically important that the chair of that committee be somebody who's got their head screwed on straight and understands the importance of environmental protection.

Jamie: So, the Subdivision Act had been around. When I first got in the legislature of course, I didn't know about how, but you could just see what people were doing with the land and these big corporations coming in. Even though the bill is maybe not magnificent, people can see where you, Sally, and your group were so helpful lobbying to get it through. And it was a close vote, both places if I remember right.

Sally: Yeah, it was not lobbying in the sense that we think of lobbying now. I mean there have been some big changes. We had the ability and the money to do TV advertising, full-page newspaper ads. We were traveling all over the state for months speaking to any organization that would listen to us. We learned how to target legislative districts looking at who was on what committees and going to talk to them when the session was out. I mean essentially that era helped those of us in the environmental community figure out how to get things done. And the Subdivision Act, the subdivision issue as well as coal became our classroom, if you will. We ran full-page ads in the paper. I don't know if you remember any of the cartoons?

Jamie: Oh, yeah. I do. I remember.

Sally: So, we were really doing everything we could to educate the public. In a way, it was kind of like introducing a new brand of toothpaste and you have to learn that it's Crest and it's not Colgate. We had that way of looking at it. Our mission was educating and selling and engaging people.

Jamie: And what were you educating and selling and engaging them about?

Sally: We were educating people about the necessity of having laws that protect the land and the buyer. Most, I would say probably don't you think, about ninety-eight percent of these lots initially were being marketed to people on the east coast, specifically New York and New Jersey. They were selling the "American dream." For practically nothing down, you can have your own little ranchette out in the middle of nowhere with no utilities.

Jamie: I'll tell you one thing on the Subdivision Act. Depending upon the number of acres, you could or could not subdivide. That was what the big issue was; they wanted a small number of acres to divide. So, the division of acreage was a big part of the Subdivision Act.

Sally: Right. And so, it was consumer protection education as well as resource protection because what was literally happening on the ground before the Subdivision Act, and after, is they were just going out there with bulldozers and making roads that were un-maintained and dust clouds everywhere.

Jamie: Yeah.

Sally: Yeah. So, there were on the ground negative environmental consequences. There was enormous consumer protection outrage. In fact, because of Tony Wolff's book, this was what prompted the attorney general in New

York to start criminal investigations on AMREP for the way in which they were advertising. We had national attention on New Mexico because of this business of carving up the Southwest that was going on.

Jamie: Now we're going to switch a little bit. Were you married to Max when Frank Bond decided to run for governor? And Max took that seat. Is that correct?

Sally: I was married to Max when Max was a Republican and ran for that seat. And there's a lot of mythology about that and I would love to set the record straight.

Jamie: Well, that's what we're talking about. In other words Max ran for the legislature and Frank Bond helped me when I was running for the legislature. That was the election when Julian Grace won because I had the Subdivision people, the Realtors, and the City trying to defeat me. I really didn't campaign that much. It was taking too much out of the family. Now, the question I was going to ask you, which I remember real clearly is that we had a leadership fight in the leadership with Raymond, the Speaker and Gene Samberson. I wasn't in the legislature obviously. Max at that time was a, and correct me if I'm wrong, Max was a Republican at that time.

Sally: He ran and was elected as a Republican.

Jamie: No question about it.

Sally: No question.

Jamie: I don't know if you know this, if Max told you. But the situation is that we wanted him to help us against Gene Samberson.

Sally: Okay. This is where the mythology's coming in, because Raymond has his story. Jerry Apodaca has his story and I have mine.

Jamie: And I have mine. And I've got Raymond's story. And you'll see if mine is almost the same as yours.

Sally: We'll see. We'll see. I was saying that there are three myths.

Jamie: Let me give my story first.

Sally: Okay. But just so that you know, Jerry Apodaca has a myth about why Max changed parties that was published in *The New Mexican*.

Jamie: That's not what I'm talking about that.

Sally: Remember who was working for Tony Anaya?

Jamie: Let me just finish my recollection. We'll see how close I am to you.

Sally: See why we're friends?

Jamie: Now let me tell you why I think I'm closer than you. I knew Max very well. He's a good guy. And I went to see Max after he got elected as a Republican. And I'm very strong against coalitions. I feel if you're going to do a coalition, you need to be in that party. I mean, I don't care what it is or what the story is. I don't take coalitions as a proper way to do things. And so, I talked to Max and I said: "I'll do everything to help you get re-elected if you will change your party affiliation. And I will guarantee you that I will be able to get help from Santa Fe Democratic Chair Carlos Martinez to keep others out of the race." Then he and Raymond made an agreement. The only commitment I had with Max and Toney Anaya is that nobody would oppose Max in a democratic primary. And that did not happen. Am I correct?

Sally: Yeah.

Jamie: We sat in the office with Toney Anaya—Max and me and Raymond. Toney said he would not help anybody run against Max in a primary. I had Carlos Martinez, the County Democratic Chair, say he wouldn't have anybody run against Max. I don't think he ever had any opposition, did he?

Sally: Yes.

Jamie: When? The second year? Or third year?

Sally: There have been several times.

Jamie: Yeah. But the first time, no. The first year, he did not have any opposition? Right?

Sally: No. The first year, no. Not in the democratic primary. Although, republicans tried to take him out a lot.

Jamie: Republicans, obviously I didn't have any control over that! As democrats go, there was a commitment that we made to Max on that deal. Now what other deals they made, I don't know. I don't know if they said "Max, you're going to be Chairman of Taxation." That's what Raymond says, but I don't know if he said, "Max, you're going to be Chairman of Appropriations." I just know that what they asked me to do, which I did, is make sure he wouldn't have any democratic opposition in a primary. Is that correct?

Sally: Uh huh.

Jamie: That's my story. Now what else?

Sally: You want to know?

Jamie: Yeah.

Sally: Okay.

Jamie: That's why I asked you.

Sally: Okay. One of the things I couldn't lay my hands on but I still have is a document that I made. It was a spreadsheet. The headings on the columns were, "Change parties. Stay republican, vote republican. Stay republican, vote with the democrats. There were a lot of options to consider." And what happened was, this is a very human story that Raymond Sanchez doesn't know about. Jerry Apodaca doesn't know about and I don't think you know about it because it was very personal to us. It was after the election. Max had an accident. Driving to our house going down Old Pecos Trail on the way to Arroyo Hondo and someone comes out of the left lane. Ran a stoplight. Ran into the side of his truck. Crashed the truck. Injured him. He ended up at the ER. It was a bad accident, a big collision. He was hurt. He went to St. Vincent's hospital. They did x-rays and one of the things they found on the x-ray was a growth on his lungs. This was in November. I've never told this story publically. Some people know about it. And so, they found this growth on his lungs and the doctor was very concerned and he said, "You better go deal with this." So, we went to Presbyterian Hospital in Albuquerque. We really thought he might die. We thought he had lung cancer. It was pretty big. And it turned out that it was, I mean they really opened him up and it was a big thing and it turned out it was fetal tissue from a twin.

Jamie: Wow.

Sally: This is a very human story. After the surgery, we had one of the most heart to heart talks I've ever had with anybody in my life about what's important. We both thought he was going to die. You're a politician. We care about the same issues. By then, he'd gotten an education going to law school and he'd been hanging out with me.

Jamie: You changed him.

Sally: He had changed from that conservative guy. So, at any event, I was saying to Max, "Come on, look what the Lucy's are doing for you? You vote with them most of the time. Why don't you just do it? Oh, because you were elected republican? So what?"

So, I had been offered a job in the Anaya administration, which I took. I was a policy aide, the first Environmental Policy aide in the office. And Max didn't want anybody to know until it actually happened. And we knew from him talking to Raymond and other people that if he changed parties, two or three other guys would change as well. And it would make it possible for Raymond to become Speaker just after Anaya got elected governor. So, literally the opening day of session, he says "Okay, I'm going to do it today." And said "But, we need to find a voter registrar." So, I go in to work and somehow I get past Sherry Scarfioni, who was like the watchdog of the governor's inner office. "Have to see the governor." I walked in, sat down and said, "Governor, Max is going to change parties." He said, "You're shitting me?" And I said, "No. But we need a registrar. Is there a registrar in the office?" "Oh yeah, Barbara." So, we called Barbara from the back. Max comes up from downstairs and he changed parties—literally in the governor's office the day of the Speakership vote. And I said, "You know what? You want to be chairman. Let's just throw this in the pot. Why don't you talk to Raymond about that?" So, they did.

Jamie: And they gave him the Taxation.

Sally: They gave him Tax.

Jamie: But the situation on my side was that Max and I met with Governor Anaya and Governor Anaya...

Sally: Yes. After he changed. Yes.

Jamie: No, before he changed.

Sally: Oh, about him running again?

Jamie: No. What we guaranteed Max before he changed...

Sally: He changed, Jamie, he changed parties the opening day of the session.

Jamie: I know, but we had talked to Max before that because he had to have an agreement. I had to talk to Carlos Martinez and I had to have that commitment. I had the commitment of the governor. We met with Max. Sitting here right now, I can see Max's face right now. I promised Max that I would guarantee "no opponent in the primary." Carlos called him on the phone and said, "I won't pose any candidate against you." Toney also made that commitment. And then when Max changed parties, it was done. That's what happened. What you say is exactly right. But if we hadn't gotten those agreements, Max would not have gone to Governor Anaya's office and changed his party affiliation. He wouldn't have done it.

Sally: He was setting it up.

Jamie: We were on the same page. Max and I were on the same page on that deal.

Sally: So, that's what happened.

Jamie: Okay. And is there anything as you think about the environment and as you look forward for the state of New Mexico, anything else you want to add? What do you think is the most important? 'Cause you've dedicated so much of your life to this.

Sally: The biggest issue here is the biggest issue for the planet and that's climate change.

After I left the legislature, my next big involvement with environmental issues came as a result of Governor King appointing me to serve on the Game and Fish Commission, and then Governor Anaya reappointing me. Because of my longstanding aversion to secrecy in government, I was committed to opening up the department and making sure that Game and Fish was accountable to the public. And that meant making sure that the game and fish were properly cared for so that you have fish to fish and wild animals to hunt. I always believed that there must be a balance. This includes land conservation. I insisted that this balance would be through open, accountable management—not backroom deals. Backroom deals can end up producing enmity and big problems.

On November 14, 2016 I sat down with my friend and colleague, Dr. Tom Arvas who served on the Game and Fish Commission with me for 21 years. Dr. Arvas is a practicing optometrist. He is a current member of the NRA Board of Directors. Tom and I, pardon the pun, don't always "see eye to eye." Despite our obvious philosophical differences on some issues, Dr. Arvas and I have found a lot of common ground over the years and we have worked together to accomplish a lot of wildlife conservation. A theme that I have tried to emphasize in this book is that partisan differences between elected officials at all levels of government in our country have stymied progress. It is critical that people figure out how to work together. I have many Republican friends and I hope that all our politically elected officials can learn how to listen to each other better and work for the common good.

Tom Arvas, OD, member of Game and Fish Commission,
served on National Rifle Association (NRA) board /
Interviewed November 14, 2016

Jamie: Tell me about yourself. Tell me about your involvement with the NRA.

Tom: Let's just start out with what I have done for a living. I'm an optometrist.

I've been practicing optometry in New Mexico now for forty-nine years, still practicing and as an optometrist, to be quite candid; I was very naive about the legislative process. So my first involvement was when I became the president of the New Mexico Optometric Association. As president, we had legislation in Santa Fe and that was my first experience in what you might call politics. After my presidency, it was only a year of presidency, the legislative chairman who was from Las Vegas said he didn't want the job any more. I said, "You know, I kind of had fun up there in Santa Fe, because we won. It's always fun when you win." I said, "Well, you know, I think I'd like to try that."

My first moment of real truth came, when about a week after I got the job, I called him up and said, "Bob, I want to meet you up in Santa Fe and I want to meet all the legislators that we know." He said, "Well, you're going to get your first lesson in politics." He says, "Those are my friends, not your friends. You're going to have to go make your friends." So that was kind of cold turkey in those days. To this day, I still enjoy the political process.

After that, I became involved with you, Jamie, in nineteen seventy-nine. We had eight years together. From then on I went to the NRA. I got involved with the NRA in about nineteen eight-seven in the committee structure. And then I was appointed to the board, or elected to the board in about nineteen eight-nine. I've been on there ever since. I just got elected to my eighth term this year. I don't believe in term limits too much.

Jamie: I do.

Tom: The thing about our relationship all these years has been, and you know Jamie, you can be difficult at times but it's the right kind of difficult. You learn from the difficulty. I know as chairman you were an outstanding mentor, if you want to call it that. What I learned from you was not only the process but also how to develop relationships and how to do what you're supposed to do when you're in the office.

Jamie: When did you go on the Game Commission and who appointed you?

Tom: King, no first was Anaya. What happened there, that was kind of an interesting thing.

Jamie: I was already on the commission. Anaya had re-appointed me.

Tom: Yeah. What happened was, I had no idea of anything about Game

Commissions or Game Departments or anything. I was an optometrist. My office was on San Pedro, right across the street from the Autry Building. Well, as fate would have it, there was a coffee shop right across the street and every morning I would go have coffee and I ran into Cisco. He was chairman of the commission. He said, "You ought to try to get involved since you enjoy hunting and you enjoy doing all this conservation work." At that time, the seat that I obtained was Johnny Jones' seat.

My next-door neighbor was a person by the name of Steve Ferrari. He ran a pre-stressed concrete business if you remember that in the old days. He said, "Well, call Johnny up. He's a pretty nice guy, and tell him what you want." I called up Johnny Jones. I said, "Hi, this is Tom Arvas. I talked to Steve Ferrari. He gave me your number and he said you're on the commission. I'd like to learn more about the commission." Never answered me at all—just hung up the phone. That kind of took me back a little bit so I went back to Cisco and said, "He answered the phone but he wouldn't even talk to me." "Well, call him again." I called him again and the same thing. He wouldn't even talk to me—just hung up the phone. That got my ire up and I thought, "Well, I'll just see about this."

I went up and talked to Governor Anaya and I said, "You know, I'd like to be on the commission." I'd been supporting him all along anyways and he said, "Well sure. We'll just dump Mr. Jones and we'll put you on." Well, Johnny Jones didn't like that and as fate would have it later on, we actually served on the commission together because another governor re-appointed Johnny Jones, so we actually served together. That was kind of an odd set of circumstances. Then I got back on again in two thousand two with Governor Richardson.

Jamie: You went on the commission when I was with Bruce King.

Tom: Right, nineteen eight-four to nineteen ninety-two.

Jamie: I was on the commission when Anaya was elected.

Tom: Right.

Jamie: Okay. Tell us about the Game Department.

Tom: Well, there are nine million acres of public land. The Game and Fish Department oversees the management of wildlife and conservation of the environment so there are animals to hunt and fish to fish. I had been hunting all my life. I bought my licenses every year, but of course I didn't know about the administrative aspects of the department. Once I got involved with the commission, it was amazing some things that were being done that just didn't sound right. Some of the policies of the department just weren't what I thought were appropriate. I believed that the only way you could support the constituent is to find out what their problems were and at that time they were having a lot of problems. Licensing was difficult. Even in those days permits were hard to get, which they still are now. I think when we were first on the commission; the budget was five million, now it's forty million. That's quite a change. So as a result of becoming more familiar with some of the problems that the department was having, I think I took fifty-one days out of my optometrist practice for Game Commission business. My wife said at that time, "No wonder we don't have money because you're going up to Santa Fe all the time."

Jamie: What did we do about opening it up, opening up the Game Department?

Tom: Oh, we demanded much more transparency; I think that would be the best way to describe it. Previously, nobody knew what anybody was doing. You just went to a meeting and they said, "Well, this is going to happen." After a while, you asked why. They didn't like that question "why"—they didn't like that too much. It was a wonderful experience. I don't regret one moment of the twenty-one years I served on the commission.

Jamie: Let's talk a little bit more about this transparency. How did we do it? What did you do?

Tom: I have to give the credit to you. You were clear: it was either right or wrong and if it was wrong we had to fix it. Some of the things that were wrong at that time was that the state of Colorado was having big problems with depredation, which basically means they had to reimburse in nineteen eighty-four their livestock owners, farm owners, and ranch owners a million dollars in depredation fees. Jamie, you, I think, were one of the creators of the landowner permit. The permit was a device for us to save the State and Gaming Department from having to reimburse hundreds of thousands of dollars for depredation. We would give landowners a permit they could sell to hunters to reimburse them for the use of the wildlife on their lands. It's still a very active process; now more so now than ever.

That was very enlightening to me that we had an opportunity to save money and give the public, the hunters, an opportunity to hunt also. Hunter opportunity was always a big thing with me.

Jamie: On the openness, you know I'm real strong on open records and open meetings. We changed procedures; we followed more the Open Meetings Act. Can you talk about that?

Tom: You were very, very strong on the Open Meetings Act. We didn't do anything out of line. We didn't have secret meetings or backroom chats, none of that; it was strictly business. When you went to a commission meeting, it was run like a machine. There hadn't been a system for the Game Commission meetings at that time. As you might imagine, a lot of the stuff that was being done in previous commissions was done on a friendly basis with commissioners. They decided in advance what the agenda was. They decided in advance on what they wanted to accomplish. The meeting wasn't even a meeting. It was just going in, well let's go ahead and do this and do that and that was it. So you enforced the Open Meetings Act. The law required that we do exactly what all openly run meetings must do. We had to follow the rules exactly. We had to post it. We had to tell people when we were going to have the meetings and what would be on the agenda. In the old days, they didn't even tell people they were having meetings.

Jamie: Did the department change a lot?

Tom: The department initially didn't, to be quite honest with you; they didn't really care too much about the public. They never had the feeling that the public was important.

Jamie: What did we do to change that?

Tom: Basically, we had the public come in to talk to us about their problems and hopefully we could solve some of their problems. In the old days it was more of, and I hate to use the words, "good ol' boy," type of thing where the commission would just come in and do what they wanted to do, and they would put out, "this is what the rule is." That all changed as a result of your experience in the legislature and David Salman's experience in the legislature. It became a much more formal atmosphere.

Jamie: Who was on there that helped us a lot?

106

Tom: David Salman helped us a lot.

Jamie: Talk about the landowners, in other words, a person has the right to public land and we took the stand as you remember to grade roads so people could hunt on public land.

Tom: Anyways, what was happening is, we have nine million acres of public land.

Jamie: The public has access to the whole thing.

Tom: The public has access to every inch of that, but we had to deal with the Land Office in terms of us having the right to hunt on that. We had to pay a fee for doing that. That fee was coming out of the Game Department coffers.

Jamie: Three hundred thousand a year.

Tom: Now it's up to a million.

Jamie: Several million. Remember when we went up there and we said to private landowners that we would put a road in to get into public land for that?

Tom: Right, right.

Jamie: Why don't you tell us about that?

Tom: The road, in other words, there were some lands that you didn't have access to that were on public lands as a result of the fact that they were blocked by private lands, so we had to negotiate with that private landowner for access. Getting access was quite difficult because private landowners can be very difficult to work with when it comes to opening up their property.

Jamie: Do you remember that we had the bulldozer go down on a number of lands and bulldozed from state land to other state land so a person could hunt? Do you remember that?

Tom: Yeah, the one that stands out in my mind that we created a road for was called the Adobe Ranch. It was a road that went from an area near

Magdalena where they have all those areas filled with devices to look at the moon and all that type of stuff. Actually, the public land that we had access to, we couldn't get to because there wasn't any road, so we actually built a road. We had a bulldozer. Jamie, you ordered the department to go in and get a bulldozer and just create a road, which we did. So now the hunters had access into that public land through private land. Of course, we got sued. We always got sued. We always prevailed. Actually the term that they used was "landlocked." That was a big fight that we had, but we did it.

Jamie: We opened it up.

Tom: Yes, we did.

Jamie: Could you tell us about the restructuring of fish hatcheries and what was going on with that?

Tom: The fish hatcheries were in a pretty bad state of repair. They were run down. Not many of our resources were being spent on the fish hatcheries at all. So you had the idea, which was a good one, to go ahead and rebuild all the fish hatcheries.

Jamie: How did we do that? Did we go to the legislature?

Tom: We went to the legislature and got money to do it.

Jamie: The legislature funded all the rebuilding of our fish hatcheries? Who carried that legislation? Do you know?

Tom: I don't remember.

Jamie: It was Kiki Saavedra.

Tom: That's right. I forget the exact amount; it was a lot of money.

Jamie: About five million was the amount we got for the fish hatcheries.

Tom: That was a lot of money in those days in nineteen eighty-eight. We went through systematically and improved every single one in the state.

Jamie: Could you talk about quality water, about the San Juan and the Pecos?

Tom: The San Juan is a fantastic fishery. It gets people from all over the world coming to fish.

Jamie: Tell about the regulation on it.

Tom: Yeah, we had a rule that said, "catch and release," which had never existed before I don't think.

Jamie: We started a catch and release requirement on the San Juan. Explain what we meant by that.

Tom: Catch and release basically means that when you catch a fish, if it doesn't meet the entry requirement, twenty-two inches, you have to put the fish back in the river again. But the fishery itself, the San Juan River and the area, it was hard to get access to it. The roads weren't that good. The public had difficulty in even getting there to fish so we had to improve the entry infrastructure.

Jamie: Tom, did we have subcommittees? Tell about the subcommittees. Remember we had different subcommittees?

Tom: There were always subcommittees from one meeting to the next. We met every month in those days, I think.

Jamie: But we had committees with people on there who were not commissioners. Tell us about that structure.

Tom: I was in charge of the Sikes Act Committee. The Sikes Act was a big thing that we did also. The Sikes Act of nineteen sixty provided for cooperation by the Departments of the Interior and Defense, along with state fish and wildlife agencies, in planning, development, and maintenance of fish and wildlife resources on military reservation throughout the United States. We were the first state in the west to develop the Sikes Act.

Jamie: But this all came from the way we put together the structure of the commission. You, David Salman and I, when we set up these different committees, we appointed people.

Tom: Lay people.

Jamie: That's right. We asked lay people to be on the committee to bring recommendations to the commission. Tell us how that all worked.

Tom: I believe the department somehow brought to our attention the fact that there was a possibility to enhance public lands with the use of federal monies but it had to be kind of a participating type of thing, which basically means that we had to actually sell a stamp, a Sikes Act stamp to the hunters and fisherman here in New Mexico to be able to match whatever the federal government gave us.

Jamie: We had a fish stamp, right?

Tom: Right.

Jamie: I introduced that in the legislature to establish the first fish stamp. What other stamps did we have?

Tom: We had many.

Jamie: We had a turkey stamp.

Tom: A turkey stamp.

Jamie: Tell about that.

Tom: I think the Wild Turkey Federation helped us in coming up with an artistic view. They looked just like postal stamps. You bought them. When you bought your license, if you wanted to have access to public lands, you had to buy a stamp.

Jamie: The stamps—that was the way we raised revenues. Tell us about Costillo Land Grant, with the stamp and the Costillo.

Tom: Costillo, if I remember right, that's in the northern part of the state.

Jamie: Up near Questa.

Tom: Up by Questa. At that time it was their property, but they couldn't do anything with any of the area. So we developed a fund for them so we could improve their property with the provision they would allow public access for hunts and fishing.

Jamie: We went to the elk stamp where we developed a big property there from Raton all the way up to Costillo. Tell us about that.

Tom: The elk stamp was very important because even in those days, I believe fifty-five percent of our revenue came from big game animals. So if we had a five million dollar budget, over two and a half million came from out-of-state, nonresident hunters. Well, in order for them to buy a license they had to want to come here, and in order for them to want to come here, there had to be a reason, and that's how we developed elk population really to what it is now.

Jamie: When we got the land, Questa became part of ours where we regulated it to once-in-a-lifetime hunting.

Tom: Lifetime hunting.

Jamie: Tell us about that.

Tom: We helped develop the Latir Lake area, which is a wonderful area. It's hard to get to. You have to walk in or have a jeep to get in there, but that was a fantastic place. We had to use the resources that we had. Resources we developed using these Sikes Act stamps to do that. For a state like ours, which was very small at that time, two and a half million was a lot of money to raise, and we did it through stamps.

Jamie: Go over the different wildlife areas and how we were able to get access to them.

Tom: There was a need to develop wildlife areas, which would be for the development of both fishing and hunting on these areas so that the residents would have access to these areas. People who would buy their licenses, but it's always been the fact that public land was never as good as private land. So what we did, we actually purchased wonderful pieces of property that we would be able to offer the public.

Jamie: Talk about the next time you came on the commission in regard to the problem we had at Terrero.

Tom: That was a disaster. The mine actually leaked.

Jamie: It was determined to be a Superfund site. The Game Department, as you remember, owned all the land where the mining was except for the mineral rights.

Tom: Right.

Jamie: So when the Superfund people came in to do that, the Game Department was the entity they were going after. What would have happened if the legislature had not stepped in? What would have happened to the Game Department if it had to fund that cleanup?

Tom: It would have cost millions of dollars.

Jamie: What would have happened to the Game and Fish Department? All of our money comes from hunting and fishing.

Tom: We wouldn't have had any.

Jamie: We'd be broke.

Tom: We'd be broke, basically broke without a dime. If we don't get that license dollar, we don't get any monies. We do get some federal monies now but it's like finding money in the street when you get federal money.

Jamie: Go over the other thing we did with antelope and the problem we had with antelope. Let me ask you the question. "You'd have a ranch that had a lot of deeded land and they also would have a lot of state land. In other words the state, if you looked at the state of New Mexico, sections of land all over New Mexico would stick out. So a rancher could have an awful lot of deeded land, but would have a lot of state land. Antelope move backwards and forwards and so those antelope, when they go on state land, are really owned by the state as wildlife."

Tom: We had to give out what they called 'landowner permits' for antelope to ranchers. So in order to convince the ranchers that we were doing the right thing, we would give them a landowner permit which they would sell to a hunter for X amount of dollars which would compensate them for the damage to the environment, if you want to call it that, by the antelope. We

112

had a ratio for so many acres, if he had X number acres of private land, we would have a ratio of so many permits depending about what size that number was.

Jamie: What would happen is, if you remember, Tom, is that the rancher would go in the draw. The state would have a draw. The whole public would apply for permits to hunt antelope on certain land. The landowner would have to let those people hunt that were in the drawing system and then they had their own permit.

Tom: It worked out fine. It still does.

Jamie: Go into the drawing system in regard to permits. On elk permits, it's basically up north. How much land would a person have to have to get an elk permit?

Tom: Initially, when we started the process, very few acres. I don't remember the exact amount, but it was very few acres you had to have to get a landowner permit. In fact, what they were doing up north is they weren't even...if a landowner complained, the game wardens all had licenses in their pockets and they could just write out a landowner permit and give it to them just to keep them from complaining. But then we actually figured out that you had to have X number of deeded acres and you had to document that the elk were on those properties X amount of time before he would be eligible for a landowner permit.

Jamie: Tell us about the problem we had in the north in regards to these permits being given mainly to ranchers that had about two hundred acres. What happened?

Tom: So what happened was the smaller landowner was the one who was getting, in his mind, the most damage because that was his livelihood. When he had cattle grazing on that property, in his mind the grass that the elk were eating was his grass for his cows.

Jamie: There was a law passed through Simon Gomez. Remember, we forced the department to give these permits to the small landowners?

Tom: That's right. Giving permits to the small landowners was something they didn't want to do because they didn't think it was appropriate to distribute those licenses to the small landowners at all. But Simon Gomez was tremendous. He came to every meeting we had in Santa Fe. Every meeting.

Jamie: Could you explain how we set up the districts?

Tom: There are five Game and Fish Districts.

Jamie: When you talk about the districts, talk about the qualification for people to be on the Game Commission. We passed that legislation.

Tom: You had to reside in a given area. There were five districts in New Mexico, (there still are five) and you had to live in that district and represent that constituency from that district, in order for you to be appointed as a commissioner.

Jamie: But there's another requirement. It is that you have one person who is a rancher, a landowner, and another who is an environmentalist.

Tom: Oh yeah, you had to have a rancher.

Jamie: I was chairman of the commission at that time. We decided when we divided the state into five regions, in that five, one had to be an environmentalist and one had to be a rancher.

Tom: Right. The reason for that, that kind of soothed the feelings of the environmental community, which never got soothed. Still to this day, they're not soothed.

Jamie: Could you talk about what we did for wildlife areas?

Tom: We really, first of all when we acquired the area, we would usually go and take a look. Also we would get federal matching funds. We'd apply the matching funds is what would happen. We'd go and buy these wildlife areas; we'd buy the Bosque del Apache for example.

Jamie: That's right, Tom. All that is owned by the Game and Fish department. We'd do that. We bought that land and we would go in with the federal government to do that. We went around and bought as much of the ranches as we could. In fact, we had a chance to buy the Vermejo, which is a big ranch.

Tom: Six hundred sixty thousand acres.

Jamie: We had a chance to buy it and Governor King vetoed it.

As we close here, I wonder if you could talk about what we did when I came on the second time to the commission. I am talking about what we did in regards to hiring somebody to do an analysis of the department.

Tom: Oh, yes.

Jamie: Tell us about that.

Tom: There's a federal organization called the Wildlife Institute out of Washington. Their job is to, if you like to think of it, to critique all the wildlife management departments. We knew we were having problems in the department. Jamie, you of all people knew it the most because you had to deal with the director. As chairman of the commission, you had to deal with the director on a daily basis.

Jamie: What did Wildlife Management do for us?

Tom: Well, the problem was that it turned out that their report, which was not what we wanted to hear, told of the inequities that were happening within the department.

Jamie: If you remember, they did the report. We paid them money for it. We paid them seventy-five thousand to do the report and don't you remember at some of the committees we'd ask when the report was going to be here?

Tom: We kept asking. And we kept getting the response "Oh, it's not done yet, it's not done yet."

Jamie: What had happened is that they came to talk to us about the twenty-five thousand due in billing. Anyway, what had happened was we thought when we hired this group that they were going to give us some marvelous recommendation because we wanted to go to the legislature.

Tom: To show them how great we were.

Jamie: So we could buy land and build a building. So we couldn't get the report. The report would not come. They came to our final meeting with a final bill of twenty-five thousand and I said at that time, if you remember,

"We're not going to pay it. It's not going to be paid." That's what we said. I got a call within hours after that saying, "Well, we sent that report to you two months ago." So when the report came, the report was very critical of the operation of the Game department.

Tom: Very critical.

Jamie: In other words, it was very, very critical that we didn't understand what was going on. In fact, it was very detailed. One thing it said in the report, if you remember, it said, "These commissioners are here for a short period of time. You can always change them." Tell us about that report.

Tom: It was a little discouraging because we thought everything was going just fine but everything wasn't going just fine. The department was not being managed correctly. Its approach to even managing the wildlife wasn't right, and that's what we're supposed to be experts at, is managing the wildlife. That kind of raised a lot of concerns on the part of the commission, especially you, because all of a sudden here we thought we were great, and all of a sudden they tell us that we're not so great. The director kept the report from us.

Jamie: What did we do at that point?

Tom: We changed the director.

Jamie: We went out in the public to do it and we filed for it. We had some very excellent people and we hired a new director. I think the whole problem came with opening up the Game department. We opened it up so much that the regular game and fish people didn't like it. Do you think that's right?

Tom: There was a policy which to this day still prevails, not quite to the extent that it did then, that there was no way to advance in the department unless somebody died or retired. There just wasn't any way to advance. So all of a sudden we found out that the director and the assistant director, they had area chiefs and the way the department was being run, was by consensus. The director would call up the chiefs, they'd meet in Santa Fe and say, "What do you think about this?" Take a vote. If four out of the five said, "This is what we want," that's the way we'd do it. The director didn't really direct.

Jamie: So we solved that problem with the new director. Can you talk about what we did with the mountain lion? What did we designate the mountain lion?

Tom: We designated the mountain lion as an endangered species.

Jamie: David Salman and I had also had previously legislated the mountain lion to be considered a game animal, that means we regulated the mountain lion. Then what did we do? We hired people, right?

Tom: We hired Dr. Morris Hornocker. I think we spent our first million dollars. That's what it ended up costing us throughout the years, and he did an extensive survey on the mountain lion.

Jamie: Why did we do a survey?

Tom: The environmental community said we were killing too many of our mountain lions.

Jamie: And what were the ranchers were saying?

Tom: The ranchers said we weren't killing enough. In fact, that was the only survey at that time that was ever done. Since then, we've done one on the bear. The mountain lion survey was the first survey and that was a lot of money to spend in those days.

Jamie: We hired Hornocker to do a survey on all the mountain lion stuff, to do it so that we'd know how many we should harvest a year, because that's the way it was set up. We needed separate regulation.

Tom: To clarify, when the Game department meets, their main job is to set regulation. So when we say we're going to harvest a thousand elk over a given period of time, the question that the environmental community had was, "Well, how do you know that you've got a thousand elk?" Always the answer was, "Well, we don't know exactly how many but it's a good estimate based on transects and all these other things that the Game department uses to find out how many animals they have." This study showed us almost exactly how many mountain lions we had, and it gave us guidelines about how mountain lions survived. We had a mountain lion that came from White Sands all the way up to Raton.

Jamie: It came the other way around. The lion went from Raton down.

Tom: They put a collar on it.

Jamie: They took him all the way down to around Alamogordo and let him go. They caught him again four months later and then named him "Koch." He went all the way back from around Alamogordo all the way up to Raton.

Tom: Can you imagine all the interstates and all the other things that he had to cross to get there?

Jamie: Like I said, they named him Koch! That lion knew where he was going and what he wanted! So moving forward, how do you think the management of the Game and Fish commission will be an important topic for the state of New Mexico?

Tom: I think it's not only an important topic, it's a requirement for the Game department to start more thinking about the future, because one of the things that we didn't talk about that I would just like to mention, is youth shooting. The reason it's a passion and it kind of ties in with the NRA, about seven or eight years ago we found out that the hunting licenses fell from twenty million nationwide down to about twelve million. We lost eight million license sales throughout the country. That was of great concern to game departments, because if game departments don't sell licenses, they don't make any money.

So one of the things that we've done, which has worked out marvelously and I've been very much involved with that, is this youth shooting. I had the opportunity one time when I was on the commission under Governor Richardson. He designated a hundred thousand a year in perpetuity, goes into youth shooting and the reason why is if you don't get a youth between the ages of eight and eleven, he's not going to be hunting.

Another thing that you kind of inspired, which we didn't do in your time, but we're doing it now, is that in the old days we used to give youth hunting licenses, but they were always the worst licenses. Now, we have two things that are happening. We give any youth who applies in New Mexico for a hunting license and doesn't get drawn, gets a cow elk permit automatically. This is a big incentive, because if you can imagine being a youth it's hard to get drawn. If you don't get drawn, you lose interest and you drop out of the numbers.

The other thing that we're doing now is giving the youth the best areas to hunt in. We're giving them the best areas to hunt in because if you don't get that child's attention and he doesn't have a good experience, he's not going to continue. To give you some idea of some numbers: Arizona has six thousand youth in its program. Arkansas has eight thousand youth in its program. Missouri has twelve thousand youth in its program.

Jamie: How many youth hunting licenses does New Mexico have?

Tom: I'd say less than a thousand.

Jamie: Tom, I appreciate you taking the time.

Tom: I enjoyed it.

Tom mentioned during his interview that Simon Gomez had come to every Commission meeting in Santa Fe when we were working on the legislation to require the department to issue licenses to smaller landowners. It was a process that took seven years. Simon Gomez was a northern New Mexican politician and he was an extraordinary grass roots organizer. He founded a group called, "Justice for Landowners." He became a good friend of mine. On November 15th, 2016 I sat down with Simon Gomez to discuss the community organizing he did and how instrumental he was in getting the legislature to amend the statute that dealt with elk permits. Simon was quoted in several newspaper articles as the Campaign Organizer. Gomez made an instrumental point that finally got the legislators' attention. He forced people to recognize that for small landowners, this was not about sport or trying to make a profit. These were honest people trying to feed their families. In an article that appeared in the *Rio Grande Sun* on Thursday, March 31, 1994, Gomez said, "Up until now, (landowners) haven't gotten a thing out of the permit program...they don't care about the bull permits. They want meat for their table, and they'll be satisfied with the cow licenses."

This interview is a story about perseverance and it is also a story about how one word can make a big difference in the way a law is interpreted.

~~~

Simon Gomez, Northern New Mexico activist, grass roots organizer /
Interviewed November 15, 2016

Jamie: Tell me about your family history.

Simon: Well, my name is Simon Gomez. My father was a businessman.
My father had the Gomez rock line. My father changed from Clydesdales
to trucks. That's true. In the nineteen twenties he used to haul ties for the
railroad with horses from Santa Clara Canyon. And then came the trucks,
okay. He would haul all the freight from Santa Fe north. He had all the
permits to haul to Rio Arriba County or Santa Fe County, Bernalillo, Taos.

Jamie: What about your father's father?

Simon: Well I didn't know him. He was a rancher from Pojoaque. I never
knew the man. My father was a business guy, okay. Do you remember Joseph
Montoya?

Jamie: Oh yeah, Joseph, Senator Montoya.

Simon: Remember he used to own Western Freight Line and Truck? That
was my father's permit. My father sold it to him.

Jamie: You've been involved in politics a little bit haven't you?

Simon: Yeah, my father, well he wasn't a politician, but he liked to be a
Democrat. That's what he liked, you know. He went through the nineteen
thirties and the depression and that time and he saw what Hoover did, okay.
My father was a very nice, a very good man. He was a very good father
and very hard working. Those people worked all day, you know. My father
started working when he was like six years old. He used to work hauling in
Los Alamos. They used to plant beans in Los Alamos. You know, they were
homesteaders there in Los Alamos. Anyway, I'm very happy to be here this
morning, especially with you, Jamie, one of my best friends. You helped me
a lot. What I did with HB 586 and what I did for the small landowners, I
couldn't have done without you.

Jamie: That was in regard to elk permits?

Simon: Yeah. We started with nothing, okay. What I saw, I would see a lot of people in these little towns like Coyote, Chama, Tierra Amarilla—all over that would tell me that you know they had forty, fifty, sixty acres, whatever they had. It might have been less or more. The elk would come in and clean them out. They had those little patches to cut them, to save hay for the wintertime, but a bunch of elk would come for a week or every night and they didn't have to cut. They'd do the cutting for them, okay. They wouldn't have anything, okay.

The sad part about it was that they would apply to Game and Fish to help them to give them an elk permit, give them some, but they wouldn't give them nothing, okay? No, the department would say, "No." In fact I had a game warden who told me, "I don't give a damn about small landowners, okay. They don't count."

Jamie: How long have those small landowners owned the land? Way before statehood? Am I right?

Simon: Yeah. The department was like, "I don't care about small landowners. They can't afford a lawyer. They can't afford nothing, you know. We can do anything we want to with them. It's the big landowners who do hire lawyers if something's going wrong, okay." That got me a little angry, too. I didn't like what he said, but anyway. Then I decided that I would start with changing the law to force them to give permits to small landowners.

Jamie: Force the Game Department?

Simon: Yes, we needed to force the Game department to give out permits fairly. Back in April nineteen eighty-eight the attorney general, Hal Stratton, wrote a letter to the Game and Fish. Of course, the Game and Fish asked him for an opinion. It wasn't done just because he wanted to do it. They asked for an opinion. He told them, as you know, the commission has not adopted a rule or regulations...he asked, "Is there a statute in place regarding the issuance of these applications?" In other words, licenses. I beat him to the punch, okay. I knew they were going to do something...whatever they wanted, okay. You know, if they let them go to the legislature they're going to say, "Well, we'll do this and we'll do that, you know." But I found an opportunity then to go and remake the law, you know, and the landowners, all of us worked together. We worked very hard. It wasn't easy. Well, you've been in the legislature. You understand how those things go. We got together. We had a meeting. I invited everybody to my office. At the time I was the county assessor in Rio Arriba County, okay. I invited a lot of people there. They all came, they were all happy and we were going to do something.

Jamie: I went to some of those meetings.

Simon: Yes, okay. See we had some in Ghost Ranch.

Jamie: How many small landowners?

Simon: There were hundreds of them.

Jamie: We're talking about three hundred small landowners who weren't getting elk permits. And you are the guy, the one person who changed all that. Go ahead and tell how you got it done.

Simon: I got some people from other places, and I got a guy by the name of Juan Lopez, and he's in charge of Abiquiu. He got me a lawyer, okay. The lawyer who helped was named Jim Quarry. He was from Albuquerque and he made the draft of the law, okay. He wrote the law. We argued. We argued for weeks, you know, and the law—it was long, and all we wanted on the law was for them to say, "You know, we're going to give...we're going to issue permits to landowners, okay, to get an elk." It didn't talk about acres, it didn't talk about nothing, just if you had land and you had elk depredation, you'd get a license. That's all we wanted, you know. So we finally came to an agreement that we were going to put that in.

This law, like I said, it was long. What I wanted was the law to say—this was the key word—landowner permit for elk, the director of the department of Game and Fish *shall*, not *may*, okay? That's the one word we argued about for two weeks. The lawyer wanted the word *may* which means 'if they wanted to' okay. The word *shall* is like the Ten Commandments, okay. Right? Okay, so I finally convinced him.

Who did you convince?

Simon: Well the Game and Fish, they were fighting me all the time.

Jamie: When did I get involved with you to get that done?

Simon: Them? They were in the legislature every year that I was there, every day that I was there.

122

Jamie: I know, but when did I get involved with them to get it corrected?

Simon: Well you got involved with me after the republican led Game and Fish. For many years I was going to the legislature and fighting. It was Carruthers during the struggles. But then, when Governor King came along and appointed you to Game and Fish, that's when things started to change.

Jamie: That's right, you got it. Then, if you remember, that beforehand the Game Department would give landowners permits. In other words before you and I got involved they'd give the large landowner permits and the small ranch owners said they wanted permits too. If you remember, the Game commission decided that yes they were going to set aside these small permits for the small landowners, which was a group of approximately three hundred. They're worth five, six thousand dollars. The landowners, the big landowners were able to get several of those permits and then the poor little guy who had maybe fifty acres, forty acres had it all their life through their family, those elk would come on and the small landowners, despite promises, couldn't get a permit. So we changed that. We changed that and it was because of you. We changed it. If you hadn't brought those three hundred landowners, if we hadn't met with them, we wouldn't have known anything about the problem. It was getting very serious. That's why you did it. Comment on that.

Simon: I did it because I would see the injustice. In fact, one day I called Bill Montoya, the ex-Game and Fish guy. I called him one day and I told him, "You know, you should be ashamed of yourself, okay." Because he was very negative about what I was doing; he didn't want me to organize. You know what I told him, I told him, "You know Bill, I don't know you very well but I don't like you, okay. I don't like you. You're one of those guys I don't know who in the hell you think you are? Okay."
   You know, but let me tell you what I did. We had a ranch. My brother had a ranch. It was only like forty acres and he couldn't keep nothing there. He'd keep his horses, like five horses, but towards the end there was nothing to eat. The elk had ate it all. I told Bill Montoya. Oh, he said, "You guys, what are you crying about? You know, you have forty acres, thirty acres and that's nothing, okay." "To you it's nothing," I told him, "To a lot of people that's their life." And it is. Okay to the little guy over in Coyote or maybe Gallina or somewhere you know that's what he has. I told him, "I'm going to do something." I told him, "I'm going to load five cows onto a trailer. I'm

123

going to find out where the hell you live in Santa Fe and I'm going to dump them in your grass in front of your house and see how you like it." I told him that.

Jamie: So we got to be pretty close didn't we?

Simon: Yeah.

Jamie: So tell us about when we would go to commission meetings when David Salman and Tom Arvas were there with me. We accomplished what you wanted. Remember that meeting when we were doing the regulations?

Simon: Well some of them I remember, yeah. I was a little loud, okay. That's the way I am, you know. I like to tell it the way it is, you know. If somebody doesn't like it, that's all right. But the thing is that yeah, those meetings, they were good meetings okay. They were nice meetings because we accomplished a lot. Jamie, you were the one that took the bull by the horns and you said, "We're going to help them." Remember, you went to Tierra Amarilla to the courthouse. We had a meeting there. You took all the commissioners, and you had Game and Fish there signing people to give them permits on precedent. Remember that?

Jamie: Yes, I remember that. We all worked together as a unit. The governor appointed good commissioners. We had people like David Salman, and Tom Arvas and even ranchers who were pretty good. We all worked together, we were one, and Republican or Democrats we had the votes to change the situation, to make things better. If you had not been doing what you did, and people don't really realize it, when you go to a meeting and there are two or three hundred small landowners there, and a person says "You know my elk is my winter food." In other words, it's not that I'm shooting the biggest bull. You had people there explaining that they actually needed to do that to feed their families. These small landowners lost all those permits because the permit system that was set up was unfair. We changed that, Simon. We did it together. Tell us, how did you put this organization together, these landowners? How did you do that?

Simon: Well, I talked to different small landowners, okay. They talked to other landowners and other landowners and then I had a meeting. You know, I had a meeting with them about what I wanted to do. They were all in it, okay. Before I knew it, everybody was in it.

Jamie: What motivated you to do this?

Simon: I saw the injustice. That motivated me. I saw the poor guy who needed a little meat for the winter. His fields were over eaten by the elk and thus he didn't have enough feed to feed his own cattle. Give him something. That motivated me.

Jamie: How many years were you in an elected office?

Simon: I ran two times and they were two year elections, okay. four years.

Jamie: Four years?

Simon: Yeah, yeah.

Jamie: What do you think of the Game Department today?

Simon: It's vicious. It's hostile. It's they, like I tell you, they made some regulations—they put something like Fort Knox, okay. The landowner doesn't have nothing. The only thing the landowner can do is appeal—that's all.

Jamie: So they've gone backwards?

Simon: They've gone backwards, way backwards, okay. Remember all those guys you gave licenses to in Chama? They took them away, and Tierra Amarilla and Coyote all over. They took the licenses back from the little guys.

Jamie: All these families that have been there before statehood? Before statehood, and they obviously didn't have a strong voice because they didn't have the attorneys and all the things to do with it.

Simon: No, they didn't know where to go or how to do it, you know. They probably talked to the game warden. The game warden told them that they didn't qualify and the hell with you. That's it.

Jamie: As we move forward, is it your opinion that we really need to revisit this whole topic and get the law back in order?

Simon: I think so, yeah. Except nowadays, I've even quit messing around with them a little, okay. It's not because I want to. It's because I just don't have the energy. I'm already at that age, you know. You know, I can't drive every day to Santa Fe and come to meetings and all that.

Jamie: And the young people, they're leaving the ranches, right? They're not staying in the family any more, the young people. They're leaving, yeah?

Simon: Yeah, most of them are leaving. They can't make a living. They all work some other place.

Jamie: So what's going to happen to all that land, do you think?

Simon: Probably they'll have it. The grandchildren, the kids and they'll probably keep it, but they won't work it the way they used to, okay.

Jamie: Over the years, in politics over the years I'd go with you and we helped Diane Denish and we helped Bruce King and we helped Bill Richardson and Simon, you were my source in Rio Arriba. In other words, you had so many good followers and such a good rapport in your community. It all comes back to meeting you in the legislature. One day when we were sort of fighting one another. You needed the legislature. At first, I didn't agree with what you were trying to do. But, as Truman says, "If you recognize the other fellow's problem you can work to find a solution through compromise." Once I recognized your problem and you saw my problem, things changed. That's why I wanted us to sit down and tell this story. We got to be close friends. In other words, I trust you.

Simon: Thank you Jamie. They have definitely gone backwards. They're even worse now.

Jamie: You could buy an elk permit on a ranch between five and eight, nine thousand dollars. So there's so many elk that you can kill a year, so they give all the permits to the large landowners and there's not any permits left for the small landowners. What they're doing is small landowners would lose that permit, but Chama may pick it up. Isn't that right?

Simon: Yeah, today they give the big landowners anything they want. Like if you want twenty, thirty, forty whatever, and then they give them a bunch of cow licenses and they don't even use them—they just turn them back.

All those landowners you had previously given permits to, they've all called me that they...not now, years ago they lost it. They took it away from them. They're not giving them anything.

Jamie: How many years ago?

Simon: Oh it's been...

Jamie: Probably about nineteen ninety-eight, nineteen ninety-nine.

Simon: Yeah, maybe twenty years.

Jamie: It all sort of happened...

Simon: This happened in nineteen ninety-four, when they gave all those permits.

Jamie: Yeah, but they quit doing it once the administration had changed. Not from Bill Richardson—with Johnson. That's when that all started to change back again.

Simon: They enacted, like I said, some new regulations.

Jamie: Well Simon, I wanted you to come talk because over the years you have helped me so much. The relationship I've had in Rio Arriba County has been entirely because of you. We've had a lot of fun together. But it all goes back to where we didn't understand one another at first. Then all this effort that you put in really taught me a lot. If you go sit in on a meeting with three hundred people and you can look in their eyes and some of them might have a little tear because they can't have an elk to feed their family. You go to a meeting like that, and you realize without you, Simon, it wouldn't have happened.

Simon: That's right. It wouldn't have happened.

~∾~

During my interview with Simon I learned that all the work we had done together had been reversed during the Johnson administration. While this interview was in some ways very sad, it also shows how important it is to keep up the fight. To make sure that for the issues you care about you enlist enough support to ensure there are others to continue to advocate. I wish there had been more Simon Gomez's to carry that issue forward.

In my interview with Dr. Tom Arvas, I mentioned that when the Terrero Mine leaked and was established as a Superfund site, the property was owned by the Game and Fish department. Once I realized what the costs would be if the federal government handled the cleanup and billed us later, I knew that the state needed to assume responsibility for cleaning up the spill. But that meant we needed to have a Natural Resources Trustee who could negotiate with the federal government. If we were going to have a Natural Resources Trustee, that meant that we needed to establish an Office of the Natural Resources Trustee. According to *The Roswell Daily Record*, in an article by Kate McGraw published on March 7th, 1993, Fred Peralta D-Taos carried HB 821. The bill created a state "natural resources trustee office to seek damages for hazardous waste dumping on state lands...the bill was passed despite its $332,000 appropriation because the money will be paid back to the state general fund from damages recovered by the trustee. The natural resources trustee bill stems from the federal Comprehensive Environmental Response, Compensation and Liability Act, also known as the CERCLA or Superfund law. The CERCLA statute required each state to designate a "trustee" for damages to natural resources including soil, air, surface or ground waters, wildlife habitat, fish, or plant life caused by the dumping of hazardous wastes on state lands or state trust lands, whether done by individual or industrial dumpers." The reporter indicated that the governor, the State Environment Department, the State Game and Fish Department and the mining industry supported the bill. That bill ultimately passed and we were able to set up the office as we had planned.

On November 1st, 2016, I sat down with my longtime friend and natural resources colleague Jim White. Jim assisted me with the creation of the Office of the Natural Resources Trustee. His expertise and leadership were crucial for the task we had at hand when the office was set up. Managing the many different players between the federal government and the multiple state agencies that got involved in the Terrero Mine site cleanup was a massive job. Not just me, but every New Mexican, should be thanking Jim White for his role in overseeing that project. As I said, in the introduction, this book is about the unsung heroes. Few people understand the financial and ecological devastation that happened in the Pecos wilderness when the Terrero Mine site needed to be cleaned up. In an article from the *Santa Fe New Mexican* by Cheryl Wittenauer, that was published on September 6th, 1990, the reporter described a second campground being closed along the Pecos due to water contamination. The reporter stated, "The New Mexico department of Game and Fish announced the partial closing of the Willow Creek Campground north of the Pecos less than a month after the Forest Service closed its Panchuela Campground in the Santa Fe National Forest's Pecos Ranger District." Jim Piatt, at the time chief of the Surface Water Quality Bureau of the state's Environmental Improvement Division stated, "samples showed concentrations in the water which, if consumed would be a significant health hazard."

Three years later, an article appeared in the *Santa Fe New Mexican* on February 17, 1993 from the Associated Press that stated that, "Contaminants might have killed fish at a state hatchery, but more tests are needed before saying how much blame rests with pollution from an abandoned mine upstream on the Pecos River...New Mexico commissioned the federal study as part of its reclamation effort at the old Terrero mine site north of the town of Pecos." Ultimately that study concluded that the Terrero Mine site was responsible. The state had a massive cleanup on its hands. Jim White saw what needed to be done and ensured that every aspect of the cleanup was handled efficiently and at a minimum cost to the taxpayer.

∽∽∽

Jim White, engineer, organized New Mexico Office of Natural Resources Trustee Office, oversaw the cleanup of the Terrero Mine site / Interviewed November 1, 2016

Jamie: Could you tell us about your background and where you worked before you became a trustee?

Jim: I worked for forty years as a vice president at Gordon, Herkenhoff and Associates. It's all engineers and most of our work was with the Highway Department. I graduated from college in nineteen fifty-six and that's about when they started building the interstate highways. So we established an office here in Santa Fe and I worked with the Highway Department, mainly on the interstate highways. I had that and of course we did a little bit of stuff for other clients including the city of Santa Fe, for example.

Jamie: And where'd you go to school?

Jim: I went to the University of New Mexico. Graduated with a bachelor of science in civil engineering. And then later on I was appointed to the Engineering Registration Board, which was the board of registration for professional engineers and land engineers. That's a lot of words but that's what the board was known as. Governor Bruce King appointed me to that position and then I served for five years. Governor Jerry Apodaca appointed me for another five years. I was chairman of that board twice.

Jamie: So, tell us about the Natural Resource Trustee Office. How did that all come about?

Jim: Well, I guess I was kind of like the man that was doing the work. The first thing that happened was that the fish hatchery up there in Pecos—they had a big storm event and they used to take all their water from a spring to work with the fish. But something happened with the supply of water so they had this storm and a lot of water from the Pecos came in and got into their system. And as a result, a lot of the young fish died. Okay, big disaster we think. So, the Environment Department starts studying that and they see that the mine at Terrero was mainly mining zinc and lead and a few other things. So anyway they started looking at what to do about this problem. AMAX owned the mine. Previously, AMAX had sold off some of the physical property, but not the mineral rights, to the Game department. Okay so, now we've got those two intermingled. And as you drive up the highway, there was a slag pile off to the side of the road. In the highway business, well we were using it instead of gravel. That was one of the few places in the area there that you could get this material. So, everybody who wanted to be building a road would go down and get this slag. Okay, so that included the Highway Department. That included the Forest Service too.

Jamie: And this had been going on for a long time.

Jim: Well, this has been going on forever. I was living in my cabin up there. The cabin was built around the mid-fifties. And so, the Forest Service was

130

using that on the roads which was right by my cabin. And my kids would go up and one of the things was there, it was a lead sulfate. Anyway, it was a thing that looked like fool's gold. So, they loved that and they wanted to go collect the fool's gold. So, they were going around and I'm sure they're not the only kids up there that ever went out and played with that lead sulfate.

Jamie: Yeah and so the situation that happened was that they were going to close that whole upper canyon of the Pecos River. If you remember, we didn't have a Natural Resource Trustee at that time.

Jim: No, we didn't.

Jamie: And then what happened is that we went to you to appoint you to run the office. Tell us how you did all that.

Jim: See, what you had there was a long time ago, when that mine was still working, they had a long tramway that went from Terrero, the mine at Terrero down to a mill site in Pecos. It was like fourteen miles long and they had these huge buckets that would carry the ore and they'd dig it out up there at Terrero through those buckets. Carry it down to the mill site in Pecos and they built a railroad over to this mill site and they would somewhat mill it into a kind of ore that could be handled.

Jamie: When Governor King appointed me to be the Natural Resource Trustee Officer, I hired you. So, tell us about that.

Jim: Yeah. All right. Well, I was working as a consulting engineer all by myself at that point in time. You came over and talked to me about the issue, since I was familiar with the area up there, having grown up there and lived there. And I was familiar from my work with Herkenhoff. I was familiar with the other people involved in the clean up mainly at the Highway Department, but also with the Forest Service and with the Environment Department. You wanted me to go to work. So, I was going to go as a consultant, but then we got to talking about it, and the people at the Department of Finance convinced me that everything would go better if I would forget about being hired as a consultant and go to work as a state employee.

Jamie: So, we did that. So, what was your job? As we were doing it, tell us what your job was.

Jim: Well, my job was to oversee the work that the state Environment Department had agreed to with the federal people to administer this Superfund stuff. We had so many entities there. Like I said before, we had the Highway Department, the Game department...

Jamie: The Forest Service.

Jim: And then of course there was the Federal Environment Department. The idea was they wanted somebody who was familiar with those entities to try to come up with a plan to fix the site.

Jamie: So, they wanted you to do that. Your biggest job was supervising all the work that's done. Tell us about that.

Jim: Yes, I was supervising the work, even doing some of the design. But I was mainly supervising the work and we were working primarily with our state Environment Department. But we also had the Federal Environment Department to contend with. That's the main thing. We had to get these designs approved. These were innovative concepts about how to fix this serious, toxic problem.

Jamie: And then you had to approve the design. You had to approve what they were going to do for us. You had to approve all that.

Jim: Yes, I had to approve all that. And so, that became kind of complicated because we had, I don't know, in the Environment Department we had this one lady. She had a PhD in soil science. Okay, I had a Bachelor of Science degree in engineering. She didn't feel too happy that I was kind of her supervisor. But I was. And we started out trying to take down the mill signs there in Pecos. Trying to figure out what could we do there? So, we did the studies. We got the surveys. We did the study and came up with a plan to re-grade the area there. Cap it with an impermeable cap and line the ditch. There was a little creek that ran through there. Still does. Then we had to dismantle the receiving end of this fourteen mile long delivery system down there. That was quite a bit of work. We had to keep the natural streams that were coming into the creek. Keep them from eroding into the leftover waste from the mill site there. But we finally came up with an acceptable solution and they found a local person there that could haul away the waste.

Jamie: Did the trucking. Hauled all that. So, you're the one who lined up Duran?

Jim: Well, I guess we probably put it out for bid, but he was about the only one.

Jamie: Well, we tried to keep it in Pecos.

Jim: Yeah, we tried to keep it in Pecos there. That was what the governor was interested in doing. If we're going to be doing all the work there, then we're not going to bring people in from who-knows-where to do it. If we can, find people in Pecos or the area there that could do it. This fellow could do it; so he did it.

Jamie: So, your position was to approve, as I said, the designs. You had to do that. You had to run the cleanup effort.

Jim: At that time we were working on cleaning up the mill site. Then we had to go up to the mining site, and that was where the start of the problem was.

Jamie: Explain the problem you had with the Highway Department. Can you explain why you had to pave? And please talk a bit about your relationship with the Highway Department because you had done a lot of work for them. That was one reason we hired you because of your relationship. So, tell us about that.

Jim: Well, I had worked with the Highway Department. I was retired, I really kind of retired from the consulting engineer business that we had with the Highway Department. But I still had the contacts over there. I still knew all the people. See this Superfund was a real pain in the neck. But the kind of genius part of the Superfund legislation was that you could get all the people that had some kind of a responsibility for a problem and the Superfund legislation required them to get together and come up with a plan. If they didn't come up with a plan that was acceptable, then the whole cost could be shifted off to any one of the individuals. That was the genius. So, the Highway Department, they'd been using this slack pile on the road up there. They were the ones who probably had the most at stake. The Game Department was using it for their business. The Forest Service was using the pile for their campground. Well, I knew all the people at the Highway Department since they had been dealing with me and I had been dealing with them for 40 years.

Jamie: But you still went to see Governor King to make sure that the Highway Department did what you requested. Isn't that correct?

Jim: Yeah.

Jamie: In other words, because of your relationship to King, you could do that.

Jim: Well, I had control. I could approve or disapprove whatever the Highway Department proposed to do to their road.

Jamie: So, you determined what the Superfund requirements were and made sure we followed those directives.

Jim: And I made sure that the Highway Department did it. It was the same thing with the Forest Service. They were a little trickier. They had a couple of campgrounds up there and of course, this nice gravel that was sitting over there waiting for somebody to use it. They took it and used it in their campgrounds. So, here we go. What do you want to do about that? Do you want to pay for the whole thing yourself because you're one of the guys? So, they had to. That's the genius there that forced everybody to work together and end up agreeing to a plan.

Jamie: How long were you running the Trustee Office?

Jim: It was about five years.

Jamie: So, the need to clean up the Pecos Canyon is the reason we were able to get you to go to work for us, because you had retired. But you had all this engineering background, and a strong relationship with the Highway Department, which I knew would be very important for the project to succeed.

Jim: And I knew a lot of the people up there. This thing had all started with the big flood and they used the water from the Pecos River for the fish. Before, they'd been using just their spring. When they used that water from the Pecos, then the little fish died.

Jamie: So, when you were running the Trustee Office, did you and I visit with AMAX on a regular basis?

134

Jim: Yes. The AMAX was involved there, of course.

Jamie: Well, they were paying for it. They paid for all of this.

Jim: Yeah. They paid for it.

Jamie: And you had to be the one to submit the bills.

Jim: So, they went and studied the people who were living there and had been drinking the water out of that river all their lives to see if there was anything they were worried about. It was lead. The zinc didn't affect people so much as it did the fish. But they were worried about the lead.

Jamie: So you had all the educational background to supervise the job. It was your total responsibility to sign off on everything right?

Jim: Well, I knew the governor pretty well.

Jamie: Real well, but with the Superfund, they required you to sign off.

Jim: Well, it was a lot of money and they were reluctant. They had to have somebody who would be the one who would sign off on it. And I was the guy. But, see the problem that you've got when you have a situation like that. You've got all these scientists, all these soil scientists, God knows whatever you got. But you're usually going to end up with some construction that requires an engineering expertise. So, that's hard to get. Sometimes it's hard to get all these people to agree that this one person you've got there is the boss.

Jamie: The only one you had to really report to was me.

Jim: Yeah, Jamie, you were the guy I would report to. We both reported to Governor King.

Jamie: Yeah. But you can see why you were hired to run the Natural Resource Trustee Office to do that. What's fortunate about it and unusual is that your family had been up there. They had the home up there so you knew what the story was. I bet you're real proud when you drive up there and see how clean it is.

Jim: Oh, yeah. It looks great. Most people drive by the mine site. Not very many people go down by where the mill was. I haven't even been there in years but it looks okay. The mine site looks beautiful. We redesigned it. They did a real good job. Took all the trees down. We re-graded it. Planted grass. Re-did the drainage.

Jamie: You were responsible to see that was done?

Jim: Yeah.

Jamie: Did you enjoy doing it? Do you feel good now?

Jim: Oh, yeah. I did enjoy doing it because I've got a cabin up there, up at the end of that road, and I go up there. That cabin is looking good. I wanted to have everything up there done correctly and looking nice, not just because I worked for the state, but because I, my wife, my kids and their kids and sooner or later, their kid's kids, my great grandchildren, are going to be going up to my property there. They're going to be driving right by all the cleanup we did.

As I mentioned, I was the first Natural Resources Trustee Officer, but later Martin Heinrich held that position before he got elected to the United States Senate. I worked closely with Senator Heinrich on a number of environmental projects. Elected in 2012, Martin Heinrich is a United States Senator for New Mexico. Heinrich serves on the Senate Energy and Natural Resources, Armed Services, and Intelligence Committees. He is the Ranking Member of the Joint Economic Committee and the Subcommittee on Emerging Threats and Capabilities.

With a background in engineering, Heinrich brings a unique perspective to the Senate, where he is focused on creating the jobs of the future and protecting the vital missions at New Mexico's national labs and military installations. He is a strong advocate for working families, a staunch ally of Indian Country, and a champion for New Mexico's public lands and growing clean energy economy.

An avid sportsman and conservationist, Heinrich works to protect New Mexico's public lands, watersheds, and wildlife for future generations. He worked with local communities to designate the Río Grande del Norte and Organ Mountains-Desert Peaks National Monuments. Heinrich also led the effort to create the Columbine-Hondo Wilderness Area, establish the Manhattan Project National Historical Park in Los Alamos, and transition the Valles Caldera National Preserve to National Park Service management. He is also leading the effort to pass bipartisan sportsmen's legislation to extend key conservation programs and improve public access to public lands for hunting, fishing, and other outdoor recreation.

With its abundance of solar and wind resources and energy research hubs, New Mexico can lead the way in combating the devastating effects of climate change and modernizing our nation's electrical grid. In 2015, Heinrich helped negotiate the long-term extension of renewable energy tax credits that support New Mexico's growing clean energy industries. Heinrich introduced legislation to prepare New Mexico's workforce for good paying clean energy jobs. He has also supported the development of renewable energy projects on public and tribal lands, the adoption of innovative energy storage and battery technologies, and improvement to the security of our nation's energy infrastructure.

Before he was elected to Congress, Heinrich served four years as an Albuquerque City Councilor and was elected as City Council President. During his time on City Council, Heinrich championed successful efforts to raise the city minimum wage, address crime through community policing, support local small businesses, make Albuquerque a leader in energy and water conservation, and fought for campaign finance reform. He also served as New Mexico's Natural Resources Trustee, working to conserve the state's outdoor heritage.

After completing a Bachelor of Science degree in Mechanical Engineering at the University of Missouri, Heinrich and his wife, Julie, moved to Albuquerque where he began his career as a contractor working on directed energy technology at Phillips Laboratories, which is now Air Force Research Laboratory at Kirtland Air Force Base. Heinrich later served in AmeriCorps for the U.S. Fish and Wildlife Service, and was the Executive Director of the Cottonwood Gulch Foundation. He also led the Coalition for New Mexico Wilderness.

Heinrich's principled leadership is driven by his working-class upbringing, his wife, Julie, his two sons, and the people of New Mexico. I have worked with Senator Heinrich on environmental issues and I asked Senator Heinrich if he might comment on our collaboration over the years.

∿∿∿

Martin Heinrich, United States Senator for New Mexico, former New Mexico Office of Natural Resources Trustee / Letter received July 15, 2017

Jamie Koch's environmental stewardship in New Mexico is legendary. As a state legislator, state Game commission chairman, and New Mexico's first Natural Resources Trustee, he turned his passion for the outdoors into action.

In the 1990s, Jamie established the Office of the Natural Resources Trustee charged with working to protect and restore the state's natural environment and the services these resources provide. His conservation record set the bar for how to successfully execute community-driven, collaborative resource management. One example that comes to mind right away is the restoration of the Pecos River watershed. When the remnants of the abandoned Terrero mine were seeping into the Pecos River watershed and Lisboa Fish Hatchery, Jamie brought the responsible private companies and state agencies to the table to negotiate a cleanup plan that has restored the health of the Pecos Wilderness for future generations to enjoy. Jamie has been a mentor to me through the years, and I have enjoyed working with him to protect the places that make New Mexico so special. Before I was elected to Congress, we worked together with community coalitions to support the creation of the Ojito Wilderness, restoration of ponderosa forests in the Zuni Mountains, and the protection of parts of the Sandia Mountains as open space in Albuquerque. And I was proud to follow in his footsteps as New Mexico's Natural Resources Trustee, working to restore the state's land and water.

As a member of the Senate Energy and Natural Resources Committee, I have looked to Jamie's example as I've worked with communities and diverse stakeholders across

New Mexico to secure major conservation gains like the designation of the Río Grande del Norte and Organ Mountains-Desert Peaks National Monuments, the establishment of the Columbine-Hondo Wilderness and Valle de Oro National Wildlife Refuge, and the transition of the Valles Caldera National Preserve to National Park Service management.

I am grateful for Jamie Koch's service to our state and his unwavering commitment to protecting and conserving our public lands, watersheds, and wildlife for all of us to enjoy.

The last person I felt it was crucial to include in this chapter was my friend Huie Ley. Huie's family owned the land adjacent to where the Terrero Mine site cleanup took place. He had a front-row seat on the proceedings and he was the one who brought the problem to my attention in the first place.

I thought it would be very helpful to hear his perspective on how this problem unfolded. I sat down to interview him on November 1, 2016. For him, and his family, it was a very personal story. As with any issue I got involved in and fought for, once I heard his story, I knew I needed to do something.

Huie Ley, former county commissioner of San Miguel County, highly involved in the cleanup of the Terrero Mine site /
Interviewed November 1, 2016

Jamie: Can you talk about your background? Sort of like a biographical sketch about you. Who you are?

Huie: Okay. My dad showed up in Cowles, New Mexico in nineteen twenty-nine. My mom was born and raised in Pecos. My mom's side of the family is the individuals who sold the mill property to AMAX back when AMAX first came in.

Jamie: What was the mill property?

Huie: It's where the concentrator was down in Los Alamitos Canon (Pecos). The Fox spur, and this is jumping ahead but the Fox spur came off the railroad. The ore from the mine went to the mill. The concentrated ore was then put on the railroad and it went to the smelters. My mom's side of the family is where the property that was sold to AMAX was and that became mill property.

Jamie: And what was AMAX?

Huie: AMAX was the mining company that came in and mined from nineteen twenty-five to nineteen thirty-nine. It ran through the depression. It was the largest employer in the state of New Mexico when it was running. Had the world's largest aerial tram at the time. Today, we have no historical markers. There is nothing about this mine anywhere in the canyon. You know, you go to different places and you see historical markers. They've got signs saying this is what went on here. It ran through the war, etc. We don't have anything that indicates what happened other than what we're going to be talking about here today. I was born and raised there, went to school in Pecos, went to New Mexico Military, graduated from St. Mike's and then I went to NMSU. I graduated from there. I did a bull fertility study for the state of New Mexico. Traveled all over the state doing this semen evaluation on bulls. Then I went back home and started running the business. Sherry and I got married in nineteen eighty. We've raised three kids there. And all three of them started in Pecos. Went to St. Mike's. Went to NMMI, except for Brandy. Brandy didn't go to NMMI. My daughter, the oldest didn't. She went to State. Conrad went to State and we got to throw you one bone. The doctor in my family, Matt, went to the University of New Mexico, the youngest.

Jamie: The smart one.

Huie: Sherry's a nurse. She was one of the first graduating classes out of NMSU in nursing back in the seventies. Then we ran the business; we took over the business from my mom and dad. They built the original store there in nineteen forty-three. My dad was the caretaker and property manager for AMAX after they closed down. We used to live across the river. We bought the dairy from the mine when the mine closed and it was across the river from the store, which is still here today.

Jamie: This is at Terrero?

Huie: This is at Terrero. We ran the dairy. Delivered milk and eggs from Terrero to Española. We had the chicken farms in Española. We delivered milk going to Española. We'd deliver eggs going back to Terrero. So, we wound up with that business in the fifties. My parents bought the dairy from the mine, from the Lapp's, who were running the dairy during the mining days. Elliott Barker headed up a purchase agreement to purchase the AMAX mining property.

Jamie: And Elliott Barker was my greatest mentor.

Huie: So, Elliott Barker looked at the fact that these tracks of land, the Mora, Willow Creek, across from me where the dairy was were all key access properties to the river for fishing. So, he said, "The state of New Mexico needs to grab those up and put them in the public domain." So, I've got a letter in my file that told my dad that he was going to have to move because Barker was going to purchase that property. My dad was going to have to move across the river or move somewhere. The letter, from the state of New Mexico Department of Game and Fish is dated August eleven, nineteen fifty. The letter states, "The purpose of this letter is to advise you that it will be necessary for us to cancel this lease six months from the date hereof as is provided in the second section of the lease. The Game Department feels that a new lease will have to be drawn up and this notice of the cancellation of the lease six months hence should not be construed in any way as jeopardizing your chance of getting a new lease from the Game Commission. We will be very glad to work with you on this at the first opportunity and see what we can work out that will meet the needs of all parties concerned." So, Hugh Woodward, the attorney for the mining company had eighty acres. We sit on three of those eighty acres now across the river. He gave that land to my dad to move over there. So, that's where the current store, house, and everything sits, is on those three acres. Sherry and I got married in nineteen eighty and we were running the store, running the horses, doing the pack trips, doing the hunting trips. Doing all that sort of stuff and we were just happier than a bunch of little larks.

And then, in the spring of nineteen ninety, unbeknownst to me, this big old sign went up in front of the store on the highway. The DOT showed up and hammered this sign in. I walked out there and looked at the sign and it says, "No access beyond this point." I said, "Holy smokes." This is the state road that accesses the wilderness that accesses all this game and fish property and all these summer homes. All these folks, all at once, here we are. It says, "No access beyond this point." I hit the panic button. I thought "Dang oh mighty. What's this all about?" I talked to the highway boys and said, "What the Sam hell, what's going on?" "I don't know. They told us to put this sign up." So, I said "Damn." So, they actually put signs up the canyon, all the way up the canyon and the one in front of the store. I mean that was final. You're going to turn around in the parking lot store and go back. Well, all the camping, all the access, all the fishing, all that stuff, that was where I came from. And I am thinking, "Damn, this is my livelihood. This is the whole deal." So, I got on the phone.

Jamie: And nobody had said one word to you? Not one word?

Huie: I had not heard a thing about it. And I'm thinking, "Where the heck did this all come from?" So, I got on the phone trying to, you know, talk to Game and Fish. Talk to whomever, whatever, and finally I got a hold of you because you were on the Game commission.

Jamie: I was chairman of the Game and Fish.

Huie: I said to you, "We're talking about closing off all access to this thing." I wasn't thinking about the remediation costs and I didn't have any of that. I got you on the phone. Bruce was governor, and of course, my dad and Bruce King had bought cattle together and stuff like that. So, I had a little bit of access there, but hell, that wasn't even in my mind.

Jamie: See, then it goes back 'cause what had happened with Elliott Barker, we [the Game and Fish Department] had bought up all that land. So, the Game Department is totally responsible for the cleanup of the lines up there 'cause we bought the land.

Huie: So, we started down this road. You got involved in it and I was involved in it. And we're sitting there and you got all these players. You got DOT, you got the Forest Service, you got the state, you got the private land holdings, you got all these multiple agencies. Somebody's got to pull everybody together and rope this thing all together and that's where you wound up in the process of getting it all done. But we worked through that thing. I mean, on the federal side it was the Jack's Creek road that had to be completely remediated. They went in and ground all the material up with regular asphalt type rotary machine. Brought all that material in and bound it with a calcium binder, laid it all back down and then paved over the top of it. The DOT on the state part of it did a temporary, that is still there today, patch by putting a little bit of material on top of the existing dirt road and then coming in and chip and sealing the road from Cowles all the way to Terrero. That was six miles of road that they had to do. The feds did their mile and a half on the upper end. And then we had to start to work with the remediation of the waste rock pile.

Jamie: See now what happened in the mean time before that is that the EPA notified us that the National Trustee in the National Trustee Office should handle all of this. We had no National Trustee, no National Trustee Office. We didn't have one. So, the negotiation, the only way you could have negotiations was if you had that. So, the state would have had to appoint a Trustee in an established department. So I decided I would be that person. Governor King went to the attorney general and said, "Can Jamie be our Trustee?" because it had to be an employee. The attorney general said, since I was chairman of the Game and Fish, I could be the Natural Resource Trustee. That's when I hired Jim White,

Huie: So, we wound up trying to get all these players together and work through the different entities.

Jamie: Huie, you were involved in this all the way along. In other words, if we had not had somebody as articulate as you, if you hadn't taken the time or if you had just thrown up your arms and said "Well, this is what we got," which is what most people would have done, things might be very different now. But not you, Huie. You reacted and did something. And so, when you stop and think, if you had not done what you did, we would be in a different situation.

Huie: Ten thousand folks in the deal. You know, just one or two people can say "yes," "no," "yes," "no." Well, so we got the Forest Service and we traded them that quarter acre. Got them out of the picture.

Jamie: Now, talk about streamlining the process.

Huie: So, we got that quarter acre in, got it in under the state so that we would not have to have the feds involved in that waste rock pile. So, we actually had two sites.

Jamie: What happened every time it rained before we cleaned it?

Huie: Well, because of the rain and the waste rock pile, minerals would leach out from the waste rock—zinc. The zinc would go into the river and it'd kill the fish. We would have these massive fish kills.

Jamie: In the fish hatchery?

Huie: Yes, in the fish hatchery.

Jamie: And the fish hatchery had a shut off valve. A deal to stop it if it rained and they didn't do that on two occasions. The Game department didn't shut off the gate and killed all the fish in the fish hatchery. They also killed all the fish from where the creek came in to all the way down through Pecos.

Huie: So, what they would do at the fish hatchery is they had a diversion. They'd shut off the incoming flow from the river and recycle the water so that they'd keep the hatchery from getting zapped. Well, we didn't quite get that done a couple of times. So, that gets into the press, gets into the public eye. At that point in time, the public sentiment was very much about "clean up the mine sites all over the United States."

Jamie: As you know, I'm the one who put together the Environment Improvement Agency. I was the one who had passed that legislation.

Huie: See, if it had gone Superfund, because what I was gonna tell you is the waste rock pile is physically manipulated material that was left from the mine, immediately adjacent to the mine. The high graded ore was put on the tram, taken to the concentrator, so down in Pecos now we have these large settling ponds that have been manipulated. Have leaching going into the subsurface, going into the water, all kinds of things. So, there were two sites and both of them were going to take major amounts of money. I knew if we could clean them up internally in the state, we were going to be a whole lot better off. But, if the EPA came in on the federal side and built a Superfund site, then we would have been dead ducks in the water. I mean, they would have taken years to study everything before getting around to cleaning up. All this, even as it was, I thought we drug our feet quite a bit 'cause we tested all the folks in the Canyon for lead.

Jamie: That's where the Environment Department wanted us to do it. But what we were able to do is get the state to pay that cost, not the Game department.

Huie: So, we got that all lined out. Got everything pretty much squared away. One of the other things that we secured in this cleanup was Mickey Lang. When he was head of the Game and Fish back in the late sixties, he had given what we call a golf course, and the Forest Service now calls it "The Links," like "golf links." "Links track." It was a nine hole golf course that ran during the mining days. The miners played golf up there. Matson's house, the superintendent of the mines, his house set up there on the edge of the golf course. Quite a few houses were up there. Mickey traded that land to the Forest Service with the intention that the Forest Service would develop a facility, a camping facility there. And the Game and Fish properties down here wouldn't be the ones taking all of the impact from the public's access to the Pecos River. They could develop a handful of campsites but mainly, it would be day-use parking for the fisherman. Get the campers up off the river. Built them a real plum of a campground up here that had all the amenities and everything. Well, Forest Service would not develop that facility because of the underlying mineral rights issue. They didn't have the mineral rights so they would not move forward. The life span of the facility was not going to be good enough to protect their investment because they didn't have the mineral rights. So, one of the things that we negotiated in the compact is that when the cap that is on the waste rock pile is maintained for eight consecutive quarters, then the mineral rights will transfer to the state. The state has the mineral rights. It's in their deal and in exchange for that, the state has the site to take care of for the rest of time. But we have not transferred that as of today. It's still hanging out there and I can't get any traction with it. I don't know why we can't get that moved but it's one of those deals.

Anyway, on the east side of it, we came in and dug about a twenty-five foot deep trench to stop the leach through the waste rock pile. We dropped a rubber, vinyl liner that goes down into that ditch, comes out of the ditch, goes over the top of the waste rock pile and encapsulates it in a plastic barrier. Then we came back over the top of that and covered it with topsoil, and grass and trees are growing on it now. Matter of fact, they started taking trees off of it because they don't want the trees to penetrate the plastic, so they're taking the trees off. So, now we created a really nice grassy hillside.

Jamie: I was so happy when that cleanup finally was finished. I can remember when Elliott Barker and I went in the wilderness. Prior to the cleanup, every time we passed that site, Elliott Barker just cussed it. He would say, "This is the worst thing ever." Every time we drove by, he'd say it should have been cleaned up. Every time we drove by, Elliot would give me hell.

Huie: So, we got that one all remediated and then started on the one down in Pecos. And I was the county commissioner then, at that point in time. *Tererro* is a book that Leon McDuff wrote about the mine and all this stuff. His dad was the fifth guy hired for the mining company. His dad's the one who built the super structured bridges that go up the canyon. There's only one left and it's in the historical registry. He built big wood-beam bridges and that's really what opened up access to that entire canyon to a greater degree. Some of the folks will say it opened up and killed everything. And others will say it opened it up and created everything. So, it's a matter of opinion. But from a tourism standpoint, that access to the wilderness, which is the two hundred thirty-five thousand acres, was an economic boom for the state, for the community.

Jamie: How much traffic do you get? What is your average amount of traffic, roughly, during the summer months?

Huie: You know, the weekend warriors as we call them now days are what we deal with. And we'll run about two thousand five hundred individuals up the canyon on a Friday, Saturday, Sunday and they're just there for the weekend. There are no real amenities for them in terms of water, camping facilities, that sort of stuff.

Jamie: So, what would have happened if the Superfund had closed down the canyon?

Huie: Oh, that'd been it. We would've been dead-in-the-water. There wouldn't be any economic benefit for the community at all. I mean, Pecos would be dried up even worse than what it is today. Bedroom community for Santa Fe is where it's headed.

Jamie: What would have happened with all those residents up there? How many residents do we have up there, roughly?

Huie: There are five hundred homes in the Pecos canyon.

Jamie: What would have happened to those five hundred homes?

Huie: The same thing. During the fires, throw them all out and tell them don't come back. You're under permit because they are actually, a large percentage of those homes are on federal leases. Back in the twenties and thirties, the Forest Service was trying to develop an economic base, an income stream. Yeah. They're on federal leases over there. The Forest Service implemented this recreational cabin lease to develop an income stream for the Forest Service back when the Forest Service actually was a multiple use agency. Now they're moving into preservation. They would lease the site to an individual to build some cabins. The way they marketed it was a "fair market lease." They'd go in and appraise the land value based against private land sales and then they charged six percent of that appraised value for your lease. So, if you had an acre of land at forty thousand, you got six percent. That's what they charged you for your lease, for the annual deal. So, it was a good revenue stream and it continues to work well today. We've had those cabins there for tons and tons of years. But those are all dollars, new dollars that come to New Mexico every spring, every summer, every year, because they're not just to northern New Mexicans, but to the entire state. Some of the cabin leases come from Albuquerque, from Roswell, and even Clovis. And there are a lot of non-New Mexico residents, including folks from Texas, Oklahoma and Kansas. So all those cabins would have been cut off. They'd had no access. All the private land boys—I don't know how the EPA would have dealt with private land.

Jamie: So, you mainly worked with Jim White and me. Wasn't that true?

Huie: Yup. Rolled the deal. We're still working. We're still doing the remediation. We still hold in the silt fences.

Jamie: It took five years for them to complete the cleanup.

Huie: Yeah, so we did the cleanup on the concentrator, the concentrating site, and we got those all fixed up. One of the determinations we had to deal with was the settling ponds. Trying to say how far do you take your risk aversion? Do you do a twenty-five year floodplain, fifty year floodplain, a hundred year floodplain, a five hundred year floodplain? Well, the cost is just vertical. When you go from twenty-five to fifty to one hundred to five hundred, I mean it's just tremendous. And we'd just started laying it all out and everything and were in discussions about it. The difference between a fifty and a hundred year flood plain is a chunk of money. And we were sitting there discussing it, and they had just started to channel it and get it set up to go, and we had a hundred year event occur. The rain came down through there and took everything out. We had a huge rainstorm. It flooded the whole valley. The settling ponds became a big playground for the Pecos folks because of the sand and silt. And I said "Well, you either look at it that this is the hundred year event and we're not going to have another one for a hundred years" or this is "Hey, wake up. Do the hundred year stuff." So, we wound up going ahead and convincing AMAX to do the hundred year flood plain stuff on the settling ponds.

Jamie: So AMAX paid for all this?

Huie: Yes.

Jamie: Was there any media coverage of the hundred year event?

Huie: We don't have any coverage in the Pecos canyon no matter what happens.

Jamie: But all of that was paid for by AMAX.

Huie: Ken Paulsen was the president of Cyprus AMAX.

Jamie: What do you think the significant to long-term effect has been on what we've done?

Huie: I mean the long-term remediation, ninety percent of the people who go up there now have no idea what was there.

Jamie: Nobody knows. Maybe that's what I was telling you.

Huie: People get all excited, when there's some deer or elk eating on the hillside, on the grass up there.

Jamie: Yeah, people don't realize what the Natural Resource Trustee is. They don't even know about it. Nobody knows. The story has not been told. And to my mind, you, Huie, you have been the key. If you hadn't been there, we wouldn't be talking today obviously.

Huie: I'd be doing something else, I bet you.

Jamie: Moving forward, what do you think is going to happen?

Huie: What I would like to see happen or what I think is going to happen?

Jamie: Both ways. What would you like to see happen and what do you think will happen?

Huie: I would like to see that whole Pecos canyon as a recreational complex with Game and Fish, Forest Service, State Parks, all these different entities, the municipality, the county, all coming together and moving it as a tourist destination. That whole area was a destination for tourism for years. And we lost it. You know, you look at Cloudcroft, you look at Chama, look at Angel Fire, and look at Red River, Taos, and all these other entities. You say, "Well, how were we so far ahead of them? and then we got so far behind them?" And a lot of it is political influence. The Village was not on the forefront with tourism and all that. So, as a county commissioner, I tried to move it forward quite a bit, but the Forest Service funding and everything pretty much road blocked a lot of it. But if I could be a "King for a day," I would develop a center corridor of that thing run by State Parks, and have the Forest Service, have the outside edges of the campgrounds, like Iron Gate, Jack's Creek, Windsor. That way those place would all be accessible. And have the main corridor down here run by State Parks all the way up and down the canyon. Have State Parks run it because Game and Fish is just not in the campground business. They're hunting and fishing and that's all they really care about. They don't care about taking care of the camper and making sure the outhouse is clean. That's just not who they are. And the Forest Service is very reluctant to move anything. I mean we can't even secure the access to Iron Gate. I've been trying for years.

Jamie: Why would we want to develop more campgrounds? How does that help the environment?

Huie: Well, it's not development so much as if you don't give individuals an appropriate place to recreate, to camp by designating for example: "This is where we want you to set your trailer up," or "We're going to give you some water to drink and please put your trash here. The outhouse is here." If you don't do that, they'll find and create their own user-developed campsite and then after a while, degradation occurs because it's not taken care of, because it's not maintained. Then all at once, the Forest Service and the state says "Well hell, we can't have people there." So, they close it off.

149

Jamie: And they go find another place.

Huie: They'll find another inappropriate place. So, now what you've done instead of having one site that is well controlled, you have degraded two sites.

Jamie: And so on.

Huie: And then it just continues. And if you go up to the canyon now, we've got all these signs that the Game and Fish have up. The signs say, "No parking. No camping. No this. No that." I am suggesting that there could be signs saying, "This is where we want you to be. This is your facility. This is the water." Right now, there are only two places to get water in the canyon. One is the first campground that the Forest Service has down at Field Track and the other one is the last campground up at Jack's Creek. Everything else in between has no water. So, how do you, from an economic standpoint, how do you expect people to bring enough water to camp for a week? You can't do it.

One of those deals, remember you and I...there were concerns about the mineral rights. We're coming back to the mineral rights. Conoco was in up there securing the mineral rights. On the Game and Fish property across from me, below the cave, they drilled.

Jamie: There's a cave across there, an Indian cave that the Indians used to use.

Huie: They still do. Pecos Indians were here this summer. The cave across from me is their sacred ceremonial cave. It's blocked off access to the public and all that. But Conoco drilled a core sample and in the horse pasture in front of the store, there was an Artesian well from a core sample that the Cyprus mining company drilled back in the thirties. We drilled this one over here and damn if we didn't hit that Artesian well. And I thought "Well hell, here's an opportunity to secure water for these campers" and all this stuff. So again, you were on the Game Commission back then. I called you up and said "Hey, I got an idea." My idea did not work. My Lord, we couldn't capture the water because we couldn't case the water and the water wouldn't mix with water as it came through the different layers and we wound up plugging the hole. I mean it would have been really nice to have water for the campers.

Jamie: It's done. It's gone. So, you said, "If I were King for a day, I'd like Pecos canyon recreation complex to be reality." But what do you think will happen in the next ten years?

Huie: I don't think we'll see any development in that land federally or from the state because of the function of the economy at this point in time.

Jamie: It also depends on the governor. If you have a governor like Bruce King and Bill Richardson, those types of governors, you might. But if you don't have that kind of government, you've got a problem. It's not going to happen.

Huie: Well, and right now with Governor Martinez, her deal is that she has said she did not want to fund a piece-meal process. Well, we have let the Pecos canyon complexity get so big, five million here, five million there, five million over there. To have to come up with in today's environment, twenty-five million to build the whole facility, we're not going to find that money.

Jamie: It's not going to happen. Also, because people don't want to pay a fee. If they had to pay a fee, they would have to have water and everything else. If you don't have water, you're not going to pay a fee.

Huie: Yeah.

Jamie: We tried to get the State Park Service to take it over. And we were pretty close and it never materialized. If there were a State Park all the way up there, you'd have water and the garbage and everything else.

Huie: You would also have some security. You would have some law enforcement. Not from state police, but somebody with State Parks that goes by and sits and visits and chews the fat with the folks. Tells them "Hey, make sure you pick up your trash when you leave" and that sort of thing. You don't have to be that hard, hardcore side. But you need somebody there to make sure everybody stays in line to a certain degree.

Jamie: Now, if you did get your recreation complex, the first piece I said was that the first benefit that I understand is that the property is well maintained. And so, from an environmental standpoint, it's very good. There's also, I'm assuming, once you have your services like your water, the paved road—you would have appropriate parking and all of those things, and proper waste management and everything like that. I'm assuming there's an economic impact that's different than everybody just shows up and they don't pay a fee.

Huie: Definitely.

Jamie: Let's talk about the economic impact just for a second.

Huie: The economic side of it. Currently, you have people like real-life, high desert anglers who come in. They bring clients in from Santa Fe and fish some of the waters, but they're day use. They're just in and out. If you had a longer span of time that folks would stay—whether it's campers or the day use folks, the better the amenities are, the longer you're going to have somebody stay in the community. If you stay in the community five days, you're going to need to go down and purchase some fuel. You say "Well hell, I'm tired of eating my own food. I'm going to go to the restaurant and get something to eat." Or, "I forgot to get hot dogs and marshmallows (or whatever), or I ran out of them." Or "The raccoons ate them, or whatever." So, the longer you can get somebody to extend his or her stay, it extends the season for the community because there's facilities there for people to use and stay in and you can get beyond the June through August. With proper facilities, you can get into May and get into October, so you've extended the economic impact because of the length of the season, and you can by the length of stay. Right now, if you look at a lot of the hunters and stuff, three days is about the max that they stay. So, you need to give them more so that it's easier for them to stay longer. And then, they're going to impact the community. Because right now, ninety percent of the people who walk through the door of my store have never been there before.

Jamie: And so, to go full circle on what we've been discussing, if we had been a Superfund site, we would not even be envisioning future campsites, etc. Because if we hadn't done what we did, the state couldn't afford the fifty to a hundred million AMAX was claiming it would cost to clean up the site. Instead, we managed, with Jim White and others, to devise a plan that cost about five to six million and we got AMAX to pay for it. If AMAX didn't pay, many people's lives would have been affected and people would have left. And you see why it's so important.

Huie: Well, there's one other thing, back to when I was "King for a day." I'd take that damn lynx track, that's nine hundred acres. Take that back away from the Forest Service. I'd say, "You did not fulfill your contractual agreement."

Jamie: Yeah.

Huie: "Yeah, you didn't develop this campground. That this was our intent on trading this to you was we were going to develop this campground. You didn't do it. Give us the property back or we'll trade you back or give you something." And then the state would have a facility.

Jamie: So, in the future, if the state can get that land back from the Forest Service, that would be a wonderful place for a developed campground.

Huie: Yes.

Jamie: Just so I'm clear. This was supposed to be done in the nineteen sixties right?

Huie: Yes, in the sixties.

Jamie: Back in the sixties.

Huie: That was at the cap on the mine to transfer the mineral rights that underlies this lynx track.

Jamie: Okay, so that's another thing that's still hanging out there?

Huie: That's still hanging out there. Yup.

Jamie: Unfinished business.

Huie: Unfinished business.

4

Carry the battle to them. Don't let them bring it to you. Put them on the
defensive and don't ever apologize for anything.
—President Harry S. Truman

In 1975 I was defeated in the legislature. I knew I had angered many different groups of people by passing bills that I thought were in the best interest of all New Mexicans, not just a select few. I realized I could be much more impactful raising money for strong candidates than in the legislature. Plus, at that time, I had different priorities. Nene and I were raising our daughters—Amy and Julie. The legislature is very hard on families. I've sometimes been called "The Kingmaker." In 2007, the *New Mexico Business Weekly* published interviews with fourteen power brokers. I was one of the people they interviewed. I was pleased because the headline of my profile read, "The Kingmaker: Jamie Koch Tells It Like It Is." Plus, there was a picture of me at age seventy throwing the shot put. In the story the author, Haley Wachdorf said, "If you're the gambling type, you probably don't want to bet against Koch—because he usually wins." I would agree with that except I don't always place time limits on how long it should take to win. If I don't win the first time, I usually dust myself off and explore new tactics. Then I keep trying until I do win. The article went on to talk about the major fundraising that I did for various causes including the March of Dimes and United Way, as well as the many political campaigns where I chaired the fundraising efforts. The article discussed how I participated in an ethics task force in 1992, which was writing legislation to reform the state's election rules. It stated that, "Koch threw in a last-minute addition that candidates running for state office could not pay for their campaigns with money raised for a federal election campaign." I had done that to prevent Bill Richardson from running for governor in 1992. But as I've told many people, politics is funny; your opponent today may be your friend tomorrow so better not to burn bridges. I remember when David Salman, and Bill Richardson and I sat down together in 1998. I said the only reason I'm coming out of retirement is because of Bill Richardson, because I could see if we could have somebody of his stature come back to New Mexico and run the state; the state could benefit and it sure did.

By 2001, I was chairing the fundraising committee of 'Richardson for Governor' which raised more than five million. In the *New Mexico Business Weekly* article I said, "I think the world of Bill Richardson, but if I don't agree with him, I just tell him. The problem you have is that if you disagree with someone's policies, you need to tell them that before it comes out in the paper. My pattern is the same. I am very blunt. I'll tell you exactly what I think. Maybe I shouldn't do that, but I don't believe in playing games." I have enormous respect for Governor Richardson. Of all the governors I worked with, I think I was able to accomplish the most with Governor Richardson. Together, we managed to get over one billion dollars worth of capital outlay for the University of New Mexico. I told him to hire David Contarino to manage the campaign and David ultimately became Governor Richardson's Chief of Staff.

I believe that New Mexico benefited enormously from the political savvy and the vision that Bill Richardson brought to our state. Because of his background as a former cabinet secretary for the Department of Energy appointed by President Bill Clinton and from his time as a congressman and as an ambassador to the United Nations, he had a much bigger lens from which to evaluate situations. Time after time, his ability to look at the chessboard and come up with the winning combination of moves always inspired me. We had a lot of good governors but no one like Bill Richardson. I think ultimately, historians will agree with me, that what Governor Richardson did for New Mexico in his first four years will never be replicated.

~~~

David Contarino, campaign manager and chief consultant for
Governor Bill Richardson, first chief of staff for Governor
Richardson / Letter of December 20, 2016

As Democratic Party Chair, Jamie's staunch advocacy for Democrats
and for a positive vision for New Mexico was unparalleled. Jamie was
a fighter in the best sense of the word. He fought for candidates and
policies to improve schools. He fought to raise wages and expand health
care for all New Mexicans. He also fiercely protected the interests of his
candidates in an ethical and effective manner. In 2002, when his counter-
part, Republican Party Chair John Dendahl offered $100,000 to induce
the Green Party to run candidates in congressional races to siphon
votes from our Democratic candidates and help Republicans win, Jamie
would have none of it. He called out Dendahl for his attempted bribe,
demanded his resignation and put enough public pressure on him so
that the whole sordid deal was scuttled. As Finance Chair for Governor
Richardson, Jamie relentlessly focused on raising the resources that the
campaign needed to compete, putting his extensive contacts and energy
to use for the cause. Thanks to his leadership, our campaign broke every
fundraising record in the book. I salute Jamie for his talent, his loyalty
and his tireless support of Democrats and Democratic principles.

∽∽∽

Bill Richardson, governor of New Mexico /
Interviewed December 8, 2016

Bill: I was governor of New Mexico. I was a congressman and I first met you
when I was running for congress. You helped me. We had various interactions when I was in congress, but my main interactions with you were when
I decided to run for governor and the first person I went to was you.

Jamie: Why was that?

Bill: I had been in Washington for fifteen years. I'd been a cabinet secretary. I'd been an ambassador and I wanted to run for governor. I wanted
somebody I could trust who knew everybody, who would give me advice,

who would be honest with me, and that person was definitely you. We sat in the living room of David Salman, a former legislator from Mora, a great environmentalist and we kind of started thinking about the governorship because at the time David Salman was a likely candidate, but he decided not to run. I went to you. We had breakfast and I said, "Jamie, I want to run for governor. What do I need to do?" You told me several things. One, you said, "You need to hire David Contarino, who ran Senator Bingaman's campaign. He's the best political operative you can find." That's one thing you said. Then I said, "You need to help me raise money." You said, "I'll be your campaign finance chairman." That's two. Three, you said, "You need to campaign like you really want this. You have to go everywhere and not assume because of your titles and your background that you're going to get the job. You have got to show New Mexicans that you want it, because you've been away. That's what you need to do." Whenever I had to consult about who I would name as a coordinator in northern New Mexico, in southern New Mexico, who was my campaign staff besides Contarino, I'd go to you. You were a shadow campaign manager overseeing my campaign, including in the pre-primary convention, defeating Gary King and Ray Powell, Jr. You were the architect of us getting the pre-primary votes. My two opponents did not get the required twenty percent. So we had an easy primary. We had no primary.

Jamie: That's right.

Bill: Then in the general election, through your fundraising and through your strategizing, not just on campaign operations, but you know a lot about financing, natural resources, environment, but most importantly you knew the state so well. You knew where the levers of power were, what to say about the university system, what to say about education. You were probably the most valuable person in my operation, in the totality of what I needed to get elected. And I was elected with the biggest margin since Jack Campbell in nineteen sixty-four, and I attribute that success from the early support from you, Jamie Koch. You assembled a group of advisors for the transition. You assembled a group of supporters to raise money for the inaugural, and then you played the most important role in the selection of my cabinet and the selection of my team to start off, to kick off the governorship. What you were able to do, because you were a longtime legislator, a political player, and a business leader, see you mixed politics and business better than anybody else. You would give me honest advice, saying, "Bill, stay away from this guy. Stay away from this idea. Don't do this," but you would do it privately. You never embarrassed anybody. You never like would bad mouth somebody in their face. I followed your advice and all of your advice was very good. So once I was elected governor, when I was the governor-elect, I turned to you and I said, "Jamie, now we've got to form a government." You said, "You want to be a good governor who's bipartisan. You need to talk to one person to start out because the biggest problem is the budget. His name is David Harris, and Harris has worked for Republicans and Democrats. He'll work for anybody as long as he has power."

Jamie: That's right.

Bill: You know there was one area where you said, "I want to have a major impact. I want to impact the natural resources area." I said, "Well, what do you mean?" You said, "Well, I'll find you a Game and Fish director. I'll find you a secretary for Natural Resources. I'll find you an Energy person." I said, "Okay Jamie, but you know, you have got to run them by me." I said, "I need a Republican woman who's an environmentalist." You said, "I know just the one, Joanna Prukop" and then you said, "But I have to find her. I don't know where she is." I said, "Okay, you find her," and you found her.

Jamie: Yeah, she was in West Virginia, back east.

Bill: So sight unseen, I named a Game and Fish director because this was your pick. You had taken me horseback riding with Huie Ley.

Jamie: Yeah.

Bill: Yeah, in Pecos.

Jamie: We were going to shoot grouse and this is true. I said to myself "I bet Bill can't shoot real well," and suddenly this grouse gets up and flies between two trees for just a second and you killed that grouse. Remember that?

Bill: Then you took me hunting. You took me hunting at Ted Turner's ranch and we got that, what the hell was that?

Jamie: Ibex.

Bill: Yeah, an ibex. Anyway, so you named the Natural Resources Secretary, and Game and Fish, sight unseen. This was your love, game and fish, you

159

know the fishing, hunting, hiking, horseback riding—this was your arena. Then you got me a horse. I said, "Jamie, I want a horse," so you helped me get a horse, a Missouri fox-trotter, right?

Jamie: That's right.

Bill: Okay. We had a personal relationship, too. I'd say, "Jamie, you know I need to find some equipment for the mansion, some gym equipment," and you would find it.

Jamie: Yeah, we built the gym in the basement because you needed a work-out spot.

Bill: Yeah, because I was getting really fat. Then you named the first Energy Secretary, Ron Curry. Then you also did something that's very important. I was going to fire all the Johnson appointees, because I wanted my own team, and you came to me and you said, "Don't fire Michelle Lujan Grisham. I knew her dad, Buddy."

Jamie: Buddy Lujan.

Bill: Buddy Lujan. She's really good. The seniors love her. We went to meet her and you know my first meeting with Michelle was not good. I said, "Jamie, I don't want to...Jesus, I mean she works for Johnson. I've got, you know Patsy Trujillo wants it, my people." You said, "No, no, you gotta name her. She will be really good or you'll have a revolt of all the senior citizens." Then all the seniors started going crazy because I hadn't renamed her. You were right, so I named her head of Aging and Long Term Services. I kept her and then in two thousand four I named her to be Secretary of Health. You were determined, you said, "She knows senior issues and she is good at her agency and the senior citizens love her. So it'll be a good thing for the administration." So I named her. So you named maybe four cabinet secretaries, recommending them, and one who was outside of natural resources area and that was Michelle.

Jamie: But I never asked you for anything. I'll never forget sitting in Rio Chama. I was sitting and I don't remember who I was sitting with and you came over and said, "What would you like to be appointed on?" I said, "Oh I'd like to be on the Board of Regents." You looked at me and you said, "You'd like the Board of Regents?" You said, "Oh, we'll think about it." I

160

didn't say any more. I hadn't even thought of that idea until you asked me that question. I hadn't even thought about it.

Bill: No, you never asked. You would never ask for anything for yourself. I mean, you'd recommend for others, but I remember talking to my wife, to Barbara, I said, "You know there's one person who I think if they want me to make the lieutenant governor, which I can't, I would do it. That's Jamie." She said, "You're right. Whatever he wants."

And so I kind of casually, but I knew in my mind that Jamie loved the University of New Mexico, because he started, we started going to games as governor-elect and I said, "He likes this. He likes this Regents thing," and the university was a mess at the time. So when he casually said that, I said, "Well, yeah." So you were my first appointment to the Regents, and then I reappointed you.

You told me, "We need a flagship university that leads in economic development and technology and culture and in athletics." You knew I loved athletics. You knew I loved the university for Latin America and scholarships and Native Americans and diversity. You knew that. So, Jamie, you and I got a lot done through your advice during my first term. I took your advice on a lot of university initiatives. I took your suggestions about a Student Success Center, on The Pit, on the budget for the university, on the cigarette tax, which I was against. I'm against taxes. I took your advice on many things and it was always good advice.

Jamie: One thing when you would say something on the campaign you would stay with it. And to reverse that, I knew that was a big deal.

Bill: But it was a very creative bill that you came up with where the cigarette tax would go to education. It wouldn't go to the budget. It would go to education, to the university system, and you made sure that the University of New Mexico got the share that it needed.

Jamie: The tax revenue was forty-five million.

Bill: Forty-five million and then...

Jamie: We went into your office. I had Dr. Eaton, myself, David Harris and Dr. Cheryl Willman. We went into your office to talk about the cigarette tax and I don't know if you remember because you just were normal casual. I knew what you were going to do about it, but I didn't tell them. You got up and left the room and I followed you out of the room. You came back in the room and you gave us the forty-five million. When you came back into the room, you said, "I'm going to do it."

Bill: But you talked me into it, because I was against taxes in general. You came up with a concept. You were a major force with labor unions. They listened to you. They followed you. Right-to-work, the project labor agreement...

Jamie: That was the biggest thing ever.

Bill: That, I forgot about that. Project labor agreements where labor and management work together. It was also the politics of the Democratic Party.

Jamie: The hospital came under budget. No one could believe it.

Bill: Right.

Jamie: It totally came under the budget. I did lose six hundred thousand commission income from the non-union contractors, but the labor agreement was outstanding. Talk to anybody and they'll let you know. It came under budget by so far.

Bill: It should have been followed in other construction in the state but has not been. It's a legacy because of the way that hospital was built. Yeah, but it was your thinking just across the board: for university budgets, for the Health Sciences Center, for athletics, for a science and technology center. I was very good to the University of New Mexico because of you, Jamie Koch. I was good to all the universities.

Jamie: Yeah, you were good for higher education in New Mexico. The amount of money that the University of New Mexico got because of you was a little over one billion. That scale of capital outlay had never been done before.

Bill: That's right.

Jamie: It was across the board. The capital outlay also included engineering buildings and student housing. People don't realize, but I've always said that the reason this happened was because Governor Johnson vetoed so much that you had a lot of resources when you walked through the door.

Bill: The gift that he gave me. He wouldn't spend on anything.

Jamie: I said, "Bill, you need to kiss Johnson on the cheek because he left you a pile of unspent money."

Bill: Yeah, yeah. And I remember New Mexico State would come to see me, the president there, and the president of Highland University would come too. They would say, "Governor, you give everything to the University of New Mexico." I said, "Well, you know, you got to find a Jamie." I remember saying that to NMSU's lobbyist.

Jamie: It was Nick Franklin.

Bill: I said, "You need to have a Jamie. You don't have a Jamie." The President of NMSU said, "No, we have Nick Franklin." I said "Well, Nick's a good man but he doesn't even live here. He's lives in California." I think your greatest legacy to the state was your contributions to the flagship university. Whether it was persuading me about someone else's proposal or coming up with initiatives on your own, or even long after I left, fighting for the university, trying to bring the Regents into a plan. I mean, what you did with the Regents was spectacular. You said, "Let's have a plan; let's do budget priorities."

Jamie: We did pretty well because we had Don Chalmers.

Bill: Chalmers was really good.

Jamie: We needed a Republican.

Bill: You came up with Chalmers.

Jamie: Yeah, I did; because he had supported you.

Bill: Yeah, he had. He was good.

Bill: You know what else, Jamie, was very helpful? My administration formed an alliance with the Chamber of Commerce in Albuquerque with Terry Cole. She helped us with the tax incentives and with the educational reform that created a Department of Higher Ed that got rid of the superintendent, and that created an educational structure and made Veronica Garcia secretary. You were key in my appointing Veronica Garcia, which I think in the long run was the right thing to do.

Jamie: I think she was good.

Bill: That was, you know, that was my best four years. The second four years were not as good, but you were instrumental in the success of the administration in Natural Resources, just in general kitchen cabinet advice. To capsulize, Jamie, you have had a more positive influence in the state than almost anybody I know. Because your contributions are unsung, unknown and your legacy involved the legislature, involved the business community, but most importantly education, higher education, our flagship university, the University of New Mexico. You know, it's a shame that the University of New Mexico is going through these problems today, and the University of New Mexico Health Sciences Center. You got a hospital named after my wife and me. You came up with it. You said, "You know what, Bill? We're gonna put your wife's name first. It's the 'Barbara and Bill Richardson.' It's not the 'Bill and Barbara.'" You are smart Jamie. You told Barbara what to concentrate on including healthcare, on immunizations, on domestic violence, which is what she did. She is very proud of her name on that hospital.

Jamie: We wouldn't have it now if it weren't for you. People don't realize that. You can see now we can't get another hospital because Governor Martinez is not supporting it. We also wouldn't have a Cancer Center if it hadn't been for you. It wouldn't have been done and people don't realize it. To name something after you and Barbara, that was a really important thing to do.

Bill: I want to mention that I wasn't the only one to benefit from your political acumen. I mean this discussion has all been about Bill Richardson, but you had a major influence in the development of Tom Udall as a political leader. In fact, the first, one of the first times that you and I didn't agree, was when I wasn't able to use funds from my federal account towards my governor's race because Udall was thinking of running. You were close to Udall. So you got this bill passed that prevented me from using my money. Then we sued the state. We won.

Jamie: That's right, you won.

Bill: I didn't hold it against you. I later found out that it was Gene Gallegos and Udall who did it, right?

Jamie: No, it was Fred Nathan.

Bill: Fred Nathan?

Jamie: Yeah, he gave me the language.

Bill: You gave it to somebody, right?

Jamie: No, we're in this committee and I had Ed Lujan sitting next to me and then they're going after Bill Richardson on this committee unanimously.

Bill: Because they all wanted to run, right? Well, I think you were instrumental in Udall's career, right?

Jamie: Yeah, I helped him a lot, yeah.

Bill: Yeah, but not as much as mine.

Jamie: Oh, not at all, no. Not even near.

Bill: You were...I know you helped Bingaman.

Jamie: Yup.

Bill: You knew these patrons in the north and you knew the Indians, the Native Americans, the Pueblos, the Navajos. The Indians trusted you, despite your being an Anglo. They knew you cared about the land and water, and so whenever I had a Northern New Mexico issue, the acequias, the land grants, I'd ask you. You knew where the barometers were. Taos, Mora, Rio Arriba, Santa Fe—you had a major influence there, Jamie. I know you had influence in the south, in Silver City and all that, Albuquerque, but politically vote getting, when you helped a certain candidate, it gave a lot of credibility to that candidate.

Jamie: The one thing that we had fun with was Johnny Dendahl.

Bill: Oh yeah. He was your friend though, wasn't he?

Jamie: Remember I said we were good friends. We were good friends, but he was going after Bill Richardson all the time. They wanted me to be state chair to go after Dendahl, and we got Dendahl taken care of. I think you remember Dendahl and I were on the radio station and they were talking about Bill had nothing but elected jobs, appointed jobs, on and on and on. I said, "Okay, let me make sure I understand, Johnny. You're saying he's on the tit?" "Yeah, I said it." "Okay. What about Domenici?" He said, "Well you could probably say that, too." I got that recording and I picked up that recording and sent it to Pete Domenici and that was the end of Dendahl, because he said it on radio, tracked him right in. Do you remember that?

Bill: I do.

Jamie: I had that recorded, delivered over to Pete's office.

Bill: What's masterful about you, Jamie, is that there's the "Jamie Koch policy" side, resources, university. Then there's the "Jamie Koch political mastermind" side. I really have not met very many people including in DC or New York that have those dual instincts and are as strong in both areas of policy and politics, like you do. In other words there's a political side. There's a policy side. The contributions to the state, it has to be highlighted by education. You have that record. On the other side, the politics, you nurtured so many of the state's most important leaders.

Jamie: As we bring this interview to a close, because we're asking every single person we're interviewing, as you look at the state now and you look forward and you think about what's needed as we move forward, what do you see?

Bill: Well, the state obviously needs a governor with a vision, which we don't have. The state needs a new Jamie Koch. You made your contribution so we shouldn't ask you to do it again. You have given the office an enormous amount, but I think future leaders could learn from this book that it's important to preserve New Mexico's institutions. I believe that the university is the central force driving this state. The University of New Mexico brings the state together because we have no major league team. We have no huge industry. The university is the unifying entity that educates and brings recreation to the state. It brings happiness, pride in the Lobos.

Jamie: The main reason I started this book, is to sit down and have a conversation with all of the people who have helped me and have worked with me to accomplish many things.

Bill: A lot you did on your own. You were already a powerful person. I didn't make you. You brought power to me initially and then when I got power I was able to enact part of your vision, which was also mine. You see the symmetry? It wasn't that we used each other. It's that we were catalysts for each other and we had similar visions. It was a friendship. It was a symbiosis.

When I sat down with Governor Richardson that day, he mentioned the fact that he never interfered with the work of the Regents. The governor was correct. He never tried to inject himself into the work of the Regents. He did, however, take some heat when I recruited his deputy chief of staff, Billy Sparks, to come work for the University of New Mexico Health Sciences Center. The *Albuquerque Journal* and others accused the governor of putting all his people at the University of New Mexico to expand his sphere of influence. This was utter nonsense. The governor was sorry to see Billy leave. Billy had done an excellent job directing the entire communication infrastructure of the governor's office including the hiring of all of the governor's appointed public information officers.

I was very happy when Billy accepted the offer to work at the University of New Mexico Health Sciences Center because Billy's ability to generate positive headlines and build support for a campaign was exactly what the University of New Mexico needed. Billy ran the Bill Clinton Presidential Campaign in the state of New Mexico with Dave Contarino in 1996. Billy had the ability to do rapid response communications like no one else. He was invaluable to Mayor Dinkins in New York City. But long before that in 1986, Billy had made a name for himself when he helped create the very famous concept of the Farm Aid Concert. Billy galvanized support among all stakeholders and executed that first historic nationally televised concert that raised over nine million dollars in one day and instantly elevated the plight of American family farmers.

I had gotten to know Billy very well when I was Chair of the

Democratic Party. In addition to his unparalleled communications/ media skills, Billy knew how to put campaigns together. When I suggested to Dr. Roth that he look at hiring Billy Sparks, I had an idea that Billy would re-brand the Health Sciences Center and help them better communicate to the public all the amazing things the doctors, the nurses, the researchers, and the staff and the students were doing. The Health Sciences Center is definitely one of the jewels in the University of New Mexico crown. But, up until Billy came on board, they had not done a very good job at telling their story. I sat down to talk to Billy on November 29, 2016.

～～～

Billy Sparks, advisor to New Mexico Democratic Party, communications director for Governor Richardson, communications director for New Mexico Health Sciences Center for Development and Disability / Interviewed November 29, 2016

Jamie: Tell us about yourself. Why did you come to New Mexico?

Billy: It's important to know that I was born in a very small mill town in North Carolina called Saxapahaw, named after one of the Indian nations that used to be there on the Saxapahaw River. The owner of the town, and when I say that I literally mean that, was the owner of the mill (Sellers Manufacturing), was B. Everett Jordan. Jordan was appointed by then Governor Hodges to replace a U.S. senator who died. So he became the United States senator and my father worked as a foreman in his mill there. They babysat for me when I was growing up, first three or four years we lived there, and I used to ask him a lot of questions about the senate. Then one of my favorite little vignettes is when I was three years old according to my mother, she came into the room and asked what I was doing, I said, "I'm reading Revelations." She said, "Why are you reading Revelations?" I said, "To see if there is time to be a senator before the world ends. It's very important to me." So I actually fell in love with the idea of the senate. I worked to become a senate page for Sam Ervin who was an amazing constitutional scholar. I became a page my junior year in high school and went to Washington.

My father had passed away at that stage. I'd never been north of Virginia and was dropped off at my own apartment on Sixth and East Capital Street, when Rufus Edmisten eventually became Chief Counsel to the Senate Watergate committee. Sam Ervin headed up the Watergate committee. After I graduated from high school, it was the height of the Vietnam War. I was from a very small county with a very low number in the draft. I was trying to figure out what to do. I talked to a lot of people. Eventually, I signed up to be a Russian linguist, so they sent me to the Defense Language Institute in Monterey, California for a year to learn Russian. I studied Russian fifty-seven weeks, six hours a day, five days a week, by Russian natives. With the caveat being that if you flunked one six week test or two weekly tests you went to Vietnam in ten days because that ended your language school contract with the army. Seriously, the contract said that if I flunked, then they sent you to Vietnam. That's when I lost most of my southern accent and I had to study in a very different kind of way. So I became a Russian interrogator for military intelligence. I was honorably discharged and then I went straight to University of North Carolina in Chapel Hill. I went into the honors program, majored in international relations and was one semester shy of getting my degree when I started working on a campaign for Howard Lee, who was the first African American to run and win a statewide election in the south since reconstruction in the eighteen seventies.

The reason I bring that story up is because that set me up in very close personal relationships with African American politicians nationwide. So Andrew Young, Jessie Jackson, Howard Lee and some others took an interest in me at that stage, so several years later I ended up working in New York for Mayor Dinkins. Dinkins was the first African American Mayor of New York. We won the election in nineteen eighty-nine, lost to Giuliani in nineteen ninety-three, and so I started working with the Democratic National Committee teaching rapid response and doing media training sessions across the country. I was at the Chicago Convention in nineteen ninety-six for Clinton's reelection campaign and they asked me if I would meet with Dave Contarino who I'd never met before. Contarino, at that point, wanted to move from full time to half time as director of the coordinating campaign, so they asked me to come to work with David Contarino. That's when we got together with each other. I came here, did that, we won the campaign as you all know, and that was a vision that the National Democratic Party had that New Mexico would be the anchor state in the mountain west to change the dynamic before Clinton's election in 1992. They had never carried a state west of Mississippi since Carter's election. New Mexico was going to be the state to change all that in the mountain west.

Jamie: This was for the Clinton campaign?

Billy: Uh huh. So I went back and served as the deputy director of his inauguration for the nationwide broadcast and worked up there. But I told everybody in DC I fell in love with New Mexico and I'd come back, and of course nobody believed me that I would. I came back and worked on Marty Chavez's gubernatorial campaign as a field organizer. I had everything from Socorro to Portales and Catron County south. I didn't know how difficult that would be at that time, but we carried Doña Ana County.

Jamie: He was running against Johnson?

Billy: He was running against Johnson, yes. The interesting thing about that campaign was that he lost Albuquerque. We actually had enough votes to win if you carried Bernalillo County, but that's where the race was kind of won and lost was here in Albuquerque. I'd just come out of that race. I went to opening day of the legislative session as a guest of Helen Garcia, who was the state rep from Doña Ana County that I had gotten to know pretty well during the campaign. And Johnson gave a State of the State, and the Democrats did nothing except applaud and stand up and sit down. I told Helen, I said, "Take me in to see Raymond, the Speaker. I want to talk to Raymond." I mentioned to him, "You should have equal time. You should have a Democratic response." They said, "That's a really good idea, what are you doing right now?" I said, "I'm in New Mexico." I got hired as the communications person at that point and then Eric Witt and I worked together.

So we actually became the first permanent staff of the Speaker that they'd had. They'd never had a communications person before. I said, "The reason you guys are losing so badly is because you're up here for sixty days and the governor is up here every day. He controls the message all year long. You guys leave town so we have got to change that dynamic." I went to work for Majority Leader Lujan and Speaker Sanchez in nineteen ninety-nine. One session I actually worked on communications for the House and the Senate.

I went to work for the senate in two thousand one as their communications director for the majority party and went through the transition from Senator Aragon to Senator Romero. Richardson had been the chairman of the Clinton campaign here in nineteen ninety-six. So I'd known him since then and had heard about him in the House. I worked in the US House in the nineteen eighties myself, so I'd heard about him and talked to him over the years. I said, "If you ever decided to do something, let me know and I'm there with you." Right after Richardson decided to run, Contarino called and said, "You want to come have a meeting and sit down and talk about this?" I told him I'd be able to switch as soon as the session was over, so I became Richardson's director of communications in March of two thousand two when he was running for the campaign. That's when you and I became much, much closer and developed a great relationship.

Jamie: Keep going.

Billy: At that point you'd been Finance Chair in the campaign, but soon thereafter you became chairman of the Democratic Party in June.

Jamie: Why did the governor want me to be chairman of the party?

Billy: I think what impressed him the most was your ability to get under the skin of John Dendahl and to actually have the kind of reputation where you could call for the kind of measures like no negative campaigning, like telling the truth in ads. Just calling Dendahl 'Johnny' was a major element in that whole dialogue between you and him, when John Dendahl was the Republican chairman at the time.

Billy: The entire time Johnson was governor, Dendahl really ruled the state. He controlled the agenda. He controlled the stories. He was unmatched in his ability to create press in a positive way for Governor Johnson throughout his entire eight years in office. You put a dramatic and sudden halt to that from the very beginning. I think when you called him out on the ads and he admitted that he'd voted for John Sanchez and you immediately called him out saying that it was obvious this thing was rigged from the beginning. They had false ads about Walter Bradley and you called him out on that. We need a lot more of that right now.

Jamie: The reason I went over there, as you said, was to neutralize Dendahl?

Billy: Well, I think you knew Bill very well. You had a good relationship with him based on your past experiences. You'd been a phenomenal Finance Director. I think you raised three hundred thousand in Santa Fe, another three hundred thousand in Albuquerque. It was his goal to have six hundred thousand raised when he announced, and you did that. People hadn't seen that kind of success in fundraising in New Mexico for a gubernatorial candidate before. Plus, you helped staff the campaign. You decided that David Contarino was somebody he should talk to; Harris was somebody he should talk to. You basically guided him on his return to New Mexico; having been out of the state as UN Ambassador and Secretary of Energy, coming back into the state to run wasn't easy. I think he needed a sounding board. One of the traits I love about you the most is your unvarnished fact telling. Speaking truths to power is one of your greatest attributes and you had no problem speaking truth to power. You weren't interested in a position. You weren't interested in a job. You didn't care about what he could do for you, but you seriously loved the state and knew more about it than ninety-nine point nine percent of the population. So having you serve as kind of a right arm in the process was critical to his being able to come back. You reminded people of his success and his positive vision for the state. You helped establish the issues that he should be talking about. You helped put together the listening tour of people he should meet with and everything and then you were extraordinarily successful in raising money.

Jamie: How did I become the party chair? Normally the governor picks his party chair, isn't that correct?

Billy: Yes. When he got the nomination, you were the top of the list.

Jamie: Did we have a Democratic House, a Democratic Senate?

Billy: We were definitely lacking in the national offices at that time.

Jamie: But here in New Mexico.

Billy: In New Mexico, Senator Domenici was very popular and effective. Even though that was an election year when Domenici was running, and I think Gloria Tristiani was running. You focused on both the judgeships and the state House and Senate and you were making sure that those things stayed Democratic and everything remained good majorities and worked well with all the people running. And you had a relationship, obviously, with the Daniels family. Diane Denish was the lieutenant gubernatorial nominee and you had worked with her father for thirty some years.

Jamie: Yeah, for forty-five years. Can you remember some of the things we did in the Democratic Party that the governor was happy that we did?

Billy: I think getting down to the grassroots level, having candidates have access to some funds they wouldn't have had otherwise, making sure that they had consistent messaging, putting a mechanism in place for brochures, direct mail, phone calls, access to polling, were important contributions to the Democratic Party. The national Republican Party really had started putting huge resources in the state legislative races. That started in the late nineteen nineties and was definitely continued here. So they tried to target us on all levels and I think you prevented that from happening. They weren't successful in trying to do that.

Jamie: Senator John Arthur Smith was running against Congressman Schiff. Tell us about how that was going. Were you aware of how that was going?

Billy: John Arthur had never run for congress. He'd been a very effective state senator.

Jamie: Polling, Bill Clinton was doing great in New Mexico. Am I correct on that?

Billy: Yeah, he won both times.

Jamie: He was doing well. Back to Senator John Arthur Smith. He had been polling pretty close to Steve, hadn't he?

Billy: He had been.

Jamie: Then the national Democratic Party pulled all the money away from John Arthur Smith.

Billy: Right.

Jamie: When they did that, it ended his campaign, so people wonder why he's not a staunch Democrat. The Democrats pulled it right out from underneath him. Am I correct on that assumption?

Billy: There was no notice either. There was no rationale behind it. It was based on what trends and the fact that it'd been a Republican seat for a long time, but they didn't look at the immediate, at what was possible. There used to be an old saying in DC that "incumbent gets ninety percent of the money. First timers get five to seven percent and everybody else gets three percent." So if you're running against somebody who's been there more than once, you're at three percent of all the funds raised gets allocated to your race, regardless of your situation. That was a mistake they made. I think they're still making it today. We only picked up six seats this cycle, nationally, in the House and we needed to pick up fifteen to twenty to be competitive with what's going on.

Jamie: Were we able to neutralize Dendahl pretty effectively do you think?

Billy: I don't think Dendahl saw you coming because from the very beginning and because you've known him for, as he says, for sixty years. You had interactions with him in a lot of different areas in Santa Fe. The fact that you're both from Santa Fe so you were able to call him on all his stuff right off the bat surprised him. I think starting off with Walter Bradley, and how they accused Walter Bradley of voting for or facilitating Manny Aragon's election in the senate, was a total falsehood. Walter never did that. You called him on it so they were on the defensive from day one. When he admitted on the radio show that he voted for John Sanchez in the primary, that he'd been for him all along, in President Bush's forum, you called him on that.

You got photographs of Bush from nine-eleven, they were using that as a fundraiser thing, being on Air Force One on nine-eleven—you called him on that. As I say, the best defense is a great offense. You created a great offense. You changed the entire dynamic of interaction. Responding within the same news cycle as your opponent was a major shift.

Jamie: The Democratic Party, where do you think it is today?

Billy: It should be more coordinated. We need a message that resonates with working people.

Jamie: What do you mean by that?

Billy: If my major goal as a liberal is protecting human rights, I will fight hard for that and that may motivate me to go vote, but I also want to feed my family. I also want to make sure that my kids can go to college or that my life is going to be protected, that I can walk on the streets safely. You have to understand the daily challenges people have in addition to the mighty goals that you have. You have to be on the street, in the farms, in the rural towns, you have to be able to understand, visit and give them credence for their concerns. I think you can't win an election purely on negative advertising. You can't win an election purely on talking about how bad your opponent is. I think they all thought they could. You have to actually...like with John Arthur Smith's race, if you see a potential, you have to commit to that. Also, Howard Dean was really right in this. We need a fifty state strategy.

There are Democrats in every state. Two years ago, the head of the DGA pulled money out of a lot of governor's races including here in New Mexico. We should be involved in every race. Democrats are Democrats and you should support them, but if you're not out there consistently and if you're not putting your money where your mouth is, you're going to lose.

Jamie: So you went to work for Governor Richardson during his administration?

Billy: I was happy to be his first appointment. The first day after the election was over we had a press conference in Santa Fe, in the Roundhouse, and he named me as his director of communications. We set about putting the state government together and you were a big part of that effort in terms of who's here, who's done what. We had to have a transition committee that was really bipartisan. We put some Republicans into the state cabinet. We reached out to all people. We put together a very diverse, bipartisan cabinet.

Jamie: When you got through with the governor's office, how did you get to the university?

Billy: You and I and Dr. Roth talked. You told me I should meet Dr. Roth. You had a statewide town hall about health sciences and the role of health sciences and you brought everybody together with the university, with the county and different people, and what direction that we needed to go in. Dr. Roth is an ER doctor. He had been in the university a long time. So you said, "I want you to have lunch with us, you and Dr. Roth." So I met Dr. Roth and really liked him. So February ninth, two thousand six I made the move. I took two days off from my job with Richardson and said farewell to what Governor Richardson called the 'heart and soul' of his administration. That was a great headline and it really made Contarino mad. He walked in and said, "What am I, the liver?" I've got the *Santa Fe New Mexican* headline framed that says, "Richardson's Heart and Soul Takes His Leave." We all laughed.

Jamie: You were definitely an important part of Richardson's success during those first four years.

Billy: You also were very important for our ability to achieve our goals. Every position I've known you to be in, you have always had definitive goals that you were able to accomplish because of your unwavering commitment to the task. Following the lunch with you and University of New Mexico Regent Eaves, you both expressed your concerns about where Health Sciences was, the kind of community, controversies that surrounded Health Sciences. You mentioned there were community groups that didn't think we were listening, that the hospital was considered just a charity hospital and not an academic medical research center. One of the first things I said when I got hired, and Dr. Roth agreed, was that we needed a vision. I believed if we could convince people that the Health Sciences Center was an asset and not a liability, we could change the entire dynamic. Actually our favorables when I started were below thirty pecent.

Jamie: I know that. Can you tell us where your favorables are now?

Billy: Eighty-six percent.

Jamie: What do you think the overall future of the university is as you see it? You got two issues affecting our future. You got one, which is the Democratic Party nationally and in New Mexico, which is a separate issue, and then the other issue is the Health Sciences Center governance we discussed.

Billy: Well, I think that you have to be realistic about where you are as a state. I think what made Richardson's tenure so different was one of the statements he made. He said, "We don't have time to do everything piece-meal. We can't do education this session, taxes the next session, economic development the next session. We have to do everything all at once because the only way you're ever going to solve this kind of thing is look at the entire picture and see what's going on." I think that made a huge difference at the time. We had a saying, "Better jobs, better schools and more money in the pockets of New Mexicans."

Right now we're back into focusing on wedge issues that separate people and don't solve a damn thing in terms of the quality of life for an individual. It's not about people any more. Now they just care about winning. That's the only question they're asking. Am I winning? Or am I losing?

When I was sixteen, Senator Ervin told me, "There's two kinds of politicians: somebody who wants a title and somebody who wants a job." He continued, "You make damn sure you work for people who want the job. Because they're actually going to do something."

I think one thing that characterizes your career as a public servant, and again, going back to my original premise about you: problem solving has always driven you. You have always prided yourself on doing everything in your power to make sure you solved problems, and that's why I admire you so much.

5

Intense feeling too often obscures the truth.
—President Harry S. Truman

I relate to President Truman's idea that intense feeling too often obscures the truth, because I grew up dyslexic and that often was a frustrating sensation for me. As a child, I knew I was smart. I knew I had ability; but in a classroom setting, I often struggled. I was lucky because my parents always made me feel important and they did a lot for me in terms of providing tutors and working diligently with me to ensure I got through school. As I got older and had to do more on my own, college work was very challenging. I spent hours studying. Things took me a lot longer than it might take someone who did not have the same learning disabilities that I did. I would spend a very long time, many hours, on a paper to get it written correctly. It was frustrating and I was not always treated with respect. For example, I had a professor in one of my courses that gave me an A+ but she put a question mark on the page. She said she put the question mark because I normally didn't do that well on timed tests in class. She said to me, "You cheated, you didn't write this." I said, "Yes, I did." I suggested that she question me and do an oral exam on the topic right then and there. So she asked me some questions and I gave all the correct answers. She said, "You're okay." I didn't get an apology but she did tell me I knew my stuff and I did a good job on writing the essay. She wasn't the only one who labeled me as not being "the sharpest tack." Those kinds of interactions had a lasting impact. I was determined to prove the doubters wrong.

In many ways, this chapter of the book is the most intensely personal. My own ability to overcome difficult circumstances in my youth and watching my daughter Amy overcome difficulties, as a child with special needs, guided my decision to get involved in the projects we discuss in this chapter. As an adult, I wanted to ensure others had the resources they needed. It is my sincere belief that, everybody deserves a chance to be successful. I realized that my parents and certain mentors had been critical and vital cheerleaders. I realized how important the academic support I had gotten early on in my school years was in terms of my self-esteem and my overall ability to succeed in the business world after graduation from college.

So, when I had an opportunity to make a difference while serving on the Board of Regents for the University of New Mexico, I knew I needed to give back in a way that would pave the way for future generations of students. I realized many student athletes were very similar to me. They may have excelled in sports but their academic course work could border on unmanageable without help. I was able to convince Governor Richardson to work with me to fund a student resource center for our student athletes. It is called the Student Success Center. On November 4, 2016 I sat down with Dr. Breda Bova to talk about the Success Center and my time on the Board of Regents.

Breda Bova, PhD, department chair for the Department of Educational Leadership, chief of staff for five past University of New Mexico presidents / Interviewed November 4, 2016

Breda: I came here as a doctoral student in nineteen seventy-five and I got my PhD from the University of New Mexico and then I became part of the faculty in the college of Ed. I became department chair for the department of educational leadership. I was an associate dean for about five years, and then I moved to the president's office. I was the chief of staff for five presidents.

Jamie: I didn't realize there was that many.

Breda: Yes. It was Louis Caldera, David Harris, David Schmidly, Paul Roth on an interim basis and then Bob Frank. I left Bob Frank two years ago and

I retired. I work part-time now for the athletic director. During that time, for sixteen years, I was what they called the FA or the faculty athletic rep.

Jamie: Could you explain what the faculty rep does?

Breda: Every "Division One" school has someone the president appoints to be their faculty representative. President Peck appointed me. The FA must certify the eligibility of the student athletes. The NCAA has a rule that student athletes have to be certified outside of the athletic department. So, I did that, and then I also did other things including chairing hearings and stuff like that. So, when I retired I decided to work for Paul Krebs, our athletic director. I've been doing some mentoring programs for female student athletes and some special projects.

Jamie: Did you go on some of the trips? Did you go on trips and help the athletes?

Breda: Yes. When I was the faculty rep we used to give the mid-term exams at the Mountain West basketball tournament. Some faculty would let the students take the exams when they came home, but several members of the faculty said "No. You've got to take it." And so, since I'm a faculty member, they would let me give the exams. And I remember one student who had nine tests that we had to give her. It was amazing. She just took them one after another. She'd say, "All right, give me the next one." So yeah, it was fun. It was great working with the students.

Jamie: Why do we have to do all that? Why do we have to help the athletes so much in their academics?

Breda: Well first of all, most of them are very good students. But, the athletic department has athletic academic advisors and they're the ones who know all the NCAA rules. So that you just can't jack around with your academic plan, they work with the academic advisors in the colleges that the student athletes are enrolled in.

Jamie: Is there a requirement that they have a certain grade point to play?

Breda: Yes. They have to pass. They have to have at least a two. But, the bigger requirement is what they call the forty-sixty-eighty rule. And the rule means that by the end of their sophomore year they have to have forty percent of all of their classes towards their degree. Then by the end of their junior year, they must have completed sixty percent and then at the end of their senior year, eighty. Some of the student athletes will take five years to finish. And if they're on track like that, they're much more likely to finish in four or five years.

Jamie: Then the NCAA looks at graduation. Tell us about that and how that works.

Breda: Yes. It was about five years ago they started an initiative to get students to complete their studies in four years. Because football, for example, after the season was over in their senior year, they might just blow off the second semester of their senior year because they wanted to go pro. Universities, if they didn't keep them enrolled, they would get points deducted and if they didn't have a good, what they call APR, annual progress rate, they could lose post-season playing time. This affected a couple of the big basketball schools back east. Connecticut lost one year, because the kids were leaving without finishing. So, we've done really well with our APR here.

Jamie: If we didn't do that, could we lose scholarships?

Breda: Yes, you can lose scholarships. And you can lose post-season play.

Jamie: So, where I'm going with this is that we were about to lose some football recruits, baseball recruits, and basketball recruits. Everybody knows when I came on the Board of Regents, I was familiar with university athletics. I remember Coach Flanagan told me a story and I can remember because I knew all the coaches before I came here. Coach Flanagan told me how they had a really good player that he wanted to have come to the university. The student's parents visited Kansas State and Kansas State had a Success Center. He lost that student to Kansas State. So, then what happened, once I jointed the Regents, sometimes I would travel with the team. We would see how these Success Centers were set up. I think the most important thing that I had an opportunity to do is the University of New Mexico six and a half million dollar Success Center. So, what I'd like for you to talk about is what's happened there? And what is our Success Center doing? And how is that helping out athletes? So, won't you tell us about the University of New Mexico Student Success Center?

Breda: Prior to us getting the Student Success Center, which is located right on the corner by The Pit, the academic advisors had been working with students in Johnson Center in a very small area.

Jamie: Johnson Center is the old gym?

Breda: Yes, it is the old gym right across from Popejoy. They had one room for the students to go in and they did study halls there. They had a few computers in there. So, when you were able to get the old technology ventures corporate building on the corner here, it was really great. Remember, before we moved into the building, Fidelity was in there for a while before their offices were built down in Mesa del Sol. They were gracious enough to leave some of their furniture there for us. Then we moved in and we have the entire, not quite the entire top floor, athletics, but we have most of it and then downstairs is all for financial aid and for admissions and the registrar. It is absolutely great. It is a spacious area and that's where my office is now. The coaches will have their own rules. Some coaches say every freshman, regardless of how smart they are, what their GPA is, has to clock in for "x" number of study hall hours a week. And some coaches will determine if the student has a really good GPA then they don't have to come to the center. But you find kids who don't have to attend will attend anyway because now they have a fuel station. We can feed students snacks. We weren't able to do that previously. It's a new rule. And so, they have bagels and peanut butter and protein drinks and items like that as well as fruit. So, you get a lot of kids who just come up there. We also have CAPS, which is the tutoring service. The tutors are up there at night from five to nine pm and they have tutoring in areas that we need it in. We're able to tell them what we need and they have the tutors. So, the place is opened basically from eight to nine-thirty every day except Friday. Sunday nights, they're open again until nine. Also, now the academic advisors have decent offices. The ones in Johnson were so small. Now, one of the men's basketball advisors has her computer but she also has a computer for the students and so she'll be able to work with them while they're on the computer and we never could have done that in Johnson. We have three computer labs. We use those for the coaches when they have to take a recruiting test. Every Division One coach has to pass a recruiting test or he or she can't recruit. It's a very leveling experience. So, the head basketball coach has to take the same test that the tennis coach takes.

Jamie: What kind of information are you looking for?

Breda: Oh, recruiting information. For example, that they know what would be a violation. The test ensures the coaches know what they can do and what they can't do. The test is based on the NCAA manual. The test is offered in May and June and we're able to get all of the coaches in the computer lab in those two sessions. Paul Krebs hired a learning specialist and we were one of the first schools in the Mountain West to have a learning specialist. And it was interesting because there were several kids a while back who were never previously diagnosed with their disability.

Jamie: Like dyslexia.

Breda: Yes, or just some cognitive issues. The learning specialist is really good at understanding what the challenge might be and getting them certified. The certification of the disability is important because then we're able to offer them compensatory kinds of help. Our learning specialist is also housed over there and compliance is also there. But the nice thing about having all of these wrap-around services there is that they're able to be around each other and help each other solve problems. So, it's not like I've got to go five buildings away to get to the compliance person. If an academic advisor sees something that might be an issue, they've got the compliance person right there. The building is really, really great.

Jamie: What effect has the Success Center had on student GPAs ?

Breda: Well, the grade points have gone up over the years and we think that a lot of it is due to the leadership that Paul Krebs has put into place. I wish that we had thought about that when we started it. Then we could have actually done some studies on it. But the grade point averages have gone up. The building has just facilitated the students and the support mechanisms coming together. We can solve problems more quickly. It's a state of the art facility and the coaches are just so pleased to be able to bring parents and families in when they're recruiting kids.

Jamie: Is the average GPA over three now?

Breda: Oh, it's over three. It's three point three.

Jamie: Yeah, I was going to say that.

Breda: Yeah, so it's very good. And some of our kids, a lot of the kids, have academic all-American or academic Mountain West conference. I worked with a young woman yesterday. She is a swimmer and she is a biochemistry major and I was helping her with her resume. I couldn't see any GPA on there. She's graduating in May. I said, "So what's your GPA? She said, three point eight nine." I told her, "You need to put that on the resume." I said, "If you can just boost it to a three point nine, you'll graduate Summa Cum Laude." So, she looked at me. She said, "What's that?" I said, "It's all Latin. 'Cum Laude', with praise, 'Magna Cum Laude', with great praise and 'Summa Cum Laude', means with all praise."

Jamie: You mentioned a lot of wrap-around services in that building. Does that include counseling?

Breda: Yes we do have a clinical psychologist. She's in the building. And we are able to refer kids to her. She works five days a week, just for us, from eight to five. And she's available in the evenings.

Jamie: Well, I think it's an interesting point because of what social media has done to our world. In terms of online bullying, people don't realize the kinds of things that happen with social media when an athlete has an off game or something like that. And all of a sudden, people are saying all kinds of nasty things about them online. Anybody can have a bad game. This is part of the process of being an athlete.

Breda: And that's another thing that Paul Krebs did—he hired her. We never had a psychologist before. She's part of the student health for the university. She is available in the evening because if something happens to one of these students, we have direct and immediate access. And so, we were one of the first in the Mountain West to have our own learning specialist and our own psychologist. And she's not, and Paul will tell you this, she's not a sports psychologist. She's a clinical psychologist. She helps the students manage the stress, which can be considerable.

Jamie: I don't know if you know the story of how we got money for this.

Breda: Well, I remember you told me.

Jamie: Well, I'm going to tell you again. In other words, the university is a great place. And normally, you have committees and committees decide what you're going to do and where things can be done. And normally, when you do that it takes maybe four or five months or a year. Whatever it takes to decide. Everybody has to agree to decide. You know, your financial person and everything and what's going to be primary and everything else. Well, I'm dyslexic and I knew how hard it was for me. So, I went to see Governor Bill Richardson, and I said, "Bill, I want you to do me a favor." [He has capital money.] "I want you to put in capital money. I already knew that we could buy the building for six point five million. Nobody knew it. Not one person knew what it took. I didn't tell them at all. That year in the budget, there was a little clause in there that said it had to be for the purpose to buy the building. I think getting the funds to buy that building and getting those funds designated as solely to be used for a Student Success Center is one of the most important things I've ever done.

Breda: We were delighted to get into that building, athletics was. And when Dave Schmidly was president, he used to use parts of the facility for a tail-gate before the football games because it has a nice patio outside and stuff like that. We've used it for some professional development things for our employees. So, it's a great, great building and we're so fortunate.

Jamie: Thank you for talking about the Success Center. Now, let's shift focus and talk about the president's office. One of the first persons I met when I came was you, Breda, and we were thrilled that you became the chief of staff for Louis Caldera. Are you familiar with the way the Regents were organized before?

Breda: We always knew about the Regents as faculty and in the dean's office and stuff. But it was never 'til I really went into the president's office that I understood just the complexity of what they have to deal with.

Jamie: And we changed it considerably from what it was. Do you remember what it was before?

Breda: Well, when you came on as president of the Regents, I remember one of the things that impressed me was your total transparency. Everything was open. The faculty, I think prior to that, never really had much access to the budget. And it wasn't that anybody was trying to hide anything but there just wasn't access to it. And when you came on board, everything was open. You set up different kinds of committees.

Jamie: We established the Regents Audit Committee and also the Lobo Development Board to develop the university properties.

Breda: Lobo Development.

Jamie: We didn't have a Regents Audit Committee prior to this. Budgets. We wouldn't get any budgeted figures at each Regent meeting. They didn't have them available. I'll tell you a story. When I first came on the Regents, I'll never forget. They asked me what I wanted to be on? And Larry Willard was president of the Regents. I said, "I want to be on finances." "Well, are you sure?" I said "Yeah, that's where I want to be." So, I went onto the Finance Committee and Larry was chairman as president of the Regents and he was also chairman of the Finance Committee.

And so, we're going through all this stuff and I said, "Do we see a budget?" "Oh, no we don't show it to you." "We don't get a budget, a monthly budget?" "No." I said, "Okay." I'll never forget, we're sitting there and Julie Weaks-Guttierrez said, "Now we're going to go to the legislature and when the legislature gives us appropriations I'm going to come back and I'm going to tell you what your tuition should be." "So, what you're telling me is when the legislators review the budget, they get to tell us what the tuition will be. And that's the way we do it?" I said, "I see." At this time, I was not president of the Regents. I said, "So what you're telling me is, we're going to increase the tuition and fees by six and a half percent? (I believe it was) And that's it?" She responded, "Yeah, that's it." I said: "And we have to vote on it in order to send the budget to the state?"

I said, "Okay, well let me just make it perfectly clear to everybody that this is the last time we're ever going to do this in this manner. It never will happen again. I'll never vote for any budget I haven't seen and I don't think it's right to do it." And the staff and the faculty didn't have anything to do with that budget. I was determined that any future budget was going to have the input of the entire university. That's why I started the Budget Summit. The Summit was a one-day series of presentations where everybody at the university knew what was in the budget. We also began requiring monthly statements.

Please tell us about you being chief of staff with the different presidents.

Breda: Louis was the former secretary of the army for President Clinton. And so, I learned terms like "stand down." I didn't know what that meant. I'd go in, I was getting ready to go in and Mitch is the scheduling person, she said, "Stand down." I said, "What does that mean?" It's funny because when I think back, Louis Caldera wanted to increase the GPA for admissions to the university, but he was so used to being in the army where you just do it. When it went from a very low two to a two point five—people just flipped out because it was going to limit access to a large number of people. Vis-à-vis the required GPA, we're there now, but we went through a process and he didn't. So, he left his mark on the university. He was good to work for. He played volleyball for West Point, men's volleyball. So, you know, he was an athlete and he supported the Lobo's. Rudy Davalos was the athletic director during that time and Rudy was not endeared to the president for different reasons and he'd always say to me, "You take care of him" when we would travel, or something like that. So, it was fine. And then when he left, David Harris came in.

Jamie: And David Harris really didn't have the educational background to do it. But he had the financial background and we thought it would be for a short period of time.

Breda: And he did a great job.

Jamie: Very skilled.

Breda: One part of me said, "Leave him there." We were able to get David Harris out and have him meet the faculty and this was when you really opened up the budget process. In these budget committees, there would be like the head of the faculty senate and the faculty budget committee, and then a couple of faculty sometimes from the Anderson School of Management who were skilled in certain areas. And so, they wound up liking David Harris. When I was in the president's office, I would always tell the president, "Harris is going to be one of your best allies because he knows where every nickel is. And if you ask him for help, he will help you. I promise you." But you know, we had a really good team. We laughed a lot and David did a lot of good things for the university. I think you were responsible for getting David Harris to the university. Then Dave Schmidly was hired. David Schmidly was at that time president of Oklahoma State and prior to that, he was president at Texas Tech. He had been a president a while and his wife, Janet, was responsible for starting the Parent Association because they had a really good Parent Association at Tech and at Oklahoma State. And so, the Parent Association goes on to this day. Dave Schmidly came at a time when we had a big budget issue. It was kind of good but it

188

was also challenging. The faculty, at that time, the faculty voted a 'vote of no confidence' against Dave Schmidly, David Harris and you. I felt really bad because I was not able to convince the faculty that they were spared a lot of pain. I told David Harris and I told Dave Schmidly, "You needed to let the faculty feel a little bit of the pain of what the budget crunch was." I mean my counterparts at UNLV and places were taking furloughs. They weren't taking them voluntarily. We didn't lay anyone off. Nobody was furloughed. The budget committee was put together with representation from all different groups including: faculty, staff, deans, and the students. One of the ideas was, you know, a couple of University of New Mexico employees would like to take a furlough so they could stay home with their kids for six months or something like that. And so, they created a way that if they wanted to, they could. But nobody was forced to take a furlough.

But the interesting thing was that you were better than Schmidly or Harris because it took a while for them to get over the hurt. It hurts a lot to have your faculty take a vote of no confidence. Jamie, I think, for you, coming from an environment where people are not very pleasant a lot of times, you were sort of used to having to deal with negative stuff. Whereas the other two weren't. But the neat thing is that David Harris now is closer to some of that faculty than any administrator has ever been. Then Dave Schmidly had a challenging health issue and he had to step aside for a while and Paul Roth came in and I thought Roth did a good job. We had some challenging issues then. We had a kid who committed suicide and Paul Roth was really good with being able to deal with crisis. He was an Emergency Room doctor so he understood crisis management very well. You know, when the parents are there, to be able to go over and say, "You know I'm really truly sorry for your loss," and to be able to sit with them. Eventually Dave Schmidly came back and he finished his contract and he went back to faculty in biology.

Jamie: The biggest issue was that we changed titles of administrators. We made them vice presidents and that was the most controversial issue. Plus, the fact is that when we went to the vote of no confidence, it was the best-organized thing I've ever seen in my life. Man, they were smart. They had people who could talk for three minutes or two minutes. Whatever their time was and they had the card to tell the time. So, they went through all this stuff. They wouldn't let me speak, which is okay. So, when we got through, I turned to Raymond Sanchez and Mel Eaves and I said, "I wouldn't vote for me either." I'm proud I got eight hundred thirty-three votes that didn't agree. It didn't bother me at all.

Breda: And it played itself out and Chaouki, who was the provost, was head of this group, and now he's the interim president. So, people like you and David Harris and Dave Schmidly were able to put that aside. Then Bob Frank became president. And that was very different. I wish he had had a mentor, too. I tried as hard as I could.

Jamie: We selected Bob and Bob decided he wanted to have a different chief of staff. The situation with you, Breda, is that you know so many people and you are so well liked by all the faculty members. But Bob Frank didn't realize the tremendous value of your relationship with the faculty and the rest of the student body.

Breda: One thing I do want to get in before we finish, is during that time when we had the vote of no confidence, I sent a book home with you for Nene. It was a book that the university architect had written. Oh, what was his name? Van Dorn Hooker, who was the second university architect for the university. And it was a wonderful book about all of the buildings on campus with pictures. I remember writing in it to Nene that you know, all of these buildings would not be here and in the state they're in if it wasn't for you, and a lot of the stuff that you and the Regents were able to do. Because it's not just buildings like the library, which you didn't have anything to do with being built, but you have to keep them up and so your time on the Board of Regents was crucial. You did things like, when you put in for a new building you insisted they had to have as part of the request, what the upkeep will be in the budget and stuff like that. So, understanding that people like you influence not just the people who work for the University of New Mexico, because the people who work for the University of New Mexico don't come by themselves. They've got families. I feel really fortunate to have learned from you. When I left Bob Frank's office, one of the things I missed the most was working with the Regents because I learned a lot from them. I really did. And I think that's really, really important. I think that budget issues challenge all institutions of higher education now, and how we're going to be able to continue to fund programs will be a very significant question.

Jamie: So, as you look to the future, because as I mentioned at the beginning, all of these interviews are not just about what we accomplished historically, but past is sometimes prolog. So, what do you see as you look forward in terms of the Regents and the university because this is a particularly timely question as we search right now for a new president?

Breda: Well, I think every member of the Board of Regents that I worked with, and there were lots of different ones, they all cared a lot about the University of New Mexico. They did in their own ways. But one of the things that I hope can happen is that whoever the next University of New Mexico president is, that they get a mentor. And they should get a mentor that they don't necessarily pick. President Frank had somebody that he really liked but his advisor was from back east and he had not a clue about New Mexico and New Mexico's different.

During my interview with Breda Bova, we discussed the significance of the Success Center for the massive gains we made in four year graduation rates and average GPA's of our student athletes. Breda also mentioned how important Paul Krebs leadership was for the growth of all twenty-two intercollegiate sports programs offered at the University of New Mexico. I was directly responsible for recruiting Paul Krebs. I had seen what he had done with the football team at Bowling Green and I knew his skills would be invaluable for our community. It is true that some of our coaches make a lot of money, but with those high salaries come even higher expectations. Paul Krebs has managed critical searches for, selection and retention or termination of many outstanding coaches. Hiring and firing coaches is a high stakes, high pressure and very, very high visibility job. It takes someone with a strong character that can stand up to pressure and have courage in his or her convictions. Paul Krebs has been able to make decisions independently and I am very proud of the progress we have made under his leadership. We have a lot of armchair quarterbacks in this state. But few people understand all the variables that enter into the calculus of each and every decision the athletic director makes about the allocation of resources in the thirty-three million budget that Paul Krebs manages. I asked Paul if he would provide some commentary for this book about the work we have done together.

Paul Krebs, former vice president for Athletics / Interviewed
December 2016

Paul: I am in my eleventh year at the University of New Mexico. I came to New Mexico from Ohio where I had served as Associate AD at Ohio State and then I served as the athletic director at Bowling Green. Bowling Green was a smaller school with a smaller budget. They were very, very competitive and won a lot of games. Jamie Koch recruited me to come to the University of New Mexico. When I sat down with Jamie he was very clear he wanted me to build the athletic programs but he also wanted to make sure we would have academic success. I remember specifically that day in the university offices talking about the academics. It was my perception that they hadn't spent a lot of time preparing for the new rules that were coming forward and they were going to have some work to do academically. They were headed for some problems with some of the new NCAA academic legislation. Also Jamie made it clear he wanted to bring all the athletic facilities up to a standard that was consistent with other flagship university athletic programs. So I knew when I got here that we had some work to do on the facilities and I was fortunate enough that when I got here Jamie had engaged Governor Richardson, so there was a lot of momentum to do some work. I think as I walked in the door, the governor made a commitment of six million for the indoor facility. And shortly after I arrived in New Mexico, we began construction on the indoor practice facility. Governor Richardson, with Jamie's help, made a commitment. We went back and subsequently got an additional amount of money to build, not only the indoor practice facilities, but we cleaned up this area, got rid of a parking lot and we created some green space around the practice facility. But the first thing we did was to create a master plan. It was obvious to me there was no long-range plan, and as a consequence as we did things, we just did them piecemeal and there was no thought of how the next project would flow with the previous project. I recognized that we needed a master plan. So the first thing we did was create a facility master plan. It was a twenty-year master plan and halfway into it, it's amazing how much of that we actually have accomplished. So we had the master plan. What the master plan did was tell us where to begin to site things. We built the indoor facility with the money that we'd gotten from the governor, began to clean up and enhance the beauty, if you will, of the athletic campus. We really tried to create some green space, get rid of parking lots, and roadways and we built the indoor practice facility, which is a real benefit for all of our teams. Football benefits the most but everybody benefits from that. The track resurfacing was actually underway when I got here. Before it got resurfaced, it was in a state of disrepair. It was damaged and had holes.

We couldn't host any track meets. We had a couple of priorities, number one, enhancing the academics had to be a priority because our previous space was really poor and worked against us in recruiting. Also, the donors' willingness to support our projects, the donors' wishes, would prioritize what happened first. A good example of that is tennis was way down the list but when the McKinnon family walked in and said, "I want to give X and I want it to go to tennis," then tennis jumped to the top of the list. So our coaches, I think, understood that.

Jamie: So we did the indoor facility, the track was underway, the next big thing was the arena. The practice piece of it was done and so when I walked in, people were talking about a twenty million...Rudy had started discussions, my predecessor, about a twenty million renovation to the arena and I said, "Timeout." Rather than say "Here's the money, let's decide what we want to do. Why don't we decide, keeping with Harry Truman's big plan here, why don't we decide what it is we want to do and then figure out how much that costs and see if we can do it, rather than say, we're gonna do twenty million." It struck me as an arbitrary number and we weren't sure if that would get us what we wanted. So we did all this, came back and said, "We need sixty, sixty-five, seventy million to do this building."

As it turned out, the economy tanked, contractors were desperate for work, so we were able to basically take what should have been a seventy or seventy million renovation and pay for it for sixty million, which was predominately state—twenty million in state money and forty million in bonds and because of my connections with the governor I really helped secure that, because that's a lot of state money for athletic facilities. It was several years of outlay, but it was twenty million in state money to renovate the basketball arena. What we were able to do was take a historic building, renovate it, bring it up to code, and it gave us a jewel for our two basketball programs (men's and women's). It's no coincidence that as we were doing this, Coach Alford decided to come here, and you saw our basketball teams take off and win a bunch of championships. I think Steve saw the practice gym, saw the renovations ongoing and realized he was walking into a very good situation.

Paul: There's really three things that make an athletic department run: people, facilities and budgets. And we were fortunate enough to have a lot of money and New Mexico's one of the only places that I know of where this can happen is you're able to get state money and obviously the money's important, but what's really important about the fact that it's state money is that it's immediately available. There's no "I've gotta wait until the donor you know, makes good on a five year pledge" and then I have the cash in hand, or I have to borrow money until I get all of it. When it's state money it's there. It's immediate and you go right away, and so you're able to get a lot of stuff done quickly. So with Jamie's help we were able to secure a lot of capital outlay so we could begin work immediately, people could see change. We have hired a lot of really good coaches. And good coaches, not only do they win games but they develop student athletes and they really push the emphasis on personal development and academics. You can't be a good coach without really emphasizing progress in the classroom, I don't think. So the timing was right that we were able to build, we were able to hire a lot of good people, and we've won a lot of championships, and finally, football seems to be on the ground and getting better, which is something that Jamie, you and I have always longed for, which was to rebuild our football program and it's taken a long time, but I think we're almost there now. In the last five years we've won more championships collectively than any five year period in the history of the university. And at the same time our graduation rates have never been better.

Jamie: Our four year graduation rate is now sixty-four compared to the university average, which is around twenty-five percent. And of course there are penalties if we don't graduate enough students in a four year period. It depends on the sport and how long your graduation rates have been bad, but it starts with losing scholarships and can be as significant as ineligible for post season. What we've been able to do is win and graduate and that's really how you, for the most part, measure an athletic department.

Paul: Early on, you suggested I call the New Mexico governor. I had just come from Ohio. In Ohio the governor's not gonna take a call from the athletic director, so his secretary calls and then says "Yes, the governor wants to meet you." I think my second or third day on the job I was going to go meet the governor. I was nervous and intimidated and didn't know what to expect and he was, his back was bothering him that day, so he was kind of sprawled out on a couch or whatever he had in there. So I said, "Governor, how you doing?" after a little chit chat I finally said, "Governor, what do you want from me? What are your expectations for me?" And he turned and he said, "Don't mess it up." He said, "You're in charge of the psyche of the state.

When you win, the state of New Mexico feels better, and when you lose, it's not good. Don't mess it up, Krebsy."

And I thought, "Well, that's a lot of pressure. The psyche of the state rests with me. Okay." And he was good. He was very good and you know what? It made a strong impression on our coaches when Bill Richardson would call Alford. He liked Alford. They got along well. And when a coach gets a call from the governor, (our coaches have huge egos), and so when they get a call from the governor it makes them feel really good. When our teams get invited to the governor's mansion, it made our coaches feel really special and it's something a little bit unique about New Mexico. So it was good. And a lot of what we've done, we couldn't have done without your leadership, Jamie. And Jamie, you're modest, you'll say, "It wasn't just me. There were all the Regents." But you gotta have somebody driving the agenda and you have to have somebody fighting and you know, we were able to get stuff done because you, Jamie, were able to convince the other Regents to do this.

Jamie: To sum things up, the development of an athletic program that's thriving and successful has a number of different components that all are interrelated, but if you only pay attention to getting the best athletes and you ignore the academic piece, you're gonna be in trouble.

Paul: If you only pay attention to what you're doing within the university itself, but you forget about your fans and what they need in order to be comfortable and to make the experience pleasant for them, you're gonna be in trouble. Then there's a marketing piece in terms of the overall "curb appeal" of the facilities that come into play. I am referring to the living, studying, and practicing facilities for the students, and for the fans, the exterior look of the facilities and the amenities that the neighborhood offers that have absolutely nothing to do with sports per se, but will ultimately have everything to do with the athletes that you get and the fans who show up. This look and feel of the facilities is a very interesting piece of the puzzle that has a very real impact on our ability to recruit both coaches and athletes.

The other piece that we have done a lot of, that has now been taken for granted, but was noticeably absent when I got here, was that athletics was initially very isolated, by choice. They didn't want to be engaged on campus. "We're gonna do our own thing." That was the mentality and there was a great deal of resentment on the part of the faculty and the academic leaders of the university. They either didn't think we were serious about school, and our graduation rates reflected that, or we had this isolation, this mentality, so there was a lot of distrust or mistrust.

195

What we've tried to do is engage our staff and that part of campus. We've reached out over the years to bridge buildings, we've done job sharing; we've engaged faculty in hiring of coaches. We sit on a number of university committees. We really try to reach out and partner with other areas of the university, and while everybody may not like athletics, I think they now see our students as serious students. We have a young man who's up for a Rhodes Scholarship, football player, and our GPAs, our graduation rates have surpassed the student body, and so the criticism that we weren't serious and we weren't getting stuff done and we weren't performing in the classroom, that's all gone away. Over time it's just gone away, it's not even there, but it was very, very noticeable when I got here. There was a huge divide between south campus and main campus. A lot of people have worked to bridge that and I'm very proud of that work because in the end, our student athletes are absolutely ambassadors for the university. We want to be, have to be, seen as part of the university, not a standalone entity that lives on its own. In the past four years the programs have had sixteen Academic All Americans, and this year there were a hundred and sixty-three Lobos who were named MW All-Academic leading the Conference.

Navigating the very competitive and complicated business side of college athletics, complying with NCAA rules and demanding high ethical standards by not only coaches but also every employee, are what I have focused on. Virtually all the recent facilities upgrades have been accomplished by donations. Over the last eleven years, I am proud of the work we have accomplished and I am very clear that it would not have happened without you, Jamie.

I am very proud of the monetary support I was able to bring in for the University of New Mexico athletics. As I discussed in the first chapter of this book, athletics always have been very important in my own life. Initially as a child, athletics kept me out of mischief. But as I matured into high school and college, I developed into a very good athlete. I was a Letterman both in High School and in College and I was inducted into the University of New Mexico Hall of Honor. One of the projects I initiated when I joined the Board of Regents for the University of New Mexico was a reorganization of the Lettermen's Association. I felt it should not be administered through the Alumni Association, but I thought the athletic department should run it. I wanted our alumni athletes to remain connected and involved with current athletic programs by supporting the programs financially, as donors, and also, most importantly, attending athletic events as spectators. I wanted to create a place where former athletes could connect with each other and be a part of our current athletic programs. I was president of the Lettermen's Alumni Association in 1981. I convinced my fellow Regents to carve out some space upstairs in the northeast corner of The Pit for the new Lettermen's Lounge. I asked Judge Frank Sedillo, a member of the Lettermen's Alumni Association, and Madison Baumann, the executive director of the Lettermen's Alumni Association, if they could offer their perspectives about the importance of the new space in The Pit and how the club has grown following the decision to have the club administered through the athletic department.

Frank Sedillo, judge Metropolitan Court, past president, Alumni Lettermen's Association, the University of New Mexico / Interviewed December 2016

Frank: I'm a Judge in Metropolitan Court. I have been an attorney now practicing for about thirty years. I'm from Albuquerque, New Mexico. I played football here for the Lobos. I also played baseball. I actually grew up about a half a mile from University Stadium, just right across the desert here on the other side of the freeway. My house was one of the first houses on the other side of the freeway, so I've been coming to Lobo football and basketball games and baseball games probably since I was about six years old—old enough to cross the desert by myself. Been a Lobo for life and plan to be, and I love the University of New Mexico and I love being a Lobo.

We had a place and the Alumni Association was great and they were wonderful and they supported us. It was wonderful to be over at Hodgin Hall, but we always felt like we were a guest. Jamie, you were president of the Lettermen's Association in 1981 when we obtained the room in Hodgin Hall. Now that we have the Lettermen's Lounge at The Pit, we feel like we're home and that's a big difference in terms of that feeling, that sentiment that you want to have in an organization like this. You have to have pride. You have to feel like you're a part of the organization. That's the only way that the Lettermen's Alumni Association is going to get bigger and better and stronger is if you feel like this is who you are, that you belong, that you're a part of this institution. There have been some internal struggles with the Lobo Club over the years and I think it's just a result of a different mission. Their purpose is very different than the Lettermen's Association's purpose. We understand it and we recognized their purpose and we want to be helpful in that. Quite frankly, I think the fact that we actually have a lounge now makes that relationship much better. We feel like it's a partnership now that we're on equal footing. We're recognized equally, and even though we have different missions, we are here to work together to make the entire university and the athletic department and the athletic programs much better. Believe it or not, having the lounge has allowed for that kind of relationship to develop and to prosper, quite frankly.

The space was so important because we were a small group. Even the people who were on the Board were fewer in number. We were fairly organized. We did quite a few things for the community. We organized. We tried to organize the Lettermen's Association for current athletes. That was, depending on the year, sometimes good, sometimes not. We had an executive director at the time who was funded by the Alumni Association. It was a small group of people, basically. We would try to organize and coordinate tailgate parties and other kinds of fundraising events, try to keep up our membership and develop our membership, but it was a struggle. It was challenging to say the least. We grew in membership and we grew in terms of involvement from the board. Right around the same time that we got the Lettermen's Lounge, we came under the auspices of the athletic department, and so at that time the athletic department undertook the responsibility of paying the salary for our executive director. We've grown quite a bit more. I think we have more exposure. I think we have more opportunities to provide services to our membership. That has also meant that we've been able to raise more money. We've been able to help the athletic department in different endeavors, even though that's not our primary function. We have just gotten bigger and better as a result of having a space.

Madison Bauman, executive director, Alumni Lettermen's Association / Interviewed December 2016

Madison: I am the executive director for our Alumni Lettermen's Association. I have been in this position for almost six years. It'll be six years come February. I was hired in the winter of twenty eleven. I was a cheerleader. I was born and raised in Albuquerque. Yes, I'm also our spirit coordinator, so I'm in charge of all our cheerleaders, dancers, and mascots, so that keeps me plenty busy as well. I was also the "Lobo for Life." I have been going to Lobo games since I was just a little kid and it was a passion of mine. I went to graduate school here at the University of New Mexico as well as my undergrad. I went to graduate school for sports administration and I was an intern here in our athletic department.

The main goal, the main mission of the organization is to provide fifth year scholarships to those individuals whose scholarship has expired. These are student athletes who are no longer eligible to receive any kind of financial benefit from the university, but they're still missing a few hours, maybe even as much as a semester or two from graduating. We want those students to graduate, so we provide fifth year scholarships to those individuals. This last year we provided fourteen partial scholarships.

When we started, we had between a hundred twenty-five and a hundred fifty members that first year. We have now grown it to be about an average of four hundred a year. We still have much loftier goals. Members pay annual dues and we have lots of different levels. Our smallest level is a fifty dollars annual membership fee. Our highest fee is our lifetime membership, which costs twenty-five hundred for a lifetime. Our highest annual membership is five hundred.

We give graduation cords, so much like any type of honor cord that a graduate would walk with in their cap and gown, it's something that is earned. You can't buy it at the bookstore. This is something that they get at their student athlete graduation and it's just to commemorate and show that this student athlete was able to achieve a high level within their sport and earn their degree. It's just a small token of our appreciation that we're able to give them. We also provide all the letterman's jackets.

I think everyone who's ever been involved with the Lettermen's Association has really helped grow it. But your involvement, Jamie, was pivotal for the organization. If we didn't have a lettermen's lounge I would not be able to recruit nearly as many members. One of the ways that we also reach out to our future lettermen is I try and make an effort to meet with our coaches who have individuals coming in who are recruits. I like to walk them through the lettermen's lounge so that they know that we do have a space where once you are done here, you're not necessarily done here. You still have a family, you're still very much a part of what the University of New Mexico athletic department is and represents. It's not just your four years here. It's a lifetime.

$\sim\sim\sim$

My own experiences with dyslexia and raising Amy who has Williams Syndrome, gave me the opportunity to understand that people with special needs can accomplish anything they set their minds to. This is the main reason I advocated for the Student Success Center.

I believe that we, as a society, need to do more to level the playing field so that everyone can reach his or her full potential. In the early 1970s, when I learned what Mary Russell was working on with New Vistas, I wanted to get involved on the board of that organization. New Vistas was organized in 1971 in response to a critical need identified by local Santa Feans: Santa Fe's lack of an integrated preschool program for children with special needs. Services for preschoolers began in February 1972. Marilyn Price, a special education teacher, worked with seven handicapped children and their families in donated space at Immanuel Lutheran Church. New Vistas also provided assistance of teacher aides, therapeutic and transportation services, snacks, equipment and supplies. In 1977 adult services began. In coordination with the New Mexico Division of Vocational Rehabilitation, New Vistas established adult work activities and assisted young adults with independent living skills. New Vistas was helping students and their families get the resources they needed so that these students would thrive from pre-kindergarten through high school. Eventually, in the early 1980s, New Vistas added Group Homes for residential independent living services. In the introduction, I mentioned that in this book I would share information about unsung heroes. I am proud to share these stories. Mary Russell is very humble but she really is one of the pioneers in New Mexico in terms of helping people with special needs. I am honored that I was able to be on the board of directors for New Vistas. I sat down with Mary Russell on November 1, 2016 to talk about New Vistas and our work together.

Mary Russell, founder of New Vistas /
Interviewed November 1, 2016

Mary: I grew up in Wisconsin and met my husband Jay while attending Smith College. Jay is a native New Mexican and after college, his military service and a few years of Jay practicing law in Oklahoma, we came to Santa

Fe in nineteen seventy. Our children graduated from St. Mike's and we now have three beautiful grandchildren. I received my undergraduate degree, a BA in Economics, in nineteen sixty-two from Kansas State University, and my Masters of Rehabilitation from the University of San Francisco in nineteen eighty-six.

Jamie: So, you formed New Vistas. I want you to talk about it. I was president of the very first board. So what I want you to do is tell us all about New Vistas, how you put it together, how all that transpired.

Mary: When we returned to Santa Fe in nineteen seventy, I joined the Santa Fe Junior Women's Club. At that time the Santa Fe chapter had approximately fifty women who were looking to do community service projects as a part of the mission of the Junior Women's Club. At that time Jeanette Miller was the president of the club and working with her very closely, as former club president, was Mary Carol Wertheim. In nineteen seventy-one, we submitted a request to the National Junior Women's Club to fund, at a very modest level, a project here in the community called the Community Improvement Program, known as CIP. We had two things going on at that time: one was to try to get kindergartens established in the state of New Mexico and Jamie, you were serving in our legislature and introduced the pre-kindergarten bill in nineteen seventy-two.

Jamie: That's right. It was HB 34, the Preschool Classes Act. We were looking for some funding to go with it, and the bill did not pass because it wasn't funded at that time.

Mary: Okay, and the second part of our project, our Community Improvement Program, was to establish a program in Santa Fe. We said at the time, for physically handicapped children, those were the terms we used then. The impetus for that came from another member of the club, and her name was Sonya Lujan.

Jamie: Sonya Lujan is the mother of Michelle Lujan Grisham, the congresswoman.

Mary: Right, the congresswoman, Michelle Lujan Grisham.

Jamie: She, Sonya, had a handicapped daughter.

Mary: That was what was the initial discussion among the women. At that time there were no public facilities in education for her visually impaired daughter, who was of preschool age at that time. The few private preschools that some of the churches ran, were uncomfortable serving children who had special needs. So, we thought that establishing a small program would be the way to go to help Sonya's daughter, Kimberly. So we did that. We did it with very modest funds that we raised in the community through some fundraising projects. At that time we didn't even have a name and volunteers of the Junior Women's Club did everything (Except for the teacher). We talked as a group about what to call this project and we decided to call it, "New Vistas." We incorporated as a nonprofit educational entity with the IRS, and two or three of the club members who were teachers themselves interviewed to have a teacher we would pay a very modest sum to, with the little bit of money that we had, I think we had three thousand dollars. And we started serving children. There were seven in the first group, in nineteen seventy-two. We were actually incorporated on December seventh, nineteen seventy-one.

Jamie: And those seven children were all preschool aged?

Mary: Well, they weren't really. Age-wise they were eligible for a public school education, but the public schools were reluctant to serve children who had difficulty communicating.

Jamie: Like our Amy.

Mary: Some had difficulty communicating, didn't have bladder control, were not mobile independently in some manner or other. And so, the children, most of them, were six or seven years old, but we called it a preschool. We opened in a church donated facility, Emmanuel Lutheran Church on Barcelona Street. Our first teacher's name was Marilyn Price. Marilyn went on to be one of the top staff people in the New Mexico Department of Health. Later, Marilyn was running the division that dealt with people with disabilities. Marilyn had an assistant in nineteen seventy-two and seventy-three. We had about the same number of children, a small number, with varied disabilities, but what we saw initially was that children with physical disabilities were not going to be our target group. It was going to be much broader and include children with mental retardation and cerebral palsy and other disabilities besides just one disability like a visual handicap. So, we expanded our search to increase the number of children, and at the same time expanded the board, the initial incorporation board, to include you, Jamie. At the time, Governor Bruce King was governor and Alice King, the First Lady, joined our board of directors. We had a very vibrant group. Jamie, you were very instrumental in what was happening.

We went to the state Board of Education and the Santa Fe Public Schools, and part of this was Marilyn's thinking. She said there is absolutely no reason the schools can't serve the children we're serving who are of school age. At the same time there was a federal lawsuit going on, which was known as Equal Education for All Children, nationally, regardless of disability or ability. I don't know the title of it. But that passed the U.S. Congress and was signed by the president in the early seventies. With that federal law in our pockets if you will, we went to Leonard DeLayo Sr., who was New Mexico's State School Superintendent for twenty-two years. The state was willing to expand services, provided: a) we got an okay from the Santa Fe Public Schools, and b) they could find the money to fund a classroom here in Santa Fe. I remember the night we went before the Santa Fe Board of Education. You had a couple of parents with you. You basically said, "You figure out a way to do this because if you give us any grief, these children are gonna be sitting on the doorstep of the administration building of the Santa Fe Public Schools the day school starts in September." And somehow we found around sixteen thousand to fund that classroom and four or five, as I recall it, of the children we were serving, plus Miss Price. We went into a classroom, found by the Santa Fe Public Schools, to start the first, what we called 'multi handicapped class' in New Mexico. Meanwhile, New Vistas continued to recruit other children, hired another teacher and continued on from that. That's how it started.

Jamie: So then it started really getting going, when you became head of it. Tell how you became head of New Vistas. You became an employee of New Vistas, could you talk about all that?

Mary: Okay, well initially, in the first year or so, it was all volunteers, as I said, except for the teacher, and those two women I mentioned earlier—Jeanette and Mary Carol. They chose me to head up the project while it was still in its early, early phase, which I did. I started to write some proposals for funding for the New Vistas portion.

Jamie: Yeah, it was a big job.

Mary: The first couple of proposals were done with people in agencies here in New Mexico we knew, for example Bob Swanson was with the division of Vocational Rehabilitation, and Phyllis Nye worked with kindergarten programs in the state of New Mexico. So we knew some people who might be interested in seeing a program for these young children.

The first proposal I wrote was a one-page letter. It was funded for around ten thousand dollars and that took care of our second year of operation. From there we continued to grow. Jamie, how long were you on the board at that time?

Jamie: I was on the board seven or eight years.

Mary: Okay, well you were on the board twice. You were off for a while and then you came back on.

Jamie: That's right.

Mary: But, in those early days, the same division of Vocational Rehabilitation came to the board and said, "Are you interested in also serving young adults who have completed their special education program, and working with them?" That was about nineteen seventy-five, so it wasn't very late. We went to a larger facility and ran two programs simultaneously in the same facility. We had employment services for adults, young adults. The early childhood preschool program was in a building over on Larry Meyer's property.

Jamie: How many years did you work for New Vistas as an employee?

Mary: From nineteen seventy-four 'til nineteen ninety-seven.

Jamie: You were a full-time employee for twenty-three years, and it was a tough job. And we expanded when we started having the students learn how to live on their own.

Mary: Okay, I'll go up to that. In the grant writing, some of what was happening in the late seventies, is there were some federal programs through, I don't know if it was Department of Education or Health. But in any case, there were invitations for early childhood, or preschool programs, to begin to have intervention at earlier and earlier ages, realizing that the sooner children could be worked with, the more likely the problems that they might be having would be diminished. So, we wrote three different proposals to the U.S. Department of Education, all of which were funded, and it was in part because one of them was to serve children in rural areas; one was to serve very young children, newborns in the home; and I think New Mexico was viewed as a place that we could really make an impact with our small population.

Jamie: We did make an impact.

Mary: We made an impact, and in fact, there are programs to this day in Los Alamos, in Espanola, in Las Vegas, all started by and patterned after our New Vistas. Initially our staff was traveling out to assist, and then eventually those programs became independent and are still operating.

Jamie: Mary, you did most of this. In other words, it was you that put it together. Yes, you had some help, but...

Mary: I wrote all the proposals.

Jamie: You wrote all the proposals, and if the proposals didn't get the funding, it wouldn't have happened. In other words, if it didn't have somebody like you, it wouldn't have happened. Can you tell me how many students we served? And where it is now?

Mary: By the nineteen eighties, in the early childhood part, we were serving seventy-five people, seventy-five children or families at any given time. Now, today, the department, I mean the part of New Vistas that still works with families with young children is seeing over five hundred families a year throughout northern New Mexico. It grew, that part grew, and has continued to have a large impact throughout New Mexico.

Jamie: You just said families and this is an important point. The more than five hundred families that they're currently serving, even back when you were serving the seventy-five, your organization was working with the whole family, not just the child getting their services and their learning at your particular facility, but also helping the families understand how to serve these special needs children? Correct?

Mary: Yes, I would say the philosophy of New Vistas children's program expanded in the first maybe three or four years to be much more inclusive and focused on the family. When we were just beginning we knew the families because they would bring the children in. We would talk to them, but with that first federal project the staff was going out into the community. Either Santa Fe or the rural communities, and working with much younger children. In those situations, we felt we could serve our mission better by providing services in the home with the parents, or the caregivers or the grandmother. The key was being able to assist the caregiver who was working on a daily basis with that child. And so that happened fairly early and that's basically the whole structure now, and there's very little that goes on in the Center per se other than parent groups, you know counseling and that sort of thing.

Jamie: What about the group homes?

Mary: Okay, so during the seventies the Santa Fe Association for Retarded Citizens, which is what it was called then, they had an active group of parents who were interested in some kind of community living program. Their desires fit in with the fact that the state of New Mexico was beginning to move adults from the Los Lunas Hospital facilities into their home communities, and so the state was willing to fund programs in the community and the Santa Fe ARC parents were looking for something in Santa Fe. There were a couple of things besides just the New Vistas board that fed into the time being right in nineteen eighty to establish the first group home. We had a community citizen, Lee Brown, C.L. Brown.

Jamie: He had a handicapped boy also.

Mary: Who provided property and housing, which is still used for the same purpose, known as group homes for people here in Santa Fe and we ran the program. We, at that time, expanded our board to include members of the Santa Fe ARC. So, it was still a New Vistas program, but it was very much influenced by the families who we were serving again, but at the adult level. And services were provided to help, first to provide a place to live for young adults, rather than to be living at their homes, and then to work with what we already had established, which was an employment program. There were some employers in the community who were always good to work with. Albertsons Grocery Store was one; the Latigo Lights, the owner of which is now deceased, but he always employed about three people over there.

Jamie: Yes.

Mary: There were several people who were reliable, consistent employers.

206

But it's challenging. The program you founded, "Project SEARCH" sounds wonderful as another way to build up the confidence and the skills of people to work in the community. But in any case, we started the group homes in 1980 and with one group home for men and one group home for women. They had six residents each. And then over time, three more were established and that continued to be our sole way of working with people for community housing for a couple of years. And then by nineteen eighty-four or nineteen eighty-five with the assistance of federal funding, we looked at what we called more independent living situations for people to live in apartments with a companion to provide support. That program continued through the time that I was at New Vistas, both kinds of living arrangements, employment, other independent living services and the early childhood program. And you came back on the board somewhere in that period because we had a lot going on. I think we had a wonderful partnership.

Jamie: Well, I do too. So what do you think was the most significant positive outcome to come out of New Vistas for the state of New Mexico in the time that you were there?

Mary: Well, probably the most significant was the public schools opening up classrooms for children with all levels and kinds of disabilities. Over time, the whole education system of New Mexico was impacted by that change. Think of all the children who never saw a classroom in their lives because they weren't toilet trained, they weren't independently mobile, or they couldn't communicate in a way that could be understood by an average teacher. Thousands of children never had that opportunity and starting in nineteen seventy-four, in New Mexico, they all have had that chance ever since then. That's probably the number one thing to me. A second thing would be the expansion that we had in the children's program, multi counties of northern New Mexico, and then our independent living program, which is another division of our programming getting federal government funding. We established centers in Las Cruces and Farmington and Santa Fe, and that had an effect upon adults whose injuries or disability had come from spinal cord, stroke, or other disabilities that had their onset in adulthood as opposed to childhood or birth. So, together those two programs have reached thousands of people in New Mexico and are still all pretty much operating. New Vistas doesn't manage all of them any more, but they're all still going. So, those would be the things.

Jamie: So, we have one last question, which we're asking, which is moving forward as you look at what the needs of this population will be into the future, what do you think will be important for the state of New Mexico as they move forward serving this population?

Mary: That's a tough one because a lot, a significant portion of the funding for some of these programs, from the state of New Mexico, is the match that is done with Medicaid and I can't remember the figure I just saw in the paper of what this next legislative session's looking at, but it's probably eighty million dollars.

Jamie: That's right, and you see Medicaid should mean you can only earn so much money on these part time jobs, so you've got to have an employer who's willing to let someone work thirty hours, because the minute they go over, every year we have to file, we have to certify that Amy's handicapped every year.

Mary: In order to get the funding, yeah.

Jamie: And so they can't work forty hours, they're limited. So most of them are under Social Security. They can only work thirty hours and that's it. If they work over, they lose their Social Security. So you have to have an employer who understands that, that they can't do it, and if you don't have an employer who understands, the person can't work because they'll take their Social Security away from them.

Mary: Well, and the state coming up with those matching funds its, what three to, four, three to one, probably about the time I retired, the state was having to deal with the high twenties, millions, twenty-seven million, now they're up to I think like eighty million, people who are eligible for Medicaid services, including people with disabilities. We're talking half a billion, half a billion for these programs, just New Mexico.

You know we see it in different places; we see it in private programs, hospital programs, public school programs, the funding is always an issue for everything and New Mexico's not a state that has lots of extra dollars around for programs. So, you know I think being able to find funding through a hospital sector, or something other than always the government, that would be ideal if there are other sources.

I'd have to say another concern that we should all have is that the makeup of the population of the children who are being served, and families, has changed as we have more families who are immigrants unable to easily locate services and more mothers with substance abuse. And so, a program like New Vistas early childhood program is seeing children who are at risk if not truly disabled. The babies born addicted are at risk for developmental delays. So that's a change in population, not for the good.

Long ago, I had a dream that [In 2017, New Vistas was 45 years old] by thirty years along, we wouldn't need a children's program, that medicine and public education and awareness would change everything. Well in fact, the needs are greater than ever.

Jamie: I think the headline that I'm hearing from you after a very long career in this space, is that the earlier people can work with families and help them to not only identify what an issue may be, but also to provide them with the skills that they need, the resources that they need to assist that child in the early stages of development, the better chances you have for that child to lead a successful life as things go down the pike, and that is a better use of resources from the public.

So, in your dream world, if you were "Queen for a day," what would you like to see if you could sort of map out what things you would like for the state in the next five years, in this space? I mean obviously your program serves people statewide right now. New Vistas obviously has grown, so what do you see will be needed in the future?

Mary: I think the challenge is being able to continue to identify those children who need the services and have the funding available so there aren't children on waiting lists from birth. You can't be on a waiting list for five years. It's a particularly difficult thing for young children. It is not right for a five year old with disabilities to not have had any services. But it happens.

So, I learned a tremendous amount about how to assist people with special needs from the time I spent on the board of New Vistas. Later on, after Amy graduated from high school, I saw how difficult it was for many special needs students to mature into adulthood because there were very few jobs for them to do. When I saw what a difference it made for Amy to be employed through Project SEARCH at Seton Hospital in Austin, Texas, I realized this was a replicable program. The program had been initiated in Cincinnati, Ohio in 1996 and has grown to become an international model.

Toward the end of my tenure on the University of New Mexico Board of Regents, I approached the University of New Mexico Hospital about creating a Project SEARCH program here in New Mexico. Project SEARCH is a program that works with employers to identify positions and train employees with special needs to fill those positions. Tanya Baker-McCue and Erica Brooks will discuss how that project got started and the tremendous success and expansion of the program here in New Mexico. As you will hear in the interview, Project SEARCH demonstrated that people with disabilities often make better employees for certain jobs than people who do not have any disabilities. On November 17, 2016 I sat down with Erica Brooks and Tanya Baker-McCue to talk about how we got Project SEARCH established in New Mexico.

~~~

Tanya Baker-McCue and Erica Brooks, Project SEARCH coordinators, the University of New Mexico Health Sciences Center for Development and Disability / Interviewed November 17, 2016

Tanya: I work at the University of New Mexico Health Sciences Center for Development and Disability and I oversee a division here called the Family and Community Partnerships Division. I have spent my life teaching special education. I have a Masters in Special Education and have done most of my life's work around family support and advocacy and systems change work. I currently write grants and do development. I oversee several state and national grants to support people with disabilities. I oversee a library and information network, a Medicaid waiver program and employment training programs, which is why I was the person who was introduced to you here at the Center. I have been doing a lot of work with youth and adults to be meaningfully employed in the community.

Jamie: Could you tell us about the program Project SEARCH? What is Project SEARCH? And what was the process you went through to be able to have a Project SEARCH program here in New Mexico?

Tanya: Well, let me just say that one day my boss, Kate Maclean, who was the executive director of the Center at the time, asked me to have lunch with one of the Regents, and that was a pretty scary prospect, but I said "Okay." She said, "Well, he wants to talk to us about a model that I haven't

210

heard about, and I don't know if you have either." And I was very struck with, first of all, the fact that you were coming to us on a kind of personal level, because your own daughter had benefited from this model in Austin, Texas. I had never heard of it before—you know it just hadn't been something I was introduced to. You were very persuasive. Your passion as a dad and then obviously your influence was very helpful. You really believed in the Center and some of the work we were doing here, and you believed in the possibility that we could collaborate on this project together. So, my mission at that point was to go and research about the program because I knew nothing about it. I started with calling the people in Austin at the Seton Hospital. Then from there, that administrator gave me some names and numbers of people in Arizona, and I wound up interviewing about three or four different states and was just so impressed right away because this was clearly a pretty high fidelity model that reflected all the things we believed in philosophically, around integrated employment, you know real employment, real wages, and going from a business model. So, I was really hooked and curious. Before you know it, I had reams of notes and contacts and people were saying they'd come and visit me, or should I go visit them, and you know this was kind of like an investigative reporting is what it started to feel like, right?

And, so we meet again and we start talking about well, and I think I was really struck with you, Jamie, being determined to make it happen. You were like, "Why aren't we doing it here? Why isn't anyone doing it here? It's such a simple model, it works, and we could do it here. I have the influence here, let's propose this..." I had never, you know, proposed anything to the Regents before, and it was a little out of my league to be honest.

Jamie: Well, I think you did a pretty good job.

Tanya: So, you know, we did a little PowerPoint and I think it was a hundred thousand dollars, or I don't even know if we had the number yet.

Jamie: We needed money.

Tanya: Yes. You were very forthright. You said, "So tell me how much money you're gonna need." We said, "Well maybe, maybe forty thousand?" And you said, "No. You will need at least a hundred." You were very clear. "Don't ask me for that little amount. You know what you really need. And you're going to need it for more than one year." You were right. So, we did propose it. But I believe it is Amy who really sold the program. Seton had

211

done a video of her discussing her work for that hospital. That really sort of sold everything because first of all, it's a video of her work in Seton, but also of her playing the piano. The video was about more than the program. It was really about disability issues, women's empowerment and leadership. It is a very moving piece.

Jamie: It was the leading ladies, young ladies in Austin. My daughter, Amy, was nominated as one of them and she was selected because of her inspiration.

Tanya: Yes, and her leadership.

Jamie: And leadership.

Tanya: It was just beautifully done. It was a short, two minute segment about her, maybe a little longer. So we, we said "Could we show this to them at the end?" And what I didn't expect was the sort of the emotional pull that happened for you and for everyone, you know on the Board of the Regents, and in the audience. So, my back is to the audience and I just remember, of course I've never presented in front of a Regent you know before, and behind me I can hear people sniffling, and I looked to my boss and I said, "Is this normal, like what do I do now?" But, it was just a really beautiful moment where everybody got it. Everybody in the room realized that this was possible. The Regents saw that this program would be meaningful and that it would connect a lot of people in the community. And that's one of the things I learned from that day. I learned you have to be brave enough, of course, that's the thing; you have to go in front of people. So, I would go and talk to the managers at the University of New Mexico later to try and get people interested, and you would find out, people would come up to you and say something like, "I have a son." Or, "I have a daughter." You know it wound up; many people were touched by the idea because overcoming a disability is part of the community. People had these experiences in their own families. I didn't have to convince people as much as I thought I would have to. Actually, it was the easiest funding I've ever gotten because we had a champion right there. Everybody said "Absolutely, this is the right thing to do." I remember Steve McKernan looking at me, realizing it was going to come out of his budget. You were the ambassador, our champion. You were there all along the way, guiding us, saying, "Okay, this is what you need to do." Then, you introduced us and got us connected right away to the HR and the recruitment department, because one of the first things we had to do was work with the various departments and get an intern. So, basically the model is a partnership between a school and a business. It is often a school to work, but it's a work internship model and it allows individuals with disabilities to have the opportunity to have a lot of work experience, to float through on a regular basis, various rotations within a hospital setting or a large organization or business. The interns wind up learning tasks, specific tasks. When you're in a hospital setting, what's so beautiful about a hospital, is that there's enough jobs and departments, it's almost like a little village or city.

Jamie: Did you have to go to Cincinnati?

Tanya: This model has a high fidelity, and part of the money that we received was to be able to pay for the initial license, so we could replicate the model exactly. So what you're paying for, for the initial license, is for the national experts to teach you exactly how the model is implemented. The founder of the model is Erin Riehle. She was a nurse in the Cincinnati Children's Hospital. She was the head of the ER department and she couldn't get the supply cabinet filled when she needed it and she kept saying, "Why can't we keep people in these jobs? Our supply cabinet's never, never filled with the supplies that we need and it is very frustrating."

And so, she had come upon a group that was looking for individuals with disabilities to get jobs. Long story short, she almost accidentally stumbled on this concept and wound up having some of the best employee relationships partnering with some folks who were getting people jobs in the hospital. And so, it kind of snowballed from there and she created this way of doing things. They really are the experts. We call them "the mothership," or the national model. We have to be licensed and you have to pay an initial license fee. What you pay for is really their travel to come and see you and ensure that you know how to do it. So, it's not like they're getting rich on it. They use those funds to come and train you. We started at the University of New Mexico with ten interns.

Jamie: But before you did that, talk about how they were surprised that you had the money to do this.

Tanya: Usually it starts from either a school or an adult organization that provides services, and then you're begging the business to work with you. And we came to the conference first, just a few months after we received the money, there happened to be the national conference, and there were people from all around the country. I mean this, I can't even remember how many, I'd have to go look, how many Project SEARCH sites there are around the country, and the world now; there's some in Ireland, England, and China. It has just exploded.

So, we go to this huge, international conference, you know thousands of people, and we tell people what we were doing because we didn't realize how unusual it was, that the business was offering us the support, and they almost fell out of their chairs, and they said, "That's never happened, ever, ever, how'd you get that dad?" And I said, "It was the dad who had influence, who wanted, who saw the possibility." I said, "It's beyond my control." But within a month of talking about it, we already had an article in the *Albuquerque Journal*. We had schools and programs coming to us, asking how they could be involved. It was like something way beyond me, almost from the beginning, it was contagious almost. My job was to just try to organize it as that was happening.

They were really impressed and we happened to be matched with the Founder of Project SEARCH as one of our people to help us to learn how to do this. So, she came out about every three months and helped plan and implement. Erin Riehle helped us develop all of the components, step by step, by meeting with the managers at the hospital. She walked us through how we could do some public open houses for both the hospital employees and for the community. To get the word out we had people like Erin and you telling their stories. We had people who shared your daughter Amy's video a couple of times. People were very welcoming, very interested, from the beginning. Even in my own family, I've had two children with cystic fibrosis, and one of my children passed away. He was medically fragile. He used a wheelchair and a G-tube. His care required lots of medical equipment. So I spent quite a lot of time in hospitals and quite a lot of time in the disability and chronic health world, so that's kind of why I do what I do around family support and working with individuals who are fragile.

Jamie: Could you explain how you have to educate the staff and the intern? In other words, normally when people go into this program, it takes about a year to get them prepared to potentially be an employee.

Tanya: This program is quite rigorous—usually about four rotations in a nine month period. So it's an internship program and for the nine months they are placed, we've actually got a classroom. Here's another part, which was unheard of, because I don't know if you know anything about space at the hospital or the University of New Mexico, but it's a premium, right?

So, we actually were able to finagle a part time classroom in the Child Life Department. So, in the new pavilion there's a nice little classroom that they use for education and for staffing. The interns use that in the morning as a place to regroup, to get some sort of soft skills training around hygiene, and you know, orientation to the hospital kinds of things for about an hour, and then they each go separately to their internship site, sometimes two in a day. So they may be placed for a couple of hours learning something in sterilization or in housekeeping or in food and cafeteria. There was an occupational therapy assistant program and there were a couple of people that did that. We had like thirty departments. These are complex, but routine tasks that somebody else might find boring after a while, but for some of these individuals with intellectual developmental disabilities, this was a career, and they were excelling. So, it was things like matching the sterilized equipment for a surgeon who's left handed. He has to have his instruments exactly lined up to his specification, and you need to kind of, you know be invested enough to pay attention and really do that well. This particular intern had the highest rate of doing it correctly of anyone they ever worked with.

Jamie: And he's handicapped.

Tanya: And he's very, yeah somebody no one ever thought would be employable. He wouldn't have gotten a chance. No one would have thought that employable.

Jamie: See, what happens is that normally these people are not looked at as being good employees and Project SEARCH shows, if it's done right, they're the best employee you can get.

Tanya: Give them the chance and then give them the training. So they were getting very good training.

Jamie: Well you had to design the training first, and that's why it's important. You know you guys designed the training for them to be successful. It's a lot more detailed than people realize.

Tanya: Right, so they have a job, yes. So, we partner with agencies. One of the important partnerships in this case was the Albuquerque Public Schools, and Best Buddies, which is an agency that provides coaching, job development and job coaching. So they work together with their staff to give individualized training to the individuals on whatever task they were learning. They infiltrate with the individual at the job with them and then they fade away as the person gets better at the skills.

Jamie: This is over a ten month training period?

Tanya: Right.

Jamie: After the ten month training period, what does the student have to do?

Tanya: Well, first of all, what happened was by the second internship we had the department asking to hire them. And we would have to say, "Well not yet." Okay, I mean you know we tried, you know we didn't want them to fail if they went in too soon. We said, "They're supposed to learn more" and they'd say, "But they're already better than any of the employees we've gotten" because they're, you know these were kind of beginning jobs that were high turnover. There were lots of other diversity issues that meant that the manager of that department really was struggling with keeping that job filled. And here was somebody who was loyal, showing up every day on time and was somebody they could count on. These managers were saying, "We get it, you don't have to show us any more." And so, sometimes we would let that happen if it was the right thing, but that was just amazing to us, that that happened so quickly.

Jamie: But then the young man or young lady is getting a salary.

Tanya: That's right, so then they, we had people right off the bat, being hired with full time salary and benefits.

Jamie: They could never find a job anywhere else.

Tanya: Yeah, they wouldn't have even been, they wouldn't have gotten in the door in a competitive market. This was a way, like any internship, I mean it's the concept of a fellowship, their internship, people get to demonstrate, they also get to learn the job, so they have an edge. So why wouldn't we do that for people with disabilities? They need that edge. So, yeah, so the typical intern would go through all that training and maybe have five different experiences, or more, of the various departments and they would, we would kind of individualize it to their strengths. We didn't just throw

216

them in places, we looked at what they were interested in, and we had about, the first year we had about seven of them got jobs at the University of New Mexico Hospital. It's not the goal to get them hired there, because you don't want to hire every class, right, then you would have too many people with disabilities all in one place, and the goal is to get people integrated and have them be in lots of industries. Because after the internship they can take those job skills and go to Presbyterian or Lovelace. Their skills are applicable anywhere in a health related field. They could also generalize their experience and apply the training to many other kinds of jobs. So we also partner them with the business community and we have a business advisory group that helps mentor and supports the interns so that they have connections to businesses. But that first year in particular, people fell so in love with the interns that the managers of the departments were their biggest champions. They wanted to hire the interns. I mean we didn't have to sell this any more—it was selling itself and people in the hospital felt like Project SEARCH was theirs. We couldn't take this away if we wanted to by the second year.

Jamie: It's been three years.

Tanya: Twenty fourteen was the first implementation year. So, we had a planning year. Part of what they make you do is have like nine months to a year planning year, and that's why the funds from the hospital were such a blessing. It gave us some salary and the license fees and then the certification fees so we could replicate in those two years to really develop it well and not just rush in and kind of throw it together. So, we met every month. All the players met and planned out every piece. We learned what we had to do. We did recruitment of the students. We got them ready. We got tee shirts. You know in the University of New Mexico, everybody has a color of a uniform or a shirt. That's very important in the identity of the University of New Mexico. The only color left was rust, and it's burnt orange. We got an emblem for Project SEARCH. The first time I saw a Project SEARCH intern working, I started to cry. I had gone into the hospital as a patient. It was emotional to see it all come together. And so they went through the hospital orientation, the folks in the Learning Department for Orientation adapted the orientation without us even asking.

Jamie: So, they were wearing these burnt orange, they were tee shirts or they were scrubs?

Tanya: They're like a scrub tee shirt; it's one of the options. They're not considered scrubs; it's something in between. And then if the intern needs to wear a scrub in their department, they wear a scrub. So, they wear that when they're not wearing whatever they might have to wear as part of their job. So, we connected them; the Project SEARCH model is once you get started, it sustains itself. We had the gift of having the time and the funds to plan properly. We were able to plant this seed and I think it has made us so much stronger and we're now looked at as one of the model states.

Jamie: Are you saying that the New Mexico programs are considered models countrywide?

Tanya: Yes worldwide.

Jamie: That goes back to your involvement. Because you put this thing together properly, so now New Mexico is reaping the benefits.

Tanya: We had the right supports.

Jamie: Now we're one of the leaders in the country, in the world.

Tanya: Right, so a lot of programs kind of, you know, slam things together and then learn things after and then say, "Oh I wish we had done it this way" and the programs aren't connected properly. But we had the luxury of really investing in the development in the beginning and taking the time we needed to learn it and working with the community.

Jamie: So how many did you graduate in the first year?

Tanya: The first cohort ten interns were hired at the University of New Mexico. Eight of those interns to this day are still employed there at the University of New Mexico, which is phenomenal. These are all individuals with pretty significant intellectual disabilities, who would probably be doing arts and crafts in a day program if this hadn't been their opportunity. These individuals are working full time with benefits at the University of New Mexico. I mean it's phenomenal, if you look at the stats nationwide for people with the same needs. People were just blown away by the success of it. The current class at the University of New Mexico has nine interns, and many of the departments already are asking if they could hire.

Jamie: They have to apply, don't they?

Tanya: Yes, they have to apply.

Jamie: In other words, they have to learn how to apply.

Tanya: So, they literally, once their internship is over, have the opportunity to go back and if there's a position available, they apply like any other person would apply competitively. They wind up being more competitive because they have the experience and the relationship. So, they often get the job.

Jamie: I think that is just fantastic.

Tanya: So what the University of New Mexico did was, because we helped invest in the Best Buddies in Albuquerque Public Schools, who we were partnering with, and these were students who were in their last year of high school. We said we needed another something in the community because we felt like we could probably double the class size. So, we approached Embassy Suites and they were interested, and so we have a second site now in Albuquerque with APS.

Jamie: But that's certified through us now, right?

Tanya: Through the University of New Mexico.

Jamie: In other words, as you're expanding to the other site, you're certifying those individuals. Are you doing that outside of Albuquerque?

Tanya: Yes, we're doing it statewide. It's expanded tremendously and I have you to thank for this.

Jamie: Remember, we won the license for the whole state!

Tanya: And they love this model because I have a statewide coordinator. So we now have expanded to Embassy Suites. We went to Gallup. There was an interest in Gallup, and we work there at the Hilton Garden Inn. The Gallup program is comprised of mostly Native folks who live in Gallup. The whole employment issue in that community is different than Albuquerque, so we really had to kind of think about things differently. There were three individuals from last year who are still trying to get employment. The other seven have gotten a job at the Hilton, which is again, phenomenal, and they got all that training. So we stay with them after the program concludes too. It's not like once the program ends, "Oh well." No, we follow them; we're developing job clubs now. The way it sustains financially is we made agreements with our the New Mexico Division of Vocational Rehabilitation (NMDVR) and our state Public Education Department and our state Developmental Disability Department of Health, and asked everybody to redirect their existing monies. They were so impressed with this that they collaborated with each other to support this. Then they gave us some monies to help coordinate it statewide and to provide the ongoing training. All of the departments that contribute wanted to be able to ensure the fidelity of the model, because that's so important as we replicate.

Jamie: So Project SEARCH goes to other places, like in Gallup, and normally they wouldn't do that under one license, but I made a case for it, and it looks like they liked it.

Tanya: They did. So, the other part is, I don't know if you've heard that we are now at Presbyterian?

Jamie: Yes.

Tanya: They wanted it downtown. I said "No, that's not fair to UNM Health Services. We're not doing it downtown." So we did it at Rust Hospital, and with Rio Rancho Public Schools and Adelante.

Jamie: So, you've got a site in Albuquerque, you've got one in Gallup, and one in Rio Rancho?

Tanya: So, we have two in Albuquerque, one in Rio Rancho and one in Gallup. We're beginning the development, as we speak, of another site for Project SEARCH in Gadsden. We'll be working with Good Samaritan Society—Las Cruces Village, an independent and assisted-living facility in Las Cruces. We just interviewed our eleven new interns last week, and they look like a great bunch!
    Project SEARCH is also looking at, and this is the first time this will have happened, a location in El Paso. However, it will be the state of New Mexico that will support the interns working in El Paso, because they are living on the border. So, we're actually talking to people in Texas to partner with New Mexico. That's a whole new adventure that we're going to start.

It's also a Spanish speaking community and a different culture, again, right? So, that'll be another new challenge, but it's a very enthusiastic team.

So, we put out a statewide application asking communities who would want to be the next. We're going to do three more developments this year beyond Gadsden. So we're going to do eight in development in total by the end of this year. We just received word yesterday that Los Alamos High School is ready to begin their planning year for a new site to launch in fall twenty eighteen.

Jamie: How about Santa Fe?

Tanya: We actually have been, several times to Santa Fe, and I would say they're not quite ready. Community Options is the provider agency and they've gone through some turnover. We're meeting with the newest director again. We've gone there quite a bit, and we also worked and met with the School for the Deaf, because they have an interest. So, we're looking at Taos. That's part of the work, pulling that team together, getting them ready and sometimes you put them on the back burner and then they're ready the next year. We sometimes will bring them to the conference or provide some technical assistance for them. Yeah, so we're always in this place of development, helping them after they've grown to still provide the technical assistance and support, and that's a lot of what Erica does now, I'm not as involved.

Jamie: Erica, can you tell us just a little bit about what you're doing on a daily basis now with the program?

Erica: Sure, so my role overall is to meet with the teams. Well, let's back up a little bit. We have a statewide expansion team here at the Centers for Disease Control and Prevention, for Project SEARCH specifically, and we meet to discuss areas and locations that we feel are ready for Project SEARCH, or that have an interest in getting a Project SEARCH Program. So, that's generally the first step—we send an application. We get any feedback, then we do an application process, or an interview process. Then we just start to build all the pieces that we need for that specific program site. Then they do a planning year, which I'm really involved in. They meet monthly as a steering committee and that includes one representative from each agency as the collaborating partnership and we go through all of the details of what it takes to do a Project SEARCH site.

Tanya: This means figuring out the funding and what's going to get paid for.

Erica: Funding, yeah. Each agency provides numbers in regards to how many students we need to carry. It's a braided funding process, so it looks a little bit different for each site, depending on what their school system works with. So, there's the funding portion, there's the student application process, there's the recruitment process, there's an assessment that the students have to go through. It's quite detailed. And that's an entire year's worth of planning. And then, the following August, they actually begin the program. So my role, I kind of step back a little bit once they begin the program. The instructor takes the lead, and I'm available for any facilitation or questions or technical assistance that they need from then on.

Jamie: So, would you describe some, if there have been any obstacles that you've had to overcome and what that has been like? Because it's all sounding really rosy and I just know these things are a little tougher.

Erica: I think Project SEARCH, Tanya and I were talking about this yesterday, I think that Project SEARCH kind of comes across as an abstract thought, that it's all really great, just like you said, and then we start to really get into the details of it and it's a full collaboration. And these agencies aren't used to that level of collaboration.

Erica: They know of each other and they know generally what the role of the other agency is supposed to be and what they're supposed to do when their specific role is finished, but there's this gap of where they're supposed to pick up. So they don't understand how they can overlap their resources and make it a really seamless transition for the students, and that causes conflict sometimes.

Tanya: It's the secret of Project SEARCH: that they all work together as one. They blend their talent and they blend their monies.

Erica: That's the secret ingredient.

Tanya: So, the school, if the school's paying for something, has its instructor at the hospital or the business. So, sometimes folks will say, "What do you mean? We can't do that, what about insurance? Blah, blah, blah." The hospital's inviting other programs in, right? So, they're mixing their resources on behalf of that intern and it is the real reason I think this works, and why it's sustainable. But they're not used to doing things that way. So that's so much of Erica's job, is to get them to play together. We always go back to this.

Erica: They do, they always kind of pull back into their specific agency and they say, "Well we can't do that. This is your responsibility" and then through discussion we find out that you can in fact do that and there are loopholes, and Project SEARCH has figured out these loopholes. And once they start that conversation and they see where they can work together, it really becomes like a family setting. I can't stress that enough.

Tanya: And then they own it.

Erica: And then they own it.

Tanya: We can't tear them apart if we wanted to.

Erica: Then I kind of fade into the background, as far as how important I am.

Tanya: I told her it's like raising teenagers. When they need you on that day, you're there. But if you hover over them, they get mad at you. It's a developmental process.

Erica: It really is. But as Tanya mentioned, we take a representative from each agency and we put them on site in a business, and really what we're doing is teaching those agency representatives how to follow a business model. And so, the business is really the focus of this. We pull from DVR, from Department of Health, from the school, but really the business is what leads this program all the way through. We follow all of their rules and regulations. We require that the students pass any orientation tests that they have. They have to get badges and complete any direct testing. The businesses determine how this program is going to go.

Tanya: Absenteeism.

Erica: Absenteeism, we follow all of their disciplinary measures. So, it really takes everybody who's used to being in charge of students in transition stepping back and giving away part of their authority.

Tanya: But still maintaining it at the same time, which is kind of a delicate balance. The reach of Project SEARCH has actually gone beyond just Project

SEARCH, because the program has turned a spotlight on the possibilities. We're now looking at other internship options for adults. We're looking at this in a broader way, as well as the importance of that collaboration. So, in the last couple of years, I have gotten other grants now modeling the collaboration of multiple agencies. Project SEARCH taught me that a big piece is teaching people how to work together in the community, basically, and putting their resources together and developing action plans.

Jamie: You go to their national meeting?

Tanya: As presenters, we are now experts!

Erica: I don't know about experts. I'm still learning every single day. We're kind of continuously knocking down barriers.

Tanya: And I think you know when you did the Gallup program there were some barriers. What were some of the barriers there?

Erica: We've sort of changed the model fidelity a little bit as far as Project SEARCH goes. Generally, you use the Project SEARCH logo, you give credit to Cincinnati and you follow the general guidelines they provide. With Gallup and with Erin's permission, we redesigned all of the documents to make them more culturally friendly.

Jamie: For the Native Americans.

Erica: Right. And so one of the fidelity pieces with Project SEARCH is to establish a business advisory council. In Gallup that's not applicable by any means because everything is so spread out and the students, some of the students travel an hour each way to get to the work site. So, finding representatives from each of those communities has been the biggest task. To make that more applicable for them, we're using the chapter houses instead. So, they're going to be inviting the chapter house leader, one every single month, to visit the site, tour, meet the interns, see what it is that we're trying to accomplish, and then keep them as a contact for when that student returns to their community after graduation. Even the logo, we have a New Mexico Project SEARCH logo, but we're going to add in some of the other aspects of their culture to that logo, but it'll be just Navajo specific.

And the transition programs within the high schools are also noticing that they're not focusing on the skills that they need to blend over.

224

Tanya: So it has spread to the other issues where they need to start doing this more in middle school and earlier in their high school careers. So we are working with the schools now to do that and so we're working with programs like Youth Development, Inc. that provide summer employment to kids who are at-risk. I don't know if you know that there are programs all over the state that help give very beginning work experience and they already pay for that. Those programs just don't include people with disabilities.

Jamie: Is there anything you want to add before we close, as far as how Project SEARCH may evolve and what New Mexico can learn from this program?

Tanya: So, we're looking at this year, entering for the first time into having our own statewide conference because we have enough cohorts that we need something here.

Jamie: It's Project SEARCH statewide.

Tanya: Yes. We are looking at having a local conference and having the speakers come here, the national folks, and then having the different programs present to each other what they're doing. We are exploring ways, opportunities, for them to share and teach each other. So, it's literally becoming a statewide technical assistance program. Budgets are being cut but nobody's cutting Project SEARCH. So far, everybody's seeing the benefit. I imagine this will continue to grow. In general, there's still a lot of discrimination and disbelief that people with disabilities, and in particular developmental kind of disabilities, are capable of working. So, this is a showcase because it's so successful in terms of getting people to collaborate with businesses.

Jamie: I know that where Amy works, at Seton Hall, in Seton, most of those people who started have been working there for five to ten years.

Tanya: How long has she been here, there?

Jamie: She's been there for five years.

Tanya: So Project SEARCH changes minds and hearts.

Erica: I love that you said that. Project SEARCH influences cultures from each agency, so the business is completely changed by it in a positive manner.

Tanya: We've seen this with all the employees at the hospital, right?

Erica: Yes, they begin to say, "We want more employees like this person."

Tanya: The morale of the other employees in the business goes up because they feel like they're doing something meaningful and they get inspired by the joy that person's bringing to their job that might have been considered mundane.

Erica: And that's huge.

Tanya: And the business gets all kinds of wonderful PR, you know it's just a win/win.

Erica: It really is a positive culture change.

Tanya: I just need to personally say, I feel so lucky that I had that opportunity, that you gave us that opportunity, that you introduced it to us. I know that you don't want this to be about you, but I will be eternally grateful that my career connected me with you, and I just want to thank you for that personally.

Erica: I agree. New Mexico really has been blessed to have you introduce Project SEARCH Jamie.

6

*Men make history and not the other way around. In periods where there is
no leadership, society stands still. Progress occurs when courageous, skillful
leaders seize the opportunity to change things for the better.*
—Harry S. Truman

As I discussed in Chapter one, I began working for Jack Daniels in 1972. Most of this book is dedicated to discussing the projects I was involved in outside of my professional career in the insurance business. However, there was one project I participated in that leveraged my insurance expertise for the benefit of all New Mexicans and that project was the creation of New Mexico Mutual Insurance Company. The passage of the Workman's Compensation Reform Act really was historic. I give a lot of credit to Speaker of the House Raymond Sanchez and Senator Marty Chavez as well as Representative Fred Peralta who co-chaired the task force.

When I think about how bad things were and how dire the situation was for New Mexico's economy, I am extremely proud of a small group of people who were determined to avert a major crisis that would have crippled businesses across the state. By 1987 it was clear that the workers compensation system was broken. New Mexico's worker's compensation benefits were, according to the Independent Insurance Agents of New Mexico (IIANM), "the most generous workers comp benefits in the nation, including almost unlimited medical care and generous disability payments. Insurance carriers were paying out $1.21 for every premium dollar collected, and the assigned risk pool was assessing insurers staggering amounts to make up for its losses."

In 1987 New Mexico's unemployment rate was 9.3% while the rest of the country was approximately 5.5%. New Mexico businesses were having a difficult time keeping up with the very high costs of the mandatory workers compensation coverage. They were also losing contracts to competitors in other states that had much lower workers comp costs. The high workers comp costs also were negatively impacting the State's ability to attract new businesses to locate here.

On June 30, 1987 The National Council on Compensation Insurance filed a 27.7% rate increase for New Mexico. Most of the remaining workers comp carriers in the state were forced to cease operations in New Mexico. Within a year there were only four carriers left. An interim legislative proposal suggested creating a state workers comp fund to bridge the gap. In April of 1988, the IIANM hosted an "Insurance Crisis Roundtable." Due to the very small number of companies writing workers' comp, the option of creating a state workers comp fund started getting more notice. During the 1989 legislative session, a bill was introduced to create a state fund for workers compensation. The bill was opposed by the IIANM and it ultimately failed.

In April 1990, the IIANM joined with the Association of Commerce and Industry and other business trade associations to hire a national workers compensation expert named Howard Bunn. Bunn helped draft workers comp reform for New Mexico. I offered a new proposal based on legislation passed in Minnesota. I wanted New Mexico to form a private mutual insurance company to help replace the lost markets. Speaker of the House, Raymond Sanchez, and Senate President, Manny Aragon, appointed a Legislative Task Force which was comprised of over 40 business and labor leaders. I became the only voting member of the task force that was permitted to be from the insurance profession because I was serving as the IIANM Legislative Chair.

On November 4, 2016 I sat down with Chris Krahling, former state superintendent of insurance and Thom Turbett, the current president and CEO of the Independent Insurance Agents of New Mexico, to talk about that Legislative Task Force and the events that led up to the creation of New Mexico Mutual Insurance Company.

Chris Krahling, former state superintendent of insurance, instrumental in the establishment of NMMCC and Thom Turbett, organized the Independent Insurance Agents of New Mexico (IIA) to support NMMCC, current president and CEO of the IIA / Interviewed November 4, 2016

Jamie: Chris, before we get into the founding of New Mexico Mutual, can you talk about your background? You were superintendent of insurance and all that sort of stuff. Then we'll get in to the workers comp.

Chris: I became involved in the insurance business in nineteen seventy-eight when I bought interest in an independent insurance agency in Albuquerque, New Mexico. Prior to that, I served as the administrative assistant to Governor Jerry Apodaca. I was active during the time that I owned the agency with the Insurance Agent's Association. I worked my way through several positions of the Agent's Association from nineteen eighty-eight to nineteen ninety-one. I started off as secretary, then treasurer, then vice president and then chairman of the board. So, I was an officer in the association during the time that this reform took place. In nineteen ninety-five, I was appointed state superintendent of insurance and I sold my insurance agency at that point in time so there wouldn't be a conflict of interest. I served as superintendent so I regulated the insurance industry during that period of time, obviously. I resigned as superintendent at the end of nineteen ninety-eight. Following that, I served as vice president of Government Affairs and Marketing for New Mexico Mutual, as vice president of Sales and Marketing for Blue Cross Blue Shield of New Mexico and then returned in two thousand three to New Mexico Mutual to serve as president and CEO for five years until I retired in the spring of two thousand eight.

Jamie: Thom, tell us about you.

Thom: I'm a native New Mexican. I've been a licensed insurance agent since I graduated college at the University of New Mexico around nineteen seventy-four. And I was an insurance agent most of the time when this reform was going on out in the street. And then I left in nineteen ninety-four to become the CEO of the Insurance Agent's Association.

Jamie: How many members are in the association?

Thom: Currently, there are roughly a hundred fifty agencies across the state that are members of the association. So, I've been here twenty-three years. In the early days, when I first took over, that was when New Mexico Mutual was first getting going. The association was actually running a major part of New Mexico Mutual in the formative years. When I first got here, we were doing most of the underwriting. We were collecting all the money. We were doing all the accounting and we had four staff members to do all of that.

Chris: And you did all the marketing.

Thom: And marketing as well.

Jamie: So, we'll come back to that. We'll come back to that because that's an important portion. What I'd like to do is for you, Chris, to tell us how you all helped put this thing together. Could you also provide a brief history of the Workers Comp Reform Act? Can you explain how we did it? Can you explain the committees and stuff? Please be sure to discuss the information you provided to the task force on the financial capabilities of all the agencies across the state. Discuss how you showed that a large loan that was required to start New Mexico Mutual could be paid back. We could guarantee it'd be successful.

Chris: It really all started, I think, with our annual convention in nineteen eighty-seven, which was at the Inn of the Mountain Gods. At that point in time, workers comp in New Mexico was becoming an issue because of the cost and because of the subjective-ness of the law and because of the backlog of cases that were in district courts. We knew we had to do something. So, the Insurance Agent's Association kind of took the lead in moving that forward by creating a taskforce to look at what we could do as a state to improve the worker's compensation situation. We asked that every company and every insurance agency donate a little bit of money so that we could hire a lobbyist to represent us with the legislature. We did that. We formed a group within the Insurance Agent's Association to represent what we believed was in the best interest of the people of New Mexico. We didn't really have a dog in the fight in terms of benefiting from it. Our dog in the fight was to make the system better for our clients who are businesses, and for their workers who receive the benefits from workers comp, and that was kind of our charge. As time marched on, over the next few years, the legislature became aware of the fact that this was a massive problem because we were losing jobs to out-of-state people.

Jamie: The insurance companies didn't want to write workman's comp insurance in New Mexico.

Chris: We were down to, at one point, about four insurance companies that we could actually place worker's compensation through as independent agencies. The assigned risk pool was growing at a rapid rate. The rates were going up considerably year after year.

Jamie: What's the assigned risk pool?

Chris: The assigned risk pool is a body created by state law to provide an outlet for employers to purchase workers compensation insurance if they are unable to purchase coverage through the standard insurance market.

Jamie: Why did it? Why? 'Cause I want to find everyone I have worker's comp.

Chris: At the time, the state required businesses with three or more employees to have worker's compensation insurance. So, businesses have to have it. Now, some don't, but the vast majority of companies do obey the law. And so, as an agent, when we couldn't place worker's comp coverage with a standard insurance company, we had to go to the assigned risk pool. And the assigned risk pool is made up of all the insurance companies doing business in New Mexico as a group. Together they are assessed every year based on the percentage of workman's comp they write in New Mexico to subsidize the assigned risk pool. That way there's adequate money in the pool to pay for losses. As time went on, the pool grew because the standard market shrunk and the assessments to the insurance industry by the pool grew as well.

Jamie: How are those assessments determined?

Chris: They were determined based on the amount of money coming into the pool versus the amount of money going out to pay claims, and if there was a shortfall, each insurance company writing comp in New Mexico would be assessed a proportional amount based on their share of the total market to cover the shortfall. So as assessments grew. There was less incentive for companies to continue doing business in New Mexico in the standard market.

Jamie: And if an insurance company decided not to write worker's comp, would they be assessed?

Chris: Well no, they would only be assessed if they wrote coverage during the year in question which had the effect of driving companies out of the workers compensation market in order to avoid paying assessments which were growing rapidly year after year.

Jamie: We had to have worker's comp. Then we had companies pull out of the state because they wouldn't write worker's comp. So, as that started happening, more and more policies went into the assigned risk pool.

Chris: That's right, and at that time a few companies were renewing policies, but they just weren't taking any new business. So what happened is that the companies that were still writing policies, and CNA Insurance Company is a good example, their assessments would go up every year drastically because they were taking a bigger percentage of the standard market. So, everything was moving toward being written through the assigned risk pool. That was a bad thing and it was costing more and more money for businesses. So, something simply had to be done to correct the law, to correct this travesty in the market place. And so, again the Agent's Association took the lead in working with the legislature to create a Legislative Task Force. What we said was, which I think is important, the solution to this problem is not a give and take issue. *Everybody* is going to have to give and the beauty of the task force that was created by the legislature under the leadership of Speaker Raymond Sanchez and Manny Aragon in the senate, was that the legislative leadership said that they would accept whatever recommendations this task force brought back to the legislature. And bear in mind, the important thing to know, is that this task force was made up of business leaders and labor leaders and you, Jamie! Everybody else who had a dog in the fight: the doctors, the lawyers, and the healthcare community, all these other folks were purposely excluded from it. The concept was if the business people who were paying the premiums, and the labor people who were receiving the benefits, could agree on what they wanted this program to look like, that would be a good thing. And to the legislators' credit, when the task force completed their work, that culminated in a special session of the legislature. We had a bill obviously, that was introduced, that completely reformed the entire workman's comp system in New Mexico. And the leaders of the legislature were true to their word, to their credit. They accepted what was presented to them by business and labor, and the bill passed and became law. It was one of the most successful legislative accomplishments, I think, in the history of the state. It was totally bi-partisan. Totally done through the input of real people in New Mexico who would be affected by the proposed law.

Jamie: So, what happened was, while we were investigating, we found out that in Minnesota there was a private company that was writing all Minnesota's worker's compensation policies. And the situation, that all of us knew, was that when the law was changed, the companies that had left New Mexico weren't going to come back in the market right away. They wanted to wait for a long period of time. They wouldn't come right back in. So, what we did was we made sure in our new proposed law that we had a company that could write this and that's how we came to create New Mexico Mutual. CNA was very helpful in those early days because they came to lobby the legislature, and CNA's attorney gave me advice because I was the past president of CNA's National Agents' Association. Remember, they were here for all this stuff? I asked the head of their underwriting, "Well now when we do this, what will your folks do?" They responded, "Well you know Jamie, when this is all finished, it'll be a couple of years before it will be us." I responded, "What do you mean? You mean to tell me after we re-do all this law that we're talking about doing and the legislators are hearing how we're going to save money and stuff, you're telling me you're not going to come back?" They said, "Well, you know, it'll be a couple of years before we do it." That's when I realized we needed to replicate the Minnesota model. I was sitting on that task force, and I said, "We have got to make sure we don't have a monopolistic situation with a state-run agency."

Chris: What we wanted to make sure was that the state, after this reform was completed, that the state would never, ever, ever end up back in the position it was prior to the reform. We never wanted it to be a situation where there was a limited market that agents could go to, to place worker's comp. So, we created this non-profit, state-funded, insurance company that was subject to all the regulations, just like every other insurance company. But it was created for two reasons. Number one, so that there would always be a market for New Mexico businesses to go to, to buy their worker's comp. And number two, one of the things we found out during this whole effort was that there was a lack of empirical data in New Mexico to base

233

decisions on with regard to claims, and with regard to premiums, and with regard to everything else that went into the workman's comp dynamic. So, we wanted a company locally that could be a repository, if you will, if that's the right word, of data. So, that five, ten years down the road, the legislature would have a place to go to, to see what actually happened and what was the result of all of these things empirically and objectively. Not from a biased perspective. So, that they could make any changes or tweak anything that was necessary to change going forward, so that we would keep current with the needs of the state. So, New Mexico Mutual was created to do that very thing. All that sounded really great except for one thing. How do we pay for that? That's where the IIANM really came into play in a big, big way and I know, Jamie, you don't want to be the credit guy here, but you were the guy. It was your tenacity. Your lobbying acumen as our legislative chair, and frankly the private company, was your brainchild. I was the president of IIANM by then. You called me one day and said, "We have got to put together credible information that we can take to the Board of Finance, because that's who we're going to ask for some money from. We need to take some information to the Board of Finance that is objective, credible information, to show how much business, how many accounts, and inde-pendent agents throughout New Mexico would write in this new company and generate a revenue stream so that the new company could pay back the loan we were asking to borrow from the state."

Jamie: So, we contacted all of these hundred plus agents out there. They all agreed that they were going to put, ('cause we're the agent and we represent), they were going to put their customers into this new company. That's why it worked. If we hadn't done that, the legislature would not have agreed to the deal.

Chris: And we accumulated several very large three ring binders. The fact of the matter is the people who worked here at the Insurance Agent's Association coordinated this with all their members and each member would fill out a little form, a one page form on each client. Every individual client they had. How much the premium was that they would move to this new company. So, when we compiled all of that, we had this stack of forms that were returned to us verifying that the various agents throughout the state, that were committing to move these specific clients into this new company to create this revenue stream to pay back the loan.

Thom: Yes, that list was prepared detailing the number of accounts and

234

premium volume that would be produced in the first year, including monthly totals each member agency would produce. A sum of just over five thousand [5,109] accounts totaling almost seven million dollars [$6,761,381] in premium volume was committed.

Chris: Jamie and I took that stack to the Board of Finance. I'll never forget this. It was a great deal. We took this stack of information of data that we received, that people signed, the agents signed to the Board of Finance. Governor King was chairing the Board of Finance. I'll never forget this. Jamie and I appear before the Board and asked for the loan, which was ten million.

Jamie: Ten million is not a shabby loan.

Chris: Yeah. How were you going to pay it back? And we said, "Here's the proof of how we're going to generate revenue. A portion of which is going to be earmarked to repay this loan." And the Board of Finance looked at that and said, "That's a good way to approach this issue."

Thom: Looking back at the nineteen ninety-one plan and comparing its fifteen year projections with what actually happened, it is uncanny how accurate those projections were.

Jamie: Except for the head of the Board of Finance. Remember that? The head of the Board of Finance didn't think it was a good deal.

Chris: Who was that? I don't remember.

Jamie: Phil Archibeque. He didn't think it was a good deal. So, he could have stopped it. But Governor King said, "You're going to approve it."

Chris: I mean it was a wonderful. It truly was a wonderful experience.

Thom: In addition, a General Agency Agreement and individual agency contracts were drafted that held agencies accountable with volume and persistency clauses. These documents were all combined in a business plan, which was finished in July nineteen ninety-one. It was authored by John Herder, a well-known actuary hired by IIANM. It also contained: projected start-up costs and loss ratios, suggested rates, underwriting guidelines, and almost everything else the new mutual company would need to quickly begin operations and succeed.

Chris: It was amazing.

Jamie: But the thing is, what you and the IIANM put together was such a fabulous presentation. I mean, you can't believe how detailed and how exact it was. It was phenomenal. People told me on the Board of Finance it was one of the best presentations ever put together. How's this going to be paid? The data was all laid out so thoroughly, you couldn't question it.

Chris: Thom, you need to take over because folks said, "Well that sounds great. But, how are you going to market this? How are you going to get this company on the street immediately? Granted you've got a bunch of clients out there, but how are you going to market it and bring them in? Underwrite it, collect the money, bill them, and handle their claims? How can you do all this stuff when the company right now is just sort of still a fantasy." That's where you guys came in.

Thom: And so, the Insurance Agent's Association came to the forefront and said, "We can serve as a managing general agent to provide all those services on behalf of this new company. We'll market it. We'll collect the premium. We'll underwrite it. We'll do all the work. We will do all the backroom grunt work until this company can really get on its feet."

Jamie: Keep going. Go on.

Chris: And that worked out wonderfully. The association and the staff here, they were staffed up as Thom told you about earlier. They did that and it was a tremendous success.

Thom: Okay. There was a slight hiccup before then. I don't know if you remember.

Jamie: Oh, yeah. Well, say what the hiccup was.

Thom: Well the hiccup was that the attorney general at the time, Hal Stratton, ruled that the company was illegal because the state couldn't give money to a private enterprise. Yeah. And these guys, to their credit, I think you came up with the idea of getting around that.

Jamie: Anti-donation.

Thom: The Anti-donation clause, yes, that's when they came up with the idea of having the board of New Mexico Mutual appointed by the governor. And that made all of that legal because now it becomes a quasi-state entity that's controlled on the board by the governor's appointments. They could contract with the Agent's Association as the managing general agent, which they did. It was written into the law. And that's how the IIANM became the original managing general agency for New Mexico Mutual. The most controversial part of the workers compensation reform had now become one of the best investments the state had ever made!

Jamie: That's right.

Thom: I came in right around that time. It was probably a year down the road when it was just starting to cook. We had hired Dolly Bauman, who was an underwriter from one of the insurance companies, the old USF&G. And she was leading the efforts, so she did most of the main underwriting. When the applications all came in here, they did the original underwriting. They took the money. We had an accountant who was keeping track of the money, and as New Mexico Mutual staffed up, they started to take over a little more of the work. It took them a long time to staff. It was a brand new company. You can imagine how long it would take for an insurance company to staff up.

Jamie: At that time we wanted to be able to write insurance immediately. So, if we hadn't done it that way, then the legislators and the business community would have really been upset. We had to start writing business. I think I put a million dollars with them in the first year.

Chris: And if we hadn't done that, we would have been in the hole financially in terms of repaying.

Jamie: And the Board of Finance would have said "'private monopoly.' We'll take it over," and it would have become a big state agency.

Thom: And that was another effort that you guys didn't talk about. The first thing you had to do before you got to do all this was to kill an effort by the legislature to create a monopolistic state fund.

Chris: Actually, it was an effort by the superintendent of insurance, Fabian Chavez.

Jamie: I knew Fabian Chavez very well. The situation was that he wanted to take this thing over. And we didn't put him on the task force. So, we were fighting the superintendent of insurance and I had to have some nice conversations with Fabian quietly. He wanted to take it over so it'd come under the department of insurance.

Thom: So, how did those conversations happen, Jamie?

Jamie: Well first of all, he married my brother's former wife. And his daughter is my niece. I just sat down with Fabian and said, "I think this is the way things ought to go. I think it'd be a better solution and we'd like to do it without getting out in the public." He became very much agreeable.

Chris: Fabian actually had a bill introduced to create a state fund for New Mexico to become a monopolistic state and everything would be sold through the state. He had a bill introduced. And I testified on the bill before the House Judiciary committee. Fabian made this beautiful presentation about why the state ought to be selling worker's comp and nobody else. The lobbyist we had at that time was a guy named Nick Franklin. Nick and I presented the opposing point of view, which is, if you put the state in worker's comp, it's no different than going to the motor vehicle department and standing in a line to buy your worker's compensation insurance. Nobody wants that. Plus, it's a deterrent to insurance agents throughout the state, all over the state where every legislator is elected from because they're going to lose money in terms of selling worker's comp. We lost the argument nine to two in that committee. Fabian won but that's as far as it ever went because I think at about that point in time is when Jamie had his little conversation with Fabian.

Jamie: And another person who was in the conversation with Fabian was the Speaker.

Thom: Raymond went with you?

Jamie: Yes. And Marty Chavez also went. So, the three of us had a nice visit.

Chris: And all of a sudden then Fabian kind of became a supporter of creating this New Mexico Mutual as an alternative. And that's how it went.

Jamie: Yeah. Then he started getting threatened for it. Go on. Go tell about how it came here. It's sort of an interesting story. Who was the first guy we hired who came from Crum and Forster?

Chris: Warren Smalley.

Thom: Yeah, so I was just going to say. Jamie hired Warren Smalley.

Jamie: The board hired Warren. I found him.

Thom: Yeah. He found him but the board hired him. And he became the first CEO of New Mexico Mutual. His main job during those early years was to staff up. He was looking for underwriters and really all they were doing in the initial years was just typing the policies. We were doing most of the work over here and then we would transport the money. The first check I wrote here in nineteen ninety-four was a million dollar check back to New Mexico Mutual. I was like, "Holy crap. I'm signing a million-dollar check on my first day on the job," which was just incredible. But that's the kind of money that was going back over to them to fund the operations. And then we would get a cut of that. The Association, in its initial years got, I think we got a five percent override on all the business our agents were placing. And it was considerable. I would say that it was amazing that the business that you guys said would come in, was coming in in buckets because the four insurance companies, they were still here.

Jamie: The question is, what do you see for the future? How's it working now? What will the issues be down the road?

Chris: New Mexico Mutual?

Jamie: Yes.

Chris: Well it's been an evolution.

Jamie: How big is it now? Do you know the writing?

Thom: It's about a hundred million.

Chris: In premium dollars, so, it's grown considerably. I was CEO there from two thousand three to two thousand eight. So, I could tell you about that time frame.

Jamie: When did New Mexico Mutual pay back the note?

Chris: We paid it back early. We paid it back two or three years early.

Thom: Two thousand one.

Chris: The reason we were able to pay it back early, we, being New Mexico Mutual, was because we had this influx of business that was coordinated through all the independent insurance agents. The company was doing well and it had excess money and excess surplus. So, rather than hold on to it, they paid the note back ahead of time. It's kind of like paying your mortgage off early. And it built our credibility as a company in New Mexico 'cause we were able to not only do what we said we were going to do financially, but we did even better than what we had projected. So, it was all a good thing. And during this timeframe, from my perspective, there was a pretty smooth transition.

Jamie: I thought it was real smooth.

Chris: I was the superintendent over part of that period of time. So, I sort of oversaw part of that, I guess. And gradually, more and more services moved from the Insurance Agent's Association as the managing general agent over to the insurance company. The underwriting, for example, and some of the claims processing started being shifted to New Mexico Mutual, as well as the billing and the accounting. All of that kind of stuff gradually moved out of the association and over to New Mexico Mutual. But one of the things that we at New Mexico Mutual always wanted to maintain was the marketing relationship with the Insurance Agent's Association because they represent the people out on the street, the agents, who are selling the product.

Jamie: They wouldn't have been there if it hadn't been for the independent agents.

Chris: That's exactly right, and that's important to emphasize. They wouldn't have been there. This company wouldn't have been there if it hadn't been for the independent agents.

Jamie: It's the largest company in the state writing worker's comp today.

Chris: It writes about a third of the voluntary business.

Thom: It might not sound big, but it is. It's incredibly large.

Chris: Voluntary means it doesn't take into account self-insured groups, like the state of New Mexico is self-insured. So, that doesn't make up part of the percentage. But all the voluntary market is the businesses out there that buy insurance from insurance agents, basically.

Thom: Keep in mind they're competing against all the huge national insurance groups.

Chris: And now, by now you know, all the national companies, they were all back in New Mexico. The national companies were saying, "This ain't so bad after all with this new law and all this other stuff. Man, I'm going back to New Mexico to make a buck in worker's comp." The incredible success story of the work comp reform and the effect that New Mexico Mutual had on the marketplace was that rates went down fifty percent, maybe even a little bit more. So gradually, the Insurance Agent's Association transitioned the services over to New Mexico Mutual and New Mexico Mutual was lucky. Warren Smalley was lucky in that he was able to buy a computer system from Minnesota. Jamie mentioned earlier that we modeled some of the creation of New Mexico Mutual after what they did in Minnesota. Well about this point in time, the time that New Mexico Mutual got going, Minnesota was upgrading their computer system. This is the way I recall it anyway. And we bought their old computer system. So, all of a sudden, not only were we moving forward in terms of organizing the company, but we actually were moving forward in terms of automating the company with a proven system that worked. I mean it's all different now. But originally, that was in place and it was a good thing because otherwise, what the hell would we have done? We don't know. So, as things moved forward over the years, the Insurance Agent's Association, bear in mind, the philosophy of the New Mexico Mutual directors, board of directors as well as officers of the company, was always to maintain the solid relationship with the Agent's Association. Not only because they're the ones that got us to where we were, but because they continued to be a viable marketing arm for our product. And so, we always paid them an override or a royalty or something that amounted to around about a half a million dollars a year that we, we being New Mexico Mutual, paid the Association for them to help us market the product, oversee the product, promote the product, promote our company, advertise our company. Thom and I used to drive around New Mexico and visit with every independent agent together as a team to promote the product: me as CEO of New Mexico Mutual, and Thom as the CEO of the Agent's Association. We at New Mexico Mutual valued what they did, what the Agent's Association continued to do for us over the years, and we rewarded them for the record. Plus, the Insurance Agent's Association acted as our lobbying arm with the legislature, which was huge. These guys, the Insurance Agent's Association has an incredible relationship with the legislature. Why? Because we had independent insurance agents in every town, in every legislative district throughout the state and they know their local legislators. So, when there was a bill that affected worker's comp in New Mexico or that affected New Mexico Mutual, the Agent's Association would take the lead on lobbying our position and their position on the bill. And we would have this incredible state wide lobbying force.

Jamie: There was always an army of testimony.

Thom: Grassroots baby.

Chris: And it worked phenomenally. I don't know that we ever lost anything. We might have had to compromise on a couple of things. But these guys, the Agent's Association, provided that service as well and that's as important as anything else.

Jamie: The other thing that was very important was the makeup of the original board. First of all, Governor King was supportive. We must recognize the contributions of Governor King. Having Governor King there made sure that we were going to be able to get done what needed to get done. He approved every individual that some of us recommended on the board. He took them. Put them on the board, people like David Hughes. If we hadn't had Governor King there, we probably would have had some trouble. Jim Snead was hired as New Mexico Mutual's attorney and he deserves credit also.

Chris: And we made sure to include labor representation on the board.

242

Jamie: That's right.

Chris: It was critical 'cause we needed to have some worker bees sitting on the board to make sure the perspective of the injured worker was being taken into consideration.

Jamie: Those requirements were all codified in the law.

Chris: In nineteen eighty-six, the legislature created the Workman's Compensation Administration. The work comp administration, up until eighty-six, all the disputes with regard to claims went to district court. It was overwhelming district courts with work. The Workman's Comp Administration became responsible for adjudicating work comp cases. Governor Anaya appointed Marty Chavez as the first director of the Workman's Comp Administration. (This is before he was in the state senate.) So, he had a background with the scope of the problem with regard to cases being jammed up in district court and the need for some real reform. And so, he wasn't operating purely as a legislator who might have had some vested interest. He was operating as someone who had been in the trenches, who understood the system. And that was invaluable, I think, to him chairing this effort.

Thom: Yeah. And the other dynamic that was going on in the late nineteen eighties and early nineties was that we were in an economic depression in New Mexico at the time. We had an unemployment rate of like almost nine percent during those years.

And the late eighties was when all this, when all the rates, were going bad. So, the labor unions were really hurting for jobs. It was really, really bad. And as you might imagine, the Democratic Party and the labor unions were very tight back then. That was a big part of it 'cause the labor unions were telling Marty and others, "Look, this is killing us."

Jamie: Well the labor unions, they're the ones that did the elimination of the set fee for the legal.

Thom: Yes, to your point, in those claims in those days, at least a third of the money was going to the attorneys. It just made sense to take that money and put it into benefits for injured workers. And that's how it was so easily solved. I mean, it's just a no brainer.

Jamie: Where is New Mexico going today? What do you see in the future?

Thom: The system?

Jamie: Be candid. Don't be bashful.

Thom: You know, the attorneys, they like their money and they're coming back in and anything they can do to destabilize the system where they can get money, they're starting to do more and more outside of the Workman's Comp Administration. And it's going the wrong way. There's more money going to the attorneys.

Jamie: How about New Mexico Mutual? How's New Mexico Mutual going?

Thom: Well, up until nineteen eighty-six, things went to District Court. Then the Workman's Comp Administration gets formed and it worked for a long time.

Jamie: Everything was working. When did this sort of sleight-of-hand start where attorneys figure out loopholes?

Thom: Yeah, it's been going on since the reform. Every year, it's like death by a million cuts. Every year there's a little something coming in that they get through the legislature. You know, a little increase in attorney's fees. Parts of the law that are in gray areas where they can get in and litigate it. There's just been a bunch. You know, it's been almost twenty-five years. So, in all that time there's been a bunch of not only legislative efforts to do that, but also our court system is what's really killing the work comp system. Our courts have ruled on a number of work comp cases against the system, and allowing more benefits that were never intended in the first place to flow into the work comp system. And you could spend the whole book on that.

Jamie: Yeah, that's a different issue. So, how's New Mexico Mutual now? In other words, are we satisfied with it? I've got my opinion. Can you tell me your opinion?

Thom: It's a mixed message. I would say they're doing really well. Their

244

funding is really, really good. They have put a lot of the money into their surplus.

Chris: They're building a new building.

Thom: They're building a new building. Their tech has gotten much, much better in the last ten years. They've invested a lot of money in the computer systems and so forth. In a lot of ways, I think their attitude is they want to become like a national insurance company and they're doing a lot of that stuff that national insurance companies do. And they're spending lots of money to do it. On the other side, they've kind of forgotten where they came from. They think that the business, the new executive team over there is all from the health insurance industry, which works very differently from P and C. On the health side, most of the business comes in through advertising, and the new people over there now see that as a way to get more business. They think they can go directly to the public and have business owners request their insurance. But, that's not really how business insurance is sold in New Mexico, certainly. It is sold through the advice of their agents. Most businesses take the advice of where to place their work comp from independent agents. Jamie you can verify that as an agent for many years. Right? How many clients did you ever have ask specifically to be put with New Mexico Mutual for their carrier?

Jamie: I never had clients asking for New Mexico Mutual to be their carrier. But on the topic of advertising, well first of all, they shouldn't be spending all the money they're doing. They should be keeping their spending lean and scrutinizing how they can keep their rates down. And that's gone. In other words, they're building a new building. They're doing all this. To me, that's completely changed from the way we set it out to be. They're starting to become a normal insurance company. Normal high paid salaries. Lots of the overhead, new buildings, new everything and that's wrong.

Thom: They're sponsoring Isotopes fireworks. They're sponsoring, they paid two hundred thousand to this cultural center for the naming rights for one of the buildings over there.

Jamie: So, what has happened, what concerns me, is it's a regular insurance company now. When you go back and look at the history, it's exactly where we didn't want it to go. Because they're acting just like that now. They're spending all kinds of money. What they should have done as they grew is to continually lower the cost of insurance.

Thom: They're a mutual insurance company. They're supposed to be, if they get extra money, they're supposed to be paying dividends to their policy-holders. They haven't done that in over ten years. Did you know that? In my mind, that is just so wrong. They've created ten new companies over there since I've been here. Maybe more. They may be up to twelve or thirteen now and they do that to add what we call tiers of different rates. It's just gotten to be quite the conglomerate of insurance companies, and by the way, I think one of the things that's happening over there that really bothers me is what they pay their board of directors. The law says they're supposed to limit the payment to the board of directors to twenty-five hundred dollars per year. Which is what happened in the first year.

Chris: So what's happened is every time they've created a new insurance company, as Thom has described, they have made the decision that the board members should be paid twenty-five hundred per year per company. When I took over as CEO we had three companies and as a result, each board member received seventy-five hundred in annual board fees. Frankly, I was never comfortable with this; however, it was the methodology that was in place when I took over and we had an attorney's opinion that said it was okay, although, I was never totally sure that I understood the rea-soning behind the opinion. Now they have ten companies or so and the board member's fees are twenty-five thousand per year. What concerned me when I was CEO, and what continues to concern me, is the fact that, in my opinion, this was never the intent of the legislature. The legislature wanted to compensate the board members for their work, but not to this degree.

Jamie: I agree.

Thom: Is that your take too?

Jamie: I agree that New Mexico Mutual is going the wrong way. If you take a look at it, they've forgotten that independent agents helped them get this done and they don't need us any more. And what's going to happen some-where down the line, there could be some legislation proposed to correct the problem.

Thom: Yeah. I've kept a list over the years. The legislative efforts, and it's a

246

pretty detailed list of what we've done, and you know it's hard to quantify it because they've got the data over there, but through our relationships over there, they have told me the amount of money that's been saved on a number of initiatives and it's well over twenty million that we've saved them in either efforts that we've stopped, or in bills that we've gotten through. For example, one of the bills we got through about ten years ago was for them to pay lump sums, which was illegal before through the work comp system. And that initiative alone enables them on really bad claims that go on forever in the work comp system. By paying out a lump sum, they're saving millions of dollars every year in claims that they would've paid before. That's just one example of something that we helped them get through on the legislative front.

Jamie: Have we covered everything?

Chris: This effort was one of the most successful legislative efforts in the history of this state in terms of how it was done. The outcome, and the continued benefit that it provides to New Mexico. Worker's comp rates are still roughly fifty percent lower than they were twenty-five years ago. And that's the proof in the pudding right there that this has worked.

Thom: It became a model for other states to emulate. And the other proof is that everybody and their brother takes credit for what happened. As Jamie said, it's amazing how many people take credit for what happened back there in that reform effort. And it's great. You know, it really was a group effort and everybody ought to be able to gain a little "atta boy" out of that effort.

Jamie: Right. However, what I'm hearing from you is that without everybody taking a collective breath and saying, "Okay, let's take stock of where we are and where we're headed," that perhaps all of this work is still at risk because you might wind up back to where you were?

Chris: That's my concern, which is why I'm so happy you're doing this. Maybe some people will remember and come to the realization.

Thom: I was a history major so I'm right with you. I think it's good. I just want to remember where we came from when we look at the history to avoid the same pitfalls going forward.

Chris: Here's how I kind of see any major piece of legislation like this. It's like a bush in your front yard. When you first plant it, it's real nice and then it blooms. And then over the years, you've got to trim it back a little bit and keep it back in the shape that it was created for in the first place. And I think we've sort of lost perspective on that. We might oughta to take another look at it. And maybe this book will help us do that.

7

If you can't stand the heat, get out of the kitchen.
—Harry S. Truman

When he casually approached my table in the restaurant and I told Governor Richardson I would like to be a Regent, I really had not thought of the University of New Mexico Board of Regents until the answer popped out of my mouth. But life can have unexpected surprises. As soon as I said it, I knew I would be able to contribute in that environment because I was interested in the university. My mother graduated from the university. My grandfather, Professor Long, was a famous biology professor at the University of New Mexico. My uncle, Malcolm Long, was a superb football player who is currently in the Hall of Honor as I am, and of course, I wanted to pay back in some way my football scholarship. My career in insurance and my time as a legislator had given me a very keen understanding of budgets and finance as well as a strict belief in the importance of open meetings and open records. Those skill sets ended up being very helpful for the projects I got involved in as a Regent. When I came onto the Board, I became aware of certain "old school" ways of doing things. Just the same way that I was intent on opening up the Game and Fish Commission, I knew that the culture of the Board of Regents needed to change. This is the longest chapter in the book because I encountered so many amazing collaborators. Over the course of the thirteen years I was involved as a Regent, I know my time was well spent because we, the Regents, were able to work as a team. I never had one action item on any major vote of the Regents that was not fully supported by my colleagues. We worked through a committee process to ensure that we were able to listen to one and another and respect each individual's areas of expertise. By valuing our individual strengths, collectively, we as the Regents made an enormous impact. In this chapter and the next we will discuss the capital outlay projects for the main campus and for the Health Sciences Center and athletics we were able to accomplish with the cooperation of the University of New Mexico Presidents, the Regents, and Governor Richardson.

I cannot overstate the importance of two of my colleagues on the Board of Regents: Mel Eaves and Gene Gallegos. Candid conversations with former University of New Mexico Regents Mel Eaves and Gene Gallegos, both highly skilled attorneys, and University of New Mexico Board of Regents liaison Mallory Reviere will help explain the culture change we initiated when I became President of the Board of Regents. Associate Vice President of Enrollment and Management, Terry Babbitt, Interim Director of HR Services, Kevin Stevenson, and Dean of Engineering and Computing, Dr. Joe Cecchi will offer their insights about some of the critical systems changes we made that allowed the Regents to better serve students, faculty and staff. I do not want to act as if everything that happened to me while I was a Regent was all a bed of roses. I have always said, that if you are going to get things done, you are going to piss people off, which is why I named this chapter from President Truman's famous quote, "If you can't stand the heat, get out of the kitchen." So I am very happy that Acting President, Chaouki Abdallah was available to meet with me to offer his important insights about what we can learn from the upheaval that occurred when the faculty held a "Vote of No Confidence." At that time, the faculty was unhappy with me, as well as President Schmidly and Vice President David Harris. As you will hear, during these conversations, I am proud of my time as a member of the Board of Regents and I wouldn't change a thing about what happened in those days. Yes, it got hot in the proverbial kitchen. It most certainly did, but if you have aspirations of being a change-maker, things will likely heat up. Leadership isn't always fun but I think our record of achievements during that time frame stands for itself.

The sheer volume of capital outlay, over a half billion dollars, which we were able to get through while Dr. David Schmidly was president of the university and Bill Richardson was governor, was quite miraculous. I continue to believe that history will prove me right that David Schmidly was maligned at the time of the "Vote of No Confidence." I know he could have done certain things better, so could I. You will see him admit it himself. But at the end of the day, President Schmidly knew how to work cooperatively with the Board of Regents. We have seen a total unraveling of higher education in New Mexico. I will address our current higher education problems in more detail in the epilogue.

I want to start with the interview I had on November 15, 2016 with the former president of the University of New Mexico, because I think it is important to recognize that although not everyone may have liked him and he could have done a lot more to connect with the faculty, still, he was a strong leader. He and the administrative team that he put in place, that he took so much heat for, actually got a lot accomplished.

~~~

David Schmidly, former president, the University of New Mexico / Interviewed November 15, 2016

David: I grew up in West Texas. I went to school in Levelland, about twenty-five miles west of Lubbock, Texas. My father was a cotton farmer, and I was the first person in my family to attend and graduate from college. My degrees are from Texas Tech University (Bachelor's and Master's); then I matriculated to the University of Illinois where I received my PhD. All of my degrees are in zoology, and I specialized in studying wildlife, particularly mammals. After completing my education, I went to work at Texas A and M where I served for twenty-five years, mostly as a professor. I was head of the Wildlife and Fisheries Sciences Department for six years and for five years I ran A and M's campus in Galveston (TAMUG). The latter position provided me with an excellent early administrative experience. TAMUG was a small school [around 1600 students] and it didn't have a large administration, so I learned how to manage every aspect of the university from dorms to food services, a library, and even a large ocean-going ship. Then I took a position at Texas Tech where I served for nine years, including three and a half as president, and the remainder as vice president for Research, Graduate Studies, and Economic Development. That was a lot of fun because it was my alma mater. When a new chancellor came on board, and he and I didn't see eye-to-eye on the direction he wanted to take, I accepted an offer from Oklahoma State University to take charge of their system of higher education.

Jamie: Over the whole system?

David: Yes, over the whole system. I worked at Oklahoma State for five years and my wife and I thought that we would most likely retire in that position. We had given thought to retiring in New Mexico, near Placitas, because of our close friendship with Terry and Nancy Yates who had lived there for over thirty years. Terry was the vice president of research at the University of New Mexico, and I knew a lot about the institution. He also was one of my former graduate students and a person I trusted. When a house came up for sale near Placitas, Janet and I bought it as a retirement home, never really expecting to work at the University of New Mexico. Then I got a call one day from Jan Greenwood, a head-hunter who was assisting the University of New Mexico Board of Regents to find a new president, and she asked me if I would be interested in the position. Janet and I talked about it. Our son was moving back from Mexico, and he was going to locate in New Mexico, so we thought it'd be a chance to get our whole family together and that's how I met you—through the search process. And I liked you and your aspirations for the university. You seemed to be a person who wanted to get things done and see things happen and I thought we could work together effectively. So, I accepted the position. I enjoyed working at the university, although it was not an easy assignment, given the budget and leadership challenges. Then, three years into my tenure, I had a major health scare. I spent twelve weeks in the hospital, during which time I was away from the university, and frankly I didn't know if I would survive. So the Regents and I agreed that I would not sit for a second term and we made that announcement to give the university plenty of time to do a search and find my replacement.

After I left the presidency and my health improved, I spent a year on sabbatical to get prepared to teach mammalogy (my specialty) one last time. I taught for one year and had a great time. Then for two years I worked as a research professor, publishing several books and articles, before fully retiring in May twenty thirteen. Now I am a Professor Emeritus at both the University of New Mexico and Texas Tech. I serve on two boards—the New Horizons Foundation in Hobbs, New Mexico, and an Austin based company, the National Campus and Community Development Corporation, that funds higher education building projects. I also do some consulting work for a company out of Florida that works with privately held family owned businesses. Most of my time is spent working on my academic books, and my wife and I travel to spend time with our two children and four grand-children. Once I walked away from the university, I walked away. I made no effort to influence anything. I tried to stay as positive and supportive as I could and stick to what I was doing without getting involved with any of the politics or controversies.

Jamie: Well the big thing is that there's a lot of things we did at the university, and the president at the university is the key to getting things done. I'd like for you to discuss some of the capital outlay we've done and sort of move and talk about that.

David: Okay, but I would like to say just a little about my impressions of the university coming in, because that is relevant to the strategies we pursued.

Jamie: Sure. Yes.

David: Like I said previously, I knew a lot about the University of New Mexico thanks to Terry Yates. I had talked with him and learned the university was a very impressive research institution. But as I looked at it, it seemed to me that the university was too Albuquerque-centric. I believed that the university needed to position itself as the state's flagship university. It needed the people in every corner of the state to understand the university was there for all of New Mexico and not just for Albuquerque. While I was president of Texas Tech, I had opened an office in Hobbs and we made "hay" in eastern New Mexico. We recruited a lot of very good high school students out of eastern New Mexico to Texas Tech. And so, I looked to reverse that when I arrived at the University of New Mexico. I wanted to see more of those kids coming to the University of New Mexico. Also, the branch campuses were of great interest to me because they served many underserved students who badly needed access to higher education. So, I very deliberately worked on a statewide approach.

I noticed something else—the university had not grown much and it was not effectively structured to succeed in recruiting students. There was no good centralized recruitment strategy. Enrollment management was virtually non-existent. That's why we created that vice president for enrollment management position. And it paid off. During my tenure as president we grew enrollment twelve percent with a twenty-four percent increase in new freshman. This growth was a tremendous help in coping with the very large budget reductions we experienced as a result of the Great Recession.

Jamie: What happened on that, that's another story. When you came in, Dr. Schmidly, you reorganized in a different way to what had been in place with Louis Caldera. The Regents removed all of the restrictions on hiring, and we gave you free reign to do what you did. And now, it's still there. I am referring to the establishment of a vice president system, which we backed one hundred percent, even though it created some political problems with the faculty and everything else. So we still are experiencing your legacy, the way you set up that leadership structure.

David: Well, somewhat.

Jamie: Pretty much still, David.

David: There were a couple of other things that I was concerned about. One was that I didn't think the university was raising much money. The endowment was very small for a flagship university. It was considerably less than any other institution I had been in charge of, and I thought the University of New Mexico Foundation was not structured correctly. It was layered inside the university and employees were doing things other than fundraising. The best fundraising institution I ever saw in my life was Texas A and M. It's a "fundraising machine." And so, I wanted to implement the Texas A and M approach to fundraising. Replicating the A and M approach meant creating a centralized, independent foundation where the employees worked for the foundation instead of the university. That way, if they were not successful at fundraising, then they could be replaced.

Jamie: Can you talk a little bit more about the changes you made at the University of New Mexico Foundation?

David: When we made a move to set up the University of New Mexico Foundation in a similar manner to Texas A and M, this was not easy to accomplish. Under this new structure, our fundraisers became employees of the foundation instead of the university. They had goals to raise money. If they didn't meet those goals, then they could more easily be replaced. The trustees were in charge of the foundation and its investments, and could remain in place so long as they were effective. To get it done, I brought in a man, John Stropp, who had worked for the A and M Foundation for almost thirty years. John was getting ready to retire and I knew him well enough to know that he would get the job done. And he got it done even though there

254

was a lot of unpleasant blood-letting. As soon as he had the new structure in place, John retired from the University of New Mexico and moved back to College Station, but now he and his wife Diane are back out here living near Placitas. The new foundation model has been a huge success and John deserves the lion's share of the credit for having the leadership qualities and tenacity to get it done.

Jamie: You also brought in his replacements?

David: Yes, after John retired and the new structure was in place, we hired Henry Nemcik. The University of New Mexico Foundation has done very well since it was restructured and has raised a record amount of private funds. In fiscal year twenty sixteen to twenty seventeen, the University of New Mexico Foundation's endowment spending distribution was fifteen million, up from just under two million in nineteen ninety.

I also wanted to strengthen the structure of the Health Sciences Center (HSC) and give them more independence. I saw the Health Sciences Center as one of the most valuable pieces of the university to the state. We had the only medical school in the state at that time and the only Level One Trauma Center to this day. Also, I was very impressed with Paul Roth and his entire leadership team. I wanted to structure them so they had more independence because of the nature of their work. We did a yearlong study, led by an outside consulting group, and came up with a separate structure for the HSC that was approved by the Board of Regents. We set them up to be a little more independent, which has now been switched back. We will have to wait to see how that works out because the Health Sciences Center is different from the main campus. It is a business that saves lives. What is required for that organization to grow is an efficient structure that is not steeped in a deep bureaucracy. Because of the excellence of the leadership team, I felt they would work better in a structure of independence as opposed to control from the top.

Jamie: You were very right in what you did. When the Health Sciences Center Board oversight was in place and Dr. Roth's leadership was nurtured, seeds were planted that allowed the Health Sciences Center to grow exponentially.

David: Another asset we had going for us was Governor Richardson who was very progressive. In my conversations with him, it was obvious that he understood the vast potential of the university for the whole state and, of course, Jamie, you were very close to him which I thought was a big plus that we needed to take advantage of. I came to know the governor through you and David Boren, who was the president of the university of Oklahoma when I was at Oklahoma State. Boren knew Richardson well. President Boren told me that he was a governor I could work with to help build the University of New Mexico. Governor Richardson was a tremendous asset in my opinion, as was the leadership in the New Mexico legislature. In every respect, we had a great team together.

Jamie: Well, I think the big thing is that when you take a look at the capital improvement at the university, we got an awful lot done. I'd like you to address that. Go over some of this capital improvement.

David: Well you know, there were three major areas. One was academic facilities. There hadn't been a lot of building going on at the university, as I recall. Also, I saw a need for improved student service facilities, including dormitories, and the third area that required attention was upgrading athletic facilities. The success we had speaks for itself, Jamie. During the time I worked with you and the other board members, on the main campus alone, we built three hundred thirty-three million worth of facilities, including a hundred seventy-one million in academic facilities, ninety-nine million in student service facilities, and sixty-three million in athletic facilities.

Jamie: For certain, there hadn't been construction in the years prior to your arrival.

David: I thought the area of student services was especially important because of its importance to student recruiting. If you're going to recruit students, you've got to have good services to support them. And then we had major challenges with some of our athletic facilities, and I felt that we had to make sure the basketball team stayed at a high level of national competition. So, the renovation of The Pit was a key project and it had already been approved.

Jamie: Yeah. There are a couple of things that happened there. First of all, when I went on the Board of Regents, I had a commitment from the governor to support our athletics. Our facilities were at the very bottom. The Pit needed to be redone because of its key role in our basketball program. If it hadn't been done, we wouldn't have been able to recruit Steve Alford or anybody else.

David: Right. One of the first recruits after I was named president was to bring in Steve Alford as our basketball coach. I had the support of Paul Krebs and the Board. I had known Steve through my association with Coach Bob Knight. And Coach Knight had told me that he felt Steve could rebuild and take our program to a national level. We couldn't have recruited Steve without renovating The Pit, and the involvement of Coach Knight was a key factor.

Jamie: Yes, I knew. The board knew what you were doing and what the situation was and we just stayed right out of it. That hire really changed our whole picture athletically. Before that, university basketball was struggling. No questions about it. But that hire was outstanding and it set the framework for a great basketball season. Also, the practice facility, which was opened just prior to your arrival, was also an important step. Rudy Davalos had said that if we don't have that practice facility, we got a problem. And it was Bill Richardson who helped us get almost ten million [$9.9] for that practice facility.

David: All of this represents a good example of what can be done when the president, the Regents, the legislature, and the governor are on the same page. Especially in a state where there's not a lot of private philanthropy. You know, when we built the football stadium at Oklahoma State, Boone Pickens wrote a two hundred fifty million dollar check. There aren't many individuals in our state that can write a check of that magnitude. So, you have to stack packets of money together. And thanks to the good teamwork that was in place, we were able to cobble all of this money together to build better facilities. Unfortunately, we had the ridiculous lawsuit and publicity over the construction of The Pit involving unfounded and untrue allegations that I had directed The Pit project to a construction firm that had constructed the football stadium at Oklahoma State. In my entire professional career, that was the most ridiculous and dumbest accusation that I was ever accused of.

Jamie: It was totally stuff like that that gets out of hand. It's not true. You had nothing to do with it, but because of the size of the university, everybody wants to write about it. The university is the big news in the state, and that blow up about The Pit construction was a mistake. You had nothing to do with awarding that contract.

David: Well, and most importantly, I didn't have the authority to do it. You guys [Regents] had to approve everything and the same thing was true at Oklahoma state. I had no authority to approve a two hundred fifty million dollar project. The company that constructed The Pit had hired my son, months after the project was completed, and the allegations accused me of directly funneling the project to them as a payback for hiring my son. Fortunately, a jury saw through the false allegations and the lawyers lost the lawsuit.

Jamie: We knew about your son's job offer. The Regents approved it. You notified the Regents about what was happening and the Regents said there was no problem. It wasn't some sneaky deal done.

David: And then of course, we did the stadium pavilion and the practice facility had already been built.

Jamie: No, it had started and Bill Richardson gave us that money too. The practice facility happened because when I was talking to Rocky Long one day, he said we need an indoor facility because when lightning comes, we can't practice. So, I went to Bill Richardson and he gave me the money to build the indoor football facility. It was at the same time he gave us almost a million to modernize our track so we could have track meets at the facility. So, those were in place. But they just got in place when you came.

David: Right. You know, here's the thing about a good flagship university with a good athletic program. It brings pride and recognition to the entire state. Governor Richardson, the legislative leadership for the most part, and you, Jamie, understood this. You put two million into a practice facility; then your football or basketball team gets better; then you appear on television more and all of the attention and advertising makes people all over the country more aware of your university. Then it becomes easier to attract students and donors because of the pride that surrounds the university and its mission.

Jamie: Look at Boise. Every time Boise had a winning football team, the enrollment went up. I mean the enrollment just would explode.

David: The investments in athletics often are paid back several times in terms of recruiting students and the image of the university around the country. So, I felt good about what was happening in athletics, and we had real good leadership in place in Paul Krebs, our vice president for athletics. He hired

Ray Birmingham to be our baseball coach and our soccer program was nationally recognized. The ski team was good. Cross-country was good. The only thing lacking was football, and we desperately wanted to do something in football, but then Rocky took off and went to San Diego. Yeah, and we went out and hired what was supposedly one of the best college recruiters in the country who's now at the University of Alabama. But he just didn't work out and it's unfortunate. We fell in a deep hole and it was hard to climb out, but I think the university football program has now recovered under Coach Davy and is positioned to regain its prominence in the Mountain West Conference.

Jamie: Why don't you go to the Success Center? Do you know the story on that? Do you know how we got the money for the Success Center?

David: Yeah, you got the money.

Jamie: You didn't know anything about it, did you?

David: No. We didn't.

Jamie: Because I learned one thing from you, David. One thing I've learned at the university is you've got to have a committee to do everything. So, if you're going to work on a project, you've got to have a committee. You've got to have someone from faculty. You've got to have somebody from staff. You've got to have the students and you have this committee that decides what direction we are going. Sherman McCorkle wanted to sell his building and I knew that. He wanted to sell for about seven million, somewhere in that area. And Kim Murphy was working for the University Real Estate Office, and he thought that we might be able to buy that building. I am sure you have heard the real estate expression "Location, location, location." I knew that building was a prime location at the corner of University and Cesar Chavez. That building was not going to remain vacant long. Real estate deals sometimes require you to "strike while the iron is hot." I was afraid we were going to lose that opportunity if we waited too long. So, I went to see Bill Richardson. I said, "I want you to do me a favor. I want you to put in your capital improvement some money to build the Student Success Center." They put it on the capital list and it said, "Building only." I didn't tell Harris. I told nobody. That's how we got it.

David: Yeah. And one of the important things about that facility was indeed,

259

its location. We needed a place for what I would call "one-stop shopping" where family and students could come and take care of all of their enrollment needs, including financial aid. We also needed a place for the student athletes to be able to study and receive tutoring. Well, that place was perfect because parking surrounded it. It was down near the athletic facilities, which was helpful with athletic recruiting and the academic performance of our student athletes. The GPA of our student athletes and their graduation rate improved significantly. We were among the best in the Mountain West Conference. And the next step in improving facilities involved student housing.

Jamie: Well, on the student housing, you know they hadn't built dorms for a long time 'cause they have to go through the legislature. We weren't aware of these companies that build dorms. We weren't aware that we could do that. You were. The situation when I came on the Board of Regents, one of the biggest problems we faced was that we didn't have dorms. The dorms hadn't been remodeled. You told us about these companies that would come and build. So, tell us about that because we would never have known about that, how to do that, without you coming. After you enlightened us, we built two new dorms. So, go ahead.

David: We had done this at Oklahoma State and now it's common all over the country. You find a private company to come in; you do a ground lease with them; and then they fund and build the dormitories. They manage or lease them, thereby earning their return on investment, and after a numbers of years (as specified in the contract), the dorms revert to you. Under this arrangement, the university doesn't have to bond its money, which can be used for other purposes, but it gets modern student housing to help with recruiting and retaining students. That was a big success story and I think now the university in terms of its student housing is now in pretty good shape.

Jamie: Well our housing, they remodeled that and then we built the other one on the main campus. The situation is, one reason we put The Lobo Village where it is, is because other than the university, the neighbors don't like us. We were going to build a parking lot. We had some property at that location where there were no neighbors. So, we could build the student housing on that land without a bunch of problems from the neighborhood or whatever. But, it was you, Dr. Schmidly, which brought that ground lease concept to the university.

David: An important aspect of managing a large flagship university is to maintain good academic and research facilities. You have to keep your facilities modern and first rate, and I am very proud of the academic projects that were built while I served as president, especially over at the Health Sciences Center. The Cancer Research and Treatment Center, the Domenici Center—those were all big projects. Then the university made a commitment to Rio Rancho that we would establish a presence there to help foster the continued growth and development of that city. We pushed hard to get the Rio Rancho campus up and going, which we were able to do.

Jamie: That's when we sat with Pat Lyons. Pat was at that time, the Land Commissioner. We went to Pat because one of the legislators, Tom Swisstack, wanted to have in Rio Rancho a situation where all the universities were in a university park. I went up to that legislator and said "We aren't going to do that. We want our own place." And that came under you, David, also.

David: A big part of our effort in Rio Rancho was getting the hospital out of the ground to serve Sandoval county. We put the finances in place to build that hospital and construction was completed just about the time that I left office.

All in all we did a remarkable amount of building in a time of challenging financial conditions in the state, without a large number of foundations or corporations to contribute. We were able to accomplish what we did because we had a really good team of people who worked together, including the university, the Regents, the governor, and the legislature.

We were able to achieve these things because, I believe, we had a positive working relationship, for the most part, between the Regents and the university. We didn't agree on everything, but that is never going to happen. All of us were pretty much on the same page in terms of what needed to happen to move the university forward. It wasn't always the most popular thing with the staff or the faculty. But you can't be an effective leader if you are trying to win popularity contests. We had to do what we did, in my view, and I think time will show that it worked out pretty well.

Jamie: I think the time that you were at the university was one of the best growth times that we've had. We didn't have any dissension on the Board of Regents. None whatsoever. We all worked together and you brought to us so many good ideas and it really helped the university.

David: Yes, and we put together a brief report highlighting some of the major accomplishments during my tenure as president. Then as you know, we had a meltdown in faculty governance that spilled over into our accreditation report. We were able to back up and address that issue and received full accreditation with a nice compliment about how we addressed the issue with faculty governance. There were probably some things I could have done differently that might have alleviated some of this problem. But we worked in a collaborative way that I don't think we ever got much credit for, including the Regents. They took after you, Jamie. They took after me. They took after David Harris. But if you recall Jamie, we had that huge budget cut.

Jamie: That's right.

David: Almost as big as the one they are going through right now.

Jamie: That's right.

David: So, we had to become more efficient and because of this governance meltdown, we had to involve the faculty and the staff more, and we did. We created that cost containment group that was very effective. We identified a lot of ways to save money, including energy. Remember that?

Jamie: Oh, tell them about your energy cost savings measures. You brought that too. I had forgotten. Go ahead and tell us about that.

David: At Oklahoma State, we had an alumna who had built a successful company to help public schools all across the country save money on their energy costs. He had contracts with about four thousand school districts all over the United States. So, when I was president of Oklahoma State, I called him one day and asked if his program would work in higher education? And he said, "Well you know, I don't know." But he said, "I'll tell you what. I'll fly my plane up there and we'll take a look and see." After seeing the campus, he was positive that his company would help us out. We worked on a pilot project and in two years we had saved OSU nineteen million in energy costs. Well, we brought that same program to the University of New Mexico, including the University of New Mexico hospital. And the University of New Mexico hospital actually won an EPA Green Star Award for energy conservation, and that's hard to do at a hospital. I think while I was president at the University of New Mexico, we avoided over twenty million in energy costs because of that energy program. That, along with a number of other initiatives, helped tremendously with our budget situation.

Jamie: You see, it goes back to when I was in the legislature. I knew it was hard to get money for dormitories and stuff like that. But again, if you take a look at The Lobo Village and Casas del Rio, you brought both of those housing options to us.

David: Many universities are turning to this public-private partnership model. They build new dormitories, new parking garages, and any other type of facility where there is a revenue source to cover the funding. They are funded, and bonded, through the public-private partnership vehicle. Because the construction is not bonded through the university, it doesn't go on your balance sheet and keeps your bond rating high. It's also more efficient in terms of timing and meeting construction deadlines.

You know, Jamie, in looking back at my five years as president of the University of New Mexico, I don't think there's much I would have done differently. You can always be a better communicator. You can always do things differently and do things better. But I felt like we had a pretty good five year run, Jamie.

Jamie: I thought we had an excellent five years. As you look back, I made many mistakes. People make mistakes, but we also had a lot of successes. I am hoping with this book that we can look at the university as a whole. I am very glad we sat down to talk today. I think you can see for you, David, there's a lot of this stuff people forget.

David: I will say there was one mistake I made. And I'm not ashamed to say it. I didn't get along with the press here at all. I made very little attempt to do anything about it, and I probably should have done more to repair things with the press.

Jamie: Well, I talk to them and they'll burn me from time to time. But, the press is a different animal.

David: Well, Jamie, you are good at managing them. I was not. And Jamie, you understood the state better than I did at the time I got here. And so, I made some mistakes. That's just the way things go. No one is perfect.

Jamie: All the mistakes I've made, you could fill this room up.

David: But you know, if you're doing something, you're going to make mistakes.

Jamie: You're going to make people unhappy.

David: But I'll tell you one thing we did not do for five years. We didn't sit on our fannies and do nothing. This story is about the institution. What the institution can do for New Mexico and how do you position the institution to achieve its potential. That's what this is all about. The rest of it is personalities, okay? And there's no state in the country that needs a better flagship university than the state of New Mexico. I mean, think about it. As a state with a low per capita income that is struggling economically, New Mexico needs a flagship university to lead the whole state. That's what's helped lift Texas up to be such an economic powerhouse. They have these wonderful institutions now all over the state that are there to uplift people and make the state successful. California has it. And New Mexico needs it.

I'm proud of the University of New Mexico. It's like any institution; it can be better. You can always do more but this state really needs it to step up and achieve its full potential. And the best way to do that is to have good leadership.

I agree with President Schmidly's assertion that you need good leadership at the helm of the flagship university in order for the institution to positively impact the entire state. The role of the Regents in guiding the creation and execution of the university's strategic plan is well documented. However, not all Regents have a legislative or financial or legal background, and that type of experience is invaluable for the type of close analysis of high-level documents that is expected of the Board of Regents. Of all the Regents I worked with while I served on the Board, Mel Eaves' ability to carefully examine every contract, every major initiative, both from a legal perspective and with his experience from serving on the House Appropriations committee (specifically working on the university budget while he was in the legislature) made his keen insights about the University of New Mexico financial management extremely valuable. Mel served on the Regents from 2003 to 2008. He was committed to the university and saw how important it was to always make sure we dotted our i's and crossed our t's. When we talk about the major accomplishments we achieved during that time frame, and the millions and millions of dollars that were being spent of taxpayer money, it would be hard to exaggerate how important it was to me that the Regents had good legal advice. Mel's participation on the Board touched virtually every aspect of the university. Mel's leadership and his integrity were stellar. Without Mel Eaves, we simply could not have accomplished what we did. I sat down with Mel on January 10, 2017 to discuss his time on the Board of Regents.

Mel Eaves, attorney, University of New Mexico Regent, board member of New Mexico Health Sciences Center, former New Mexico Legislator / Interviewed January 10, 2017

Mel: I was born in Kilgore, Texas. My family came to New Mexico in nineteen forty-seven. My father was in the oil field trucking business and he started a new oil field trucking company by the name of Jeffries-Eaves incorporated in Hobbs. He later expanded to Farmington and Denver and Casper, Wyoming and Sidney, Nebraska and Pueblo, Colorado, but we were in Hobbs from nineteen forty-seven to nineteen fifty-five. Then he moved the headquarters of the trucking company from Hobbs to Albuquerque, and that's when I moved up here. I had gone to Hobbs High School, then I went to New Mexico Military Institute and then I graduated from Valley High School in nineteen fifty-six and attended university. Well, I guess I got involved in politics because my dad was involved. He was the Democratic County chairman of Lee County in Hobbs. I got into politics almost as soon as I got up here and ended up running for the State House of Representatives in the election that was held in nineteen sixty-four—Lyndon Johnson versus Barry Goldwater. I got elected. I was twenty-four at the time. In the primary I ran against Barbara Simms of the Simms Family. They had a big farm out there right in the middle of my district. Really a lovely lady. Then in the general election I ran against Rex Mattingly, who owned a string of, I don't know, ten Standard Oil Company service stations, and I won. Bruce King was campaigning to be the Speaker of the House. It was his original term as Speaker, and I got real well acquainted with Bruce because I helped to organize the democratic legislators to support him in November of nineteen sixty-four. I served two terms and then I did not run for re-election because I started law school.

As relates to the university, this was a very important time. Tom Popejoy was president then, and Sherman Smith was his, basically executive vice president, John Perovich was the comptroller of the university at that time, basically the same job David Harris has today. Because I had attended the university and I was a loyal alum, I ended up being the person who carried the budget for the university in the House Appropriations Committee.

And as connected to the medical school, at the time in nineteen sixty-four, the University of New Mexico had a two year medical school that had been installed in the old Pepsi Cola Bottling Company plant and so a bill was introduced to expand the two year medical school to four years, and I was very instrumental in getting that bill through the House Appropriations Committee. There was a real battle to get the second two years of the medical school approved because the physicians in Albuquerque were heavily opposed to it.

Jamie: Why?

Mel: You know I've often wondered about that myself. I had a stack of telegrams. In those days a lot of the constituents communicated by telegram. That doesn't happen any more. But I had a stack of telegrams and I had a bunch of doctors come up and talk to me. And you know, they felt it wasn't necessary that a medical school in Albuquerque was needed. I think the bottom of that was a fear of competition, that's my personal opinion. This was not a political, partisan issue because there were Republicans who supported it also. It was mainly an issue of the medical association against the university doing this.

But, anyway it almost didn't pass because Representative John Mershon was chair of the House Appropriations Committee. John was very much opposed to doing this because in those days, as I recall, for every state dollar that was used to found and operate the medical school, we got a three dollar match from the federal government. And I think, I'm a little fuzzy on this, but I think the original appropriation was less than a hundred thousand and we were gonna get matching funds three to one to cover that. And Representative Mershon said, "You know Mel, it's only this small amount now, but very quickly it'll grow to the level that we cannot afford, and we can't afford to do this," and that was John's position. Ironically, his head chief administrative assistant was Marilyn Budke, who ultimately served on the hospital board and became a huge donor. After I got on the Board of

Regents, we shared memories about that period of time because you know she didn't take a position. She was supporting her chairman. However, she turned out to be one of the biggest supporters ever of the medical school and the Health Sciences Center.

The interesting part about it was when we were writing House Bill 300 for the General Appropriations Act, the provision on the university included, "would or would not include," the money from the second two years of the medical school. We knew we were going to have trouble because you normally did not defeat Representative John Mershon in front of his own committee. So, Representative Bob Mayfield, who was from Las Cruces, and I got together and we went to all of the House members, as well as senators from all of the communities in New Mexico who had an institution of higher learning. You know Portales, and obviously Las Cruces and Roswell and so forth. We all knew Representative Mershon's position on money for the institutions of higher learning was very conservative and very tight fisted. He was not a big supporter of money for higher education. And so, by doing this we put together a coalition on the Appropriations Committee and when it came time to approve the additional money for the University of New Mexico, money would also be there for the medical school. There were other things they wanted that were very important. And the same with New Mexico State and Eastern and Western, New Mexico Military Institute, all of the schools. We had a one vote majority and we outvoted Representative Mershon on every one of the issues by one vote, and John was very unhappy about that.

Jamie: That's why we're doing this, Mel.

Mel: The fifty year anniversary of the medical school was a couple of years ago, and it was really interesting because they put together a committee to write the history of what happened, and there was nobody on the committee who had actually participated, except me and John Perovich. And John Perovich was literally Tom Popejoy's right-hand person. I told the committee, "You know you really need to meet with John because I was there, but John was there at the same time, and he knows what happened. He knows about the doctors opposing it. He knows all about the fight with Representative John Mershon and the Appropriations Committee and how we had to outvote him by one vote, and he also knows how Representative Mershon did his best to get even with the University and New Mexico State." In later years, he held a grudge over that; he really held a grudge over it. Anyway, we, as a result of all these discussions, John

Perovich and I were honored as one of the founders of the medical school.

John Perovich, because he was there, I mean he was lobbying the legislature. I was one as well, and if Representative Bob Mayfield had still been alive, he would have probably been recognized also because I couldn't have gotten it done without Bob. Bob was older than I was and at that time he was chair of the House Taxation and Revenue Committee. He had more clout in the legislature than I did because he was a chair of a major committee. Anyway that was sort of my introduction to helping the university.

Jamie: And that's why I wanted you to say what it is, because people don't realize what really happened. We take for granted that we have a medical school but without you, the medical school might never have happened or certainly not until much later.

Mel: Well, what was funny, Jamie, is that they honored the New Mexico Medical Association. Actually, I think it was the Albuquerque Medical Association, as being involved in the founding. John Perovich and I said, "You gotta be kidding. They fought this with everything they could."

Jamie: That's why I'm writing this book, Mel. People throughout this book are finally being given credit for the vital roles they played in pivotal moments in our state's history.

Mel: Anyway I probably spent too much time on that.

Jamie: No, Mel, that was an important story. It's very important for people to understand whatever the battles are that we're currently going through, there are relevant examples from the past that can guide us to avoid making the same mistakes.

It's always easier to look at something that was forty or fifty years ago because people can be a little more relaxed and look at things clearly. Whereas you talk about something that's up for consideration right now and often people get completely polarized. I think it's very relevant to point out that the Medical Association fought the foundation of the medical school.

Mel: I knew it really meant a lot to John Perovich, and it meant a lot to me, too, because we were the only two people still around who were involved in that fight. To get those little medallions saying we're a founder of the medical school was sort of neat to have that. But getting back to my biography, I went to law school.

Jamie: You went to the University of New Mexico Law School?

Mel: I was admitted to Stanford and Duke, too. I could have gone to one of those schools, but I chose to go to New Mexico. I've always wondered how my life would have turned out if I'd gone to Stanford or Duke. But I stayed in New Mexico because I had been active in politics. My family knew a lot of people. I had an uncle in Farmington, one in Hobbs and my dad lived in Santa Fe. I've never been sorry I stayed here. It's an excellent law school and I got a great education and the faculty members that I met at that time have continued to be really good friends, professionally and personally, all the way up to today. Let me back up a second. When Bruce King was governor, he appointed me to the Board of Educational Finance. In those days, the Board of Educational Finance was a very prestigious appointment because all of the budgets for all of the institutions of higher learning had to be submitted to the BEF. The BEF then analyzed them. They had a big analytical staff, who then recommended to the governor and the legislature, what the appropriate, actual appropriations should be for each of the institutions of higher learning. You don't have that system any more. But it put the BEF in a very powerful position, so once again, there I was, (I think it was a six year term), and I actually resigned after Governor Anaya was elected. He didn't ask me to, but I was very unhappy. We had been in a search project for a new executive secretary of the BEF, and that search had been going on for almost a year. It was a national search. It was done at a very high level. We had five great finalists to choose from, and even though I had supported Governor Anaya and he was certainly a friend of mine, I was very unhappy with him because he ordered the board to cease the national search and to hire a friend of his as the executive secretary. When he did that, I resigned.

Jamie: What this shows, and I want to make it clear, it shows that the appointment of you, Mel, and Gene Gallegos, both were alumni of the university. You've both been involved at the university, not just when you got appointed to the Regents. When you look at the strong background that you had when you came on the Regents, that background was invaluable for your ability to truly understand the issues. People don't look at that. That's the thing that bothers me. Alumni should be appointed to the Regents. But let's talk about our time serving on the Board. What are some of the things you feel that you were able to do as a Regent?

You wrote the new Conflict of Interest policy.

Mel: Well, it was a joint effort I think.

Jamie: Well, yes it was a joint effort, but your background experience meant you really drafted the document.

Mel: We knew that this resolution that we worked on, if it was passed with the Regents, Larry would have no choice but to resign. So we passed it.

Jamie: But before we passed that, you and I sat down with Larry in Season's Restaurant and we were right up front. We didn't hide anything. We told him that he had two choices: either quit the bank or quit the Board.

Mel: I remember it well. And I think by that time, he was president of the Board of Regents.

Jamie: He was president of the Board of Regents and the Chairman of Finances.

Mel: And Jamie, every time you would ask questions of Larry about anything, one his answers, I remember him saying, "Jamie, why don't you just put on your tennis shoes? Go out there and look for yourself." He was very sarcastic. He didn't want anybody asking him questions or you know in any way getting too involved in the management of the university. Because, there's no doubt, he had been running the whole show. So, anyway, you and I, and working with other Regents, basically set the stage for Larry to resign. And that's when you were elected president of the Board of Regents.

Jamie: And you became the Finance Chair.
   That's when the minutes were put over in the library, in the basement of the library, so when we wanted to review the minutes, we had to go all the way back to the basement of the library. We had to dig through documents. I went over and looked and it was just boxes of stuff that'd take forever to find it. That is why we now have all minutes on-line and hard copies in the Regents' office.

Mel: You also made us very focused on adhering to the rules regarding meetings of public bodies as is detailed in the Open Meetings Act. You were particularly well versed in this subject because you had been involved in the passage of the Open Meetings Act and also the Public Records Act. You saw this for what it was; this was a classic example of an institution whose leadership was hiding what they were doing, and they were not operating with any transparency. I mean, we, as Regents, had to work to find out what had been going on. Having been a legislator and a lawyer, I understood the constitutional power of a Regent, which is basically unlimited. I mean if you, the Regent say something, that's what's gonna happen. I don't care if you're Paul Roth or Bob Frank or the governor; that's what's gonna happen. And so, you saw that as a classic example of why you had worked on the Open Meetings Act and the Public Records Act. Simultaneously we were basically encouraging Larry's resignation. You also were very insistent on complete transparency regarding our meetings and our minutes and our records and working with the newspaper and all those things that you know a board, a public board, should do. But none of that had been done previously. You know Larry would make decisions by himself.

Jamie: There was a total lack of transparency.

Mel: Addressing the need for transparency really sort of set the tone for the entire time we were on the Board of Regents, because we stuck with that and would not tolerate any deviation from those rules. We rewrote the Regents policies and procedures; we made numerous changes to them.

Jamie: And you were the one leading that. And those new conflict of interest rules that you wrote are they still place today?

Mel: No. This new bunch has changed them. I've seen the changes. They made a bunch of changes. Made a bunch of changes, especially with the Health Sciences Center. They made a bunch of changes by abolishing the board and all sorts of stuff. You know, when we were put on the Board, the question that Governor Bill Richardson asked me, (and it wasn't a question, he was suggesting it,) but what he'd hoped was that the university would become an engine for economic development.

Jamie: Yes. Governor Richardson had a vision of the flagship university being the driving economic force for the whole state.

Mel: So, that was a major issue, and not only was he encouraging us to leverage economic opportunities, but later on Governor Richardson was instrumental in helping get money to make those opportunities possible. That was one reason we had such an enormous capital construction and capital improvements budget. All that construction created lots of jobs, and it also made the university more able to contribute really strongly to the economic development of New Mexico. And the entire time we were there, that's what happened.

Really, the very first time the university needed new construction and didn't get it was under Governor Martinez. Governor Martinez' Department of Finance and Administration appointees refused to vote on the issue in twenty twelve when the plans to build the new hospital went in front of the state Board of Finance. That was the first time that I recall, from twenty two thousand three, until twenty twelve, that the state ever blocked the university from doing something. Since then, the university's basically gotten no money to do major capital improvement projects. The university has had no support from the governor's office or the majority of the Regents.

Jamie: You are right Mel. Things were very different when you and I served on the Regents. Can you talk about the Science and Technology Corporation?

Mel: When we were on the Board of Regents, Science and Technology Corporation was really pretty insignificant and I know you and I and other Regents, were really unimpressed with what had been done over there and the money being invested. One of the projects we worked on was trying to improve the Science and Technology Corporation to create transparency and accountability, and to set some goals. There was an awful lot of work done in that area. I just mention that generally. The details of all this are in our minutes and everything, but that was another very formative thing that we looked at.

The other thing that was right at the very beginning, a very big issue, was the Health Science Center. There were lots of things going on over there. I mean, in those days we had a Health Sciences Committee on the Board of Regents, but it was not an active, governing committee. It was basically a "feel good" committee where we'd go to meetings and whoever was reporting to us would tell us all the wonderful things they were doing and no real business took place. There was nothing really of substance that we did. You know, Jack Fortner was on the committee. He very seldom even went to the committee meetings. You had made me chair of Finance and Facilities, which was a very active committee, and good participation, but I think Jack was chair of the Health Sciences Committee and Jack approached that like he approaches most things—he doesn't do anything. Yet he's the longest serving Regent in the history of the university. It's very interesting.

We were confronted pretty quickly, with the problem of how to govern the Health Sciences Center, and the problem of how to integrate it with the university. Up until that time, you know Lomas Boulevard was the dividing line and the presidents had no real interest in the Health Sciences Center. The Health Sciences Center had pretty much established itself as a separate entity. The Health Sciences Center really didn't want the president involved either. The problem was that under Dr. Eaton there were three major components to the Health Sciences Center: one was the medical school, one was the hospital and the third one was the Health Sciences Executive team, basically. Dr. Eaton had his own group of executives there in his office. The physicians felt that insufficient money was going to the medical school and that money was being wasted on Dr. Eaton's group, which basically was just a separate group from the hospital and medical school. I don't think there was a whole lot of trust or cooperation between his group and the medical school and the hospital.

We also had a problem because Bernalillo County was unhappy. They didn't feel that the money from the tax, the annual tax that benefits the hospital, was being spent properly by the hospital.

Jamie: We revised the governance of the Health Sciences Center.

Mel: I think what the Regents did on governance at the Health Sciences Center back at that time, directly made it possible for the Health Sciences Center to grow into what it's been today. I mean that, if you step back a couple of steps and look at, take the thirty thousand foot view of this, that's what happened because without that change in governance it wouldn't have happened. And an enormous amount of our time was spent in that first couple of years on the Health Sciences Center. The clinical chairs didn't think that the School of Medicine was being properly supported. As a result they felt their salaries were not what they should be. And then the physicians had their own organization over there that basically did the billing for all of the services rendered by physicians called the University of New Mexico Medical Group. Doug Brown was the person who really advocated creating an audit committee. Because most boards of big organizations have audit committees and their job is to be sure that all the financial reporting is done accurately and honestly, that you know that you're complying with all the accounting standards, that if there's any fraud or misappropriation it gets reported and taken care of. We hired a physician from Oregon who had basically designed the governance model for the University of Oregon Health Sciences Center and who was very well respected in the field. After he went through an interview process, the Regents, with the consent of the Health Sciences Center management, selected him to come in and design a new governance system for the University of New Mexico Health Sciences Center. He worked here for about a year doing that.

Jamie: He did a good job.

Mel: Yeah, a very good guy, very competent. He came up with a plan that the Regents approved and the clinical chairs were on board with it. We also got the county's agreement to it, so it was a very constructive thing. But, you know you were very much involved in all of that because it was such a huge, important project. At the same time that was going on, the new hospital, now known as Barbara and Bill Richardson Pavilion, was in the planning stages. You got very involved in convincing some legislators to use tobacco money that was being collected by New Mexico and to give about forty-five million of that money, with the governor's consent, to help partially finance the new hospital. That was sort of a coincidence though, and I, I don't know if you remember this or not, but in my law practice, Paul Bardacke, the former AG, was my partner, and we were actually hired by Tom Udall to represent the state of New Mexico in the tobacco litigation and we recovered one point one billion for the state of New Mexico in the tobacco litigation.

Jamie: Yeah, I remember that. Your firm was involved.

Mel: Well, we represented the state. Our co-counsel was Turner Branch. I was involved in generating the money to start with, and then the legislature decided at one point, that the one billion fund, should be segregated into a separate tobacco fund and not just used for operational expenses.

It was not easy to get that money made available, but you got it. In the first year we had lots of issues facing us, and frankly, a lot of those issues were created because the past Boards of Regents had not been engaged, they really hadn't.

One of the things that you and I did, and you probably did it more than I did, was to go to faculty meetings, to go to, you know, alumni meetings, to go meet with staff counsel and one of the things you had heard and I had heard, was that the Regents were not accessible to staff, to faculty and to the people here at the university. I mean Larry did not want Regents talking to anyone because he was running the show. I know we had a lot of people tell us that this was the first time they had ever been able to talk to the Regents directly. They could talk to them in public meetings, but having separate, individual meetings with them had not been possible before you became president of the Board of Regents.

We opened up lots of communications and there were a lot of people at the university, like Julie Weaks-Gutierrez and others who didn't like that at all. They didn't think we should be talking directly.

Jamie: I asked to go have breakfast with the deans. Julie said, "You're not supposed to do that," I said, "What do you mean? I want to go have breakfast with the deans," She said, "You're not supposed to do that." I said, "Well, I'm going."

Mel: And I went with you.

Jamie: Remember that?

Mel: From then on we had regular get-togethers with the deans. They're not doing it any more, are they?

Jamie: I don't know.

Mel: Well, I think those meetings stopped.

Jamie: You can see why Mel, I'd always say to you, "Well let me get my attorney's advice," how many times did I do that, Mel? I'd say, "Well just a minute, Mel, you're my attorney" [laugh]. And your background as attorney is pretty damn good, so I had the best legal advice.

Mel: We really instituted a culture shift, because when you were president you encouraged people to communicate with staff, faculty and students. I mean, we couldn't make decisions by ourselves, but we could certainly listen and try to understand and hear firsthand what the problems were. That had not been the culture at the university. I don't think it's the culture now. I think it's gone back.

Jamie: The first six years I served with you were fantastic. There were others, too, who made that period special. Raymond Sanchez was there. Sandra Begay was very good. At first we had a rocky deal with her, but then it got to be very good. You had people like Don Chalmers, who was a super guy. Don really approached his job from the perspective of what was good for the university, not politics. He took the place of Doug Brown. Don was a supreme businessman and he often joked and called himself a Bleeding Heart Conservative. He was just a super person and that's what made it go. I mean you look at the six of us in there; those Regents made a lot of things happen. Sandra Begay at first didn't like us, but she became a good friend.

Mel: Sandra was a really good Regent. She didn't have a lot to say, but she was very studious and studied what was going on. She really tried to inform herself, and she would try to make decisions on what was best for the university. She also had no political agenda at all, none. I'm not even sure what her party affiliation was.

Jamie: Democrat.

Mel: Democrat? You know on the Board of Regents in those days it made no difference what your political affiliation was.

Jamie: It didn't make a difference. Is there anything else you want to add at this point?

Mel: I could go on and on. There were times that more than half a day, every day, when I was a Regent, I literally neglected my law practice because there was so much to do and so much to learn and so much to understand. And I know you basically gave up a huge amount of income from your insurance business because of the time you spent working on Regents issues. Additionally you helped implement the project labor agreement for the building of the Barbara and Bill Richardson Pavilion. I know you had written insurance for an awful lot of non-union contractors.

Jamie: I lost six hundred thousand in revenue.

Mel: When they cancelled their insurance policies with you.

Jamie: But that doesn't matter because the hospital came under budget. Taxpayers saved money. And I made up the income elsewhere.

Mel: The governor asked us to do it through a project labor agreement. Of course I knew quite a bit about those because in my early years in law practice, the first four or five years, my partner was Roland Kool and we represented all the labor unions in New Mexico. I knew all the building trade unions at that time pretty well. I had done a lot of labor law myself in those early years.

Jamie: Mel, you were instrumental in the drafting of all our agreements.

Mel: I knew the head of Jaynes Corporation pretty well, and they didn't have the job yet at that point, but I asked would they still be interested in bidding the job if there was a project labor agreement. They thought it was a great idea, but it was really controversial. We caught a lot of flak.

Jamie: Got a lot of flak, but it was really a good thing because Steve McKernan tells me all the time, he didn't believe it when he got started that it was gonna be as good as it was, but ultimately he thought it was outstanding.

Mel: I went to a bunch of meetings in Steve's office with him and all of the other people who were in charge of that project. I mean we were having like weekly meetings about this project labor agreement in Steve's office. Steve's a very smart guy. He knew what the governor's position was and he knew the governor had appointed us as Regents. So Steve tried to make this work and he did. I told Steve, I said, "If this isn't gonna work and it's gonna be a problem, you tell me because I don't want to do something that's gonna be a problem. You know if this isn't gonna be good for the university I don't want to do it." But he made it work and Steve McKernan is one of the stars at the university. Again, he is totally nonpolitical, he's all business. He focuses on what's good for the University Health Sciences Center.

Jamie: So, looking forward for the state of New Mexico, with regards to the University of New Mexico Health Sciences Center and the university, since our conversations have revolved fundamentally around the role of the Regents, the role of the president, and how important governance is and the culture of that governance, what do you see will be important for the state, for the future of the state, moving forward, what do you think is gonna be important for New Mexico to grow and prosper?

Mel: For the university?

Jamie: Bearing in mind the relationship the university has as the flagship university of the state, what's gonna be important is if the university's prospering, that helps the state, because the university employs so many people.

Mel: Well, I think the methods used to fund the university now are not gonna work in the future because the state does not have the money. The university's gotten too large. The state does not have the money and the university's gonna have to be more self-supporting than it is now. And the Health Sciences Center is self-supporting. They still rely on grants and federal money and contributions, but only seven percent of the total budget comes from the state. I think the main campus is gonna have to become more self-supporting. Tuition is too high. You can't keep raising it. The university has gone through a huge growth in physical plant and the overhead is enormous. I just don't think that the two principal sources of money, being the state and tuition, are gonna be sufficient. I mean obviously the foundation, I don't know what two, three hundred million probably, but that money can't be used for operations, so you can't rely on donations to support it. There's going to have to be a more entrepreneurial management of the university. I think that's gonna be a very difficult thing to do because the people at the university don't think that way. Jamie, you tried to encourage a look at what faculty members are doing, how many courses they're teaching, how many hours they're in their offices, you know, what are they really contributing to the university and to the students. And I mean, you almost got lynched for it because the faculty does not want that kind of oversight. And yet they don't produce the money that needs to be produced to support the institution. Professors aren't trained to do that. That's not where the educational system is...and you know these professors. You know like in engineering and medicine and law, they can go out and hire out all their professors as expert witnesses and make several hundred bucks an hour at the same time they're on the state payroll. And the university has not been innovative at all in trying to develop a new source of funding to improve the current sources. The problem is that the main campus has become dependent on a bunch of money from the Health Sciences Center.

Jamie: That's exactly right.

Mel: I haven't watched it, but there's probably at least one to two million a year that is basically given to the main campus. They make up reasons for it and all that stuff, but I mean it's basically given. David Harris figures out how much he wants and they say "Okay, this is what we're gonna have to have." And if the main campus didn't have that, the main campus would be in even worse shape than they are right now. I mean for the Health Science Center's sake, I would rather see a separate board. I wish there wasn't the current Board of Regents in control of the Health Sciences Center. I wish

278

they hadn't dissolved the Health Sciences Center oversight we created. But I don't know what in the world the legislature would do to provide funding for the main campus, if the Health Sciences Center wasn't helping.

Jamie: Mel, this problem is just growing more and more. It's gonna get worse, because one guy's gonna have the money and the other's not gonna have the money.

Mel: Jamie, you know one of the things we didn't talk about today, but one of the big problems the university has, is maintenance of all the physical plant, and the legislature didn't give us any money for maintenance.

Jamie: Not any more.

Mel: You've got all this physical plant. You've got to figure out where the money's gonna come from to maintain it, because we don't even have the money to pay the operating costs of the university right now. There's gonna have to be a very entrepreneurial shift in the way the university raises its money, and I don't know how that's gonna happen. The current faculty, the way it's constituted, they have got their hand out, and you know they've been doing it that way for so long, I don't know how they'd change it. I think it's going to be a real problem as we go forward. The current Board of Regents' solution is to cut expenses. Cutting expenses is also what Governor Martinez wants to do. But the university's not set up to stand still and go backwards. If you're not going forward, you're going to lose your role as a preeminent research university. You've got to be progressing. If you don't have progress, you're going to die; you're going to wither on the vine. They have been cutting, cutting, cutting; that's not going to do it.

As you can see, Mel Eaves was the architect of many initiatives we executed while I was on the Board of Regents. When Mel left at the end of 2008, someone had huge shoes to fill. We were extremely fortunate that Governor Richardson appointed Gene Gallegos to take Mel's place. Gene served from December 31st, 2008 through December 31st, 2014. In addition to being a University of New Mexico alumna, both as an undergraduate and a graduate of the law school, Gene had also served on the Regents from 1991 to 1996, so he was no stranger to the university. Gene and I had known each from our early days in the Jaycees, and of course we had continued to work with each other through various political campaigns, including Bruce King's and Bill Richardson's gubernatorial campaigns. Gene is an attorney and has an extensive financial background also. He served for fifteen years on Audit Committee for the Board of Northwestern Mutual Insurance Company, a Fortune 100 company, so he really knew how things were supposed to be run. But perhaps most importantly, Gene had a lot of experience in New Mexico politics at every level—from the county up to the National level. It is hard to explain just how much paperwork must be thoroughly read and digested prior to every Board of Regents Meeting. Gene served on the Finance Committee, Science and Technology Committee and he was chairman of the Audit Committee so the other Regents really relied on Gene to summarize accurately a considerable amount of critical data. Gene's attention to detail and his ability to hone in on the most salient pieces of information we needed to know in order to make decisions was extremely important. There are so many questions that come up and Gene, because of his legal, financial and political background, was someone all the Regents leaned on to provide his advice and his insights. Gene was masterful at digesting the budget and helping all of the Regents translate the numbers into meaningful priorities. Gene also could help the Regents navigate the political establishment. On December 8th, 2016 I sat down with Gene Gallegos to discuss the projects we worked on together.

Gene Gallegos, attorney, served twelve years as a University of New Mexico Regent / Interviewed December 8, 2016

Gene: My full name is Jake Eugene Gallegos. I was born and raised in Tucumcari, New Mexico. Went to high school at Tucumcari and then went to the University of New Mexico, undergraduate and law school. Small town. Small town boy.

Jamie: How did you and I meet?

Gene: We met in the Jaycees.

Jamie: We had a bunch of young guys. Give a little background on yourself, Gene. Talk about your legal background.

Gene: Well, my family, my father was a lawyer and a judge. He served as district judge in what's the 10th Judicial District, which is Quay County, De Baca County, and Harding County, which are comprised of small towns and a farming and ranching economy. I didn't have plans particularly to go to law school, it just sort of happened after I graduated from college. I thought, "Well, I can go to law school." I had no plan necessarily to practice law; I was just thinking it would be a good education. After the first year, I found that I really, really loved it. After I graduated from law school, I was an assistant US attorney for a year in Albuquerque. Then I got a call from the then attorney general of New Mexico and he offered me a job, and a raise so I came to Santa Fe.

Earl Hartley was the attorney general then, so I was assistant attorney general for one year and one of the assignments I had was attorney for the State Corporation Commission, which regulated motor carriers. So I began to learn the business of motor carrier regulation and actually, sat on some, what they call, joint boards, hearing certificate applications.

Russell Jones was a prominent motor carrier lawyer, representing Navajo Freight Line and other companies. He kind of recruited me and I went into practice with him. We did a civil practice but predominantly did motor carrier.

At the University of New Mexico, I played college tennis and was active in my fraternity and always loved sports. I was at the gym every afternoon to play pickup basketball. I've always followed the University of New Mexico athletics. Jamie, you and I had that in common right away, an interest in the University of New Mexico athletics. So after the two years I've mentioned in public service, that was it and I went into private practice and have been in private practice ever since, and in Santa Fe.

Jamie: You got involved a little bit in politics. Why don't you go over that?

Gene: My involvement in politics, I would say, as far as really getting deeply involved, occurred in nineteen sixty-eight. I became an activist, what you might call an antiwar activist in support of Gene McCarthy, who was running for president. Of course, we know that story in sixty-eight. But as a result, people were coming to me who were antiwar McCarthy activists. Some arrived at my office one day and simply said, "Gene, would you help us? Would you lead our group? Because we don't have very many local people who know anybody." A lot of the antiwar movement consisted of persons who had never been active politically or were part of the hippie culture.

So during the Santa Fe County Convention, we were running Carlos Martinez for county chairman against the entrenched establishment, which included George Gonzalez, mayor of Santa Fe at the time, and his cousin, Johnnie Vigil, who was the Democratic county chair at the time.

George's son is now the mayor of Santa Fe. I ended up running against George Gonzalez for congress in the Democratic primary in nineteen seventy-two. But anyway, I was involved in leadership during the county convention, the state convention, and I was a McCarthy delegate to the National Democratic Convention in Chicago.

Jamie: That's where they had the riot, right?

Gene: Yeah. I was actually in Chicago a week before the convention because I was on the Rules Committee and the Rules Committee was addressing a lot of party reform issues, so I was there a week before the full convention started. That's a book to write one of these days.

I ended up running for Congress in nineteen seventy-two, which was the McGovern/Nixon year. Not a great year for democrats. A lot of what happens in the national election of course influences the general election/ congressional election.

My opponent, Manuel Lujan, was the incumbent congressman. I won the Democratic primary. In the first poll, I was at about two or three percent. The candidates I ran against included: Mike Alarid who was a state senator and who had been lieutenant governor, George Gonzalez, who was mayor of Santa Fe and popular, because he had a radio station and was well known, and a couple of others. I started at the bottom but I ended up winning that primary.

In the general election, I ran, about eleven thousand votes ahead of McGovern, but, that wasn't going to do it.

I lost by a margin of about four thousand votes. I believe McGovern only won South Dakota and DC. It was a landslide.

I did not run for office again. In retrospect it was a blessing not to be elected, and being in congress and raising money constantly.

However, that race had set a fundraising record for a Congressional race except John Kerry's race in Massachusetts topped it. It exceeded all other campaigns in terms of total money raised. So we really had a lot of support and we had great, great funding support. Meanwhile, you were in the legislature at that time. How many terms did you serve?

Jamie: Three

Gene: I never ran for any other office, state or otherwise. I just stayed active politically after that.

Jamie: You supported Governor Bruce King a lot like I did, both of us. When did you get appointed on the Board of Regents?

Gene: The first time, I was appointed on the Board of Regents I served from nineteen ninety-one to nineteen ninety-six. Bruce King appointed me.

Jamie: What was it like then on the Regents?

Gene: We had a good board. It included a successful businessman, Ken Johns, who I really respected and worked with. I was chair of the Finance and Facilities Committee for all six years, which is really what I wanted to do. Finance and facilities, as you know, is where most of the really meaningful decisions are made.

And you know, in the meeting of Finance and Facilities I wouldn't take a work day out of everybody's time as is the current practice. I would have meetings in the evening. When there are committee meetings you occupy faculty and staff for hours needlessly. The way it was done in my second term those people are sitting around instead of working. They're sitting around for a six hour meeting when they are only going to be called on for ten minutes. To me, that was not the way to do it. We did it after work. Our meeting would start at five or six in the evening and go to eleven at night.

Roberta Ramo Cooper was president of the Board a couple of years. Penny Rembe was president of the Board two years. There was none of this business of "one person is the president of the Board for posterity" like the present Board. It was accepted. It was an unwritten rule, but it was understood as is the case with a Regent, would serve two years as president and go on. I was not that interested in being president of the Board, because I cared more about chairing finance and facilities.

During the nineteen ninety-one to nineteen ninety-six term our university president was not strong. It was Richard Peck. But we believed that if you're going to have a good successor candidates pool the next time you're selecting a president, you've got to demonstrate that there's stability, that whoever was the prior president was able to serve his contractual term.

Most university presidents only have a shelf life of six or seven or eight years at best.

Peck served his full term. Then we had an interim president who was chair of the Psychology Department. He left New Mexico to become the provost at Duke.

Then time goes by. I was a supporter of Bill Richardson, sort of, in a strange kind of way, because I had run for congress. Bill, sort of a carpetbagger, comes to New Mexico. The first job Bill gets is to be in-house director of the Democratic Party.

Jamie: He was an employee of the Democratic Party.

Gene: That way he could get acquainted with everybody politically influential. In the meantime after I ran for congress, Roberto Mondragon ran. He was wiped out. Bill was positioning himself to run for congress, so he came and we talked. I shared ideas, just as I did with Jerry Apodaca, who came to me when he prepared to run for governor. I gave him the lay of the land and particularly recommended professionals. If you're going to run a campaign you've got to have the right professional people who are going to do your media and manage an organization.

Anyway, I got to know Bill. He ran for congress and he ran against Tom Udall the first time. After he was in congress we were friendly, and when he decided to run for governor I was very much a supporter. Candidly, that often bears on how one is appointed as a Regent. A real interest in and support of the University of New Mexico is equally important. This governor's so clueless there are members of the Board that are not really people who have a foothold in the state and a relationship with the University of New Mexico.

I let it be known to Governor Richardson that I'd like to serve as a Regent again. I wouldn't make any bones about it. He asked me if I was interested. I said, "Yeah, I really would like to serve." So I was appointed and finished my second term at the end of twenty fourteen.

Jamie: How was the second term different from the first term?

Gene: The second six year term was really quite different. I was surprised at how different. One thing was very positive. Previously the board did not have an audit committee. And you really shouldn't have an organization and a Board that doesn't have a functioning audit committee. That committee really allows the Regents to have an independent kind of a function, which can investigate finances on everybody no matter who they are. You were responsible creating the audit committee. I don't know how you came up with the idea, but you did.

Jamie: I came up with the idea because of just what you said. Normally you would have an audit committee. Game and Fish had an audit committee. Businesses have audit committees. We needed our own office and we hired our own auditor. It still is the most important committee we've got, as far as I'm concerned. The committee was limited to only three Regents at a time; so you never violated the Open Meetings Act or the Inspection of Public Records Act because you automatically had a quorum. Additionally, we were frequently reviewing financial, legal and personnel issues so the sessions were normally closed sessions. The majority of the meetings were dealing with financial matters. Obviously, Gene, you really made that function work.

Gene: It helped that I served on the board of Northwestern Mutual Insurance Company. It's a Fortune 100 company and I was on that audit committee for fifteen years. I knew how things are supposed to work. When you have an audit committee you are to have at least one member who is qualified with financial expertise.

Gene: I had the experience of working on that company's audit committee. We worked with Price Waterhouse and we had executive sessions where we met with internal audit. Management was excluded. We did business the way you're supposed to in an audit committee. So when I came on this Board of Regents, that was one of the positives. I was chair of the audit committee. I also served on Finance and Facilities.

Some Regent appointees did not have a firm allegiance to the University of New Mexico that comes with being a university alum and a New Mexican. They weren't alumni of the University of New Mexico. They were appointed serendipitously by the governor. It was different from the first Board on which I served.

What I would say about service on the Board of Regents is that to me, and Jamie you shared this, two things are really important. One, is you're not there for any kind of personal benefit. It's completely a volunteer service to gain nothing by it personally. Two, you have to work at it. That means you have to spend a lot of time, and not just in meetings, but time in reading and preparation and outside meetings and that type of thing. There were some members of the second board who did not seem to honor those two principles.

Jamie: What kind of accomplishments do you think we had in your six year term?

Gene: We improved the graduation rates. Retention rates improved. Faculty was strengthened in some positions. We made some progress in addressing unfunded retirement and health insurance liabilities.

Jamie: We improved the provost, don't you think?

Gene: I think so. I think we made a real improvement. Absolutely, come to think of it, a hundred percent improvement in the provost position.

There were some accomplishments. The legislative funding, fortunately, was pretty good for two or three years, because the state was doing well financially at that time. We were able to accomplish some things. And I think we brought some stability to the athletic department and to management of the Gallup campus. Arts and Science had had a very weak chair and we appointed a good chair in that position. There were accomplishments. But there were problems that you just were frustrated about that you really can't change.

Jamie: Like what?

Gene: Well, I think the administration has been overstaffed. I think the relationship between the number of faculty and the number of staff is completely out of balance. Staff positions have just almost become full-employment source for Albuquerque. Don Chalmers and I sought to close the Los Alamos branch. It is far from cost effective and never supported locally by property tax. There doesn't seem to be any will to efficiently conduct university business and cut cost. I say this whether it was Richard Peck or whether it was David Schmidly or Bob Frank. It's the same way with governors. They get into an office and none of them recognize that you have a big organization to run and you ought to try, your first priority ought to be to make it function efficiently and make things work. They usually have other agendas.

The disappointment is, what can you do? A lot of it depends on who you're going to have as your financial vice president. Presidents tend to just hand over the business part of it to that vice president. We had a good one in my first term, I thought, Dave McKinney. He was a really a strong financial vice president.

Another thing about this Board of Regents, when you're dealing with a president and you have a contract with a president. The Regents have a responsibility to conduct an evaluation. Which brings us back to what I said, you know, if you're going to do it right as a Regent, you've really got to work. You've got to sacrifice your time.

Jamie: You and Don Chalmers worked on President Frank's contract. Why don't you talk about that a bit?

Gene: We did have a good businessman on the board in Don. We negotiated and drafted the contract. Unfortunately Don had cancer and his last year or two of service it was very tough for him. Don Chalmers had automobile dealerships. He was very much a businessperson. However, having said that, this brings up something else that should be mentioned. I think it's a mistake to overload the Board of Regents with Albuquerque people because there is almost an inevitable situation that may arise where their own business interests collide with the university's interest. Obviously, you're going to have members from Albuquerque and maybe a couple from Albuquerque. To load up with Albuquerque members means that you're placing some people in that kind of a potential conflict situation.

Jamie: One thing I want to mention, Gene, you were so important on the Regents because of your legal background. You and Don were recommended by all the Regents to do President Frank's contract. We sort of overruled the president at that time. A number of us said we wanted you and Don on it. Could you talk about how you put that contract together?

Gene: Bob Frank had his personal attorney. His attorney wasn't that effective, by the way. As a template, we probably started with a contract that we'd had with President Schmidly. However, we tailored it. We wanted to set objective targets for Bob Frank so it wasn't to be just a subjective kind of judgment about his performance.

So we built in targets like graduation rates, and retention rates, and provided that there should be bonuses if those goals were achieved. We wrote, I think a pretty good contract as far as what was expected of him so that he would know what was expected. That placed a corresponding responsibility on the Regents to observe the objectives that were set forth in the contract. Not just to put it in a drawer and forget about it. If you don't evaluate the president on an annual basis against objective, verifiable targets, everything becomes personal or subjective. It is the responsibility of the president of the Board of Regents to lead that evaluation.

We drafted the contract, worked through it. We had some back and forth with Bob Frank's lawyer, but Don and I came up with the present contract that they have to work with. That was not the only instance of doing legal work, Jamie, another was negotiations with American Colleges Corporation. They are a proprietary firm that builds student housing. So instead of the university bonding for funds, they contract to build the student housing on a lease of the University of New Mexico land. ACC came forward, of course, with promises of what it was going to do for the university. Look at all the success we've had. Then here comes the contract. You have a University of New Mexico Real Estate Department that tends with little question to accept, "Oh, well, here's the contract from the ACC." So I and Don ended up spending hours and hours over the contract and finding provisions of it that are not satisfactory and having to argue how the University of New Mexico is to be paid, what the acceptable terms are going to be. I just felt that responsibility to the taxpayer.

Jamie: See, that was the value of your participation, Gene. Mel was similar when he was there. Not criticizing the legal staff at the university however, when you have, with your background and knowledge, you were really doing the attorney's work. When you lose that insight within the Regents, you've got a problem.

Gene: The problem with the recent dispute between President Frank and the Board is that it is made difficult to attract a new qualified person to be the next president. Our Board, my first term, recognized that. Whether we were happy with Richard Peck or not, we weren't going to make it public. We weren't going to create the image that the Regents would not allow the president to serve out his term and leave gracefully. You've got to be thinking not just about this president. You've got to be thinking about the next one.

Jamie: The lack of annual evaluations is really a problem.

Gene: Yes. If you don't have a file that shows year after year of negative evaluations, then all of a sudden you want to terminate for cause, the president has a lawsuit.

Jamie: That's what they did, Gene. While I was there, we didn't have the last two years of evaluations. By the way, who pays for the lawsuit?

Gene: Well, the university's going to have to defend it and that's going to be costly.

Jamie: So, that's the taxpayer?

Gene: Yes, the taxpayer. That's why the second time, General Hossmer and I took the responsibility and we did the evaluation. We spent a lot of time on the evaluation letter. It had some negative comments. It referenced performances that were not satisfactory. It was affirmative as stating expected actions. We expect this and this. He had an evaluation one time, out of five years. The contract, of course, says that he's supposed to have an annual evaluation.

Jamie: In April.

Gene: And anybody who knows human resources employment knows if you're going to fire somebody you've got to have a file. You have to build your case.

Jamie: What is your opinion of the situation at the Health Sciences Center?

Gene: That's interesting because that also, having served two terms and not back-to-back, but what you might call sort of different eras, it helps with your perspective. Because my first term, the head of Health Sciences was not Paul Roth. Paul was dean of the Medical School. He wasn't the honcho over the whole Health Sciences.

Jamie: Dr. Eaton was head of the HSC.

Gene: Bill Johnson was president in charge of the hospital. You remember him? This is before Steve McKernan and he did a hell of a job. The hospital always had a seventy-five or eighty million dollar reserve. At the end of a fiscal year, the University of New Mexico would loan money to the state because the state needed money to match their Medicare reimbursement. The University of New Mexico hospital would loan the Health Department of the state twenty-five million for sixty days. It was a less complicated era in the early nineteen nineties compared with now.

The problem was, here's what really happened is, the last two years of President Schmidly's term, he was ill. He was often in Houston for treatment. Dr. Paul Roth commissioned a study, a consulting group to come in and interview everybody and come up with a report. The report said, "You know, your Health Sciences Center really needs to have separate governance. It just has different missions and a different kind of finance structure than the rest of the university."

This report justified introduction to the Board of amendments to the form of the governance of Health Sciences and changes to the university policy manual. I was opposed to it. Jamie, you were opposed to it. Basically, I said, "This is one university. We're one university. We're not two universities. We're not a north of Lomas University and a south of Lomas University." That's what was really being accomplished.

The changes placed Paul Roth, really on an organization virtually parallel with a university president with the HSC title chancellor. That's how that whole thing came down with HSC having its own board. Instead of business coming through finance and facilities, or student affairs, they would have their board and then everything would come directly to the Regents. It was a power play to pull the authority over that function, the medical school, the cancer center, the Carrie Tingley Children's Hospital and on and on and on, basically under their own governance. The chancellor has his own board.

That was a mistake. Recently the current Regents in some strange manner I am told, reversed the separation of HSC. They made a determination to basically unscramble that egg and try and bring control back under the president of the university over the whole Health Sciences enterprises.

Jamie: Let me ask you a question on that. Health Science is about a two billion dollar budget.

Gene: I think, that's pretty close to it because the whole University of New Mexico budget is three billion and...

Jamie: About eight hundred million is the university.

Gene: Roughly, about two to one.

Jamie: What you've got on the Health Sciences is that they're able to generate money a little bit better than the main university. We have tuition fees or what we get from the legislature. Do you think we're approaching the time that we need to separate Health Science from the main campus, and have legislation introduce a constitutional amendment to be voted on by the public, creating two separate boards appointed by the governor and confirmed by the senate?

Gene: No, I definitely don't think so. I think, either you have the Health Sciences Center that's part of the university or it is independent. It's not unusual to be entirely separate. The University of Arizona and the university medical facilities are an example. I can name several others.

Jamie: Colorado.

Gene: I can name others where the medical functions really are separate.

Jamie: That's what I am advocating. I believe we should have a seven member governor appointed University of New Mexico Health Sciences board, and that new board would have to be part of a constitutional amendment.

Gene: And if that's what they want to do, then you do it.

Jamie: I'm not saying that's what they want. I'm just saying from what I've seen when you have a two billion dollar institution, and an eight hundred million dollar institution, obviously when one gets in trouble, and it's the small one, the smaller institution is always going to be looking for a handout.

Gene: Well, it creates a tension because there are people on the north campus, who just see anything that's done to reinforce singular governance as a ploy to access HSC funds. I don't think that's really the reason. I think you either have one university or if you think that doesn't work, then the whole medical apparatus should be truly separate.

But you know, Jamie, one thing I've never understood. Here we have the hospital and we have all this medical staff and some of the best, some of the best in the state. Unfortunately, the UNM Hospital has to do so much of the indigent work. Everybody, you know, St. Joseph's and Presbyterian say: "If you can't pay, you go to UNMH." Which hurts, but I've never understood why we didn't simply have an HMO for our faculty that would be where the service, the healthcare and services was provided by our own doctors and nurses.

Jamie: I've been trying to get that done forever.

291

Gene: Instead, they've got insurance and they've got Presbyterian, and they've got Lovelace, and of course your outside providers have a margin. They obviously have a profit margin in there. Why not have it as almost a co-op kind of thing, like Kaiser Permanente. That was how Kaiser, that HMO started for the Kaiser employees. But here we have hospital, doctors, specialists and yet, our staff if they need medical care, they're going under their Presbyterian insurance. We'd received explanations for this structure but they were not persuasive.

Jamie: I agree. All university employees, both main campus and north campus, should have medical insurance through the university, not a private insurer. So Gene, you are anticipating my next question. We are asking everyone that is participating in the book to offer their ideas about the future. As you look forward for New Mexico, what do you think is going to be very important for the state to grow and prosper in the future?

Gene: Well, I sit here and frequently, in fact, I ran into somebody at lunch today and we had a conversation. I sit here and I look at Texas, which is an economic engine. Colorado, Arizona, they're not Texas, but they're doing well, they're prospering and here we are, right between those states. In fact, across the line, even parts of Mexico, Chihuahua State, is probably prospering. The first thing is a change in mentality. There's an attitude in New Mexico, that first of all, we're poor. And secondly, we're not good at what we do and if we try something, we're not going to succeed. It's a negative attitude. How do you overcome that? I've racked my brain about how you overcome it.

But I think, it's going to take leadership. We've never had a governor, including Bill Richardson, who could change that overall mentality. Richardson really wanted state government to be well run and to be customer-friendly and collect taxes efficiently and do things like that. A good school system would make a big difference. We tried to fund education, but we're not going to prosper unless there's some attitudinal change and how you achieve that, I don't know.

You know, you get some people who come in who are really competent. For example, we have a good football coach. Bob Davie is a quality, competent individual. He's intelligent. He's articulate. He's been around. You know, he coached at Notre Dame. He's building a program. Then I recently read a very negative comment in the *Albuquerque Journal*, the person wrote, "Well, you know, the football team, they won eight games, but it was against poor teams." That kind of derogatory viewpoint is dragging our whole state down. Why don't they give scholarships to New Mexico high school players? Of course, the answer is, "If you did, you'd sure as hell never win a game." But just that kind of attitude hurts us. We have some very talented students coming up in New Mexico, but without supporting and nurturing that talent those individuals leave.

Negative attitudes permeate everything we do and we need to change that. Until we change the mentality, New Mexico will continue to lag behind the rest of the country.

I agree with Gene about the need for an attitudinal shift in New Mexico. When I was appointed to the Board of Regents, I initiated rule changes that Mel Eaves and I wrote to require more transparency regarding Board activities. On the 10th of December, 2016 I sat down with Mallory Reviere who is the special assistant to the University of New Mexico Board of Regents. Mallory took the place of Ellen Wenzel who was the first special assistant for the Regents. I sat down with Mallory because Mallory can attest to the fact that she serves as the "Face of the Regents." She is the person people can request board minutes from. If someone wishes to meet with a member of the Board of Regents, she facilitates that meeting. I insisted that the Regents have their own budget and their own administrative person. Prior, that function was carried out by someone in the president's office and thereby subsumed in the president's budget. I felt it was important that the Regents had the opportunity to interact with members of the public directly without filtering.

Mallory Reviere, special assistant to the University of New Mexico Board of Regents / Interviewed December 10, 2016

Mallory: I've lived in New Mexico since two thousand eight. I'm originally from Texas but after graduating from Texas A&M, my husband and I went to work for British Petroleum. We had a number of years living overseas. After living overseas for fifteen years we came to New Mexico. We came to Albuquerque and we worked in a business that we were about forty percent owners in, and when we were ready to sell the business, I decided I wanted to go back to work. I thought I'd like to work at the university. That's how I came to the University of New Mexico. Our children were getting to be college age and we knew they would be coming to the University of New Mexico.

I happened to apply at the University of New Mexico when the very first special assistant to the Board of Regents was retiring. Ellen Wenzel retired in twenty thirteen. She had been the first special assistant to the Board of Regents. In two thousand five, you created both the position and the office itself. Previously, the support for the Board of Regents had come out of the office of the president of the university. I believe you saw there was a real need for there to be a separate, autonomous office created for the Board, with a person there to man the office and to be a central point of contact. It was important for that person to be a resource for the Regents and to be a central point of contact for incoming, and then of course outgoing, communications.

It was essential that there was an office to support the Board. Additionally, there are the nuances of the Open Meetings Act, which restricts the Regents communication among themselves. Having a special assistant to the Board and an office allows there to be much smoother communications in compliance with the Open Meetings Act.

Jamie: First of all, before Ellen Wenzel came, when the work was being handled in the president's office, we didn't have an employee and that person really reported to the president. We felt it should be separated and we should have our own person and our own budget, because we are independent of the president. The president reports to the Board of Regents—not the other way around. You mentioned the Open Meetings Act. What do you have to do there and what is the time factor required to notify the public? And how you do that?

Mallory: Yes, a very critical part of the job is to be very familiar with the Open Meetings Act and to comply with it. There are restrictions on how the members of that body can meet, and so a quorum of members cannot meet unless the public has been notified of the meeting agenda a minimum of seventy-two hours in advance. At this point, the University of New Mexico policy is that they're noticed ten working days in advance. So those notices for the regular meetings go out ten days before the meeting and then the agenda must be available to the public at least seventy-two hours before the meeting.

Jamie: And are the minutes of the Regents meetings available to the public? Are they able to pull them up easily?

Mallory: Yes.

Jamie: Could you explain that? In the past, when I came on the board, all the minutes for each month were given to the library to be archived. That made it very difficult to find that information. Explain the access the public has now to the minutes of all the committees.

Mallory: The minutes of the past eight years of all the committees are posted online on the public website of the university. Additionally, there's a public Regents website that also has the minutes. We also have a lobo vault repository that is managed by the library and they've got minutes going back to nineteen ten.

Jamie: As you look forward, what do you think is going to be important for the Board of Regents?

Mallory: I think that's a great question. Regents, like all governing boards, face the great challenge to properly oversee without getting pulled into the weeds. The Regents need to be able to be the visionaries to hold up that vision, an ideal that we all want to be attainable.

Jamie: The president of the Regents is the one who formats the way the board runs. It's set up very carefully to do it that way. It's the president of the Regents, not anybody else, who is the one who establishes how the Regents function. The president handles all the committee appointments.

Mallory: Yes, the president of the Board of Regents has quite a lot of power.

Mallory: I mean, the university president has power, but he or she must rally people around the vision. Jamie, you were wonderful at communicating your vision to others and uniting people around a common goal, to take things forward. And so that kind of goes back to my comment about how Regents are continually pulled into the details. It's just a natural pull, but to be able to separate one's self from that force, resist being pulled into the day-to-day issues and to hold the vision out there to the community, that's the challenge.

I agree with Mallory, that the Regents need to keep promoting broad visionary changes that help the university grow and stay competitive. However, in my opinion, up until I arrived, the Regents frequently got so invested in long range planning that sometimes they lost sight of the needs of their constituents. In a university setting, your constituents are the students and the faculty and the staff, but especially the students who were often overlooked. I have talked about how Mel and I rewrote many of the policies for the Regents. I have also mentioned how I restructured the board committees when I became president of the Board of Regents. In this chapter, I wanted to spend some time talking about the efforts I made to connect the Regents with the students. I was fortunate that when I became president of the Board, at that same time, there was a brilliant young man, Kevin Stevenson, who had become president of the Association of Students of the University of New Mexico. Kevin's leadership helped me better understand how we could implement immediate changes that had a big impact. Uniting the campus community is an important part of a four year academic experience. Athletics can bring people together and raise morale. The students knew this. They had been fighting for this, and I am glad I was at the right place at the right time and I was able to convince people we needed to listen to the students and implement what they were asking for.

Because of Kevin's excellent negotiating skills and his exceptional communication skills, the university ended up hiring him to work in the president's office. You will see in this interview how he succinctly sums up the major issues facing nearly all institutions of higher education. He currently serves as the Director of Human Resources Business Services for the university. On December 15th, 2016, I sat down with Kevin to discuss our interaction while I was serving on the Board and the projects we worked on together.

Kevin Stevenson, director of Human Resources Business Services for the University of New Mexico, past president of the University of New Mexico student body / Interviewed December 15, 2016

Kevin: I'm a native New Mexican. Born and raised. I am a first generation college student. Grew up in Rio Rancho. Moved all the way across the river for college. While I was in school in undergrad, I got involved with student government. The first time I met you, Jamie, was actually at a student senate meeting. You had come to talk to us about the presidential search that the Regents were kicking off. It was a long time ago and that search ended up with President Caldera. I think it's a noteworthy place to start because that was the first time in anyone's recent memory that a Regent actually showed up at a student senate meeting and took the time to come and not just talk to you, but also listen to these folks in student government. And so that was the first time we ever met you.

Jamie: What was your title then?

Kevin: At that point, I was just a kid on the senate. From there I moved into the role as Association of Students of the University of New Mexico president, and that was when I really got to know you and really started working with you. There were two big things that I worked with you on when I was a student. At the point when I was a student, for the prior twenty or twenty-five years, there had been a lot of unhappiness between the students and the athletics department. The previous athletic director had moved the student section in The Pit for men's basketball games and had gotten rid of it for a variety of reasons. Over that period of time, students had tried unsuccessfully to convince the athletics department to give them back a student section. Both you and I, having a pension for athletics, and we thought it would be good for Lobo athletics. We had an ability to work together. It allowed us to do something really cool. We put the student section back in The Pit. And this was something that we had talked about. The students really wanted this and we both thought it would be good for the university as a whole.

    The basketball coach at the time, Coach McKay, really wanted it and thought it would be great for the environment in The Pit. And you know, the thing that sticks with me about this is we're nineteen, twenty, and twenty-one year olds. We don't know what the hell we're doing. And so you try to convince people to do what you want and the only way you know how. We had students signing petitions and we were writing letters in *The Daily*

Lobo and trying to use whatever platform we had to make this come to fruition. I remember sitting in my office in the basement of the Student Union building with you and I think that's worthwhile. It's important to note because I didn't drive to Santa Fe to meet with you at Daniels Insurance. I didn't come over here to Scholes Hall to meet with you in the Regents office. You actually came to the basement into the student government office to meet with me and talk about what were my priorities. What do we want to do? And the student section in The Pit came up. And you said, "Well I think we can do this." And you took out your phone and you put it on the table and you dialed Rudy Davalos, put it on speakerphone and said "Rudy, I'm sitting here with Kevin Stevenson, the president of the students. And we need to get this student section done."

And Rudy said, "Well okay, I think we can make that happen. I'll get in touch with Kevin." Then you hung up the phone. Weeks later, we had arranged to put a student section in The Pit. Starting the next season, we had the section behind the basket next to the visitor's bench designated as the Student Section. Our Student Fee Board voted to increase student fees to provide additional financial support to athletics, both as a thank you for the student section, and also to offset some of the donors that athletics had decided to move out of their seats to give students their seats. And at no time, whether it was in the newspaper articles that followed or at the press conference where the section was announced, did you take any credit for this. You really let this look and feel like it was something that the students accomplished. It was awesome to be able to work with you on that. But it was one of those things that we had tried to do unsuccessfully for fifteen or twenty years. Then one thing in the equation changed, and that was the entrance of you, Jamie Koch, and the problem was solved and the deal was done. The kids are still getting free tickets sitting behind the basket in their Student Section in The Pit today.

Jamie: Could you talk about the Student Fee Board?

Kevin: So, we have, the university has, a student board of seven, maybe nine people now, but a handful of students that make recommendations to the Regents on how much they should pay in student fees. And also, where and what departments should receive those fees. When I was an undergraduate, I served as a member of the board and then chaired the board one year. And over time, this is one of those things where the students and the administration don't always see eye to eye about how their money should be spent. Or what they should invest in, or how much they should pay.

298

Jamie: What are some of the fees used for?

Kevin: So, we have the four big ones: the library, the student health center, athletics and IT. The idea is that rather than tuition, which just goes into kind of a big bucket that pays for everything to run, that fees are earmarked for specific things that provide benefits to students or offer tangible stuff. There are fees that go to Popejoy Hall, which give students half-price tickets, things like that. And over time, that Board is going to work either with or sometimes against the Regents to get fees of an appropriate amount put in the right places. And I think athletics is one of the places that has seen a real increase in fees over the past ten or fifteen years. Depending on how you look at it, the increases haven't even been enough and they're still not where they should be. One of the things I'm proud of and thankful to you for, was the ability to work together on some of those things instead of kind of that opposition. I think the student seats in The Pit are a good example of having a nice partnership and collaboration to achieve mutual goals.

Jamie: I wanted to sit down with you today because you have an important perspective. You graduated from here. And you came to work here, so you've seen more changes than normal. Over the last eleven years you've worked with all five presidents, so, just tell us what some of your impressions have been.

Kevin: You know, I think that the university is in a good place. I think we do a good job or we have done a good job of playing what at times is a pretty difficult hand of cards. We're in a pretty difficult budget situation. It's been a long time since we were in a really nice budget situation. Going back to when I was a student and one of the things that you created was the annual Budget Summit. I'm sure you hear this from a lot of other folks, but it's worth mentioning. The university itself, and the openness and transparency and the inclusiveness of the university, was very different in two thousand two, before you came on to the Board. Because of your leadership and your commitment to transparency and openness in government, a lot changed. I think that one way to think of it is we have the luxury of complaining about things today that we didn't even know were happening fifteen years ago. We might not like them and we might complain about them but at least we know they're going on. The university's budget and our Regent committee meetings were held in closed session. They weren't open. They weren't noticed. People didn't attend. The Regents, under your leadership, were committed to a new level of openness and transparency. It fundamentally changed the way the university operated and how the constituencies within the university operated. You, and President Caldera at the time, created the Budget Summit. Instead of just having our CFO and our Regents behind a closed door build the university's budget, you decided we were going to bring all the stakeholders together to hear what they actually thought. What should we spend our money on? As students, we were given the opportunity to develop budget scenarios. We were able to provide input about how much we wanted our tuition to increase. These are the programs and activities that we want dollars invested in. Now the budget summit is very routine. People, I think, really take it for granted that they have a say in these processes, that they're able to peek into the budget process and have a voice in how things are done. It was a pretty radical change from fifteen years ago. Jamie, you really changed the level of transparency and you know that means that everybody can see a lot more of the warts of this place. But it also has facilitated, I think, moving us forward in a very real way because we've been able to tap into the expertise of everybody across the campus community—not just the administration, but the faculty, the staff, the students, etc.

Jamie: So moving forward, what do you think is going to be important for the university?

Kevin: I think we've done a reasonable job kind of balancing competing goals or competing priorities. How do you simultaneously push forward academic excellence and student success in a flagship research university, while maintaining relatively open admissions so that anybody in the state of New Mexico who wants to attend the University of New Mexico, has the opportunity to attend the University of New Mexico, while at the same time, keeping a relatively low tuition so that it's affordable? In a very traditional higher ed model, those things are very, very much in conflict. I think that we've done a really good job over the past decade of improving our student success. We have done a good job of improving graduation rates and improving retention rates and improving the quality of our degree. We have also improved the quality of our faculty. I think we're in a place where we have to think hard about prioritizing what the university is going to be and to whom moving forward.

When we were doing the search for President Schmidly, when you were president of the Board, one of the things that we did was meet with all of the living past presidents of the university to talk to them about what's needed in a president. What does it take for someone to be successful?

When we were meeting with Dick Peck, he told us a story about when he was hired in the early nineties to be president. He went to Harvard to a new President's Institute. And being at Harvard, it was case-driven. They were in a discussion session, and the case that had been passed out was the University of New Mexico, and why it's impossible for a president to succeed.

Jamie: I didn't know that.

Kevin: So, the Cliff Notes were basically that you have this collision of competing forces where you have a governor appointed board with a very rural power base in the legislature, a low-cost, open access institution with a faculty that looks very much like a flagship research institution or an elite East Coast college. And you have these fundamental differences that no one here, maybe since Tom Popejoy, has really been able to reconcile—how to make all of these things fit together. I think that's the biggest challenge. We're in a state that needs so much in so many places and demands so much from the things that we do and the people that are here. You know, it's unclear that we still have the luxury of trying to be "all things to all people." And you know, moving forward, you think about the person we're looking for with this new search. I spent the morning before I was here reviewing a draft of the position profile that we're going to use to recruit the new president, thinking about how do we come to terms with some of the trade-offs that have to be made? We're in a situation because of, whether it's declining state funding, whether it's the number of high school graduates in New Mexico plateauing or decreasing, increased competition for traditional college students, general uncertainty about the value of a college education, just in general. How do you keep this place moving forward when a couple of things that for the past hundred twenty-five years we've always been able to count on are no longer available to us to count on. There are three things that have really changed the landscape: that the state would give us more money next year than we got this year, that the Regents would let us charge more for tuition next year than we charge this year, and that more kids will show up to take classes next year than they did this year

All of those spigots are being turned off. You know the questions we need to ask ourselves are not: "How much new money will the funding formula at the state level generate for us?" It's: "How much, what can we do to minimize the amount of money that will be cut?" You know, it's not: "How do we go recruit new students to fund ourselves through growth?" But it's: "How do we tap into new markets to offset the declines in our

301

traditional enrollment base?" I think that things are more pleasant and things are certainly easier when you have a nice, positive derivative, and the slope is up on your resources. That's not the case. We're in a really challenging time. We've got a kind of "come to Jesus moment" about what the university is. Do we need to be smaller and more exclusive? Do we need to be larger and more open and focus on some pieces of the mission more than others? Do we double down on providing instruction and education to in-state students at the expense of our research or service missions? And what does that mean for us as the flagship institution of the state? So, there are really, really lofty questions and issues to grapple with. I think that higher ed, as an industry nationwide, is grappling with many of these issues. But these things are really exacerbated in New Mexico. You know, maybe it's because we're fifteen or twenty years ahead of everybody else in terms of demographic trends. Maybe it's because we're trying to balance these competing missions of access and excellence, even though that's a dumbed down way of saying it. It's a difficult thing that we're trying to do. I think it's impressive how well we've done with it over the past ten or fifteen years. But this really is a critical moment, I think, for the institution in terms of how are we going to re-make ourselves, re-invent ourselves, re-envision ourselves so that we can be successful for whatever higher education looks like in the next twenty-five years.

As you can see, Kevin Stevenson highlighted the challenges we currently face—but one of the reasons I like Kevin so much is he has a balanced viewpoint. He mentioned the positive successes we have had with four year graduation rates and our overall improved graduation rates. In this book we have talked with many people about the problems New Mexico faces, but we do have some important successes to celebrate. According to the *Albuquerque Journal* editorial on May 17, 2017, "Incentives put in place at the University of New Mexico during the tenure of former President Bob Frank and continued under acting President Chaouki Abdallah are showing results in the gold standard of higher education—four year graduation rates." I concur with the *Albuquerque Journal* that those incentives are showing results. I am very pleased to highlight in this book the individual, Terry Babbitt, who was the author of those incentives. Terry has been with the university for approximately 20 years. Every president since 1997 has seen his significant contributions, and as in the case of the *Journal* editorial I just quoted, most of those presidents have taken the credit for his achievements. So it was important to me that we unpack exactly what the incentives are that are working. Terry Babbitt is a powerful public speaker. He has the ability to crunch numbers on the spot and access highly detailed information about our student body from his own memory. He understands the subtleties of recruitment and retention because he has made it his life's work. He has never asked for credit, but the improved four year graduation results are, as the *Journal* notes, "undeniable: from 15.8% in the 2012-2013 school year to 21.7% in 2015-2016 to upward of 25% this year. Acting President Abdallah points out...this investment will pay off 100 times into both the personal benefit of the students and their parents but also the state." I sat down with Associate Vice President of Enrollment Management, Terry Babbitt, on December 15th, 2016.

Terry Babbitt, associate vice president, Enrollment Management Division (Chief Enrollment Officer), the University of New Mexico / Interviewed December 15, 2016

Terry: I'm currently the associate vice president of the Enrollment Management Division at the University of New Mexico. That is essentially the chief enrollment officer and we have admissions of new students, financial aid, registration processes, and student support/retention areas that report to me. I have been at the University of New Mexico about twenty years and before that I was from the State of Oklahoma. Like you, I made my way through college playing football. I don't know if you ever knew that, but I was at the University of Oklahoma, and then at a smaller institution in Oklahoma. I was working in admissions and that turned into a fulltime admissions career, twenty-six years ago.

I did a lot of traveling, high school to high school, recruiting the whole state of Texas, much of New Mexico, and always was doing recruitment and admissions. So, sometimes related to athletics, sometimes, most of the time obviously, my career merged just to admissions for all students and I ended up in New Mexico. My great grandfather was a foreman at the Phillips Ranch by Cimarron, many years ago when it was still owned by Frank and Wade Phillips. So, we had a strong family connection to this part of the country, so I decided just to make a career move here twenty years ago. I ran recruitment and admissions and worked all the way up running different areas in the enrollment services components to the position I currently serve in.

Jamie: So, how did we meet?

Terry: When you first came on the Board of Regents, I think I remember the first meeting. It was your first year, two thousand three, and it was the budget time of year and they were running through this budget process and you said, "Look, we're not gonna run it this way any more." That was your first meeting, or the first meeting I was at about the University of New Mexico budget process and your involvement, so I remember it pretty clearly.

Jamie: That was thirteen years ago.

Terry: They had just run budgets through the Regents Committee without much scrutiny, or you know, oversight. Of course, the Board's primary role, one of them, is fiscal oversight for the institution, and so you had made a point that we're gonna go through this a little bit differently. I think that was the first time I was there with you, Jamie. And then you know our paths crossed a lot over the years as you became more integrated in the student plight, and the student plight for us, still to this day. But beginning those years, there was an emerging crisis with student debt, affordability. The University of New Mexico has a unique role as an accessible research university. Forty percent of the students come from parental educational attainment that is high and need is low, and then we have another forty to fifty percent where parental education attainment is low and need is high. So, we serve a very diverse population with a lot of different needs, and this complicates our philosophical and operational strategies to make the University of New Mexico students be successful. So, as student loan problems emerged, affordability emerged. Jamie, you and I talked a lot over the years about maintaining affordability, tuition structures that allowed students to take more credits for cheaper prices, guaranteed tuition rates that people could count on. But we also struggled with trying to have reasonable tuition that could support the infrastructure that a research university needs. We had lots of discussions about how do we serve the highest need with the most support, and how are we going to be a great institution with strong programs like athletics and other support that will attract students that want that type of experience as well. So, it's a very complex interaction to try to serve a lot of diverse people.

Jamie: So, regarding our graduation rate. Tell us how you've worked over the years, because you know when we read in the paper about our graduation rate, well you're the one that really needs to be credited. Tell us about how you worked to increase the graduation rate, and also you might mention that when somebody leaves and goes to another college, that they may graduate, but we get them as a non-graduate.

Terry: Sure. I think when you came onto the Board, the six year graduation rate was in the low forty percent range, so less than half the students were graduating in six years. That's a very hard number to move because there are many factors affecting student success: their intentions, the affordability, their academic performance and their preparation in high school. Again, in many instances these days, immigration status can be a factor. English as a second language, and other remedial needs can impact the length of time required. You just can go on and on.

Jamie: So the forty percent range was in two thousand three? Right?

Terry: Yes, it was probably a little bit lower, and you know we had lofty goals; we needed a lot of support from areas on campus. The board had to drive a lot of decisions that helped move that number, and this year we're at fifty percent. We went up ten percentage points, which doesn't seem large, but it's probably the largest increase in the country among our peer groups on the six year rate. And the same thing with the four year graduation rate. We've emphasized the four year graduation rate more as you were leaving the Board. We want people to complete in four years. We kind of got away from that because we gave people credit for doing other activities, and even a chance to work. We have a large population of our students that work.

Terry: So, ten percentage point gains and graduation rates over that time period, is a pretty substantial movement. It's not just from one initiative or one group—it takes the Board agreeing that was the metric that we wanted to measure.

Jamie: Well you know, Terry, that's actually an interesting story because you and I both worked out the details to incentivize students to graduate in four years. However, the last time I was on the Board, the governor's staff knew that I was trying to ensure we had incentives for people to graduate in four years and keep the tuition rate from increasing. So, I knew the messenger would be very important for the success of this proposed initiative. For a variety of reasons, and their initials are "politics in New Mexico," I knew I would not be the right messenger. Rob Doughty, to his credit, agreed to present our plan. The governor's office signed off on the plan. This was a situation, similar to others in my career, where I wanted to see the outcome and I didn't care about who got the credit. You, Terry, are the same way.

Terry: We have a lot in common. I will never forget all the times you talked about dyslexia, and I am not sure if you know that dyslexia impacts my family as well, so a lot of us resonate with that. Our goal in making better preparation has to be, "how do we," "how can we" improve their chances entering the university by requiring more preparation? But, we also do not want to exclude students who we should be serving. It's a fine balance. You'll find people in the state who think every student in New Mexico should be able to come to the University of New Mexico and flunk out, borrow money, if they owe it back, and have their credit ruined for the rest of their life. But, we have a bigger responsibility of stewardship to try to help students prepare, and to admit the students who we think can be successful. And that's what we've really balanced over those years with some enhanced preparation for students. We increased support programs; we also increased financial aid for students with need. There's a litany of things that had to fall into place: cooperation, leadership from the Board, many different entities on campus and a strategic idea of how to get there. So that's probably one of the biggest accomplishments over that period is to actually improve the completion rates for students who begin at the University of New Mexico. The lottery success scholarship was an instrumental aspect of all of this. When I came to the University of New Mexico, we were really down in the dumps in enrollment. In nineteen ninety-six, our freshman class was sixteen hundred students. Then the lottery came in. We changed some practices and nowadays we're double that number of freshman—over thirty-three hundred. A lot of that's attributable to the lottery. I give the state and the legislature a lot of credit. The lottery allowed resident students to get tuition essentially four and a half years, and that made a big difference. Our migration rates from New Mexico used to be twenty-three, twenty-four percent, meaning "out migration," meaning about twenty-three percent of our high school seniors would leave the state, and now it's twelve or thirteen percent. So, in this book you are giving credit to others, and I'm giving credit to the state and the legislature for implementing a program that really helped a lot of our students succeed. It's timely because it's in jeopardy again this legislative session.

Jamie: Go over the guaranteed four year level tuition.

Terry: Sure. The guaranteed tuition model started to emerge probably in twenty ten or so and we started talking about it. You had asked about it, and we ran several models during those times. We modeled where like if you had a five percent tuition increase as you came in as a freshman, then that was locked. That rate is guaranteed for four to six years. We ran various models: four, five and six years. But, in essence, you know as long as people made progress then, and did the things they needed to do, then their tuition rate wouldn't change. So we surveyed the parents. They liked it conceptually and we really went through probably a couple of years of modeling different things and the Board talking about different things back and forth. Finally after you made the deal and asked Rob Doughty to present, we had a concept where we could guarantee a tuition number, along with an incentive to graduate in four years. The incentive was that you got your last semester's tuition paid for. That's the ultimate model that ended up going out there.

We'll have our first recipients of that this spring. It was an effective incentive for drawing students. It really helped our new student enrollment. We promoted it and the first year that we really pushed that out to new freshman, beginning students in particular, we had a six percent increase. So it's about a two hundred freshman increase that we give a lot of credit to that program for achieving. Then we had another increase last year. So, two years of increases since the incentive was rolled out and you know new students are the heart of our long-term enrollment. I think that was another big step—an innovation that we had, that you participated in, that was instrumental. You were able to pull the right levers at the right time to make that happen, because we had tried unsuccessfully to get a few models out prior to that for almost every year.

Jamie: You have talked about graduation rates and what we have done in that area. Can you talk about recruitment?

Terry: Yes, we have utilized a systematic approach, as many people might know that work on the inside, but I don't think it's that obvious on the outside. I'll tie it to the branding. I mean our big challenge at the University of New Mexico has recently been, and the whole state of New Mexico, is that we are a relatively small state, two million people. But we have approximately thirty-two higher education institutions or campuses, and our demographic is shrinking. So, you combine those factors and we have enrollment challenges. We can't just make it. We're a large university for the size of our state. People talk about the Arizona State University's massive enrollment, sixty thousand and all that, per capita for our population; we're bigger than them. So, our population compared, our enrollment compared to our state population is actually bigger. But that's because we have a lot of adult students. We have commuter students. We have online students. We have traditional eighteen-year-old students. Our freshman are eighteen point three years old, all thirty-three hundred of them. So we have a mix of segments we have to try to serve to meet enrollment.

But, to your point, the demographics and challenges of New Mexico will continue to be that any growth we do have will have to be from populations that generally have a little lower success rate. For our students who speak English as a second language, those populations grow a little bit. They generally might have more need. They might have more preparation challenges, so any growth we do have in New Mexico is projected to be from those areas. From an enrollment standpoint, we have to try to be broader than New Mexico in meeting our targets. That means we have to get out-of-state students. We have to be really good at international enrollment, which we historically have not been that strong at. We systematically identify prospects in really highly targeted states. Jamie, you and I talked about this a lot of times. It is states you would expect, like Colorado, Arizona, Texas, and within the last six or seven years, California has emerged to be our top feeder state from out-of-state.

Jamie: Another issue is our online learning. Explain where you are on that.

Terry: Our big enrollment challenge at the University of New Mexico hasn't been in, even despite some of those challenges, it's not usually not in beginning freshman or your traditional eighteen-year-old class that we make. We have, our challenge is to bring in nine to ten thousand new students every year, because we graduate about five thousand and there was attrition for another four thousand or so. But ultimately the great recession beginning around two thousand eight really fueled adult and part-time enrollment at the University of New Mexico. Our enrollment grew to record heights. It's very clear in the data from two thousand eight to twenty twelve that enrollment grew. But ultimately, the adult students who came during the recession have been leaving school. So you know the value of education, whether they're moving out of state or some of them going back to work, since twenty twelve there's contraction in enrollment. So, from record enrollment we've gone down, still better than pre-recession numbers, but mostly adult part-time learners have left our traditional system.

It has been essential for us to try to develop more managed online programs, we call them, where adult learners—they may be in a job, they may not be—they may be trying to advance or just get a new skill. The managed online programs are where they can come in and take online classes in eight week formats instead of sixteen, get class work and be on a track to get another credential. Sometimes it's a certificate. It could be a master's degree, it could be bachelor's degree, but that's what you are referring to about online learning, and that's critical for us if we're going to regain some enrollments or maintain some of those adult kind of nontraditional learners. That's where the market is. That's where profit institutions grew over the years. That's where traditional institutions are kind of reaching their own strengths to get some online segments. We're not going to become an online university, but the Board has been supportive, and you certainly were very vocal that if we don't do more of this online environment, it's a lost segment that eventually we'll lose totally.

So, we have a managed program plan. We have multiple degrees and some engineering areas, business and psychology. Very important ones are due to come on board this spring. We've made progress. We have an RN to BSN program that you approved where students with an RN license, (they most likely got it at a community college,) associate's degree, can have a path to a bachelor's degree, which is just better management opportunities. It's an advanced opportunity obviously for them and they can do it all online. So, those are some advances we've made and we've still got some work to do there, but I think during the last year to two years you were on the Board, that approved us moving in that direction.

Jamie: Can you talk about how we recruit people?

Terry: Sure, it's a very systematic process. You don't just wait for them to come in. We try to identify prospects, juniors to sophomores in high school who are a good fit for the University of New Mexico and meet our criteria, all around the country. We have analytics programs where we look at our student body. We look at where they're from. We utilize geo-demography which helps identify what students are a good fit for the university from around the country. And then we go and develop prospects by buying ACT names, SAT names, PSAT names, of people who are taking these tests, as early as sophomores, and build these prospect pools. Then we have to apply, just like any marketing customer relationship, management tools that we use—digital marketing, behavioral engagement, where we have communication plans for those students, specifically for segments of where they are.

Like California students who we think are interested in affordability, we're sending different messaging. Based on our comparison group, our competition would be like Arizona State. They can come here for eight thousand dollars cheaper, and so for groups that we think affordability is a question, we'll target messages for that group from California.

We have stiff competition. There are less high school graduates out there than ever before, and we compete heavily with Arizona State, Colorado State, University of Arizona, University of Colorado, Texas Tech, for a lot of these students in these same markets. So it's a very competitive environment.

Jamie: Aren't you sort of the author of all this stuff?

Terry: Yeah, I pretty much guide those strategies.

Jamie: The reason I wanted to interview you, the main reason I wanted you to be in this book, Terry, is we look in the paper and it says, "The University of New Mexico has increased their graduation rate," but in this case, it really is, "Terry Babbitt who has increased the graduation rate." People don't recognize that here we have this system designed, and you can see what the results are. It's not the president and it's not the provost who designed and continues to tweak that system—it's you.

So, as we move forward, as you think about some of the challenges, what do you think is going to be important for the university moving forward?

Terry: I think that at the University of New Mexico internally, we just have to keep some continuity. I've worked with you longer than I've worked with any president or provost. So, you know leadership, vision at one level and the people doing the work. I think that continuity is more important than probably anything. Those people being on the same page is crucial. I think that's why people at my level, which are, you know, high mid-level, (I'm not a top level, but a high level,) do need to remain engaged with Regents. That's where we get a lot of work done and administration should encourage that, I think, and ours luckily has. But, I think we have to stay focused on success at the University of New Mexico. For example, we need to graduate students. We need to graduate them on time. We need to keep our eye on that. Our national perception is only diminished by, really by lower graduation rates.

Our research is great—you know our Health Sciences, certain high profile programs. Engineering is good. We have great things to tout in those

310

areas, but our success internally, moving forward with high graduation, high student success—I think that's the most important thing for us to do internally. That's pretty common for places, but we just have a long way to go because our mission is enviable. We have a forty percent Hispano population. University of Texas, which is a very high Hispano state, they only have twenty percent. So, where we are is where people are going to be and aspire to be in terms of enrollment demographics. We've got to do the hard work and make them be successful. We can't just say, "Oh, we've got all these Hispano students and their parents didn't go to college and they don't have money and that's why they didn't graduate." That's not acceptable. We've got to overcome the obstacles and we've got to graduate people. I think that's the internal main thing. External things obviously impact us, so I would be a fool to ignore it. I've worked at public universities my whole life and it's no different—no better, no worse—about the politics. That's why we're a public institution. We're accountable to the public.

I hope that state leaders will value the impact of the University of New Mexico. They'll have to start making hard decisions about these thirty-two campuses around the state in terms of who can get funded and who can't. New Mexico just can't fund all the public school stuff they try to and thirty-two college campuses. I know it's hard. I think that the value of the University of New Mexico as a flagship institution and Health Sciences as a landmark research institution and provider of patient care has to be valued at a higher level than it is.

We have talked a lot in this book about what it means for the University of New Mexico to be the flagship university for the state. A lot of responsibility rests with the deans and department chairs to ensure that the quality of the education we are providing meets the high standard that being a flagship institution implies. In a subsequent chapter I spend time with folks from the Health Sciences that will discuss the critical medical research that the University of New Mexico provides that has been recognized nationally. On the main campus, one of the "jewels in the crown" is the University's School of Engineering and Computing. We have some very distinguished faculty in this school and the dean, Joe Cecchi, PhD, has brought a tremendous amount of expertise and leadership to the department. His own quest to keep challenging himself by going through the Executive MBA program is a testament to his indomitable spirit. He is the best kind of leader because his colleagues and students are not asked to push themselves any harder than he pushes himself. Having said that, he pushes himself pretty hard! Joe will discuss how the MBA helped him understand the best management of resources and why it was so relevant for him to be a successful dean to learn business skills and not solely focus on the academic mission, but also the most cost effective way to realize that vision. On January 15th, 2017 I sat down with Joe to discuss his many years of teaching and leadership at the university.

∾∾∾

Joe Cecchi, PhD, dean of School of Engineering and Computing / Interviewed January 15, 2017

Joe: I was born in Chicago, Illinois in the first half of the last century. I was born not long after World War II, which is significant because the Manhattan Project has had a lot to do with my career. But I was born in time for Sputnik and I went to high school in the aftermath of Sputnik. In those days, the schools had ramped up on their teaching of math and science and I benefited from that, and so those are pivotal events in my youth that really set me on a course to study physics and engineering and really have led to the career that I've had. I was the first in my family to go to college. I went to a small liberal arts college in Illinois—Knox College. I majored in physics. It was a good place, because I had a broad education and later in my career, that came in handy because it was more about managing people than doing technology. I went off to Harvard to get my PhD in physics. The professor I worked with won the Nobel Prize. Probably six other professors I had there at Harvard were Nobel laureates or would become so at some time. So, it was a very exciting place, and I joined the faculty at Princeton University. I began doing research in the energy field and I was there for twenty-one years. And a friend of mine from the University of New Mexico, Steve Brueck, called me up and told me there was a position open as the chair of Chemical and Nuclear Engineering. I applied for that position and was fortunate enough to be selected, and so in January of nineteen ninety-four, I came to the University of New Mexico as professor of chemical engineering and as the department chair for that department.

Jamie: And when you came in nineteen ninety-four, the Regents were not an open book, were they?

Joe: No.

Jamie: How were they structured then?

Joe: You know as department chair, I don't think I ever went to the Regent meetings. It just wasn't something department chairs did. I only started going when I became dean in two thousand. Bill Gordon was the university president and Larry Willard was the president of the Regents. It was very different. It was a small meeting. They didn't meet very often. I think it was under your leadership that we went to a monthly meeting, which is what we still do. Back then it was maybe every two months and maybe not even every two months. I don't recall there were the committees.

Jamie: And Larry was in charge of the finance committee. He did have a finance committee.

Joe: That's right. That's right. I never attended any of those meetings. So, it was really quite different at that time. As I said, I don't, it was not the norm for department chairs to go to Regents' meetings at that time. In fact, all the people wouldn't have fit in the room if everybody that goes today went then. So, clearly there were fewer people attending the meeting.

I was department chair for the next six years and our provost at the time, Paul Fleury, a very well-known person was lured away by Yale. I always thought it was good that the University of New Mexico could be Yale's farm club. The provost appointed me interim dean in two thousand and then had a national search, in which I was selected to be the dean in early two thousand one. I will skip ahead to when we met I think at this point, because we met in two thousand three. I was a member of the presidential search committee at that time, and you had just come onboard in January of that year, if I recall correctly, and you joined the search committee along with Regent Eaves, and Regent Maria Griego-Raby, the three of you were the Regents on the search committee.

My first close encounters with you were in those committee meetings and also in the interviews because you sat with the deans when we interviewed the candidates. But when you became president of the Board in two thousand four, you immediately brought to the Board a process that was much more inclusive. You recognized that the business of the Regents is important to everybody at the University of New Mexico, and that everyone, a lot of people, should participate and understand the governance. I think it was a much more open governance and inclusive of many more people, and so, that began the style of the Regents meetings that we have now in a much larger room because it was attended by many more people. Also, you instituted the protocol of doing the detailed business through committees and then coming forward with suggestions from the committees at the open sessions of the Regents, and that's still the way it is today. I attend every Regents meeting and most committee meetings, at least the committee meetings of academics, student affairs and research and finance and facilities, because of course, what goes on in those committees and the subsequent Regents meetings is very important to the School of Engineering.

So I was dean. I was in my ninth year as dean and we did have some instability at the top, and one of the consequences was that the president hired a provost with whom I did not see eye to eye, and I agreed to step down. I think that provost wanted me to step down a little sooner than I thought was appropriate. I wanted to serve out my term and I think I got your backing to do that, and even the president at the time and a few other people who convinced the provost that we should have a transition at that point. But I've always been grateful for the support you gave me at that time, and it was a good time to step down. Nine years is a long time as dean and we'd gotten a lot done. We had built the Centennial Engineering Center with a great deal of support from the University of New Mexico, both in terms of funding from the state and from GO bonds and Severance Tax bonds. But also, that was the first time at least in a long time, and that was through I think the leadership of Vice President Harris, that the University of New Mexico sold a bond in order to build buildings. He recognized the need and I think you were with him every step of the way.

Jamie: We did not think that the money would come in one session. Might get five million the next, and then when Harris came on, we went the bond route. One of the first buildings we built was Engineering.

Joe: And also, the Cancer Center came out of that bond and a few other things, and I think to recognize we had the capacity and therefore didn't have to be dependent solely on the state money was really a major step forward. This campus looks totally different than it would have if that didn't happen. But I do remember that it took the leadership of the Regents as well, because the bond agencies wanted to see that the University of New Mexico leadership goes all the way up to the top, and I know that all of you stood behind David in those proposals and the result is we've got a lot of buildings today and we've continued to do that. That was an exciting thing. It took six years to get the money for that building, but without the bond, we'd been looking at just building half of it and then coming along years later and building the second half. That bond enabled us to build the entirety of Centennial Engineering Center, and it is today the largest building on main campus, and it's a phenomenal facility that really wouldn't be there without your leadership, Jamie, because you were president of the Regents. That building was completed in two thousand eight.

We moved in. I got to live in there for a year. I was happy and of course, all of us even when we would become chairs or deans are still faculty members, and I was really happy to go back to the faculty in two thousand nine. Do more teaching, getting more research done. Hard to do those things when you have responsibility of being dean, and I did a few other things in that time. I actually decided to get an MBA and went to Anderson in their Executive MBA program and got my MBA so that I could learn all the mistakes I made when I was dean, and then, as you know, I took a year off to go to Abu Dhabi and work in a new university in Abu Dhabi. I spent a year there helping them ramp up. It was partnered with MIT and we got a lot of interesting things done. But a year turned out to be enough. We have a lot of family here and my wife, Amy Wohlert, came along also. She also worked for the university so we did this experience together, but we agreed a year was enough. I came back in twenty twelve just when President Frank was starting his term.

Jamie: What year did you get your MBA from Anderson?

Joe: My MBA was in twenty eleven. My bachelor's degree was in nineteen sixty-eight and my PhD was in nineteen seventy-two.

Jamie: How long did it take you to get the MBA?

Joe: It was a two year program with three summers. It's the full MBA degree. It's not a watered down degree. It's the full MBA, but it's in a cohort and it's very interesting because it's filled with people in their careers. We go through as a cohort and I've got close friends from that experience that I still have. I think they did a great job so I'm a real fan of that program. I'm very happy I did it.

In early twenty fourteen, the then dean of engineering was not getting along with provost Abdallah. I think there was just something, a little stress between them, and provost Abdallah decided to make a change. In February of twenty fourteen, he asked me to come back to be the dean again, and I did that in addition to my role of managing work for the National Labs.

But I said that I didn't want to do that [the dean position] forever. I would do it long enough to position us for a very good national search for a new dean. In fact, we just completed that search and we have four great candidates that the provost is trying to decide on. I will step down the thirtieth of June as dean. There were two deans in between my two terms and the transition just wasn't managed very well. This time, I took the position specifically to help Chaouki manage the transition and I think we will have a very smooth, seamless transition in terms of that. I will have served twelve years as dean. The other I think notable event was after many years of service to the Board, you stepped down. Then Governor Martinez re-appointed you back to the Board and it was my privilege actually to go to the hearing on your confirmation and testify on your behalf that as Regent. I think it was clear that you always had the interest of the university first. In fact, you had transformed the process under which the Regents operate to really ensure that there was participation by all parts of the university. The faculty, the staff, student governments, and both undergraduate and graduate, and of course, all the administrators thought you were an exceptional steward, especially as president of the Regents, and indeed the committee confirmed your re-appointment.

You served for another year after that and we were very glad to have your wisdom back. You were chair of F and F, of Finance and Facilities at the time, and one of the things that we brought forward to you was the issue of differential undergraduate tuition. Our expenses are much greater. You know, we were the only professional school not to have differential tuition. Our salaries are higher, our costs are higher and I think that you and the committee understood that. There was some reluctance generally in Regents to approve any kind of tuition hike. I made the case at the Regents meeting and you allowed me to bring, had students come forward and speak, and I'm very pleased that it actually passed the full Board unanimously: seven to zero. The adoption of our proposal has been very important funding in these tough times because that has helped us stabilize things. So I'm really grateful for that.

Jamie: The one thing is that with you, remember when I came on the Board of Regents, I met with the deans for lunch a number of times?

Joe: Yes, you did.

Jamie: And I remember I asked you about that and nobody had done that in the past. In fact, some individuals were critical of me for meeting with the deans. I always remember how cordial you were. You are the only dean I've had a relationship with for thirteen years.

Joe: Well, the fact that you wanted to spend time with us meant a lot to me, and I think you did that because you cared. You wanted to understand what we did as deans and you wanted to build a relationship with the faculty and staff.

Jamie: What do you see in the future with the university?

Joe: Well you know, like all state universities the financial challenges are important. Chaouki and I are reading a book called *Re-engineering University* by an economist who was actually a professor at Stanford and then he took on, he actually was a vice-provost at one time I think. But he eventually took on David Harris' job. He took on the actual management of administration and finance. It's a very quantitative book about how to restructure university budgets so that universities can succeed, and how to contain costs and so forth and so on. I think that this is the only way forward for us to understand better how we can do more with less. The biggest point in there, which is going to be a challenging conversation with faculty, is to kind of change the way faculty teaching is handled and so forth. I won't go into details but I think, both the provost and I think, that the ideas contained in this book are well worth looking at and trying—and again, it's quantitative.

You can measure the output and adjust things so it's not just taking a flyer and trying something. But he approaches it as an economist and I think it makes a lot of sense. It isn't about turning us into a trade school. A central point of this is that we have two missions. One is to graduate our students and give them the right education. But the second is to be an institution that has a set of values that make society a better place, and this is what is unique about universities. We have to find ways to fund both of those. He's got some very good points. I think the future is going to be best for those universities that are able to look hard at what the challenges are and the changes to be made and make them, and I think Chaouki has been that way throughout his time as provost and that's resulted in greater retention, in higher graduation rates. I know that he would like to continue and I think that's promising. A lot of it is going to depend on what happens to the economy of New Mexico and we all hope that that improves when the price of oil and gas increases.

Jamie: I just want to jump back 'cause I am interested in something you said. You indicated this time you felt that you really could have a seamless transition to the new dean, that you didn't have the first time around. Can you talk about that? It is an important moment in the university's history, and let's face it—there is a tremendous upheaval going on. What, in your eyes, would make for a seamless transition? And that could be, 'cause you're a numbers guy, that could be a longer time frame for the transition. You know, maybe a compressed time frame isn't the right thing right now. Maybe, I mean I'm just asking because you bring a lot to the table and I'd like to get...

Joe: Let me give you my perspective on what could have been handled differently from, the past two transitions. As I already pointed out, the provost at the time in two thousand nine and I did not see eye to eye, and I think that when I stepped down, her goal was to change the direction very much from my direction because I guess she didn't agree with what I was doing. But that's hard to do, because we have limited resources, and not to take advantage of the things that are already there is a mistake. So, there was a pretty rough two years for that interim dean trying to work under her. You know, steer things in a new direction and not really have the resources. Then there was a national search to bring another dean in from the outside. But the provost also hired that dean and again, the person brought in maybe didn't fully understand what he was getting into, and in particular, he never established a relationship with Chaouki, who soon became the new provost. So in both cases, there was no continuity. They were like starting fresh. When I went back in, in twenty fourteen, I restored things as best as I could. I got us back on the track that the faculty wanted to be on, and then, in the search for the new dean, we've looked for people who would understand what we built. We have a lot of strengths and we need a leader to capitalize on that rather than going off on some new tangent...so that's the bottom line answer is to "really, really take advantage of the assets."

Jamie: So in terms of the whole university, not just the School of Engineering, what do you think will be important?

Joe: Build on the strengths that we have so we are ready to face the challenges of the future in a realistic way. As of the first of January, I will have served under six presidents and seven provosts, and continuity is important. You know, we really need to get on a footing where we can all have sustainability. I guess, this is a hard thing. We're in the middle of it and it's kind of hard to see how it's going to come out. But certainly the appointment of Chaouki as interim president will help a great deal for the continuity. He's a great provost and he will be a great president. I think it really comes back to knowing what your strengths are and building on those things. Getting everyone to agree about what the strengths are and then working together to really leverage those assets.

You can see why I wanted to include a conversation with Joe Cecchi. He and I share a lot of the same ideas about what it takes to lead an institution. I also appreciate that he, like me, served in a leadership role, went away but never burned bridges, and was able to come back and guide the department again when things had gotten on shaky ground. I have talked about my belief that it is just essential not to burn bridges. But the saying, "Careful not to burn bridges, you just might need to cross back..." is really true. Joe mentioned that I served on the Board of Regents and then later was re-appointed to serve on the Board a second time. I have been a public servant for approximately 60 years. So I definitely have seen the pendulum swing back and forth in politics. It just doesn't pay to hold grudges. I like to think I am pretty consistent in my view points. However, whatever end of the spectrum you may be on politically, one thing I've always tried to do is maintain civil discourse. I don't believe in shouting matches or profanity-laden tirades. In the past, I have had major disagreements with folks that I have a lot of respect for. I mentioned the faculty "Vote of No Confidence" that occurred when Dr. Schmidly was president. One of the principal organizers of that vote was our current interim president, Chaouki Abdallah, who at the time was a department chair. Although, I did not agree with the things that were said about me during that public hearing, I appreciated the tremendous organizing that resulted in a very well run meeting that day. I also appreciated that the provost gave the faculty a forum in which to air their grievances and that was very important for the faculty. I saw that Provost Abdallah was doing his job and he was doing it very well. On December 15th, 2016, I sat down with our interim president to discuss the "Vote of No Confidence" as well as the current search for a new president. You will see in the interview that Chaouki was a little surprised to learn that I pressed very hard for him to be chosen as our interim president. I have included the interview in this book because I wanted to give plenty of in-depth discussion to what was undoubtedly the most challenging time in my career as a public servant. I also wanted to demonstrate that although the interim president and I were on very opposite sides of the fence at that time, we have moved on and we both continue to advocate very passionately for the university. We continue to respect each other and have since become much more unified with regards to our ideas about what will be important moving forward.

∾∾∾

Chaouki Abdallah, interim president of the University of New Mexico, past provost, the University of New Mexico / Interviewed December 15, 2016

Chaouki: I was born in Lebanon in nineteen fifty-nine. I come from a family of eight—five boys and three girls. Actually, neither one of my parents finished elementary school, but my mother had always wanted us to study and to go to college. She instilled in us, from a very early age, the importance of education. I remember discussions when I was five or six, when she was talking to me about college and that if I didn't do well in school, she'd sit me down and explain to me the importance of education. All eight siblings graduated from college. I have three brothers, who are engineers, one sister who's an architect, one sister who's a pharmacist, and one brother who's an MD. My father was a stonemason. I was doing very well in Lebanon and having a great time until nineteen seventy-five when I was around sixteen when the war started. It started as little skirmishes that were kind of close to where I lived in Beirut. Then it got worse and worse. Eventually we stopped going to school and I went back to the village where my parents lived. I come from a very small village, three hundred people. Everybody knows everybody and everybody gets into everybody's business. So, I went there and finished high school close to my village, and then I started the university. There was a lull in the war, and I finished my first year and then the war started again in my second year so I couldn't finish it. We could no longer go to college.

I had relatives in the U.S. My father's aunt and his uncle came a long time ago to the states and they went to work in the steel mills in Pennsylvania.

So, that's all we knew—I mean we didn't know anyone else and we had no other contacts. My great aunt was the only surviving relative. And my great aunt suggested to my older brother and me that the school close to them in Youngstown, Ohio, was a really good engineering school, because we were both in engineering school. So in nineteen seventy-nine we both came to the States.

Anyway, I already had one year of college, but since my parents were paying for my education, I knew I had to finish quickly, so I finished in two and a half years. I went back home to Lebanon because I wanted to help them. It didn't work out as the war was still raging, and so I came back again. This time I went to Georgia Tech, which is a very good engineering school. Youngstown was excellent for what I needed at the time and I did my Master's at Georgia Tech and I caught the attention of the person who became my advisor, since I did well in his class. He offered me a scholarship, which was a lifesaver because they were borrowing the money to send me. My brother finished a year after I did and he went to graduate school too, but we were still unable to go home because the war was raging. My parents had six other kids to put through school. My parents would borrow money for our education, and everyone in the village would send me money, basically, because of my mother. Everybody would tell my mother, "We know you need money for your son's education."

So I finished my Master's and went to work in Florida. I worked two years in Florida, at a company, but I really wanted to go back and get my PhD so that I can teach. I wanted to be a professor. So, I went back to get my PhD. It took me about three and a half years after that and I met my wife during that time.

Jamie: Where did you get the PhD?

Chaouki: Georgia Tech, I went back to Georgia Tech and I got it. The University of New Mexico was my first academic job and I was attracted here by a person named Peter Dorato. I don't know if you knew Peter. He was on the faculty, and he was an outspoken person, but he was a really smart guy and a really, really nice person. He took me under his wing academically and made sure that I was introduced to the right people in academia and research. He helped me a lot with that. He was my mentor here. I have had some incredibly supportive people besides my parents, who have been just amazing. I've had three people who left their mark on me. I would say it was my high school teacher, who really taught me the beauty of math and science because before that I was a lot less interested in science. He took me on and helped me. I wasn't that great a student, and he saw something in me and he spent a lot of his own time working with me. The second person who was very influential was my Georgia Tech advisor who's been an amazing friend and colleague, and then lastly, my third mentor was Peter Dorato here at the University of New Mexico. These are the people who helped me the most in my professional career.

Anyway, I came here in nineteen eighty-eight. I became an assistant professor, went through the ranks, became an associate, then full professor. I married in nineteen ninety. My wife, Catherine and I dated long distance—we got engaged in nineteen eighty-eight and then we married two years later. She graduated on a Friday and we married the Sunday after on July fourteenth, nineteen ninety. She then came with me to Albuquerque and we've had a wonderful life ever since.

I went one year to Tennessee during that period, then came back to the University of New Mexico. I became the associate chair for Graduate Affairs in my department. The Electrical and Computer Engineering is the largest department on main campus, probably the largest in terms of funding and graduate students. The department does very well because of its faculty and staff. There are a lot of good people there, and after I became associate chair, I became the chair of that department and then that's when my troubles started around two thousand five when I became the chair of the department. I was happy being a chair for the first five years, and then I was renewed for the next five years and I was starting to get antsy. I wanted to go back on the faculty at the time. And it was a good time to make a change, because we were hiring a new dean of engineering and that's the time when the previous provost at the University of New Mexico took a job elsewhere. So, I was nominated for the provost position, an interim provost position, and things moved very quickly. It's a fog right now, but I remember I got a message like on Friday—"You're nominated to the interim provost position." It was my choice to apply or not, so I talked it over with my wife and she said, "Go for it! What do have to lose?" And I talked to some other people I trusted and they all said, "You should do it." I thought to myself, "I'm not a dean." And they said, "Oh what do you have to lose, do it." So, I applied like on Monday, and very quickly, maybe Wednesday or Friday I found out I was a finalist.

Jamie: Who appointed you as a finalist?

Chaouki: Who appointed me? I don't know. The search committee, I think. I don't know, I mean all I knew at the time was that I got an email saying,

"Congratulations, you've been nominated." Maybe I should go back and look. Then, as a finalist, the message came also from some group, some search committee member, "Now you're a finalist," so prepare a talk or something. So, then I did the talk and the interviews. And then within a few days after that I was told to meet with the president. I got a call from the president's office that said...

Jamie: Who was the president?

Chaouki: Schmidly, David Schmidly, the message was that he wanted to see me at nine o'clock Monday morning. I remember this part distinctly because I'm like "Okay, I don't know what that means, I got it or I didn't get it," but either way I was going to step down and go back on the faculty because I was getting tired of being chair and I didn't want to do that any more.

Jamie: So, David called you for provost, right?

Chaouki: Say what?

Jamie: David was calling you for provost, is that correct?

Chaouki: David? Yeah, yeah, yeah, he's the one. So, he called me in to tell me "Congratulations. I want you to be the interim provost." It was an interim position. He was in his last year, approximately July, of his last year as president. And I think the search had started for the regular position, I mean for the next president. So, I said, "Okay, great." I told him what I thought about the role and he told me what he thought. I didn't know him that well. I mean obviously, I had very little interaction with the president at the time. I had interviewed with David Harris and with David Schmidly and with Paul Roth, as well as with the faculty.

Anyway, I became interim provost and I went to Google what a provost does, because I didn't know what the hell a provost does. Then I called my friends at other institutions, and I asked them, "Tell me if your provost is doing a good job." And some told me "No, you know I hate her" or "He's not good," and some told me, "Yeah she's great." So, I picked three of those names and I was able to talk to, to visit or spend time with a couple of them. I went and visited one and the other one I had a three hour talk with, to see what is it that they do, and how do they do it. I learned a lot more from that than almost anything else. And that's what I'm going to do now. I'm going to talk to other presidents and see about the job. I mean I sat down with the previous University of New Mexico provost and I also went around and talked to people around campus. You also invited me to Santa Fe. I went and saw you and Gene Gallegos in Santa Fe. I talked to a lot of people to try to get the lay of the land, but really, frankly, I didn't know the scope of the job at all. I don't think people are trained for these positions, just like I don't think I am ready right now to be an acting president, but I figured I can learn it.

Jamie: Let me put a little in here. When I met you, you don't know this, but David Schmidly does, when I met you, I was impressed by your firmness. No bullshit, (excuse the language) whatever. So, I had recommended to David that they make you provost.

Chaouki: I did not know that.

Jamie: And in fact I told David that I've seen a lot of provosts, most of them I didn't think had the backbone or the personality to be a provost. And what you don't know is when we hired Bob Frank as president, the first person I talked to Frank about was you. I said, "You need to keep Chaouki, keep Chaouki," I said. "Chaouki has done more to settle down the faculty than we've had before." So, I guess you didn't know that?

Chaouki: No, I did not, I mean you know I suspected.

Jamie: I didn't tell people that.

Chaouki: But I suspected if the Regents did not want it to happen, it wouldn't have happened. I suspected that much. To me, each one of these positions that I have held is the one I needed to do a good job at, so I'm not looking for the next one. I was satisfied, like I said, being a chair and planned to step down. As you know when I was a provost for the first six months or whatever, I wasn't planning that I would be in that role forever. I thought that the new president is going to come in and replace me. I'll do whatever I can in the meantime. I think you're right—the faculty is still very important. I still have a rapport with the faculty. I still meet with small groups of the faculty and I will continue to do that as acting president.

I think when you get into these positions you lose touch with some things. You see the forest, you don't see the trees, and everybody is seeing their own tree, their own problems. So, I hope I didn't disappoint in the last six years. I had my first meeting with Bob Frank in the president's house because I hadn't met him before. [I wasn't there during his interview.] I told him basically, "Look, I don't know if we can work together. You seem to have a style. I have a style. You know you said a few things in public that I saw, which I don't agree with."

Jamie: That goes back to why I liked you right from the beginning very much, not because of what happened with Schmidly and the vote of no-confidence, but at that time I saw that you are a man of your principles. I thought that would be helpful because the provost has to be that kind of a strong person. You have to really be able to have the faculty supporting you, because if the faculty doesn't support you, you've got problems.

Chaouki: You're right, you're absolutely right. If the faculty doesn't support you, even if you have the support of the president and the Regents, you have a problem. On the other hand, at times you have to push back on the faculty. I mean I see the provost, or any one of these positions, as a conduit, both up and down. So, I need to translate their concerns. I need to take it in and explain to the president and to the Regents, that these are important issues and we need to address them. If I can address them, I will, but in many cases concerns have to do with resources. We've talked a lot about resources. In other cases I have to tell the faculty, "No, you can't do this. You can't get it." And it's not because it is morally suspect or it's not a good thing to do. It's because there's another side to this.

Anyway, my style is that when I talk with people in private I can be as frank as possible. When I go in public I need to be more diplomatic. I don't like secrets, but I also don't like leaks. I will give you an example. When I was leaving President Schmidly's office that morning that he offered me the interim provost position. I think the meeting lasted from nine to nine-thirty. I was walking back and I was getting ready to call my wife. I had not told her yet that I was offered the position. I got a phone call from the *Albuquerque Journal* asking me what my salary was going to be. I hadn't even talked to *anybody* yet! So that tells you how much, you know things get discussed quickly. They called me and I said, "I don't know, we didn't even discuss it."

Jamie: I wonder how come they called you.

Chaouki: I'm sorry?

Jamie: I wonder how come they called you.

Chaouki: You know, you tell me. You know the *Journal* better than I do. Either, I mean they knew a lot more, and this is, I guess what I'm saying is, I tell people, "If you don't want something to be found out, if you want to keep a secret, don't tell anyone."

Jamie: Well, I'll tell you that Kent is a good, personal friend of mine.

Chaouki: Yeah, I sit down with him a lot these days.

Jamie: And I told Kent about you.

Chaouki: Okay.

Jamie: I told him in great detail about you.

Chaouki: So, that explains that one. [laughs]

Jamie: So, that's something you didn't know.

Chaouki: No, I mean I knew you were friends. I mean he told me multiple times, "You know I talk to Jamie, but I didn't know at the time."

Jamie: Can you just go back because you've addressed the fact that at the time you became provost you really had to talk to people to figure out what a provost does—right? So what does a provost do?

Chaouki: So, a provost is really the chief academic officer. The provost does what the president used to do inside the university before the job got too big for one person to manage. So, the job used to be that of a president; the president was responsible for both inside and outside. Then the job of the president got to be so big on the outside that the academic side, everything that's academic, became the portfolio of this other person, who takes care of the academic programs, the faculty, the students, and the research. The best analogy, which is not mine, but I like to use it, is that the provost is like an orchestra conductor. The colleges within the university are so different. You've got the music department in the College of Fine Arts, you've got the school of law, and you've got the school of engineering. You know our engineering faculty here are closer to engineering faculty at New Mexico State or at Colorado State, or at UT Austin, or at MIT, than they are to a philosophy professor here. The departments are so different. The way we measure them is different. The way they evaluate each other is different. The way they teach is different. Everything is different. So, you've got these different parts: think of them as the string part, the wind part of the orchestra, the piano, and everything else, and you have to make them work and sound good together. Sometimes one college is giving more, and others are taking. If you look at the budget, at the contributions of different colleges, some give, some take, but everybody ultimately gives to the state and to the students. And the provost is the conductor, and if I had to say what a successful provost is, it's someone who can knock down the walls between all of them, produce resources by working with finance folks and with the Board and with the president. The provost gets the needed resources and makes sure that they are advocating always for the academic mission.

Jamie: So, how did you meet me?

Chaouki: I had heard your name multiple times. I had heard of the Regents and I thought the Regents were people in robes. I mean frankly, I was minding my own business. I met you probably around two thousand seven or eight.

Jamie: Two thousand eight.

Chaouki: Two thousand eight? Yeah, so there was some tightening of the belt at the university. I had an assistant, a department administrator, who was a middle-aged single woman who worked so hard. She was an incredible worker and she came to me one time crying. She told me that she went to the University of Phoenix to get her MBA and she owed more money at the time than when she finished. She owed so much money, I forgot, thirty thousand, fifty thousand and she was making you know around thirty-five thousand. And I felt really bad. I mean she was working really hard and was amazing to begin with. So, I went and requested a raise for her, because at the time there was a hiring freeze or something. I requested, I forget, three, five thousand extra per year, which we had in our budget, and it was denied. I was really upset about that and during that time, it came out that David Schmidly's son was being considered for a position at the University of New Mexico. It also came out David Harris got a bonus. And there was a group of faculty at the time that was really upset with these actions.

Jamie: Also Schmidly had changed the administrator's titles all to vice presidents.

Chaouki: Right, that was right before then. So there was a lot of unhappiness at the University of New Mexico.

Jamie: We didn't know what that really meant, so a vice president, obviously a vice president did get a nice income, salary. But with that salary came heightened expectations.

Chaouki: So, the folks on the ground, or on the front line, were not, were not being talked to. To me it was personal with our department administrator, but there were a lot of issues around that time. We were told that we didn't have money, we didn't have money, and then these things came out. At the time, there was a group of faculty that was meeting, and one of my faculty colleagues would go to their meetings, and sometimes he would tell me what they discussed. But I really had no idea what it was. I learned later that this was a group that was led by Rich Wood. I don't think he was the faculty senate president, or maybe it was during that time, I'm not sure.

Anyway, one time I was invited to go to one of those meetings. I went and I listened and thought they were right. They were complaining about how we needed to make a fundamental change and how the administration was not listening and how the Regents are out of touch. I started learning more about it, and I went to a few more meetings. And I think now, looking back at it, I was one of the few engineers. I was not the only department chair, but I think I was one of the few engineers. There were very strong groups on one side who wanted to burn down Scholes Hall and some who wanted to go to the governor. There were others who were trying to work things out. At the end we settled on a course of action. I think they came to Schmidly. I wasn't part of the delegation. I think they came to him with some requests. All I know is that eventually we had organized a vote and I was part of the people organizing. I was also asked if I would speak at the public meeting. We debated a lot, back and forth on what to do, who should be speaking, and so on. And you know there were people who wanted everybody to speak and there were people who said we shouldn't do anything, or that we should work it behind the scenes. Eventually, I think Rich was very skillful, he was able to convince us to control the message into something that would be strong, but not disastrous. Rich was, as I understand now, still talking to people behind the scene. He was talking to Schmidly, but I don't know if he was talking to you or the Regents. Rich would come in and try to explain to the group what we can ask or not ask for. Some people wanted the president to be fired while others wanted the university budget to be divided a particular way. There were a lot of ideas like that. Anyway, we organized the no-confidence vote and it was a spring afternoon that we went to this large meeting. I spoke at it and then we took the no confidence vote.

Jamie: How about eight hundred thirty-three votes? I got the most of anybody, I'm proud of that.

Chaouki: No, it was like five hundred.

Jamie: No, eight hundred thirty-three.

Chaouki: Seriously? I don't know, I don't remember. Okay, it was a lot.

Jamie: Well, let me fill in just briefly. I've never been to a function that was so well organized. I was very impressed. I was chairman of the Democratic Party and I've never, ever seen something that was done so well. They had organized it in such a manner that everybody had a certain amount of time to speak. They told me I couldn't speak, and then everybody had so much time to speak. People were told to raise their card. It was beautiful. I was sitting next to Raymond Sanchez and I said, "You know Raymond, I'd vote against me now."

Chaouki: I had never met you at that time, but you were the president of the Board and the Board was very, very disliked. People believed that the Regents were controlling everything, and frankly, there were rumors, or discussions, that the governor at the time, Bill Richardson, was putting his people in and they're controlling the university. By the way, that was the mood across the United States, that the universities are becoming more like corporations. They're becoming companies like, and they're hiring these upper level people to manage us. Now, having been on this side, I understand why you need people with certain kinds of skills. The university is like a city right now. It's not what people think of the university. The university has businesses. It's a hospital; it's athletics; it's police; it's a lot of parts that need other parts.

I do feel that the gap between the lowest-paid employees and the highest-paid employees has widened so much. It used to be three to one or maybe five to one. Now we have people at the University of New Mexico who make maybe thirty thousand and we have the highest paid employees, making more than three hundred thousand, so that's ten times. Now, is it justified? I think that the market demands it. As an example, to hire faculty in engineering or business I have to pay more than we pay somebody in history. That's what the market is; that's what I tell people. It's our modern society that values things differently. My wife is an engineering consultant, and she charges a lot of money compared to a policeman who puts his life on the line, or a teacher who educates our children, but that's what the market dictates.

Jamie: In all fairness, our faculty is not paid well in comparison to other universities. I've always said we needed to get caught up. Anyway, tell me about our meeting we had here in this little room.

Chaouki: After the vote of no confidence, Rich Wood came to some of us and said, "The vote is now behind us. We made our point, but now we gotta work together and we gotta pick up the pieces." I give a lot of credit to Rich because after we made our point, he quickly started working to unite the various parties. Rich organized this meeting, and I don't know how we were selected. There were five or six of us and we had a meeting with Schmidly separately, and then we had a meeting in here, in the board room. It was David Harris, you, and I think it was David Schmidly too. Everyone spoke and I think Rich tried to set the stage for the meeting. You spoke and other people spoke, and then it got a little bit heated. Maggie Washburne said, "You know I've been here a long time. I'm from here, and for the sake of New Mexico and the University of New Mexico, you and David Harris ought to resign," or something to that effect. Now, I was accused of saying that later, and I keep saying I didn't say it, but at the time I agreed with it and I felt that you guys were screwing up. I think I didn't say it, but I agreed with it.

Jamie: No, I can vouch for you that you didn't say it.

Chaouki: Anyway, Harris or you said, (you probably said), "And how many of you aren't from New Mexico? Or something to that effect..."

Jamie: Yeah, I may have said that, but the most important thing I said was, "I'm not gonna resign."

Chaouki: I remember that. "I'm not gonna resign." So, then let's see what happened after that?

Jamie: The eight hundred thirty-three votes against me didn't really bother me since in politics you get used to stuff like this. But what did concern

330

me is that I was president of the Regents, and I didn't feel I should stay as president of the Regents under these circumstances.

Chaouki: Yeah, you became the issue—you and Harris became the issue.

Jamie: Yeah, and so what I did is that I sat down with Bill Richardson and we negotiated who would be president, which would be Raymond Sanchez.

Chaouki: Was Raymond on the board at the time?

Jamie: Uh huh.

Chaouki: Oh, okay.

Jamie: Raymond Sanchez.

Chaouki: I don't remember.

Jamie: I became chairman of Lobo Development, went onto the Finance Committee and the Audit Committee. When I was president, I did not serve on any of the committees. The Regents supported Schmidly completely and we did not get involved in personnel matters.

Chaouki: Yeah, yeah.

Jamie: So when Schmidly was hired, Schmidly said he was going to implement a new system and all that, and we said, "We're gonna support your program, what it is." We didn't question it. We supported it, and that's what we did. Now, tell me more about our relationship.

Chaouki: I don't think we had any encounter or discussions after that day for a long time until after I was selected as provost. I mean I didn't know what happened behind the scenes. I mean you obviously had something to do with my selection, I didn't know. The only thing I knew at the time is that I got a phone call from somebody to tell me I had to meet with David Harris and I said, "Why?" And they said, "Well, he wants to meet you." I asked, "Is he meeting with the other two candidates?" There were two other candidates: Antoinette Sedillo-Lopez and Jim Linnell, who was the dean of Fine Arts at the time. And I thought "Jim was going to be the next provost because he was a dean." I said, "Is he meeting with them?" They said, "No, just you." I said, "Well, I can't, I can't do that. If he meets with all of us, separately with each of us, that would be okay."

Jamie: So, right there you were establishing a culture of fairness, right?

Chaouki: Well, what I was establishing is a culture of not owing something to anybody, because I did not feel like I needed to owe anybody anything. I knew at the time that I'm one of the three finalists. I wondered, "Why are they asking me to do this unless there's some vetting process by David Harris?" Now, the Regents didn't ask to meet with me, but I met with the president at the time. I met with the president, which was appropriate, and each one of the three finalists met with the president. But David Harris was unusual to me when I found out he was not meeting with the others. So then we all met with David Harris and that turned out to be a good thing for all of us. David and I established a good relationship because of that first meeting.

Behind the scenes, obviously they were talking. I believe you and Schmidly and Harris and Paul Roth, and I don't know who else was involved with this. The bottom line is, I was announced as the interim provost, and I think I got a phone call from you shortly thereafter, congratulating me and saying you wanted to meet with me. So, I drove up to Santa Fe and I had lunch with you and Regent Gallegos. We had a very frank heart to heart and I said, "Look, you know I was on the opposite side. I know you have a job to do, and I also have a job to do. I'll be honest with you. I want your support and your help" and you told me a lot of things that I don't recall now. By that time I think you and the other Regents were starting to search for a new president.

Since then, you and I have worked on a lot of issues together, both through the Regents and other items. You would call me and we'd talk about some ideas. We worked on a couple of things like raises for the faculty. You offered multiple times to give your proposals for the faculty pay, and I would come in with something general and then sometimes you would say, "Well I want something a little bit more detailed." But the money for compensation would not materialize either because of the budget situation or other reasons. The first two years as provost, I struggled. I put together a five year proposal. I said, "This is what I would need in order to rebuild the faculty." We were coming out of the recession at that point. The faculty on main campus went down by almost twenty percent at the time. It was a miserable time. When I walked in as interim provost, the math department and the English departments were in bad shape. The math department especially was losing about three people a month. They went down from about thirty to eighteen faculty, and the English department was facing similar challenges.

I made this proposal to the Regents. The Regents supported it very strongly. I wanted twenty additional faculty a year, and I wanted a lot of money put into students. The Board supported it, and for two years they funded it completely, three and a half million above and beyond the base budget. Then the budget started going south. I think the next year they allocated two million and then nothing. Since then we've been cutting our budget. Hopefully we're not spiraling down, but are in a holding pattern.

I worked a lot with you after that, as you know, on many of these issues—sometimes on the same side, sometimes on different sides. You know we had one conversation, I think it was your last year as a Regent where you were thinking about doing something, adding something to athletics, and I said, "This won't go over very well." And you listened and you said, "Okay, I'm gonna listen to you and I'm not gonna do it." I appreciated that. I appreciated and I learned a lot from watching you operate, because you would prepare very well and people would think that you were talking off the cuff, but I don't think you could have remembered all of these things without checking and preparing. Sometimes you would say, "Well when we did this, such and such happened." And somebody would say, "I don't know." And you'd say, "Well, I'll tell you, it was in nineteen eighty-five in the such and such meeting and so on." So, you probably had these things written down someplace.

Jamie: I had, what I do sometimes, I already know the answer but I ask the question and I'd see if I'd get the answer back from somebody in the meeting.

Chaouki: Yeah, but you had too much data, so you probably prepared it, unless your memory is a lot more amazing than mine, because I can't remember what happened in a particular meeting five years ago.

Jamie: Well, the fact is, the strength of the university rests with the faculty. If you don't have a good faculty, your graduates aren't going to be top notch.

Chaouki: Yeah.

Jamie: And our faculty, when you look at the faculty, I've always said it's just like the athletic football coach. Certain faculty should get bonuses or be looked at a little bit differently so you can keep the faculty. Because we had this system that where a faculty member can go somewhere, what's the story on that?

Chaouki: Right, so here's the deal. So, actually in most colleges and schools at the University of New Mexico, most of them, with the exception of the law school that has a different system, there is a merit system and merit pay for the faculty. Meaning, faculty members get evaluated and rewarded every year when there is money. When there isn't money, they still get their evaluation even though they may not get extra compensation.

Jamie: Well, if I'm a faculty member and I got an offer to...

Chaouki: Right, so I was gonna get to that.

Jamie: Okay, go ahead.

Chaouki: Here's what happens. When we hire faculty, we hire at the market and we compete with the top schools in the U.S. When I was a chair, I would conduct my survey of what people are paying for this type of faculty in electrical and computer engineering nationwide and in the southwest, because, as you know the costs are different across the nation. Then, I would look at what UT Austin is paying, what Arizona State is paying, what New Mexico State is paying (we're higher than New Mexico State but we're lower than the others), and I'd take the average starting pay. I then know the dollar amount I need to compete with our peers. I go with that, and we start out in a good place. During their stay here, however, if times are okay, the faculty gets, based on their performance, raises or not. But, here's the catch; after their fifth or sixth year, the faculty members have proven themselves. When they first come in they're a blank slate, and we support them. We do everything to help them grow their professional credentials. But after five or six years we know which ones are going to be stars. We know they're doing great research, they're good teachers, and they are becoming visible, nationally. Well, at this point let's say we hired them as an example in engineering. Let's say for eighty thousand and they're making maybe ninety-five. Well, UT Austin may be looking for some people and our faculty starts popping up on the national scale. You know, if I'm a chair elsewhere with new money, I can hire somebody at eighty or eighty-five thousand, or I can get this faculty from the University of New Mexico who has proven himself or herself, for, they're only making ninety-five. So, what if I give them a hundred thousand or a hundred and ten, because I'm recruiting now for these special ones.

So, this is what we face a lot, is we have the stars—the people who can easily move to another institution, and are being competed for nationwide. I end up as a provost, or as a dean having to provide a counter offer. A dean would come to me as provost, and he would say, "You know the woman who's in the Natural Academy of Science, Patricia Crown? She is being recruited away." Patricia Crown is an amazing person and faculty member. She became a member of the National Academy of Sciences; she's an anthropologist. She became a member of the National Academy of Sciences, which is incredible since it is the highest honor any scientist can have. She's one of only three at our university. We have Art Kaufman in the medical school, a member of the National Academy of Medicine, and we have one in engineering, Professor Jeff Brinker. In the morning, she got the phone call that she got in the National Academy of Sciences, and in the afternoon, Arizona State was calling her. Now, she came to me, she went to her dean, but she didn't ask money for herself. Arizona State was throwing a lot of money at her. She was making like, I don't recall a hundred thousand or maybe a hundred twenty, and they were offering her around a hundred eighty. She didn't ask more money for her; she asked for her department. She said, "I need two more faculty positions in here. I need my lab physical infrastructure to be fixed and so on..." That's the type of faculty we have, and those are the ones I want to keep. So, we moved heaven and earth to try to do that because I didn't want to lose Patricia Crown.

Jamie: Don't you sometimes match what they've been offered?

Chaouki: Sometimes. Most of the time we can't match. Very few times we're able to match. When I was first starting as provost, yes, I was able to match some. I mean, you know it's not unheard of for somebody to be offered a twenty-five or thirty percent raise, so we cannot afford to match.

Jamie: See where I'm coming from, I've been telling you for a long time we need to identify those faculty members and raise their salaries, raise those salaries to be competitive with our competitors.

Chaouki: No, but here's the reason for that. The theory is absolutely correct. The practicality of it is when you don't have raises for everybody for three or four years, when you only get two or three percent, the tendency, even for the faculty being recruited, is to say "Give everybody the same small raise". Since I cannot do large-scale preventive retention, I try to do that on an individual basis. Most of the issues at the University of New Mexico now are morale problems, or campus climate problems. Most everybody understands the money is tight. I have about a hundred fifty to two hundred faculty members who need to be preempted before someone contacts them. Because you know, when people are contacted, they have already made the list of mental things that they want changed. Sometime they're upset and often they have made a decision to leave, and then we don't want somebody to stay just because of the money. I want them to feel appreciated.

I lost three people in the last two years in engineering that I could not match—three, who are really good faculty. You know I wish I had money to match and I could do it. But the fact is if I were to do that, there will be somebody else, or a group of people who are close performance-wise, maybe not in the same league, but they're close. And usually, there's another problem. The men are more aggressive at doing this, so you see more men being retained than women. In general, the men are more aggressive in going and getting offers and coming back asking, "Is the University of New Mexico going to retain me?" So, we end up with this problem that we're having to correct. Also that the woman who's just as good, but she's not as aggressive, is getting external offers from say, UT Austin, then asking to be retained.

Jamie: So, a couple questions: you talk about morale being bad right now. How does it affect faculty when we see such a turnover in presidents? Let's contrast that with Dr. Paul Roth, longest running dean of a medical school in the country?

Chaouki: There's definitely advantages to longevity. I mean our best president was probably Popejoy, and as you know he was here for twenty some years. I don't know how long he was president. Did you know President Popejoy?

Jamie: Yeah, Popejoy was a good friend of my dad, and when I went to Oklahoma State, Popejoy got me to come back here to play football.

Chaouki: Oh, I didn't know that.

Jamie: My grandfather was a Biology Professor at UNM.

Chaouki: Yeah, yeah I knew that.

Jamie: My mother graduated nineteen eighteen, and Popejoy was a good friend of my dad's.

Chaouki: I think there's benefit to longevity. On the other hand, I think after a while, maybe ten years or two terms, is really appropriate. After that, unless circumstances require you to keep somebody, I think the system benefits from rejuvenation. This is nothing personal about Paul. I like Paul a lot. I think he does a great job. I think that after a while in these positions, you don't accumulate friends, because you have to make decisions. You hope that people will respect you when you leave, but every time you make a decision you may lose one person or somebody who the decision did not go in their favor. The job of a university president right now is very difficult, both because the internal pressures, you know the economic pressures, and frankly, the political and external pressures. I mean in public universities, presidents get a lot of requests and pressure from legislators, governors, the public at large, and the newspapers. Everybody is second guessing you or wanting you to do something specific. In a way, that's why I think the job of a university president is more like that of a mayor more than anything else. You have multiple constituencies, and nobody, including you, is aware of the full picture. That's why you need to have the support of your Board, but also the trust of the faculty.

Now, how does that affect me as the provost of the faculty? I'm hoping to go back as provost as long as the next president, you know, wants me to stay on—probably for a few more years and then, you know, retire from the University of New Mexico or go elsewhere. As provost of the faculty at the University of New Mexico, I have built a structure that I hope will survive the people who are in those positions. I have a great team upstairs in the provost's office, but, if one or more of those people were to leave, we're not starting from scratch.

The challenge for us is not that we're getting worse at the University of New Mexico. It's that we're not moving as fast as everybody else. That's where the University of New Mexico needs your consistency and leadership. I wish we'd have a president for two terms or ten years. Someone who will set the trajectory, talk to the Regents, but then the Regents need to also be "noses in and fingers out."

Jamie: That's exactly right.

Chaouki: Noses in, fingers out. You know fingers cannot be in the business of monkeying with everyone's details.

337

Jamie: And also the Regents should be limited to two terms. In other words, I only accepted the one year because of the finances, but we should be only chosen for two terms maximum.

Chaouki: Yeah, yeah, I mean there are a lot of ideas, and you know the faculty, at one time, we talked to Governor Richardson about having an ex-faculty as a Regent.

Jamie: Bill Richardson never did get involved as much as the existing governor. I never remember Bill Richardson calling and dictating us to do anything. But, really the Regents should be two terms maximum, and the average term for a president between five and six years.

In addition to the terms, are there other things that you think are important for us to consider in the future? And this is a particularly great question to ask you now that you're in this interim president role. What do you think is gonna be important for the university moving forward, to grow and prosper?

Chaouki: Let me tell you what I see my role as acting president is, and what I hope I can accomplish in the next six months. I need to focus a lot, inside campus on the climate issues for the next six months. Now, for the longer term, if I were in this position, which I won't be long term, but what I think the University of New Mexico needs to have, and this is probably more of a state issue, is a higher education plan. You know the state of New Mexico actually funds higher education at a very good level—thirteen to fourteen percent of the budget, which is pretty good. The trouble is, the state has never had a coherent higher education plan. We have a lot of different groups, a lot of different universities, a lot of different campuses, a lot of different constituencies who want a piece of the pie. Governor Richardson told us one time, "If I were to give you a dollar, I need to give New Mexico State a dollar, New Mexico Tech a dollar, I need to give Eastern fifty cents, I need to give Western fifty cents, and I don't have that kind of money." Until the state focuses its attention, or its resources, the University of New Mexico as the flagship is gonna have to figure out a way to get resources elsewhere. Now, where is that gonna come from?

What we need is not only a longer term plan for tuition, but also for enrollment. You know, we're not going to get it from the state. Our state is not growing, and in fact we just got the projections recently, which show a dip in the next few years. A dip in the number of high school graduates, the

338

birth rates, and so on. If we don't get a lot of immigrants from other states or from out of the country, we cannot expect growth. Demographically, New Mexico is shrinking, which means that the tax base is shrinking, and the number of high school graduates is shrinking. So, how are we going to produce new resources for higher education? Well, we're gonna have to recruit elsewhere. We're going to teach more online, as we talked about at one time, and I'm proposing to scale it up again. We're going to have to generate revenues outside the traditional sources. Now, if the state again decides in the future, to merge some colleges or campuses and to focus on some institutions and have others play supporting roles or close them, that's a different thing. Frankly, I don't see that happening. I don't see that there's political will and it would probably be very difficult to tell a small town that they're going to need to close their campus, because that's an economic engine for that town.

Jamie: Let me ask you one final question. Health Sciences has nearly a billion dollar budget.

Chaouki: Right, one point seven million.

Jamie: And the university's about eight hundred million.

Chaouki: Right, correct.

Jamie: It seems to me that we need to potentially look at some time in the future splitting that off. In other words, that the Health Science would have a separate board run by the governor, confirmed by the senate.
So, what's your comment?

Chaouki: So, my comment on that is twofold. One is, I think there is strength to having the two together, but you're right, that HSC is the eight thousand pound gorilla. Some universities have done exactly what you said and it worked out, while others have merged, or they created new health sciences centers. Of that two billion approximately, the largest portion belongs to the hospital. [$1,345,000,000] The education part of Health Sciences is not necessarily huge, but I guess I can go either way as far as I'm concerned. Health Sciences is a very difficult operation to manage. You know they have doctors and they're dealing with questions of life and death. Frankly, I don't have a strong opinion one way or the other. I don't think it's necessarily good or bad to have it separate in some places.

Jamie: I have one quick question. Just because I think that it really, it caught you by surprise to learn that I was the one that had recommended you to President Schmidly. So, knowing that you led the troops against me, are you surprised? I think it's a very interesting thing, because believe me, you're not the first person in the course of all my years in public life that initially has been on the opposite side of the deal from me and then we end up back together.

Chaouki: So, I mean I respect you. I think both because of your skills, but also because I do feel honestly that your heart, throughout this, was with the university. You wanted to do what, in your mind and your judgment, was best for the university. At times we have differed, and I feel like this with a lot of people, so I don't take things personally because I think in management you have to cooperate and make deals.

You know there is one hill I will die on, as General Hosmer told me: "You know you pick the hill you're going to die on. You decide what you cannot live with, everything else you know you're going to live to fight another day." So I respect that. I mean I know you have had a long life in politics and in New Mexico. It reminds me of a story from my past. My best friend from high school is a guy who started out in a fistfight with me. This reminds me, that you learn to interact with people differently. I appreciate the sparring, but also the support. I thank you for supporting me to be provost, and I hope I lived up to the promise, to whatever you saw in me that prompted that recommendation.

8

The buck stops here.
—Harry S. Truman

In Chapter seven, I discussed a lot of the changes I initiated as president of the Board of Regents for the University of New Mexico. Several of the interviews mention the annual Budget Summit that was started when I became the Board president. My passion for open government and fiscal accountability has been a dominant theme throughout this book. In this chapter, I interview key players that managed the financial transactions on the numerous facilities and real estate deals I was involved with during my time on the Board of Regents. I also include a conversation I had with the University of New Mexico's lobbyists at that time, Marc Saavedra and Joe Thompson, because I firmly believe we could not have accomplished what we did vis-à-vis the massive amount of capital outlay we were able to get appropriated without the lobbying team we had in place. Executive Vice President David Harris will explain his financial background in state government and offer some commentary on the various projects we collaborated on. With Kim Murphy and Commissioner Pat Lyons I will discuss the land swap deals we did with Mesa del Sol and Rio Rancho land parcels to create the University of New Mexico Sandoval Regional Medical Center and to give back 220 acres to the Cochiti Pueblo.

~~~

When I sat down with Governor Richardson to interview him for this book, he mentioned that one of the first people I had suggested Richardson should tap to address the state's budget problem was David Harris. David Harris is just about the best financial wizard I know. When I became a member of the Board of Regents at the university, once again, I felt David's financial expertise was needed. When I talk about the numbers—say about $1,092,000,000 worth of capital outlay on main campus, health science, athletic facilities and Rio Rancho—it sounds so simple, "We did this or that" but the reality is that each one of those deals was incredibly complex and required a tremendous amount of close supervision. Just the same way it was important to me to have very good legal advice on these massive capital outlay projects, it was critical to have very strong financial people ensuring that the taxpayer dollar was properly managed at every stage of the process. Additionally, when we would go to the trouble of holding budget summits to get input from across the campus on what priorities students and staff and faculty cared about, that was beautiful; but at the end of the day, you still have to figure out how to pay for it. If you increase funding in one place that usually means something else must get cut. If you want it to survive, over the long haul, adjustments to the budget must be clearly justified and explained in a public format. David Harris was very good at figuring out ways to make the priorities happen. Naturally, David has encountered criticism, as did I, but that comes with the territory. On November 17, 2016, I sat down with David Harris in his office at the University of New Mexico. David Harris's job is not an easy one and that's why I included him in this book. When I think about what David has to manage I am reminded of Abraham Lincoln's famous quote, "You can please some of the people some of the time, all of the people some of the time, some of the people all of the time, but you can never please all of the people all of the time."

David Harris, executive vice president, the University of New Mexico, twenty-seven years New Mexico state government, director Legislative Finance Committee for the New Mexico Legislature, financial consultant to Governor Bill Richardson / Interviewed December 2016

David: I was born in Mississippi in nineteen forty-four during the war. But my parents moved to Albuquerque right after the war to work out at Sandia Corporation. So, I've lived here all my life. I went to college at Eastern in Portales. I really feel blessed that I've been able to gain a real sympathy and understanding for Hispanic culture. The values, the things you do and don't do. I mainly learned it at the Highway Department the hard way because it's easy to offend people. And when you do that, you usually get paid back and that's the way it works. In politics, if somebody offends you, if you're patient, you can usually pay them back sometime.

David: So, I've been really lucky and I think knowing you and knowing the support you have given me and I have given you. We've developed a very close relationship. We're not always, not everything we do is amicable. Sometimes it's contentious but that's the way it is. It's not personal. I mean... we're trying to get stuff done.

David: That's the one thing I've learned in New Mexico over my lifetime is the opinion makers in New Mexico are very few in number. So, you usually see the same people going up the ladder and coming down the ladder. And there aren't that many of them and if there are people who you owe an obligation to, you can do it if you're patient. You have to be patient in this business, right Jamie?

Jamie: Yes. How did we meet?

David: I actually have known you from two different career perspectives that I've had. I've worked about twenty-seven years full time in and around the state government. Four of those years I worked in Los Alamos for the county. But about half of my career was working for the legislature, specifically the Legislative Finance Committee.

Jamie: What'd you do there?

David: Well, I started as a budget analyst. I actually started my career there. It was my first job in public service. I worked there about six years as a budget analyst. It's a very interesting place to work.

Jamie: Did you analyze the university's budgets too?

David: Well through the progression of the six years, you know, as you gain more experience, a greater knowledge of state government, you take on larger and more complex departments or activities. So, by the end of the time of my six years as a budget analyst, of course I'd done everything: Higher Education, Public Education, Highway Department, all of the Executive Agencies. So, by the end of six years, I had a very good understanding of the finances of all of state government and the revenue that supported state government because I had done the tax department for several years as well. So, you know, I was very fortunate to work for a great person, Marilyn Budke, who gave us, there were seven of us actually working there at the time. I think they have about sixty on their staff now, but we didn't have computers. We had calculators. I was just able to gain a knowledge that really carried me through the rest of my career because not that many people actually understand intimately public finance. That was the first time I encountered you, Jamie. You were in the legislature and it was actually my first session as an analyst. I had made some critical recommendations of executive agencies and you, of course, were really close with Governor King. They took exception to the things I said and so, you know, we had a little tussle. Well, they put you up to it but it was very interesting because you demanded at the end of the encounter that we would have a joint hearing with the Senate Finance Committee. There was a senator over there, Senator Aubrey Dunn, who I had become really close to in just a short few weeks. So, when we get in there and I start catching a lot of grief and Jamie, you really know how to poke at people because you understand people's buttons, and Senator Dunn, thank God, came to my rescue, or I don't think I would have continued. But that's the first time I knew you were a legislator.

Jamie: Can you talk about Johnson?

David: Yeah. Well, after that I moved into the Executive branch. I started at the Highway Department. I was Finance Director there and the head of computing. And then I moved back into the Department of Finance Administration and did a couple of good jobs in DFA—property control and state budget division. But then, I left state government and went to Los Alamos, which was really an eye-opening experience for me because in state government, your job is dependent on who you know. In Los Alamos, it's dependent on what you know. So I went up there in nineteen eighty-four and I came back to the Legislative Finance Committee in nineteen eighty-nine. It was actually my second time around at the LFC. I was recruited to return by Speaker Raymond Sanchez, and the reason that they recruited me was that they wanted to get someone in there who was trained by Marilyn. So, they asked me if I'd do it. I spent another six years at the LFC.

Jamie: And that was running it?

David: Yes, I was running it as the director.

Jamie: And did they have something to do with the university?

David: Oh, yes. Times were challenging then during my time there. We didn't have a lot of money. We had to be really careful about the things we did. The second time I encountered you in a real way was when you had been appointed as the Natural Resource Trustee of New Mexico, which is a role that the EPA requires of each state. The state designates someone who would be a guardian of our environment, essentially. And there was an issue that you brought to the LFC because you know all the ins and outs and how to get things done. You brought it to the LFC that there had been a serious problem up in Pecos where the Highway Department had spread some material that had leached into the river and killed all the fish. It was a real problem. And so, we had to actually appropriate money and you were involved, I think, with the mine that caused the problem in the first place.

Jamie: It was because of my involvement with the Game Department. The mine was on Game and Fish land. The property got designated as a Superfund site. The Superfund was going to close the Pecos. That's when I found out about the need for a Natural Resource Trustee. We didn't have one.

David: We're supposed to have one.

Jamie: But the question was, could I be the trustee, because it said it had to be an employee. But the reason I was approved was because I was chairman of the Game and Fish. The attorney general said I could be classified as an employee. Then I went to the Finance Committee.

David: You came to our committee and said, we need money to remediate the site. It was five million. So, you know my committee leaders sat down with me. How can we solve this problem? And we came up with an elegant solution, which was that, the Highway Department, that caused the problem, paid for it. And it was great. So anyway, you know, Jamie, you really had the ability to come to talk to the right people at the right time. And that's how you get things done. It's true you weren't looking for credit, even though that site now has a park named after you.

Jamie: (laughing) You always take shots at me.

David: So, the thing with Johnson. I didn't really have much to do with you during the Johnson administration.

Jamie: In other words, What'd you do with Johnson?

David: Well, I was sitting at my desk one day in the Capitol building on the fourth floor and one of Johnson's transition guys, who was a legislator, came in my office and said, "What's your direct dial number?" So, I gave him my number. Pretty soon, my phone rings. The voice says, "David, this is Gary Johnson. How'd you like to have lunch with me?" I said, "No way. I'm not having any lunch with you in public. I'd be happy to talk to you, but not lunch." So, we met downstairs in the basement in Senator McKibben's office and he said, "You know, I need somebody to work for me who understands state government." I was the only democrat who worked in the Johnson regime.

Jamie: Well, what did you do for Johnson?

David: Well, I was the secretary of department of Finance Authority. But he, you know, I had this eucharistic view that I could actually help make things better, which is foolish because no one person can make anything better in something like state government. Of course, me working for Governor Johnson, it just started a war actually.

Jamie: Who was the war with?

David: It was Manny and Raymond and their entire posse against us.

Jamie: Was it because you were working for them and now you were working with the enemy?

David: Yes, and furthermore, I took all my staff with me. They hated that. I knew I was going to be controversial. I needed people around me who knew how I operated. You know, Johnson was great to work for, actually. But more important, Lou Gallegos, the chief of staff, I never would've been able to survive that without him. He was a great guy who really understood everything. And he was kind of my comrade. He was the guy I worked with but Johnson was great. You know, he said, "Here's a key to the private elevator. I want you to know you can come in my office anytime. It doesn't matter who I'm meeting with. It doesn't matter what I'm doing. If you have something you need to talk to me about, just walk right in." That's the way it worked for all the years I worked there. It was great. He was a great guy to work for actually. But controversial you know, because he vetoed everything.

Jamie: Now, am I correct? He vetoed a lot of capital outlay money?

David: He vetoed everything.

Jamie: Go ahead.

David: He vetoed thousands of line items in House Bill 2. Manny and Raymond and Max, all these guys, were playing a game. They were always over-appropriating, knowing that we would have to balance the budget. That's what we did. We did our job and we left state government in really good shape financially. So, when Richardson came in, he inherited a good financial landscape. But by then, I had retired and you know, all of a sudden, I'm on vacation out in California. And I get this call. "Hey, this is Jamie Koch." You said, "You remember me?" You know, blah, blah, blah. And you said, "I have recruited this guy, Bill Richardson, to run for governor. We have promised him he would have a well-financed campaign, that he would have the best staff and that we would make him governor." You said unfortunately, "Richardson is making all these promises about finances."

Jamie: We went to a political rally and Richardson kept saying what they were going to do and I said, "Oh my God."

David: So you went and I convinced Richardson, that he couldn't make these promises unless you can pay for them. And when you were a Regent, anytime we talked about doing something, you'd always say, "How're you going to pay for it?"

Jamie: So, Marilyn Budke. I called Marilyn Budke. I asked her, "Marilyn, do you know how to get a hold of this David Harris? I want to talk to him." She said, "Well, I think he's retired." So, she got me the number to call you.

David: She probably got it from Paula Tackett. Anyway, you called me on the phone, saying: "You know, we put this campaign together. We think it's going to be an incredible campaign and we need somebody with some finance experience 'cause they're making a lot of promises." So, I said "Well I don't know this guy, Richardson. But I'd be happy to talk to him." I had never met him. I didn't know anything about him. And you said, "Well, could you fly back right away?" And I said, "Well, you know actually, I'm on vacation. But I will afterwards." You said, "Well, I think you need to come right away." So, you went and talked to the governor and the governor said, "You know, let the guy have his vacation." So, when I got back from vacation, you took me in there to the office. And actually, the governor interviewed me for three hours. It was unreal. I'm not a campaign guy. That's not my strength, but from the kind of campaign they were running, it was really intelligent. It was all based on policy. Everything that he talked about was based on policy changes that we would make that would actually make New Mexico a better place. And so, Rick Holmans and I worked on these policies. We poll tested every one of them and had focus groups for feedback on these things. We put together policies that we knew the public would like. And then we'd have rollout events.

Jamie: David, you would tell us if it was financially feasible.

David: Yes, I would let you guys know if you could do it or not. So, we had thirty-three formal policies at the end of the time that we rolled out. We did every one of them in a public rollout with the press there. Billy Sparks was great about creating events, of course.

Jamie: While we were doing these rollouts, the press knew who David Harris was.

David: And the Republicans knew me.

Jamie: Yeah. But your presence was very important because your credibility was great. So, when Bill was announcing all this stuff, they knew it was financially feasible.

David: So, my commitment was up 'til the day of the election. That's when my contract was over. So, I was at home on election night watching the returns and Richardson calls me and says, "Well David, I'm going to take over the Capitol. I'm going to storm the Capitol tomorrow and start the transition. There will be no vacation. We are going right to work. And I want you to be on my transition team." I said, "Ah shit. You know, I thought I was done with this. I'm retired, you know?" So, I said "Okay, well I'll give you another sixty days." You know, I didn't think it would kill me. And so, we went up to the Capitol. We set up our office and it was a phenomenal amount of work. I would say we were working at least seventy hours a week. We would start early in the morning. We'd go late at night. My role was to build his first budget, which I did single-handedly without any help and it was a damn good budget. But the other thing was...

Jamie: It's a shame David that you're not very confident.

David: No. But it was a good budget. We needed to get a hundred bills drafted that represented all of our policy commitments. So, of course I knew the Legislative Council very well and we got all those hundred bills drafted by them. Cost us nothing. All we did was take our policy documents. They used our policy documents to draft the legislation. But then, beyond that, we completely re-populated state government. From Election Day until the day that the governor took office, we filled every exempt position. Every board, every Board of Regents, every commission. We were really working our asses off and we'd sit around this table and we'd all have our cell phones out there. We had this huge organization chart. It was little sticky notes and we'd put the names in there and we built a true government. By the time Richardson hit the ground on January first, we had our whole crew hired. We were running. The legislature comes up within the third week. The first thing the governor did after the election in the transition, he came to my office and he said, "You are my second most valuable person outside of Contarino. I want you to be my DFA Secretary." And I said "No, I've already done that. I'm not doing that again. You're not sucking me into state government." So, he said, "Well, I want you to be close to me. Will you be my deputy chief of staff?" So, I said, "Not for long. But I'll help you get through the session." So, that's what we did. We introduced our hundred bills and everything got bogged down in the legislative process, like everything always does. 'Cause if you want to kill bills, just put money in them. And so, we were getting down to about the last ten days of the session and the governor was getting pretty frustrated because nothing was happening. So, I came up with this bright idea that we go down and we meet with the leaders in Manny's office. And we'd make an appeal to them that we needed these bills. We promised them to the public and we needed them. And Manny took the bait and he said, "You know what? We're going to pass every damn one of these bills." So, that's what we did. We passed ninety-eight bills of our hundred in the last ten days of the session. I gotta give Manny credit. He was as good as his word. I felt really good about that. But I wasn't going to stay there. And of course, one of the things that we did is that we put you on the Board of Regents of the University of New Mexico. Jamie, you could've had anything you wanted but you told us, "That's the only thing I want." And that's what we did. It's true. That's what happened. Toward the end of the session the governor said, "Will you go over and run the finance authority for me?"

Jamie: Didn't you help put it together originally, the Finance Authority?

David: Yes, it actually happened in my office in the LFC. We knew we were going to have a special session sometime in the fall over tax reform because that was one of the commitments we made in the campaign. And so, I worked on the tax reform and I worked at the finance authority. When we came to the special session, neither the governor nor the legislators wanted to reform any taxes. So, that was off the table virtually immediately because the governor was smart.

Jamie: No taxes. You heard that?

David: The governor was smart. He was like a Republican—he didn't want to be known for raising taxes. And he had good business points, by the way. So, the only thing we got out of the special session was the funding package for the Highway Department. It was about a one point six billion dollar package. We did that bond package at the Finance Authority. It was the biggest deal they had ever done there. We had no staff to do it. We were totally dependent on contract stuff. But during the time I was working there, you were talking to me and saying, "We've got a really screwed up mess here at the university." And we were talking back and forth. You said, "I'd like for you to sit down with this president we hired 'cause he's lost. He needs help." I did. I met with the president a couple of times.

Jamie: That was Caldera.

David: And you kept poking away at Caldera. And pretty soon, Caldera asked me to go to dinner and he said, "I want you to come down here and go to work for me. I really need the help."

Jamie: See, it's important what happened here. Julie Weaks-Gutierrez was the head of...

David: She was here before me.

Jamie: She was the head of finance. And Larry Willard, at that time, was president of the Regents when I became a Regent. With President Caldera, university budgets and everything else, it was a mess. How it was being done was a mess. It was not organized properly. We didn't have good relationships with the legislature.

Closed operation. So, that's why I went to you, David and said, "David, you've got to go to work for the university."

Well, what happened is that we had the most capital improvement we've ever had.

David: We changed everything here in the time that you were a Regent. It's now an open operation. That's real important. It had not been before.

Jamie: David, we're very fortunate to have you, because the way you set up the finances laid a strong foundation. Obviously, the state was having trouble with the oil and gas revenue, but David, all the capital improvements we got, all of these things we got, we got because of the relationship you had, and I had, with the governor.

David: Don't forget the governor had a lot of money then.

Jamie: Yeah, 'cause you made sure he had a lot of money left over from Johnson. So, Bill Richardson should have given Johnson a kiss on the cheek. Then we came to the cigarette tax that Governor Richardson was not going to sign.

David: Well, one day he called me into his office. And you, Jamie, had been smart during the campaign to sit down with Steve McKernan, and Steve said, "We need to build this new facility. But we can't put our finances together. We need more money." So, one day the governor called me into his office and it was Jamie, Phil Eaton and Cheryl Willman. Dave Contarino and I got called into the office. The governor said, "What can we do to help these guys?" And I said, "We need to raise the cigarette tax. It's too low. It encourages people to smoke, and that's what we need to do." And so, we put it together. We brought forty million in to build that hospital. But I think if you were to look at the University of New Mexico, we have improved this place from one end to the other during the time that you were a Regent. If you start over here on the north campus, we've got the Cancer Center, which is world-class. We've got the new hospital, you know the Richardson Pavilion, which kind of saved their bacon actually. We've got buildings all over the main campus, and then I think something that was really important to you, Jamie, was that we've completely been able to modernize our athletic facilities. I don't think we have any that we haven't improved, do we? It's almost two billion that we've done.

Jamie: See the truth is, really I'm not very good on finances and stuff like that. I would not have been successful as president of the Regents if I had not had you around. David, you helped me so much. In other words, if I hadn't had you, if you had not helped me with the budgets, helped me with financing these things, it would never have happened.

David: Well we opened the place up. We started producing monthly financial reports.

Jamie: I couldn't believe it when I went to the Finance Committee meeting. There were no monthly financial reports. I couldn't believe it.

David: The Regents didn't know anything and here they were: the fiduciaries. We did the monthly financial statements. We created a budget process that put the Regents in charge of it and not the administration, which is how it should be. We created all these facilities. The place is a far more open environment and I think a lot of people on campus don't like that, but it's the way it should be. It's a public institution. But I think of one last story I would tell about my history with you that goes way, way back obviously. One night, well when we were out in San Francisco at the Emerald Bowl, you said, "David, I don't want this to be a surprise to you. But over the next year, we're going to replace the president. It's not working out. It's going to take a little while but it's going to happen. And I don't want it to be upsetting to you or for you to think that it impacts your job." And so, that's what the Regents did. Jamie, you, set out to build a coalition of votes. They set up a process. They got a lawyer. It was all pretty surgical the way they did it. It was his lawyer and their lawyer negotiating a walk-away package.

But then, when they finally put it together, you called me one night. I can't remember where I was but you said, "The Regents want you to be acting president for ninety days."

Jamie: The reason for that was because of your finance background.

David: Well you said, "In those ninety days, we want you to do three things: we want you to: hire an athletic director, hire a provost and hire a university counsel. And then at the end of that, you'll be done. We'll get somebody else. So, that's what we did." We first worked real hard to get Paul Krebs. First we hired Reed Dasenbrock to be provost. And then, we hired Patrick Apodaca to be university counsel. And my ninety days were about up and Paul Roth and Reed went to the Regents and said, "We kind of like the way this is working. We'd just like to leave it like this." And so, that's what we did. We did it for about eighteen months while they searched for a new president. And let me tell you, it was really hard 'cause I had to do my current job and the acting president job, because we didn't have the money to pay for both. But the Regents have been really good to me. They never reduced my salary back down when the new president came in, and every time a new president comes, they tell them, "They can't fool with me." So, you know it's been good. But I think, you, Jamie, don't get enough credit for your ability to really create really complex strategies. Because a lot of the stuff we do, it may look easy but it isn't.

Jamie: That's why I'm doing the book this way. We sat down with Kim Murphy this morning for about an hour or two going over all the work he did at Mesa del Sol, Rio Rancho.

David: It took years to do those deals. We've done so many things I can't remember them all or list them all. Just the deal we put together in Rio Rancho; that was a big deal. You know, when we traded out that land with the land commissioner. We got land that's got exceptional value in the future for almost nothing.

Jamie: We got nine million.

David: Well, but more than that, we got the legislature to pass a tax so we could pay for our operation (the University of New Mexico West) in Rio Rancho. And then we got the voters out there to go along with it. So, I mean we've done a lot of stuff like that. These things that we do, even though people out in the public or the press or anywhere else would think they're just simple things—they're not.

Well I'm doing three jobs now. But when I was doing president, it was a fourth job. It's a heavy impact on a family to be president of the university. It's not just one person. You have to work the day shift and then you almost always have to work the night shift too. So, it's difficult, and Jamie, you told me when I was coming here, "This experience is going to change your life. Not financially (which has been really good). But it's going to open your eyes up to an experience that you can't imagine." For me, I like the athletic stuff and I like the stuff at Popejoy. That's what I especially get in to.

Jamie: We have done so much together. Athletic facilities: redid the track, the practice facility for basketball, the indoor football practice facility, redid all the tennis courts, redid men's baseball, created the Letterman's Room in The Pit, the entire Pit renovation, the University of New Mexico West campus, the Sandoval Regional Medical Center, the Barbara and Bill Richardson Pavilion at the University of New Mexico Hospital, the Cancer Center, the Domenici buildings on the north campus, the new residence on the main campus, the Student Success Center, the Lobo Village, the Engineering building. It has really been a phenomenal amount of building improvements for this campus.

David: And, these deals we do are complicated. But if you don't really look at all the complexities, you don't really make a good deal. You don't always get to make a great deal, but you always want to make a good deal at least. And that's what we tried to do. Right, Jamie?

Jamie: David—please tell me about you hiring Steve Beffort who passed away in June of twenty fourteen, and also the forming of Lobo Development. (Formed October 2007)

David: In two thousand four, after evaluating the condition of facilities, and knowing that significant capital outlay funds were available from the legislature, we embarked on a program to upgrade the University of New Mexico Facilities across the board: at HSC, Athletics, and Main Campus. The manager of this program was Steve Beffort, a retired senior manager, Sears Roebuck. Under his guidance we completed just over one billion [$1,092,069,902] in improvements. Under your leadership, we also established the Lobo Development Committee and as president of the Regents and being on the Finance Committee, you led the effort.

354

Jamie: David, could you explain what we did to improve health insurance at the University of New Mexico?

David: One area where the university benefited greatly was from your knowledge of insurance. In two thousand six you recommended that we self-insure our employee health insurance. In other words, eliminate the necessity of relying on an insurance company for providing health benefits. We studied this in–depth and realized that self-insurance was a great solution. We promptly brought this to the Regents and with your leadership it was brought to fruition. As a result, our costs have been dramatically lower than the industry.

One complication, however, was the financial burden of providing these benefits for the University of New Mexico retirees. Several solutions were developed to negate this impact, including establishment of a voluntary employee benefits association to help pay for future benefits, and dropping retirement benefits to new employees.

Overall, the great advantage we had was the expertise that you brought to these deliberations.

Jamie: Thank you, David, for giving me the opportunity to share that knowledge with the university. That's why I wanted to sit down with you.

So, as you look to the future of New Mexico and you think about the University of New Mexico in particular, what do you think will be important? I mean, you and I have worked together a lot. What kind of lessons could be learned for the future?

David: Well, everybody always thought that you were a highly partisan individual and I think in some regards, you are. You are a strong democrat. But you are also very pragmatic. You know if you want to get things done, you've got to be willing to talk to everybody. You have always been willing to do something that I won't, and that's go out and engage the press. I don't like to do that because they burn you. But you do it. I think it's crazy. But, it just shows what you are about. I think the future for New Mexico right now, if you're to look at it, doesn't look very good. We're losing population. Our economy is not where it should be. You can blame it on politics but I think that's silly and shallow. I think it's much greater than that. Our congressional delegation, for some reason, can't even protect the federal jobs that we have here, and it's just because I don't think we have a unified vision of what we want New Mexico to be. And that's a very sad thing.

~~~

I agree with David that New Mexico needs a unified vision. When I sat down with Governor Richardson, he also spoke about the need for a clear vision for New Mexico. In order to get over a billion dollars in capital outlay for the University of New Mexico, our lobbyists had to communicate succinctly to all of our state representatives and state senators a rationale for why the University of New Mexico needed these new buildings. It was not an easy task. Anyone who has spent any time around lawmakers know that they are besieged with hundreds of requests daily. Marc Saavedra and Joe Thompson will describe the awesome teamwork they employed to get the job done. They frequently put in ten or twelve hour days. Lobbyists are often portrayed in a negative light and that's why I thought it was essential to sit down with these two incredibly talented negotiators. When I decided to write this book, I told my friends and my family that this was not all about me. I said I would finally make sure that we would give credit where credit was due. When we talk about what I was able to accomplish while I was serving on the Board of Regents for the University of New Mexico, it just would be wrong not to mention the outstanding job that Joe Thompson and Marc Saavedra have done fighting for every piece of legislation the University of New Mexico needed and perhaps more importantly, ensuring that competing legislation died. There is definitely a finite pie, and when you have thirty-two entities competing for every higher education dollar available, you can imagine how tense it can get. I sat down with Marc Saavedra and Joe Thompson on December 15, 2016.

~~~

Marc Saavedra and Joe Thompson, University of New Mexico lobbyists / Interviewed December 15, 2016

Marc: I was born and raised here in Albuquerque, New Mexico. I've been working with legislature a long time. This will be my twenty-sixth session [at the time of this interview] coming up. And between Joe and I combined, we have probably forty years working with legislature. How I came to really get to know you, Jamie, is I started working on contract in two thousand

356

six and then I became a full time employee in June of that year. I was the director of the Office of Government Relations. You and David Harris were instrumental in bringing me to the University of New Mexico at that time.

Jamie: What'd you do before that?

Marc: Before that, I was the Core Administrator for the Metropolitan Courts. I was there when we built the Metropolitan Court facility. I started with the courts as a budget analyst at the District Court. That was back in nineteen ninety-six. That's where I started learning about the legislative process. So, that's where I really started getting a lot of experience with the appropriation process of the state legislature and I also learned a lot about building budgets, understanding the budget process, the capital outlay process, when we build facilities, etc. And so, that's one of the reasons why at that time, David Harris was asking me to come work here, because I was going to bring that experience. And at that time, we really didn't have a strong or a focused Office of Government Relations.

What I mean by that is that I was starting to work with the Regents, working with you, because you were the president of the Regents. We created a government relations policy for the university. It was a unified policy that had all government relations efforts coordinated through our office. We brought all the stakeholders together which came from the faculty, the staff, the graduate students, the Associated Students of the University of New Mexico, of course the Regents, the alumni, and the Foundation. And so, all these groups needed to be coordinated. We focused on anywhere from three to five goals that all of us could agree on. I think when you have a big institution like the University of New Mexico, you tend to have a free-for-all. There was some organization but you still also had a lot of folks going up to Santa Fe lobbying on behalf of their own specific projects to where we actually built a hundred line items on research public service projects here at the University of New Mexico that were mostly developed from personal faculty licensed with legislators and there really wasn't a focus on instruction in the general part of the budget.

Joe: I first came to New Mexico from Colorado in nineteen eighty-nine and I went to law school right away out in California. The first summer I came back Justice Pamela Minzner got me a job as a clerk down at the Court. I came back in nineteen ninety-two and ran a congressional race against then Congressman Bill Richardson. We got about thirty-two percent of the vote. Then I came back and ran in nineteen ninety-four another congressional race against Bill Richardson, the Republican revolution. We got about two percent better. But as a result of being on that ninety-four campaign, I had a chance to meet Governor Johnson. So, I went to work right away as the chief of staff for lieutenant governor Walter Bradley. Then, after a year or so, Governor Johnson brought me down as his special council and legislative liaison. So, I did that for a couple of years. Then I ran for the legislature and I was in the legislature for three terms. I was in the legislature under the last two years of Governor Johnson. Then I had four years with Governor Richardson. I left the legislature and immediately in January of two thousand five, came to work for David Harris and you as a contract lobbyist for the University of New Mexico. It was a very interesting time because one of the main pitfalls, as Marc said, that the University of New Mexico faced is we had an incredible amount of improvisation happening by faculty and deans and athletic directors and other folks.

I think one of the things that really enabled us to succeed beyond anybody's wildest dreams was that we were focused by you and David Harris. You really insisted that instead of having a bunch of disparate requests going into legislators, we needed to be really focused. And so, we would have a list of priorities and we would concentrate on those priorities. We decided, these are our priorities and this is where we want to perform. At any time, if there was a question outside of that, then you run it up the flagpole. So, we had a really distinct and clear objective. The thing that was the most fascinating to me was the relationship, the incredibly positive relationship, between athletics and main campus and how much athletics helped us in our main campus efforts. That was something that I remember you talking about in the beginning, and I understood it and I wanted to believe it. But it turned out to be absolutely true. The best example I can give you is we had done The Pit and we were working on a general obligation bond issue, which is every two years. We were working on something for the biology building and Marc wanted it to be the priority.

And yet, when it came to general obligation bond issues, we were not getting the same percentage as what we were bringing to the table, so to speak. So, Marc had us really focus on telling it that way. But then, he also had us focused on using all of our assets. So, that was just one of those years where we had Coach Alford—he ended up going twenty-seven to three in basketball. I'm not a basketball fan but he had a tremendous year. We brought Coach Alford up to the session. We were struggling on the biology building. You were there Jamie. We were all there at the Capitol and it was amazing. We took Coach Alford through the Capitol. He was introduced and we were able to suddenly have these incredibly normal and healthy and positive conversations with these people, and it allowed us to make incredible advances on our biology effort. I mean, like an eight million dollar difference. That was when it really became clear that it's not just some effort by a bunch of former jocks, which clearly Jamie, you are one. It was really about utilizing every part of the university to advance all the interests of the university.

Marc: I just want to bounce back to you in terms of lots of strengths. In terms of what we already knew about you, Jamie. Going up to the Capitol with you, I mean, your relationships with members and your historical relationships with people. Just watching you—the way you work. When people went up to you and people wanted to talk to you 'cause you had helped a lot of these people or understood there's a relationship. And that's one of the things we all understood from you, to David Harris, to Joe, and we also had Raymond Sanchez at that time. We all had relationships up there—but your relationships just go further back. It made a difference when we were right up there. So, we'd walk around with you and you would sit and talk to people and you generated goodwill. And that's what is really important in session is when you have that goodwill. Then people are going to help you do things. The other thing I think we all worked really well together on was this. I remember when I first started for the University of New Mexico and I'd always joke because I always worked for these agencies that were not the biggest fans of the University of New Mexico. (Mostly the rural legislators of Santa Fe).

It was you and other folks who really wanted to start building up the concept of a flagship institution. We really have an institution that should be out there taking the lead in the community and so, in order to do that, we had to educate the legislature on what the University of New Mexico really was about. People had these notions and some of them negative. Arthur Smith said, "What's the University of New Mexico's mission?" And something that simple made us realize that we needed to start from the beginning. That's why you would go up there and we'd take your lead and we'd all sit down with legislators, and we'd sit down with the governor, and we'd sit down with staff. And that's where we began to streamline what our mission was. So, like Joe said, we had capital outlay and we made it really tight in terms of instruction, general instruction over facilities like biology, chemistry, engineering. And we had athletic facilities and then also we really improved the general instruction by highlighting the core budget of the institution.

Schools like NMSU were eating our lunch. They were going after the funding formula. They were generating dollars in formula. You were president of the Regents and David Harris was a vice president, when we realized the funding formula issue. We realized, we're the biggest university. We have the biggest budget and we really need to take a lead. We need to develop a formula that generates outcomes and performance and then design our agenda around those outcomes. So, we looked at student success. Graduating out our students. Research. Things like that and that's kind of how we developed targets. We worked around that agenda.

Jamie: Can you be a little more specific about some of the tactics you used?

Marc: One thing we implemented was how we hit every Bernalillo county legislator or alums of the university legislators and developed one of the strongest, I think to this day, one of the strongest methods for getting the university capitalized from individual legislators.

Jamie: Well you, the two of you. The university. We were tough and we got what we wanted, but we had the dream-team—people just don't realize how critical you both were to the outcome. If we didn't have you guys, it wouldn't have happened.

Marc: I like the story where Joe watched GI Jane with Senator Beffort and her husband, Steve, because he went all the way out to their house in Paako on a Saturday evening to get a capital outlay form signed because it was due that Sunday. So, that was one of the things where Joe went above and beyond, and that's what we'd do. We'd get there probably around six-thirty or seven in the morning and we'd work until around eight or nine o'clock that evening. Sometimes, we'd go until three or four in the morning towards the end of the session and people would honestly say between Joe and I, that we had two of the strongest work ethics in the legislature. We knew that you had to be there. So, having that work ethic. Spending hours. Being sincerely genuine with these people. Developing relationships and trust. You'll never hear Joe say one bad thing about a person, ever. Also, that old rule "If you have nothing good to say, don't say it at all." But also, just in terms of, if you're not honest or up front with people in legislature, you'll get burned.

Jamie: Joe took care of the Republicans. Marc took care of Democrats. They worked together.

Joe: Well, and we did do something that nobody had done up to that point.

The way, particularly severance tax bond projects are set up, and the way they preferred to do them on a committee, is you would submit a form—a capital outlay request form—and it would have the big number. It'd say, what's the total project cost? So, let's say you have a five hundred thousand dollar project or an eight hundred thousand project. Well, legislators are politicians and they have to get elected at home. And we were trying to make a case to them that "no, this will help you politically." It's also the right thing to do to spend money outside your district at the University of New Mexico for athletics. And the way we were able to do it is we didn't have a legislator sponsor eight hundred thousand.

We would break it up into chunks, so we'd be asking them to sponsor fifty thousand. And we'd go get twenty of them. And so in the end, we'd overfund, which was important because anytime you're underfunded, you're susceptible to veto. We also then are having this incredible kind of grassroots team thing that included, you, Harris, Schmidly and Marc. We were part of a team and it's fun to be a part of the team. And that made it really fun for us, too. Also, Marc is the most competitive person I've ever seen. I'd come back to him and I'd go "Okay, we got seven hundred sixty thousand. We need eight hundred thousand" and he'd go, "Well where's the other forty thousand?" And he'd go and grab the napkins on the way out too. I mean—we just kept going. And it was really fun because then we were meeting all of our goals. It started to show the benefit of being really precise, really organized and executing it right. And doing it with a smile on your face. So, what we saw was legislators started to prefer to give money to our projects because they knew they weren't going to be underfunded. They knew that they weren't going to be giving fifty grand and nobody else was going to give it. But we could tell them "No, we've got these seventeen people are in this with you." And they would go, "Great." So, they ended up revealing what they were funding and it allowed us to be really fluid.

Jamie: There wasn't anybody else.

Joe: We created a machine and it worked for us for many years. I mean we started to see—Albuquerque Public Schools [APS] started to do a similar strategy. But I haven't really seen anybody else do it. And you can't do it just because you're trying or because you're fundamentally sound. You have to have something and we have the best thing there is—we have the University of New Mexico. So, it's not like we were trying to convince people to do something that they didn't want to do.

Marc: We also had to improve the University of New Mexico's image too. What I mean by that is that before, everybody just saw the University of New Mexico as like this big organization that didn't really play with other folks and kind of kept to themselves. We had to change that—we're talking about grassroots. We also promoted the Health Sciences Center. The Health Sciences Center is everywhere throughout the state. And so, Billy Sparks created a map that showed all the services and programs sponsored and supported by the University of New Mexico Health Sciences Center. Then on top of that, we created these maps that showed where all the alumni students were throughout the state of New Mexico. We also had to study a lot. Two things we would do when we visited with a legislator is: we would let them know "This is how many alumni are living in your district." And then we would let those alumni know "This is what your legislator did for the University of New Mexico." And that's how it helped the rural legislators, because knowing and growing up with a father who was a legislator for thirty-eight years, I understood the importance for these members in terms of them having data to show to their constituents.

Jamie: Your father? Say a little more about your father.

Marc: So, of course my father is Henry Kiki Saavedra. And I think he was on the House Appropriation Committee the entire thirty-eight years.

Jamie: He served on the Appropriations Committee my first term. So, he's a young fellow.

Marc: You and my father have a lot of respect for each other and are old friends. And that was also fun to watch. You just don't see the statesmen any more. And that's the thing I think people need to understand about you, is that you focused on what was good for the university. It wasn't what was good for Jamie. We were up there to take care of business. And there were expectations set upon us and we were up there to perform. One thing we did on the formula, on the capital outlay, is we used a little, simple formula of "how much square footage our institution has for teaching facilities" and "what's our student enrollment in the state." And so, it's like a forty-eight to thirty-two. You have almost forty-eight percent of the enrollment in the four years but only thirty-two percent of the square footage.

That formula is how we said, "This amount is what we really should be getting in capital outlay. Our request is based on that." And no one could really argue with it 'cause it is what it is.

Joe: Well and I think it does raise the issue of collegiality. Of the camaraderie that comes along with working up there at the legislature which is an incredible honor. I was the chairman of the Santa Fe County Republican Party and you were, I think at that time, the chairman of the State Democratic Party.

Jamie: We beat you soundly.

Joe: Many times. But we, it was very interesting 'cause I was working really closely with our state chairman, John Dendahl, who was a really interesting man. I know that he had genuine respect for you, Jamie. I remember you telling us, "You guys should help anybody who asks for help. If they need something from us, give it to them in terms of information or whatever." You were very clear about helping others. It didn't matter if they were a political friend or anything. Jamie said, "Just do your job."

Another thing I think is important is that I had a Republican and a Democrat on our team, but both of them had to get along or it wouldn't have worked. I can get along with a Republican just as well as Democrats. I'm very clear on why this is successful. It's been because we had a lobbying team that was able to get our legislation passed. We had a governor who would sign it. The effort that you all put in, the hours you put in during the legislative sessions was very difficult for all of you and your home life.

Marc: I'd say we probably, what would you say, we were putting in ten to twelve hour days regularly.

Joe: Yeah, it's just bad luck to leave.

Marc: You just don't want to leave. That's the thing, so you're there a long time.

Joe: That's also kind of part of the fun of it, too, is that it's like the old days of playing football and two-a-day practices and being so tired. You're still kind of laughing. You're supposed to be sleeping but you're goofing around laughing with your buddies because it's fun. And so, I think that you and I give Marc a lot of credit for this, since he set such incredibly high expectations for all of us. He instilled the commands from you and Harris but you know, it's not like you were asking us to do something you weren't doing. We were all doing it. And so, it made it more fun to know that you weren't toiling by yourself. If we called you and said "We've got a problem. We're here with this person." Boom. You would come down there in minutes.

We had some massive pieces of legislation that would impact the governance structure. So, New Mexico's an interesting state. It relies heavily on boards and commissions as a way of propagating policy and regulations. There are six hundred government appointees and the governor appoints the vast majority of them. The Regents are appointed by the governor, confirmed by the senate. There have been lots of efforts to try and change that to maybe constitutionally add somebody from the faculty or do some other thing that would dilute the executive power.

Marc: It was very impressive to see, to watch you work. You had every single member, every member. We would take members to you. You'd go on your own and I don't think you had one member you didn't talk to. You met with every single member.

Joe: And we've lost Regents before. You know, we know what it's like to lose them. And we also know what it's like, legislators particularly if somebody is a really high-end senators are asking, "You know, they're saying, are you just going to do what the governor says? Are you going to be your own person?" I saw Jamie. He said "Listen, I'm going to do exactly what I think is right every time." And that's what they want to hear. They want to see independence combined with the expertise.

Marc: And the other thing I think that people forget in terms of this process, is the work that it takes internally. So, you have the external part. You have the members, the legislature, you have the governor and you've got your local government who we also find ourselves working with as well. But I tell people, I don't know if it was lobbying but I spent just as much time working internally. And I think that it is also just as important to recognize that the university is tough because of the politics within the institution.

Jamie: So, as you look forward for the state of New Mexico to grow and prosper, particularly the university because that's the topic we've been addressing today, what do you think is going to be important moving forward?

Joe: I think at the university the great challenge for us is it's a different time, in terms of journalism. It's a different time in terms of the way the blogs work. It's a different time in the way that these requests for public records

364

happen. So, we're going to have to adapt. We're going to have to find a way to embrace the transparency that you have championed since the beginning. At the same time, we have to reconcile that with the fact that not everybody who's asking for stuff is operating at the highest level of integrity.

Marc: I think in terms of the future of the state is that we need to continue to support our institutions. We need, whether it's the University of New Mexico, New Mexico State, or Central New Mexico Community College, I think in terms of the state and the diverse economy, we can't rely on oil and gas any more. We just can't. Oil and gas should be treated as a non-recurring source of income for the state budget. We've got to find a more diverse way of funding the state's budget. Look at Innovate ABQ, those kinds of projects. I think the university will always be a center for helping those economic development ventures.

Lobbyists are often vilified by the media and in my opinion given an unfair rap. I don't mean the University of New Mexico's lobbyists in particular. I mean lobbyists in general. They serve an important function to help legislators decipher the massive amount of legislative drafts that legislators are debating in an average legislative session. Another University of New Mexico office that doesn't get any credit for what it does so brilliantly is the University of New Mexico Real Estate Office. An institution as large as the University of New Mexico has vast amounts of real estate that must be managed. As you will hear in this interview, real estate deals can turn into millions of dollars for the university, as it did on the Mesa del Sol deal with the State Land Office. On November 17, 2016 I sat down with Kim Murphy. For twenty-three years Kim was the director of the University of New Mexico Real Estate Office. You will hear him describe the painstaking process he and his staff went through to make the land swap deals viable.

Kim Murphy, former director of the University of New Mexico Real Estate Department / Interviewed November 17, 2016

Kim: For twenty-three years, I was the director of Real Estate at the University of New Mexico, beginning in nineteen ninety through two thousand thirteen. I went to University of New Mexico as an undergraduate. I graduated in nineteen seventy. I worked with an oil and gas company in Texas, but then eventually found my way into real estate in Tulsa, Oklahoma. I went to graduate school at the University of Colorado. I got a Master's degree. I worked in real estate in the Denver area for about thirteen years. The real estate business is kind of cyclical. And so, when the savings and loan crisis hit really hard in Colorado, I had an opportunity to do some consulting work for the University of New Mexico. Alan Pricket was the director of real estate at that time. This was in nineteen eighty-seven and I helped the university work on a master plan for Mesa del Sol. My involvement with Mesa del Sol goes back many, many years. Ultimately, in my capacity as the Real Estate director, with the assistance of the private developer Forest City Covington, and with the Land Commissioner, Pat Lyons, I was able to complete a significant transaction at that property that allowed that property to become developed.

Jamie: What property is that?

Kim: By the public sector, the property at Mesa del Sol, approximately three thousand acres.

Jamie: And where is that located?

Kim: It's located south of the Albuquerque International Sunport, within the city limits.

Jamie: It's one of the biggest pieces of properties in the city limits, wasn't it?

Kim: Absolutely. Many had said it was the largest undeveloped tract of land within close proximity to a major metropolitan downtown area that they could recall. And when you became president of the Regents, almost immediately there was keen interest in pursuing Mesa del Sol, moving that forward. The prior commissioner, Ray Powell, had gone through a selection process.

Jamie: Tell us about that.

Kim: Well there was a fairly extensive process by which a private developer was named and authorized to negotiate a deal.

Jamie: Why was Ray Powell involved? Why would the State Land Commissioner be involved when the university had the land there? Why was Ray Powell involved?

Kim: Well, as you said, Ray Powell was the commissioner at that time.

Jamie: Yeah, but we already had acreage there.

Kim: The total acreage of the property was roughly ten thousand acres and we had four hundred eighty acres we owned ourselves right in the middle of the property. Because we were the primary beneficiaries, the land commissioners typically involved us in any activity that would involve Mesa del Sol. Ray Powell went through the selection process of nationally exposing the property to qualified developers. He ended up selecting a partnership that consisted of Forest City Covington out of Cleveland, Ohio. Forest City Covington is a very prominent national real estate development company. So, the developer had been named. Kind of the broad outline of a transaction was discussed, but then Ray Powell's term ended without any action to move it forward. This was in two thousand three, the year that you came onto the Board of Regents. When Land Commissioner Pat Lyons came in, with your help and the Regents' help, as well as with Pat Lyon's cooperation, we began to discuss the nature of a transaction that would allow that property to be placed in private hands and developed for the benefit of the university.

Jamie: Can you talk about if there were any obstacles to make that happen?

Kim: There were a tremendous number of obstacles. A large part goes to the rules and regulations that apply to State Trust land. State Trust land in New Mexico is a very protected asset. Many states that got lands from the federal government to put into trusts, without protections on disposing of land, essentially got rid of those lands very early in statehood. And as a consequence, they have no State Trust lands. By the time New Mexico became a territory and then a state, the federal government decided to impose some restrictions on the ability of the state to dispose of the land. The land had to be fair market value. In order to sell it, it had to be done in a competitive process and there are lots of restrictions. So, as a consequence, New Mexico still has quite a bit of its State Trust land, as does Arizona and other western states. The pace of being able to put together a transaction was really largely constrained by the State Land Office requirements. One of the things that we did do, and this was allowed by law, is there was a provision that allowed for the land office to do exchanges with other government land entities. This opened the door for the university to participate in a three-party transaction whereby the university would exchange some of its other real estate, non-institutional, non-academic real estate. We had quite a bit of land.

Jamie: That's statewide, wasn't it?

Kim: Yes. The land parcels were throughout the state.

Jamie: You mean all the land that the university had accumulated statewide, you looked at all of it?

Kim: Yes, we did. And we, working with the land office, we identified tracts of land that would be beneficial to them that we could exchange with them and through this exchange, we would acquire say, trust land at Mesa del Sol in a particular location configuration that was approved by Forest City Covington. Then we would end up selling that property to the private developers. So, the university really facilitated a transaction that got the State Trust land in private hands in a way that really the land office could not have done and would not have done otherwise. I think frankly we did it in a way that benefited the land office, benefited the university and certainly benefited Forest City Covington. We began to work on it in late two thousand three. As you can see it was a very complex transaction. It not only was a three-party transaction involving the public exchange, but then the sale to Forest City Covington, it also involved multiple properties. The three thousand acres was done in two phases because the land office had initially only indicated through a public notice that one thousand five hundred acres would be available. When Forest City Covington came in, they said "You know, we really, given the capital investment that we have to make in this totally vacant land, in terms of major infrastructure, roads, water lines, sewer lines, all those things. We really need to have more acreage" and the Land Commissioner was in favor of that. And so, it ended up doubling to three thousand acres. But that meant that a number of properties on our side, on the university side, were involved in the exchange.

Jamie: It was a win/win. That's what you're saying?

Kim: It was. It really was. But again, I want to underscore the complexity.

Two phases of an exchange took place. Multiple properties. After the exchange, it was a sale of three thousand acres. That sale itself was complicated because it involved two pieces. It involved a cash payment up front of nine million one hundred thousand dollars to us. But it also involved what I call a "carried interest." In other words, we had the right and they had the obligation to pay us fifteen percent of the net income from the development of the land. And then in addition to that is a separate provision: we got fifteen percent of what we call the "vertical construction." In other words, if they went out and built a spec building that they rented to someone else (which they did on three occasions) then, we had the right to participate in those separate transactions. So you see, the sale was complicated because it involved the cash payment but also, this fifteen percent net interest. It took a long time to put this transaction together.

Jamie: When did Cochiti come in to this? Didn't we do something with Cochiti land?

Kim: Well, the primary piece of land that we owned that was part of our exchange with the land office was what's called Cañada de Cochiti, or also the Jim Young Ranch.

Jamie: And how many acres was that?

Kim: That was about twelve thousand acres, I believe. A portion of that property that abutted Bandelier National Monument was called Horn Mesa that has tremendous historic significance to the Cochitis. When we had identified the Cañada de Cochiti as an exchange property, there were discussions that occurred with the Cochitis. It was decided that it would be important for them, and for the university, and for the land office to recognize that historic relationship.

Jamie: Of Horn Mesa?

Kim: To the Horn Mesa.

Jamie: And how many acres was Horn Mesa?

Kim: A little over two hundred. About two hundred twelve acres.

Jamie: So, that two hundred acres, what happened with it?

Kim: Well, we agreed to carve that out and the university transferred that property to the Cochitis.

Jamie: So now you've acquired the Cochiti land as part of the trade for Mesa del Sol? Is that correct?

Kim: You mean the Cañada de Cochiti?

Jamie: Yeah.

Kim: Yeah, the balance of the property, the Cañada de Cochiti, was an exchange property for Mesa del Sol.

Jamie: Did Mesa del Sol, did that also include Rio Rancho at the same time?

Kim: No, that was a separate transaction.

Jamie: Okay, I wanted to separate that.

Kim: Yeah. Interestingly enough, the university, when it transferred that two hundred acres, we retained the right to use that property for research and educational purposes. So essentially, we retained the right to use the property in the way that we would have done in any case.

Jamie: People don't realize. How long did it take to do this? Just give a rough estimate, how many hours, time-wise in negotiations did you have to do before you brought it to the Regents.

Kim: Well, I'm just going from memory. But it took about a year and a half of constant work. We met as a group, after the basics of the deal were negotiated. We had to have a working group that involved the land office, Forest City Covington and the university people to work out all the details.

Jamie: Who led that?

Kim: Well, I was the lead on that. In some cases, we met weekly to go through issues, and in some cases, it was bi-weekly. We had an agenda for each one of those meetings of things that we would cover. We had assignments that people had to work on when we came back for subsequent meetings so that we could keep things moving along.

Jamie: So, after Mesa del Sol, that's where Rio Rancho comes in? Tell us about Rio Rancho.

Kim: Well, after the Mesa del Sol transaction, there was interest in establishing a campus on the west side. The university actually did a number of studies about population growth, where new growth is likely to occur and what opportunities might exist for a campus within the metropolitan area. This is a model that has been used at Arizona State University and I'm sure other places that have large metropolitan areas. They really can't bring everybody to the main campus. So, they create these separate campuses. I wouldn't call them a branch campus but a separate campus.

Jamie: It's like a west side university building. It's not like Gallup or Taos or any of those. It's still part of the university governed by the same board at the university.

Swisstack was the legislator for Rio Rancho. He had asked me to come before his committee because of what they wanted to do at Rio Rancho. They had what they call an Educational Park where they wanted to have: New Mexico State, New Mexico Tech and the University of New Mexico. I said, "We won't do that. We'd want our own campus." Well, that's where they had decided their City Hall would be. We came to be involved in that because we wanted to have a campus there. We also wanted the hospital there.

Kim: Yeah, they were in scattered locations, their administrative offices were in scattered locations, so of course they moved. They were starting to build this town center and that coincided with this idea of a campus out there for the University of New Mexico. Again, we worked with Pat Lyons at the State Land Office to do yet another exchange where we acquired a little over two hundred acres there.

Jamie: Because we gave some of that acreage to CNM, Central New Mexico Community College.

Kim: Right, correct. We sold it to the college.

Jamie: Sold it to Central New Mexico Community College. Yeah. Excuse me.

Kim: So once again, we, largely because of our success at Mesa del Sol, we established a good working relationship with the land commissioner.

Jamie: And you're the one that identified the other land to do that swap? Correct?

Kim: Yeah, that's right.

Jamie: How long did it take to put that together?

Kim: Well, it moved quicker than Mesa del Sol, but it still took probably the better part of a year I would guess. It may have taken even longer, because again, the land office had their own requirements. We have, as a state institution, we have our own procedures and requirements and it's just time consuming. The only thing I would add is of course, acquiring the property up there was just the first step. The next step had to do with CNM. CNM became very interested in putting a facility up there as well. So, we worked out a separate transaction with them where they could acquire a portion of what we had acquired for their campus. We occupied it and paid rent. Then a few years later, we were able to buy the building from them, and ended up in an ownership position of the building. Rio Rancho now has the town hall and the arena there, along with the CNM facility, the University of New Mexico academic facility and later came the hospital. I think this has been a tremendous success. So, once again we were able to do good for us because we were able to establish academic programs in an area with a large amount of growth. We were able to provide clinical services to a population that was under served. We were able to help the City of Rio Rancho by making their town center a more robust and complete service center, and the land commissioner was able to add value to its remaining lands in that area. That deal was a massive win-win for many parties involved.

Jamie: And we contributed a lot of jobs coming out of that hospital.

Kim: Absolutely.

Jamie: Tell us about Lobo Village.

Kim: Lobo Village, the other major project that I was involved in, particularly at the end of my career at the University of New Mexico, was student housing. Personally, for me, (aside from Mesa del Sol), it was probably one of the most satisfying experiences.

Jamie: Tell us all about it.

Kim: Because our housing stock was very old and dated, even though we had built "a new dorm," it was probably twenty years old at that time. And then our other dorms were dated from the fifties. There was a lot of discussion about how the university should proceed to either expand or upgrade the student housing on campus. It was commonly recognized, and we'd had a number of studies done by consultants that came in and said, "You need more housing. You need better housing." It's been proven that students who are in university housing for at least a large part of their undergraduate tenure tend to perform better academically. They stay connected to the university longer and again, that has benefits to them and to the institution. So, we struggled with how. We recognized the need. How do we really do that? Providing student housing was going to an extremely expensive proposition. We decided that we would look at what's called "a privatized housing model." In many instances, that word "privatized" has a negative connotation but it shouldn't. It just is using the resources and capabilities and expertise of the private sector to meet your needs. And the key here is "meet your needs." You have got to negotiate with the right partner. So, we went through a selection process. Again, a national selection process and engaged a firm called American Campus Communities. Who at the time was, and still is, one of the national leaders in providing private student housing on campuses at universities. This model is not unusual. In the last ten or fifteen years, almost every college and university has some part of their housing stock in a public/private partnership arrangement. We developed a strategic housing plan. I'm going to compliment you again. One of the things you insisted on when we started on this project is that the campus community was going to participate at every level. So, we organized a whole series of what we called information center sessions, workshops. These were hands-on kind of things to involve the entire campus community. Then we went out, those of us who are in charge, we went out and spoke to other groups. The faculty senate, the campus planning committee, the provost office and their various committees, to make sure they were informed about what was going on. Our real need initially was for upper division housing. I knew this first hand because my niece was here at that time when we started this project, as a freshman. Like many parents, they want their children to have the on-campus college experience. So, she stayed in the dorm as a freshman. Of course, the lottery scholarship helped families fund some of these things that normally they wouldn't otherwise be able to do. She stayed in the dorms as a freshman and as a sophomore. She left campus housing in her junior year, because that housing no longer met their need. You've got to keep them there as sophomores and then as juniors, hopefully. So, it was recognized that the first project ought to be an upper division project focused on those upper division students, not freshmen. Sophomores and juniors were our target audience. We looked at a couple sites on south campus and it was decided it ought to be on south campus. So, that started the Lobo Village, which is our upper division housing.

Jamie: Our occupancy did almost ninety percent of that, didn't it?

Kim: Yeah, very high.

Jamie: How many beds out there now?

Kim: Eight hundred sixty-four beds.

Jamie: Do we have about ninety-five percent occupancy?

Kim: Yes.

Kim: But the suites, they're four-bedroom suites and each student has a separate bedroom. They share a common kitchen and living area as well. The amenities are tremendous. There's a large swimming pool with a lot of cabanas and other things that students like to do to hang out. And there's a big exercise area and there's a game room. There's a theater. These are all things that keep students occupied when they're not studying. It's been very successful. We didn't have to spend any money to get this benefit of eight hundred sixty-four beds. In addition to that, American Campus Communities pays our ground rent. We generate income from their use of our land as well.

Jamie: You see what a big part the real estate office has had to play in the Mesa del Sol, Rio Rancho, and the creation of our upper division residential housing. You can see the work that's been done by you when you were the head of that. And the number of hours and time that it's taken to get it finished. As you ponder what was accomplished in that process and you look to the future, what do you think will be important for future real estate deals for the university?

Kim: I think a couple of things. I think first and foremost, it was actually a commitment to long-term investment and a long-term relationship. Many of our transactions are just "Hey, go out and buy this property 'cause we need to expand the campus or we need to rent some space for a program that we don't have space on campus. Go out and do that." They are fairly short-term. I mean they can be accomplished in usually a matter of months. Our Regents and our administration, at very critical points in our long history, have shown long-term vision. Yes, we got nine million one hundred thousand in two thousand nine and that's really great. It's even better than the initial deal because we are still a partner in the Mesa del Sol development, and we continue to reap financial benefits from that contract.

Jamie: You are the one who created those opportunities. The Regents voted on what you did, but that's why you are so important. People need to understand this. Future generations need to understand how these deals were put together.

Kim: Yeah. It's the long-term vision and it's recognizing long-term relationships. When I think in terms of the public/private partnership part of it, we were all motivated, we saw that it could be advantageous for each of our organizations, but also, advantageous for New Mexico to move a project of this scale forward. I think it's really a model of how public institutions and the private sector can work together. I'm going to digress just a minute here because I think you know some of this. The University of New Mexico has been involved in acquiring real estate for what I call "investment purposes" since the nineteen twenties. That's how we acquired the property at Winrock that we ended up selling for over twenty-six million. Over the time that we had that property, we generated over sixty million of income for the University of New Mexico. We acquired that property interestingly enough in the twenties. We acquired, where Winrock sits and where the Snow Heights subdivision goes to the east of there, over to Wyoming. We acquired I think about three hundred acres. In nineteen twenty, that was State Trust land and the university acquired it on a real estate contract, a thirty-year real estate contract with three and a half percent interest annually. We paid fair market value for the property, which I believe was about fifty dollars an acre in nineteen twenty. You've got to just imagine what the metropolitan area looked like then. There was nothing out there. There was probably nothing planned out there. But you could see that growth was kind of moving in that direction, so the university was very far-sighted and acquired this property on a thirty-year contract, interest only, with the principal due in the thirtiethh year. Well, that coincided almost exactly with the extension, or the construction of, the I-Forty Interchange. By that time, development was occurring out in that area. Subdivision development was occurring out there. There were some schools out there and so forth. So, Winthrop Rockefeller came to town and said, "I'd like to do a regional shopping center right here on university land." So we entered into a long-term ground lease with them on the shopping center and some of the peripheral land.

The university generated over sixty million of income on that property. And I just mention that because I think the Regents that came in, with your foresight on a lot of these issues, had the same vision. They recognized "let's make good decisions for us today because we have real needs today, but let's not ignore the fact that there are long-term opportunities out there as well that we need to leverage."

I think I would maybe add a little different twist on that because, back in nineteen seventy, I thought the institution was a really big place. I came from a small town. The campus, I'm going to call it sophistication but that's probably not the right word. It was very under-developed and I mean we did all the right things. We had teachers and we had research and we kind of stuck to our knitting and did all those kind of things. But, you look at where the institution is today, you know twenty-five years later, and it is a totally different institution. There is a lot more sophistication, capability, excitement, interest. Back then, we were almost kind of inward looking. We really didn't reach out to the mayor or the state administration that I could tell. And the outcomes were not always that great. So, we were pretty insular at that time and I think as the university expanded, and we took on these new initiatives, people realized, "Hey, we can do a lot more things if we just kind of think outside of the box. And don't assume that everyone is going to shut us down. Let's at least try to build alliances and relationships rather than assume that they're not going to work." I think we're just a lot more open to those kinds of transactions and relationships. Mesa del Sol and the American Campus Communities projects were new ways of doing things. I think that those projects show how successful we can be if we are willing to embrace new ways of doing things.

During my interview with Kim Murphy, we briefly touched on

the importance of Horn Mesa to Cochiti Pueblo. The land that was returned to the Cochiti included the well-known Dixon Apple Orchard. In order to properly explain how significant the return of those two hundred acres was to the Cochiti people, I knew I needed to sit down with someone from Cochiti Pueblo who could explain how sacred that land is. Regis Pecos is a former governor of Cochiti Pueblo. During the negotiations with the land office and the federal government Regis represented the Cochiti people. He had been a key player during the negotiations that went on between the Army Corps of Engineers and the Cochiti Pueblo when Cochiti Lake was being built. I had also gotten to know Regis from his work at the New Mexico legislature in his position as chief of staff for former Speaker of the House, Ben Lujan. Regis Pecos was one of the people who testified in support of me during the "Vote of No Confidence." In 2009, when I was interviewed by the *New Mexico Business Weekly* as one of their "Powerbrokers" I mentioned that giving back Horn Mesa to the Cochiti Pueblo was one of the most rewarding things I accomplished in my entire career. During the interview with Regis Pecos, the spiritual significance of this land was reiterated and more than ever I felt proud of my decision to get that land back to its rightful owners. As you will see in this interview, the return of that land was a much bigger deal than even I knew. The things that were revealed to me that day made me very proud, but also gave me goose bumps because I felt that I was part of an historical event that was much larger than anybody knew at the time. Truman has another saying that I feel encapsulates what happened for me as a result of the return of Horn Mesa. President Truman said, "There is nothing new in the world except the history you do not know." I sat down with Regis Pecos on November 15, 2016 and learned some history I did not know.

Regis Pecos, former governor of Cochiti Pueblo /
Interviewed November 15, 2016

Jamie: Tell us all about you.

Regis: I was born and raised in Cochiti. Went to school locally, to the Bernalillo public schools. Graduated from there, went on to do my undergraduate work at Princeton, graduated from there and on my way to law school my plans were interrupted at a time when the fight between the Pueblo and the Corps of Engineers was coming to a head.

Jamie: That was to build the lake, right?

Regis: That is the construction of the tenth largest manmade lake in the world. And of course the story behind that is a very long, but a very classic one similar to the North Dakota fight that is going on, similar players. The Corps of Engineers being the giant among those players. The Pueblo at the time was challenged with an incredible subjection to the threats of a powerful government. The Cochiti people were being forced to accept the construction of Cochiti Lake upon a very huge percentage of their cultural lands. Those lands would be lost, as well as the threat to the most revered cultural place of significance to the origin of Cochiti people. That threat became a reality, as we discovered in the deposition in the suit against the United States and the United States Corps of Engineers, that in the construction of a manmade lake that it is obviously an "alluvial construction of a lake," which means that the wall of the lake is created and the place where we as Pueblo people revered as the most significant of holy places is what mainstream society would define as a "geological structure."

Underneath and the majority submerged underground with an exposure of what would be called later the cathedral of the Pueblo people. In all of the challenges it was the one place that the elders wanted protected for those reasons, and it was the one place that the Corps of Engineers, engineers and technicians alike, agreed could be the only place that they could really put the mouth of the lake that would channel the impounded water creating Cochiti Lake, and the forceful nature of the outlet back into the Rio Grande could only be in this kind of solid geological formation. That was one of the first devastations we suffered in the construction of Cochiti Lake, was the ruination of that holy place.

And so as that challenge emerged, I had just finished my undergraduate education at Princeton. I was on the way to law school. The tribal council and elders petitioned and formally requested of my late father whether he would give them permission to do something totally unprecedented, and that was to ask for my service to the council, understanding that service in the council is held only by those who have served six principle positions, and once one has served in those six principle positions, then you become a lifetime member.

I had not yet served in those roles, but the need was so great that they petitioned my father for his permission to allow the Cacique, the religious leader, to appoint me to the council. This was unprecedented. And so my father provided permission and I was appointed to the Tribal Council. I have served thirty years as a member of that council subsequent to serving as lieutenant governor and governor multiple terms much later in my life. But that was my entrance into the deliberations of the council, for the sole purpose of chronicling the developments that gave rise to the construction of Cochiti Lake, which I had assumed the responsibility to document.

I later on became the director of the state office of Indian Affairs, appointed by Governor Anaya. Served in that capacity until I left there to fulfill my service as governor of Cochiti after sixteen years. So I served under Anaya, King, Johnson, and Caruthers, all four governors, as the Director of the State Office of Indian Affairs. Upon completion of my service as governor of the Cochiti Pueblo, I had a reprieve for a couple of weeks until the late Speaker called me one day and asked if I might consider coming to work for him as the Speaker's chief of staff. I obviously graciously accepted his proposal and I served as his chief of staff for all of his ten years as Speaker and after he passed then I went to serve as the chief of staff and the director of policy and administrative affairs for then Representative Rick Miera, until his retirement, and upon his retirement I left to go back fulltime to the indigenous think-tank that I co-founded in nineteen ninety-six. The think-tank is focused on bringing Pueblo people together to respond to the challenges of our time. We reflect upon the past regarding policies and laws and how it is that we respond in the present to assure that what future generations inherit from us is driven with the same resilience and perseverance of all those who have gone before us. We recognized that the challenges we face today are deeply rooted in history.

And so I continue to do that. Next year we will celebrate our twentieth year. We run multiple community institutes to discuss, in very frank and honest ways, the challenges of our times from land loss, to language maintenance, to indigenous laws and customs, to resource management, to health disparities, to tax policy, to education, to health disparities, to community development, the full breadth and scope of issues that challenge our present day pueblo communities. And so we create institutes for tribal leaders, for cultural leaders, for members of our community concerned about issues, young professionals, senior executive folks in the private, state and federal sectors.

We established a Pueblo PhD cohort and we graduated the largest cohort of Pueblo doctorates two years ago—ten, the largest number in the nation. We now have another ten candidates in their second year. We have a high school policy academy that focuses on introduction of young people to the same history of policies, laws, at the tribal, state and federal levels. They do research and study at the Woodrow Wilson School of Public and International Affairs at Princeton. We're in our tenth year, and through that program we have put almost three hundred fifty young people who are now returning, graduating from college and now entering their professional careers. So a really huge scope across the full spectrum has been accomplished through that work. In the process of all of that engagement, both professionally, I did have an opportunity to do my graduate work at UC Berkeley, and then later at the John F. Kennedy School at Harvard, largely driven by those early experiences of the devastation by the tenth largest manmade lakes. And then a few years later, the simultaneous response to the challenge that we found out through the process were very much an interrelated investment on the part of the federal government that Cochiti Lake and the construction was not solely a singular mission.

Associated with that was the social and economic experiment, the first of its kind, to develop a major private investment for a retirement community that in its master plan would bring forty thousand people on the reservation that required concession for leasing ninety-nine years of our reservation, the last of our homelands, to build this retirement community.

Jamie: That's the city of Cochiti?

Regis: Exactly.

Jamie: Are you familiar with that?

Regis: It was a part of a development scheme that created Colorado City, Sun City, California City, and a string of major investments by the Hunt International Resources Corporation.

Jamie: So Cochiti is a municipality?

Regis: It was the first departure from the minimal twenty-five year lease agreements amending that federal statute to allow for a ninety-nine year lease agreement. It was the first tribally created non-Indian municipality on a reservation. There were many, many complications to that whole development. Without getting into the specifics which would be a whole other book on its own, that eventually resulted in the development of Cochiti Lake, the development of the town, and in the process, looking at the reacquisition of Cañada de Cochiti and Horn Mesa. So here was a sixty-year effort. My grandfather worked on this, my father worked on this, and I chaired the last thirty years of that effort on behalf of the Pueblo.

Jamie: Correct me if I'm wrong on this. I remember when I went to your tribal meeting, and it's my understanding that the people who used to own the apple orchard had told the Cochiti Pueblo when they died they were going to give the land back to the Cochiti Pueblo. Am I correct on that?

Regis: Absolutely.

Jamie: And so then what they did when they died, their descendants did not give it back to the Cochiti Pueblo, instead they gave it to the university.

Regis: Right.

Jamie: I heard that and I got mad. I was aware that the situation was that the Cochiti people had treated this family nicely. You all had gotten along great. The Pueblo had been told clearly by the family, "When he died we're gonna return that land," and then they turned around and gave it all to the university. Do you want to talk about that?

Regis: Right. So those lands have a long history of ownership. It eventually started with one permit secured for gold and silver mining in that Cañada area. It resulted then in the abandonment of gold and silver mining later on in the territorial days, but in that kind of conveyance an exchange of lands, a gentleman from New York actually became interested in one thing—assuming ownership of those grants in that entire Cañada land that resulted over the years in building this unique mountain apple orchard that became known as the Dixon Apple Orchard.

Jamie: This is the guy who bought the land?

Regis: Uh huh. Mr. Young.

Jamie: And he's the one who said, when he bought the land, that when he passed away it would go to Cochiti?

Regis: No. Mr. Young then conveyed in another exchange to the Dixon family, and so we're getting close to a time in history that connects us to you, but in that conveyance to the Dixons then they developed a very close relationship with the Pueblo. My grandfather knew Old Man Dixon and had a very close relationship. My father knew the Dixons, I knew them later on in their older years, and then the Dixon family then pretty much had concluded that upon their retirement in the management of the Dixon apple farm that given that long, genuine, I'll say genuine relationship with the people of Cochiti, that they would convey knowing that that entire nine thousand two hundred acres of aboriginal Cochiti land would be given to the Cochiti when they could no longer manage the apple farm.

Along the way comes the granddaughter, Becky, and Becky came into the picture and wanted to continue managing the farm, but then came the politics of other land interests indirectly now creating for a conflict scenario that eventually ended up in the conveyance of those lands to, not Cochiti, but to the University of New Mexico.

Jamie: When I found that out I knew there was a problem. In other words, again, with the Native Americans, we'd said something, then we didn't do what we said we were gonna do.

Regis: Uh huh.

Jamie: Which is not unusual.

Regis: So in that conveyance of the lands to the University of New Mexico, it was a real devastation, because at that point we thought we were so close with the genuine relationship with the Dixons, the Old Dixon and Mrs. Dixon, that upon their retirement that they would convey that property to Cochiti. So anticipating the return of the land, when the land was conveyed to the University of New Mexico, that was very devastating to a generation of elders who would see that happen and their lives would end knowing that those lands would not come back to Cochiti. Now comes another genera-tion in this period that saw, and that was my father, and now me as the next generation, saw the devastation now a second time when New Mexico, who in our relationship were fostering what I thought was a genuine relationship that eventually the university would work out something to convey that property, now the Bandelier National Monument. So in all of these stories...

Jamie: Yeah, Horn Mesa goes right up to that.

382

Regis: Yeah, well, Horn Mesa is here, Bandelier is here, but in all of the origin stories, all of the migration stories contained in the prayers and the songs to this day all mention Horn Mesa, Cañada de Cochiti in different Cochiti names, Frijoles Canyon all the way up to Bandelier. That is the route of migration to the current Cochiti Pueblo. So along the way are the stone mountains, the shrine revered by hunting societies to this day. Frijoles, the home of the Pueblos from San Marcos, from San Felipe, from Santa Domingo, from Zia, all at the time of migration still as one, speaking one language, until they separated at a time to their current locations, but Cochiti eventually built its home, so here is Cañada de Cochiti. Here's the apple orchard farm, here, on top is Horn Mesa. Okay? So Horn Mesa is the original home site of Cochiti. It was the refuge that Cochiti gave to Santo Domingo, to San Felipe, to Zia, to Jemez, to the Pueblo people from San Marcos down the road here. During the Pueblo Revolt, Cochiti, at the top of that mesa, used that to protect all of those who were fleeing the persecution and the genocide by the conquistadors. That was a place that eventually became a very prominent part of history, pre-Pueblo Revolt, during the Pueblo Revolt and in the aftermath of the Pueblo Revolt. That was the sanctuary of Pueblo people, of present day Jemez, Zia, Santa Ana, Sandia, San Felipe, Santa Domingo and Cochiti. So it was a very special place as people moved and migrated to their current locations. The Cochiti remained on top of Horn Mesa. So Horn Mesa is actually contained in that nine thousand two hundred acres that eventually ended up in the hands of the University of New Mexico. So the University of New Mexico, largely through you, found out that history of devastation now a second time.

So one of the first efforts was that if we could not acquire the nine thousand two hundred acres, it was your effort to convince the Board of Regents that here was the most precious homelands of the present Cochiti people upon which was the sanctuary of all the survivors of the Pueblo Revolt that results in the survivors to this day. You understood that in a way that very few people did. In my mind, in my heart, I will always be grateful for having been blessed with our friendship, that in that kind of relationship you came to recognize that you would take it upon yourself to right some terrible wrongs in history. And so you proceeded to engage in a dialogue with your colleagues on the Board and with leaders at the university, to figure out a way to give the two hundred-plus acres upon which Horn Mesa sits as an important recognition of this relationship.

Jamie: The faculty wanted to be able to do their archaeological studying on that site, and I could see right off the bat, this was going to be difficult. That's when I got in trouble with the faculty, because I said, "No—the Cochitis don't want us on their religious site."

Regis: Let me go back to this other simultaneous development, because this is important in the overall scheme. So now one of the things that was discovered and now the state, Sandoval County wanted to exploit now a revered other part of the reservation or now no longer part of the reservation. So now the discovery internationally, nationally and the state with another incredibly revered area geologically. Only two places of this kind exist in the world—one here, and one on the other side of the world. And that is what was previously known as 'Tent Rocks,' that formation—what later became Kasha-Katuwe, in the Cochiti name.

So one of the things that happened was that it became now a National Monument, right? The only entrance to the Monument, however, was through the reservation. So here was another challenge. How could we maximize providing public access through the reservation, the only place to get to this newly designated National Monument? So now that became a whole other development that was evolving with the Bureau of Land Management. Because we had lost the opportunity to secure Cañada de Cochiti because of the conveyance to the University of New Mexico, we now created a whole other strategy that we would now enter into a joint management development and agreement between Cochiti, the Bureau of Land Management over the National Monument so that we would have some management control over the west portion of other important and revered cultural sites.

So now to the east we were devastated by the construction of Cochiti Lake, to the north was the fight with Bandelier National Monument, the National Park Service, of an existing indigenous people, a living culture, and they wanted exclusive rights over the domain of what was once our homeland as an extension of the National Park. And so the battle became between the National Park Service, the University of New Mexico, Cochiti, and now the Bureau of Land Management. The Bureau of Land Management partnership was a strategic move on our part, because if we entered into this joint management with Bandelier to the west, Bandelier has land that abuts what is now the University of New Mexico's property. So the strategy was how could we jointly manage that, extend our reach in places that otherwise we were excluded from, and eventually try to leverage that agreement over that nine thousand two hundred-acre property that now was in the hands of the University of New Mexico.

So we were making great progress, and in the midst of that progress came this request by the University of New Mexico faculty through the Department of Anthropology and the Department of Geology. One, to have access into that area for scientific purposes and two, to have access into what were very sensitive areas. So enters Jamie Koch as our champion. We were developing with good faith in hopes that if we provided for a good faith effort into an agreement to allow even though these were entering into very important, revered areas, to just on the fringe start to challenge us internationally that here we were getting closer to violating our own internal conveyance and tenets with regard to being the protectors, being the guardians, being the stewards of important cultural resources and human remains in that area.

And so now it really became an issue that we would only allow for certain access for those purposes in good faith. They didn't want what we were offering and now we were creating havoc publically exposing what we thought was a private negotiation between us and the university, and we came up into a situation much like the situation at the site that was devastated at Cochiti Lake, okay? Because the fight then became one with additional threats, to build a hydroelectric power plant at that site. The Federal Energy Regulatory Commission now entered the picture and in order for us to prevent hydroelectric power at that site, we now were driven to go through all of the steps, all the way to the highest level with the Federal Energy Regulatory Commission. We had to have a private hearing. So all of these things were happening simultaneously.

So we had secured a private hearing. Now here's the difficulty and why your entrance into this picture at that time is monumentally profound. Because what we now were challenged with at the Federal Energy Regulatory Commission in a private hearing was for the council to appoint someone to make the arguments along with our attorneys about why a second devastation could not happen based on religious access and freedom and protection of that site. The Department of Justice ruled that because our native indigenous religions were unorthodox, it did not fall within the Department of Justice protection under the Constitution. So now we were left hanging with no protections, and in order to save that site from a second devastation the council was being asked to have a member provide for testimony with regard to why this was revered. In doing so, that person would violate important Pueblo covenants of secrecy. You know—the heart of the tenet of the maintenance of that in cultural ways.

And in order for someone to protect this site upon return to the Pueblo would be ostracized and potentially banned from our community— all for the sake of testifying—breaking the covenants held sacred internally.

So while that was going on, this other challenge internally was one being pushed, and we couldn't fight this successfully with something in the back yard that was challenging—that had repercussions here. So that's when you stood with us in terms of holding to the framework of that initial set of policies and procedures of access to that place—but limited.

And when you took that stand, there was a major revolt by the faculty, largely by the Department of Anthropology and Geology, but you stood your ground.

Jamie: That was one of the issues when I got the "no voter confidence."

Regis: And that's when, for us, it was costly to you, but you took that chance, standing on the principle...

Jamie: I had good fights.

Regis: ...understanding how critical this was to this other bigger fight. We eventually prevailed on both fronts. We walked away from the Federal Energy Regulatory Commission and this is where the beginnings of a relationship with Governor Richardson started to evolve, because then, in order not to break with our covenants and providing testimony before FERC, we chose to walk away from that. Then we engaged Congressman Richardson to sponsor legislation so tight to protect hydroelectric power at that site. And the repercussions are great because one of the things that happened was in that legislation moving forward, the rules of the U.S. Senate were such that if someone put a hold on legislation, it was anonymous. So you never knew who would stop your legislation. You wouldn't have any idea who to talk to, who to convince to let it go, or why we're doing it.

Senator McCain is eventually who we found out stood in the way, and his response is that "If you give Indian people this right based on sacred site protection, they'll stop every damn water project in the southwest." And so eventually overcoming that, legislation passed that prevented hydroelectric power at that site.

So meanwhile this was going on internally. You stood your ground on what I felt to this day was unprecedented. One person would stand to advocate for us in ways that gave us a chance to not compromise in similar ways what we were being asked to compromise at FERC. That movement, that singular movement that you contributed here, that was reinforced here, created the current American Indian Religious Freedom movement. That's how deep your stance contributed to this movement, because until that time, pressure at the local level, pressure at the federal level, we didn't have the protections that what was in place with the American Indian Religious Freedom was found out to be without any teeth. It was a matter of policy. This created for the second major movement in the current history of the amendments to the American Indian Religious Freedom, based on this very incident of being forced to concede certain areas against your own tenets and covenants which you helped to prevent an academic institution for scholarly academic purposes to not cross, because in doing so it would force us to concede our stewardship, our guardianship and our protecting to those places. And you helped negotiate a mutual outcome of benefit, protecting us from having one, fail in what the pueblos told us we had failed in the construction of Cochiti Lake that sacred site was devastated. Publicly ridiculed. So here could have been another devastating example, but you rose to help us in that fight. But you just didn't stand up to help in that fight. You helped to broker something that I think now becomes a lesson for me in my work that you could hold your ground on principle core values that can result in mutual benefits derived from mutual respect extended and accorded in that scenario.

So the university got what it needed, with limited access into these places for scientific and academic purposes. We were saved by your advocacy. We were not forced to break with internal covenants of pueblo secrecy at the heart of pueblo existence today. So that was the first big fight, and I think in that you rose to another level of both leadership and respect, so that sometime later when this whole other challenge came back to surface now for a third time could have been devastating, that the exchange would now result from the University of New Mexico who we worked hard to accommodate in great hopes that in that accommodation they would be sympathetic that at some point they could convey that property in some form or fashion that might be mutually worked out as we were able to work out something that became a really difficult set of challenges.

Jamie: So what deal did you do? I want you to tell me what you all did.

Regis: We're getting close. This is a really important part of the story because now the third devastation results in New Mexico trading nine thousand two hundred acres to the state land office in exchange for Mesa Del Sol. So now one more time we were devastated and at that point I said "I may not see the return or the reacquisition of these lands in my lifetime." So now the politics shift. So now Commissioner Lyons enters into a long-term lease with the Malines, the granddaughter and her husband to manage the apple farm. So now it became a complicated scenario with now a second and third party in the mix.

Now the situation is becoming remote. It was like when you drop something in a puddle or in a pond, and the waves start to take it away, and seemingly there's no way you can jump in to move it back. That was how this land seemingly was floating away and eventually we would never see it again. So in the mix you made another important contribution that kept the hope alive, because now in that exchange you insisted that at least "let's give Cochiti what it wants most," just like in the proposed construction of Cochiti Lake. The elders cried and said, "If it must be done and if we are going to see our lands devastated, all we want is for you to not hurt this place of worship." But of course that was the first place dynamited, right?

In that whole scenario it replayed itself, but in your understanding and your sympathy and in your wisdom you said, "We can't have the Cochiti people be devastated one more time of another place so revered. Why don't we do the right thing?" And then you proposed that in the conveyance of the property to the State, let's do the right thing and let's give Cochiti Pueblo at least the two hundred acres upon which the old Cochiti village of refuge, the sanctuary, revered to this day in prayers and songs and ceremony. You kept the spirit alive that we did not lose faith because one more time you championed the cause. I came at your request after many, many months of your talking to your colleagues and they're agreeing that this is the right thing to do. You moved to have them consider testimony from us. We came down and I became the appointee to testify to all of you, and I believe in the records expressed our appreciation to your leadership, to your wisdom that gave us the opportunity. I reached deep into my heart to say what might be compelling to convince your colleagues that they ought to support you, that as they conveyed the lands to the state, they at least give the Cochiti their homelands.

So Horn Mesa, with your intervention, became a reality. And so Horn Mesa was returned to the Pueblo and you saw the great emotion in that formal conveyance that took place. That maintained the spirit that as long as we held to our faith that people from other walks of life might cross our paths in our journey. And now here's the second time that you crossed our path to something that was important, that one, gave us reason to continue our faith. And so with all of that work we now had at least a foot in the door.

So from that point we now won as a result of the largest fire in the state's history, devastated in the first eleven hours almost thirty thousand acres of the lands adjacent to that area.

Jamie: The apple orchard.

Regis: And in that devastation the burn was so hot that if you saw pictures of that area then and today, it must be what is as close as it must be to setting foot on the moon. It was charred to depths that everyone assessed said that with the first rainfall would turn that place into concrete, like a parking lot, because of the severe deal, the burn and the depth of that burn and when the first rains came, the first floods came. And as the rain continued it devastated and eventually took all of what were the homes of the Youngs, the Dixons, the Malenes, and washed them down into the river. And it now resulted in lands devalued, ones that resulted in the Malenes wanting to get out, but not so graciously. They were demanding huge amounts of money and the elders said, "Whatever it takes. This is our last opportunity. Bite your tongue and do what is necessary to reacquire those lands." So we moved.

Jamie: But they didn't own the land. The land office owned it.

Regis: Well, here's the kind of cutthroat and hostage holding scenarios that came. The Malenes were only paying over seventy-five years, a hundred dollars a year and some small percentage of the gross proceeds.

Jamie: From the apples.

Regis: Yes, from the apple orchard. We paid in the first month to the state more money than the Malenes would have paid in seventy-five years. So the Malenes insisted, you're correct, they only had a lease on the property to manage it, but they wanted a return as if they owned the property. So they were asking for millions of dollars for something they didn't own, but the commissioner wanted to accommodate them, to get them out of the lease to make way for us to enter negotiations. So after Lyons left, Ray Powell continued those negotiations. Ray Powell's father, Ray Powell Sr....

Jamie: I knew him very well.

Regis: Had a great relationship with you and had a great relationship as you developed with Cochiti at that point. It wasn't coincidence that now you crossed the path with Ray Powell's father and now Ray Powell sits in a pivotal role to make some decisions with regard to how to accommodate our request, at whatever cost. So now the Malenes wanted at least one million eight hundred thousand. We eventually paid that amount to get them out of the lease so that we would now have a clean table to negotiate with the state.

So now there was a convergence with you in the picture, with Ray Powell in the picture, and now what we thought would never happen in our lifetimes, began to move in ways that created the ultimate opportunity—that we negotiated a lease after buying out the Malenes. We entered into a five year lease with the State Land Office at fair market value. We would purchase the land and we would then trade that land, those parcels of land, of similar value with the state, and the state would then convey the property of Cañada de Cochiti to us.

Jamie: This is the Desert Inn.

Regis: So now as properties were being assessed, the property right across the street from the State Land Office became available.

It eventually came to be that was their prime realty that they wanted. And so we invested the asking price for it and acquired that property, all for about five minutes in the exchange and conveyed that to the state, and the state returned forever...

Jamie: I got a call from Aubrey Dunn. You're probably not aware of it, you might be. Aubrey is the land commissioner now. He called me, which really surprised me. I knew his father very well. His father was a good friend of mine. Aubrey called me to come to see him. He had his chief of staff, a lady, very nice lady, and they said, "We want to see what you think we can do here," and in regards to that he said, "What we want to do, we want to see what you thought." And he said, "What we're thinking of doing is getting the Pueblo to buy the Desert Inn and then we swap back," and he said, "It's a better lease. What do you think?" I said, "It's the greatest thing I've ever heard of." I said, "You can't believe how great the deal is." He said, "Well, we wanted to make sure of that." I said, "It's the greatest thing I've heard you do. Aubrey, do it." And he did.

So now all that land is back to the Cochitis where it should have been from the very beginning. The university should never have been the beneficiary on that.

Regis: So that's the story in short, but it has many other points that are critical, but the role that you played at a very personal level I will be forever grateful. Because what I saw as a culmination of sixty years of efforts, you

390

came into the picture not by coincidence, but as I have shared with Elders, that we were blessed to have someone with your principled leadership enter the picture and be able to hold your ground on some very principled core values that over the time that I've known you we share deeply.

Jamie: Well, there were other people. Don't forget I had all the Regents and they all voted, you know. You know, one person can't do it all. You have to work together to do it.

Regis: Well, that epitomizes who you are. That exemplifies who Jamie Koch is, that you'll never take credit solely, you as an individual. You always are so gracious to always share everything that you do with everyone else, and that's to be admired of a person...

Jamie: I appreciate that.

Regis: ...that I'll say defines your hallmark as a person and a person in public service.

Jamie: I've had a good time. I've had a lot of friends.

Regis: Well, I think when you do the things that you've done in your life you have many friends, and those friends are friends forever because of the genuine way that you do things.

Jamie: Well, I appreciate that.

Regis: Advocacy achieved that outcome. To do it in any other way would have caused conflict. To make that journey tougher than it was and I think that it all can be attributed to the way that you approached it, and it's a remarkable accomplishment that unless we talk about it firsthand will never be known. And yet the movement that it helped to spark and fuel on very principled grounds that results in people from all walks of life joining together largely by understanding what it takes to do the right thing, that is a very powerful and deeply compassionate demonstration of the deepest kind of understanding. There's just no other way to put that, and now the story moves on its own to be shared. The current issue in North Dakota is part of this narrative. It's the same players engaged in similar acts of devastation, and what the story and the outcome from here is now the narrative shared by people there. And so it really is, a classic David and Goliath fight, and when all this ended up in the way that it did, and we prevailed against the United States, and we prevailed against the town of Cochiti Lake, and we prevailed in reacquiring our revered homelands. All of that is to say that when we hold true to our core values and we are guided by them, and it is maintained by our faith, and we are joined in that work, to be the stewards, the guardians and protectors of the gifts of the Creator. When other people from other walks of life come to cross our journey, Jamie Koch is one such person who will ever be remembered.

And I'm very happy that you're doing this because the documentation about critical players in this movement should be known by children generations from now.

∾∾∾

Based on my interview with David Harris wherein we discussed the $1,092,069,902 of capital outlay improvements on main campus, health science and athletic facilities, I want to include the individuals responsible for making this happen.

∾

Chris Vallejos, associate vice president of Institutional Support Services (ISS), the University of New Mexico

I worked very closely with Chris Vallejos, the Associate VP of Institutional Support Services (ISS) and Tom Neale, the Director of Real Estate at the University of New Mexico when I was President of the Board of Regents, Chairman of the Finance Committee and Chairman of Lobo Development.

Chris has been a University of New Mexico employee since 1986 and is responsible for the planning, direction and coordination of major business development projects and initiatives for the university. Chris oversees fifteen divisions at the University of New Mexico including Real Estate & Commercial Development and Facilities and Utilities Management. He provides strategic oversight, consultation and support to various university-owned facility management and development enterprises.

Tom Neale, director of the University of New Mexico Real Estate Department

Tom has been with the University of New Mexico for over a decade and is responsible for major areas of property management, leasing and acquisitions, providing comprehensive real estate services for all entities of the university. Tom supervises a staff of eight full-time employees. After earning his BS in Real Estate from Florida State University, Tom was a commercial real estate appraiser and consultant specializing in income-producing real estate. Such properties included multi-tenant office buildings, industrial properties, shopping centers, multi-family housing, lodging facilities, residential subdivisions, and a variety of special purpose properties.

I am including a list of the major University of New Mexico capital projects from 2003 through 2016 to support and strengthen the University of New Mexico's mission, national reputation for excellence and ability to serve students, faculty and staff. The projects have included construction of education buildings and the University of New Mexico west campus in Rio Rancho as well as the University of New Mexico Health Sciences Center which features a number of new buildings and expansions, including the University of New Mexico Cancer Center. Athletics has also seen renovations and improvements to all facilities.

NEW FACILITIES

Major Capital Projects 2003 to 2015
Obtained from the Institutional Support Services and the Director of Real Estate at the University of New Mexico

Acc Lobo Village (Student Housing)	$40,000,000
ACC Casas del Rio (Student Housing)	$39,000,000

Chemistry (Clark Hall Renovations)	$19,499,000
The Pit	$60,899,655
Centennial Engineering Center	$41,181,992
Science and Math Learning Center (Phase I and II)	$27,030,000
Mitchell Hall Renovations	$7,998,685
School of Architecture and Planning	$8,000,000
Dominici Hall (Phase I and II)	$20,307,503
McKinnon Family Tennis Center	$1,356,338
1650 University TI's	$10,852,557
College of Education	$8,500,000
Cancer Center	$75,627,942
Scholes Hall Renovations	$2,200,000
Collaborative Teaching and Learning Building	$9,000,000
Barbara and Bill Richardson Pavilion – UNMH	$233,800,000
John and June Perovich Business Center	$9,500,000
Hodgin Hall Renovations	$2,937,497
Farris Engineering Center	$25,526,400
McKinnon Center for Management at Anderson School	$24,714,281
Yale Parking Structure	$17,750,815
University of New Mexico West	$11,300,000
Castetter Hall (Phase I-IV)	$26,019,000
Physics and Astronomy and Interdisciplinary Science (PAIS)	
	$65,746,710
Johnson Center Expansion and Renewal	$35,000,000
Communication and Journalism	$3,780,000
Sevilleta Addition Phase 2	$2,425,000
Tamarind Institute Renovations	$4,916,527
Fine Arts Library	$3,000,000
Student Success Center	$6,500,000
University Stadium	$3,000,000
Mesa del Sol IFDM	$11,800,000
Rudy Davalos Practice Facility	$9,900,000
University Track Improvements	$850,000

394

Sandoval Regional Medical Center	$140,000,000
Innovate Albuquerque	$35,000,000
University of New Mexico Community-Based Clinics	
(SW Mesa, North Valley, SE Heights)	$10,950,000
Interdisciplinary Film and Digital Media School @ MDS	$10,500,000
933 Bradford SE (UNMH HOPE Building)	$12,000,000
Gallup Technology Center	$13,700,000
Total:	$1,092,069,902

9

A pessimist is one who makes difficulties of his opportunities and an optimist is one who makes opportunities of his difficulties.
—Harry S. Truman

The thirteen years I spent working as a Regent for the University of New Mexico were incredibly busy and productive years. So far, I have limited the previous chapters in this book on the University of New Mexico affairs to discussions with my collaborators on the Main Campus. But I also spent a considerable amount of time on Health Sciences Center projects. But before I get into the big strategic planning and capital outlay projects that I was involved in, like everything else, there's a back-story to why I became very passionate about the Health Sciences Center.

When I was on a hunting trip in 1999 it is a bit embarrassing to admit that my dog basically blew a hole in my hand, by accident of course, but that's exactly what happened. I am lucky to have the hand in such good condition today. I learned through personal experience what a Level I Trauma Center is all about and why it is so important in a crisis, when every decision is time sensitive, to have access to the very best specialists. Dr. Moneim was able to put my hand back together and I am forever grateful for his meticulous work and the excellent care I received from the nurses and physical and occupational therapists at the University of New Mexico Hospital. I learned later that if I had been reliant on a regional medical center for the management of my care during that accident the outcomes could have been very different. Until I damaged my hand, like most people, I hadn't considered the complexity of all the nerves and veins and tendons that must be carefully navigated during any reconstructive surgery. It turns out, hands can be rather complicated and there is lots of room for error. After that ordeal was over, I became like many who have undergone a medical trial. I was imbued with a sense of purpose about wanting to give back to the Health Sciences Center and to help them expand their operation so more New Mexicans could receive the outstanding level of care I did.

I had a second scare in 2007 when I passed out during a high level executive meeting with the president of the University of New Mexico and several members of his executive team. They immediately rushed me to the ER and shortly thereafter wheeled me into emergency surgery to have a pacemaker installed. Again, I was extremely lucky. I was able, in the space of an hour, to smoothly transition from the small boardroom in Scholes Hall to our Level I Trauma ER, to immediately undergoing surgery with a world-class cardiologist from an academic medical research center that specializes in cutting edge treatments. I owe my life to Dr. Laskey, the Chief of the Cardiology Division, and the other nurses and docs that took care of me that day. Because the University of New Mexico Hospital was right there, I know I benefited from the team of experts that took over in my hour of need. So I feel passionately about telling this story because unfortunately, people just don't realize how lucky we are in New Mexico to have a hospital staffed with the doctors that other doctors call for help, and a Cancer Center that's ranked on par with the Mayo Clinic and Sloan-Kettering and MD Anderson. We need to allow these brilliant doctors and administrators to boldly lead our state into the future because they have ideas about how we can solve some of the most pressing medical issues of our times.

The University of New Mexico Health Sciences Center is now a two billion dollar organization that employs nearly 11,000 people. However, the path to the organization's current level of growth was anything but smooth. In my interview with former Regent Mel Eaves, you will recall he discussed how back in the late 1960s, the Albuquerque Physicians Association was initially opposed to the concept of a medical school. In order to provide the proper perspective on the various challenges we faced along the way with the founding of the University of New Mexico Health Sciences Center, I sat down with three individuals:

Dr. Phil Eaton, Professor Emeritus, VP Health Sciences; Dr. Paul Roth, the University of New Mexico Health Sciences Center Chancellor; and Steve McKernan, the CEO of the University of New Mexico Hospital. All three of these outstanding leaders have shepherded various aspects of the University of New Mexico Health Sciences Center's growth over the years. In my interview with former Regent, Gene Gallegos, we discussed the problems inherent in the current governance structure. Dr. Roth and I will discuss that issue more in-depth. New Mexico is at a crossroads and the University of New Mexico Health Sciences Center is an important key to help build the economy for New Mexico's future. I asked Dr. Eaton, the first Executive Vice President of the Health Sciences Center, to provide some background about how the Health Sciences Center got started. I spoke with Dr. Eaton because most people just don't realize how pivotal he was when we were trying to get the cigarette tax passed, which was necessary to fund the new wing of the Hospital and the building of the Cancer Center. The cigarette tax would not have passed, it would not have happened, if Phil Eaton had not gone up to the legislature day after day, visiting with the legislators face to face. He developed the rapport with the legislators that was necessary to get those appropriations fully supported by every member of the legislature. And that's what people don't realize. Now we've got all these facilities. We got it done, but I wanted people to realize the effort that went into getting that cigarette tax approved that provided funding for the Cancer Center and Barbara and Bill Richardson Pavilion in the Hospital. It was not by any means a foregone conclusion.

Phil Eaton, MD, professor emeritus, former vice president of the
University of New Mexico Health Sciences Center /
Interviewed February 2017

Phil: When I became the second vice president of the Health Sciences Center in nineteen ninety-eight, initially it was an interim appointment. The interim appointment lasted almost three years. It was so exciting because I'd been here a long time, thirty years. The institution was very exciting to me because the opportunities to make a difference to the people in New Mexico and to science were so real. Now all of a sudden, I was in a position to be able to make things happen. I developed a twenty-year strategic plan, which meant I looked at what I felt the institution needed, what was it going to look like in twenty years, and what had to be done so that it was in a position to be really effective. I knew that the elements of that in one sense was the physical plant. The second element had to be administrative structure. The third element was that it had to have a culture that would welcome and recruit and retain the highest caliber of science as possible. That was very simple. The way I operated, what I knew was that money follows vision. You don't have to raise money. I knew the money would flow if the vision was compelling.

There were two people I was in constant communications with—my finance officer, Bob Earnest and my attorney, Stephanie Wilson. 'Cause there were two things I had to have. The first was, I had to have somebody that knew a whole lot more about money than I did. And I had to know somebody that knew a whole lot more about my interface with the public, which basically meant a lawyer, than I did. I knew that I had to have a really solid relationship with the legislature here and in Washington. The two things to make that happen was: I had to be able to use money, and I had to not do something stupid legally. As a part of that, it was really important to have a close relationship with the Regents. So, that's basically how I met you. I made it a point to interact personally on a face-to-face basis with the Regents all the time. The way I operated, I really didn't make appointments with people. I'd call up and say, "Mind if I drop over and have a cup of coffee? I've got something I want to talk to you about." That's the way I worked, not just with the Regents. That's the way I worked with the whole place and especially with the people who were directly under me, which was basically Steve McKernan, CEO of the hospital, the deans of schools of medicine, nursing, and pharmacy, and all of my senior staff. At that time Paul Roth was the dean of the School of Medicine, and I had these weekly meetings with this complete leadership group. The important thing about that meeting was I wanted to hear everybody, every single person, telling me what was going on and how I could help them, and how my staff could insure that things were on track. At that meeting I listened to each and every person, selecting the issues that were burning at that particular moment, asking for their input. I put them on the table and I asked everybody to tell me what they thought, every single person. I mentioned before the elements that had to be prepared to be effective in twenty years. I had to have leadership at the level of the deans and the hospital and the School of Medicine and know that they were buying in and supporting the culture. I couldn't do that if I didn't listen to them.

They'd say to me, "Where are we going to get the money?" And I said "Well, let's put down what the possibilities are and we'll put it together. If this is what we're going to do, we're going to do it and the money will come in. Any time there's a group that you feel I should speak to, put it on my schedule, letting me know what it is and why. Just remember, I must be able to speak if they are to know how we are making a difference." I said "If things go wrong, it's my fault not yours. I don't want you ever to think that if something goes wrong, that heads are going to roll." I'm completely responsible for every single thing that happens around here, always, from the bottom up. I take responsibility for leading this place, from the person who parks the cars to the people who write my speeches. By the way, when you write a speech for me, just remember I probably won't use it because I only speak extemporaneously. But I really want to know what you think I ought to be saying. But don't feel bad if I don't say exactly what you said or anything that you said. That kind of gives you a setting in which I operated and I've got to tell you, it was so exciting and gratifying.

The end of my time came nine years later, and things weren't finished. There were a bunch of infrastructure things that weren't done. I had it all set to go but it hadn't been completed. I asked Mary Kenney, "What am I going to do? All these plans I have for transforming the campus so they could be where we wanted to go." She said to me, "Dr. Eaton, don't worry about it. They don't know how you pulled it off to happen. They won't know how to stop it either." That stuck in my mind for a long time. Everybody had a role. My role wasn't doing anything except finding the people, identifying the vision for where to go and what the steps were to take. And then, find the people who could make it happen. Let me tell you what that means. Everybody wants to do a good job. Everybody wants to make a difference. That's my assumption that everybody wants to make a difference. All I did was to make it possible for people to make a difference. The Regents could make a difference so I talked to them a lot.

For example, I knew that Domenici was a very, very significant senator and highly committed to the state. When I was in this position, one of the things I needed to do was to get to know Pete well so that I could be in a position to help him make a difference in New Mexico. I went to Washington and met with him there and I found out what he wanted to do. One of the things that he wanted to do was to do brain imaging because Los Alamos had developed a new type of brain imaging called the magneto encephalography. There was a political mess about who was in charge. Dr. Leonard Napolitano (former dean of the medical school) had asked me to solve the problem years before I became the VP. That's how I began learning about what leadership was. He called me and said, "I want you to solve the problem." He didn't tell me how to do it. He just said, "Do it." I had to find out what it was all about. Why were they going to locate the building at the VA? What this imaging technology could do was to understand how the brain was working in people whose brains weren't working well. I knew that Senator Domenici had a schizophrenic daughter. I went to Senator Domenici and I let him know this was the first biomedical advance that had the chance of quantitating the way schizophrenic patients were thinking, and even how to diagnose schizophrenia. We could put this thing around their head and see how they were thinking, and we could tell you who had schizophrenia, even if they didn't know it. That also meant that if we had a way of intervening to help cure them or improve them. We had a quantitative way to know if it was working if we could look at the hard data of their post treatment scan. That's how he and I became extremely good friends, that common interest. So, I didn't have to ask for money. When we let Senator Domenici's chief of staff know that we might have a new building named after Domenici, the money materialized. I just followed your instructions. You would tell me exactly whom I should visit with and I would have those meetings. I listened to you and that made all the difference.

Steve McKernan was also really a great help to me in how to actually put together a long-term strategic plan. He was very, very helpful in that. When it came to the hospital, we sat down and I said, "Well, what are we going to do to make this happen, Steve?" Steve came up with two things. One was the importance of having a good relationship and going to the leadership of the Native American populations in New Mexico. He and I went up and met with the various leaders. Then Steve said, "You've got to make sure that the county is on board with us on this hospital." We met with the county. I asked "Steve, who do I need to talk to?" since Steve knew all the people involved. We were meeting their needs and my role was to let them know, "This is for you." This is really what it's all about.

Jamie, you were essential with the New Mexico legislature. I had been totally unfamiliar with the legislature. I had never even darkened the door, so we hired a lobbyist to help me out, Dick Menzer. Also, Jamie, you suggested I get to know Marilyn Budke. I would go up to legislature every month when in session. I would meet with Marilyn on a regular basis, taking her to lunch, for years and years and years. She would say, "Well, these are the people. Let me tell you about them. And here's what happened forty years ago and twenty years ago" and so on and so forth. "You know this guy, Jamie Koch? He's one of the people who can help you. Here's who else can help you in this regard" so on and so forth. Every month I would go up and have lunch with her for a couple of hours. Well, I liked the legislators and I think the feeling was mutual. I had great respect for them and I felt like they were extremely respectful of me as well. Senator Manny Aragon, at that point, was invaluable as one of the key legislators of about four people including Tim Jennings, to pass the cigarette tax to fund the hospital. This was so important because Governor Richardson was against it. He did not want to raise any taxes.

You and I had to really garner support for the Hospital and the Cancer Center, both in the House and in the Senate. We'd go up to legislature every day. We'd get there early in the morning and spend all day there. We'd get home at midnight. We would spend all day, every day doing that. I'd sit there and you would have already told me, "Well here's the R's and here's the D's. These are the people that are making a difference" and you would tell me a little bit about each person and all these things. I would sit there and I'd see one of the guys I needed to speak with get up and leave, either going to the restroom or get coffee. I'd get up and I'd go out and I'd see him in the hallway. I would say or they would say, "Hi Dr. Eaton, how are you doing? Just wanted to tell you, I'm happy you're here. Here's what we're doing." This would be helpful to me. What I found out was waiting for that opportunity was my job. I would have no problem waiting six hours if I could talk or spend one minute with the right person.

I would say, "We're looking to make a difference. I know that you would like to make a difference too. This is a way you can do it." In a capsule, that's what I had to say and I had to be able to say it immediately. Then, I would stop by their office in each case and follow-up. The legislators weren't there of course. To ensure the legislator did not forget our hallway discussion, I had to know the name of everybody in the office. It was very personal. I knew who they were and why they were there. I'm talking about the secretaries and the whole staff. They would say, "Dr. Eaton, come on in. Have a cup of coffee." I would sit down and have a cup of coffee. Then I would send a note. "It was so good to talk to you today Senator, Representative, whoever he/she was. I think that this can really help the children of New Mexico and your thing or whatever." Hand written was key. I would say to their staffers, "Make sure Senator, Representative gets this." What I'm trying to say is, even though it was hours and hours of work, it was so much fun and so easy to do because I knew what we were going to be able to do with that money. And slowly but surely, you and I and the lobbying team, all of us working together, we got everybody on board, including Governor Richardson. I always said if we communicated the vision to the right people, the money would flow, and it did. Last year the National Cancer Institute designated our Cancer Center as a Comprehensive Cancer Center, which is the highest level they award. The new designation made our Cancer Center one of only forty-seven cancer centers in the country that have that designation.

Dr. Eaton mentioned how important Steve McKernan was and I couldn't agree more. Steve McKernan was the CEO of the University of New Mexico Hospital. I have the utmost respect for Steve. He ran a very efficient organization. Steve McKernan was not interested in partisan politics. He was interested in providing outstanding healthcare to all New Mexicans. He set an example of integrity that is truly inspiring. Steve is a no-nonsense person. He doesn't always have the smoothest bedside manner. But I appreciate that he is not really into small talk. If you have a meeting with him, he wants people to get to the point quickly. New Mexicans have benefited from his ability to amass significant reserves. Since the current hospital is frequently at full capacity, since 2013, Steve and the rest of the University of New Mexico Health Sciences Center leadership had been trying to get a second new hospital built. Because of Steve McKernan's financial acumen and managerial savvy, if the governor would play ball, there is plenty of cash on hand to build a replacement hospital. On February 3rd, 2017 I sat down with Steve McKernan to talk about what we were able to accomplish together for healthcare in New Mexico and his thoughts about what will be needed to address New Mexico's healthcare needs in the future. During the interview Steve mentioned that his first job in New Mexico was working for the Boy Scouts Philmont Ranch. Steve's long association with the Boy Scouts sums up a lot about Steve. The Scout motto is: "Be Prepared" which means you are always in a state of readiness in mind and body to do your duty. Steve McKernan really embodies the Boy Scout's motto. He is always prepared.

Steve McKernan, former CEO, the University of New Mexico Hospital / Interviewed February 3, 2017

[Note: This interview was conducted while Steve McKernan was still CEO of the University of New Mexico Hospital.]

Jamie: Steve, can you tell us a little bit about yourself?

Steve: I was born and raised in Pennsylvania. I went to college at St. Bonaventure University in New York. During my summers in college I worked in northern New Mexico at the Philmont Scout Ranch. When I graduated from college I had worked another summer at Philmont and retained a job here in Albuquerque with the accounting firm of Deloitte Haskins and Sells. My association with the hospital and the University of New Mexico came about because Deloitte Haskins and Sells was the auditor on the hospital. I graduated college in nineteen seventy-eight, relocated to Albuquerque in September of that year, took that job, worked here. Well, I worked around rural New Mexico at a lot of towns—Clovis, Portales, Hobbs, Silver City, Deming, Gallup, Farmington and Santa Fe, doing audit jobs for the accounting firm.

One of the jobs they had was at the University of New Mexico Hospital doing the audit for the hospital. When I was out doing the audit in nineteen eighty, they had an open position and asked me to join the hospital. So I started as an accounting manager in the accounting department that year. And I have been with the hospital since that time—so almost thirty years.

Jamie: Well, first of all, talk about the hospital board, the way it's set up now.

Steve: Sure, a little bit about the hospital itself. The hospital is almost unique in the United States in the context that the hospital was started as a joint venture between the Indian Health Service and Bernalillo County. There's an underlying federal law, and a contract that deeded land along Lomas, east of Stanford, to the county to build a hospital for the uninsured and Native Americans. The hospital opened in nineteen fifty-four. There's also a state statute—the Hospital Funding Act that allows counties to build hospitals. In that legislation and in the federal contract, it required that the hospital have a separate board. So, it wasn't the county commissioners over the hospital or anybody else—it had to have its separate board.

In nineteen sixty-four the medical school opened. By nineteen sixty-eight it needed a place to have teaching for its medical students and its newly initiated graduate medical education, or intern residency program. The county and the university entered into a joint powers agreement to run the hospital together, through the hospital board, which had regents and county commissioners and other people on it. The information I had received on it, principally from John Perovich, who was a onetime president of the university and its chief financial officer for almost forty years.

Jamie: Yeah, for a long time.

Steve: For a long time it was a very contentious relationship between the county and the university. Mostly because the county retained authority over the finances and the university had the responsibility of running the operations. So, running the operations with no authority over the finances made it a very difficult task. This went on until about nineteen seventy-six, where the state stepped in. The Legislative Finance Committee and their analysts did a review of the hospital and determined that it would be best that the hospital be leased to the university and be part of the university operations. The Hospital Funding Act was amended in nineteen seventy-eight. It allowed a county to lease its public hospital for a class A county to the University of New Mexico, referenced in Article Twelve of the Constitution. Somebody knew what he or she was doing when they drafted that statute.

Jamie: They sure did, Marilyn Budke probably.

Steve: Yes, it probably was Marilyn. So that lease was put together and that statute was amended. The hospital was leased to the university for one dollar a year and the university took over total operations. That statute, the nineteen fifty-two contract, and the lease, specified that there would be a hospital board. Initially it was five members: one from the county, one that was nominated by the All Indian Pueblo Council, and three others that were appointed by the Regents. And the name was changed from Bernalillo County Medical Center to the University of New Mexico Hospital.

It started in nineteen eighty. The hospital had significant financial issues that year. Many of those issues were actually solved because of good management, not necessarily on my part, but because of a number of people around here. Also, the very significant involvement of the School of Medicine and being able to develop Centers of Excellence in trauma, in children, in cancer, and a variety of other programs was a very important strategic decision. Changes in federal reimbursement law occurred during

406

the mid nineteen-eighties that very much improved the finances of the hospital and transformed it from a losing, break-even organization to actually a very successful financial organization.

During that period of time there were some expansions to the hospital in terms of its physical facility, but a lot of it was originally built in nineteen fifty-four and we had some very significant infrastructure problems with it. Mostly because it was built as a public hospital with no thought of a teaching mission, and it had developed into a teaching hospital. To be able to teach requires a different type of hospital: more space, a different type of infrastructure than you get with a normal public hospital.

I got to know you around two thousand three. Marilyn Budke introduced me to you. Marilyn Budke had been appointed to the Hospital Board of trustees. You and Marilyn had discussed a number of things and one of them was the inadequacy of the facilities. So, Marilyn brought you down and we had a conversation. At that time we had been doing some preplanning about expansion of the hospital. I had just received the documents from the architect. I showed them to you and you said, "Well, what's it going to take to build this facility?" Because you had been here, you had had multiple operations on your hand, and you said, "I see the conditions your employees work in and they're inadequate, so we need to fix this." You were very direct about that and you said, "Tell me what you need." And I said, "We're gonna need money," and you said, "Well, let's start working on that."

So, you looked at the plans and you thought they were reasonable. You understood the legislative process. You understood the executive process. You understood the state of New Mexico very well, and believed; I think you believed that the state could be helpful in kick-starting this project. We went up to the LFC one day and I believe it was Jamie, Marilyn and I, and we met with Ben Altamirano, Lucky Varela, Kiki Saavedra and David Abbey. Marilyn led the conversation and indicated to the LFC and the legislators that University of New Mexico Hospital budgeted approximately a two hundred million dollar project. She explained that more than twenty percent of the patients came from outside Bernalillo County, and therefore the legislature ought to be involved with twenty percent of the financing of the facility. So the hospital would need forty million. The legislators pushed back, they laughed a little bit, kidded around with Marilyn, and Marilyn did not break a smile. And they said, "Okay, Marilyn, tell us what you really need" and Marilyn said, "Forty million." And they got serious and said, "Oh no, come on, Marilyn, tell us what the real number is." And Marilyn said, "Forty million." They said, "No, Marilyn we can't do forty million"

407

and Marilyn said, "It's forty million." Jamie, you said, "I'll figure out a way to get it, but we're telling you guys, it's forty million."

So, as Richardson took office and the legislative session came up Jamie, you and Marilyn walked the halls and talked to people, bent a few arms, stomped on some feet, cornered some people and generated enough support that they were able to include a significant cigarette tax increase that would produce enough money to finance about sixty million of bonds. It might have been more.

Jamie: Yeah, a little more than that.

Steve: A little bit more than that, so there'd be some operational support, plus there was sixty million in bonds. You coordinated with the fourth floor and had them completely on board. That legislation was passed, the cigarette tax was imposed, it went over to the State Finance Authority and the bonds were issued by the Finance Authority. Forty million came to the University of New Mexico Hospital, and actually you got a twofer out of the transaction because you started the initiation of the funding for the new Cancer Center, which would be twenty million. Then we got a threefer, or a hat trick out of the deal. I believe it was in the following year, because there was a significant amount of severance tax money and you got the legislature to throw an additional twenty million into the University of New Mexico to buy the equipment that would be needed for the facility. So, the total amount of support from the state ended up being sixty million for the University of New Mexico Hospital and twenty million in that instance for the Cancer Center. You went on and worked with Phil Eaton and Dr. Willman in getting significant additional support for the Cancer Center. I was not as involved in that transaction, so I don't remember all the things that went on, but for the Richardson Pavilion, which ended up being about a two hundred fifty million dollar project, we received about sixty million from the state, and then we issued about a hundred and ninety million of bonds.

The FHA insured the bonds we issued, and the important thing about that was the FHA does hospital bond insurance. In those days, they had the same rules as they had for a house mortgage. You had to put at least twenty percent down. So, unless we had the sixty million to be able to front to the FHA as a down payment, they would not have allowed us to issue the bonds. So, it was not, it was important in the context that we needed the funding to make the project work. It was equally important that the state showed its commitment to be able to get, to convince, the FHA to issue the insurance on the bonds. By then you were on the Board of Regents and we worked with you because then we had to bid the project and we had to make sure we'd have the capability of building a two hundred fifty million dollar project, which was one of the biggest state, solely state financed building projects ever in the state. Obviously, Los Alamos and Sandia have done bigger projects than that, but if you're just talking about a single state project, two hundred fifty million I think was the biggest one.

One of the things that also you brought to the table was the possibility of using what was called a "project labor agreement." Now, project labor agreements are common in states like New York and California. They're agreements between labor unions, the trade labor unions, the contractor and the owner, (in this case, the University of New Mexico, with concurrence of the FHA), which means if the owner agrees to certain conditions, the unions will agree to make sure there will be no work stoppage, work slowdown, or anything that would affect, from a labor perspective, the building of the project. These are allowed under state law, but to my recollection, they had never been used in the state of New Mexico up until that time. And mustering up enough labor to build a project that was this big, which was over five hundred thousand feet, [I think it's 550,000 square feet], and have a build which was close to two hundred million dollars on the build itself, requires an enormous amount of coordination. Being able to have a project labor agreement meant we took one of the variables that could stop a project off the table because we had total assurance that labor would be on board.

That became important because the University of New Mexico Hospital also has service unions, and the service unions were not as excited about building the hospital. It doesn't mean the employees weren't excited. The employees really wanted the hospital, but a union represents them. If the service union had gone to the trade unions and told them to slow down or stop, they could have created a very difficult situation. At that time, because we're talking about building in two thousand five, six, opening in two thousand seven, actually the economy in the United States was doing very well, the economy in New Mexico was doing very well, and there were shortages of skilled tradesmen to be able to build a project like this. Just to give you an example, there was a place on the critical path for building the project, where at one time we had say forty or fifty electricians, tradesmen, journeyman electricians on the project, but within two weeks they had to go to over two hundred twenty journeyman electricians. There aren't that many journeyman electricians in the Albuquerque market. So when you go down to Union Hall and you make a call, they had to go to Texas, California, Arizona and Colorado to go find journeyman electricians. And because the project labor agreement, and some of the conditions under that, which meant we had to meet on at least a monthly basis, (usually every two weeks), to coordinate the project. All the different trade executives would be sitting in a room and the contractor could say, "We need these calls happening on this time and then we're gonna have these drawdowns on this time and are you gonna meet them or not?" Well, the project labor agreement guaranteed that the trade unions would meet the calls and would facilitate the drawdowns and would make sure anybody who showed up on the project was drug free, totally trained, safety oriented and would be on time and on task during the whole project.

So, I think we go to the end, the real, only condition was that we had to support prevailing wage, but given that New Mexico has a Little Davis-Bacon Act, we were, and we're a public organization, we were locked into Little Davis-Bacon in any situation, which means we had to pay prevailing wage. So, in that context there was no additional cost to the project than what we would have paid. We had a little additional cost because we had to have an external organization monitor the project labor agreement and be able to mediate any disputes. We didn't have any effective disputes at all on the project, but you still had to have that going on. So, we had adequate labor to build a very large project and that worked very well.

Jamie: Yeah, one thing that I don't know if you knew, Steve, when I was State Democratic Chair, Brian Condit, who represented the unions, was very close, as you know, to Bill Richardson. Governor Richardson had been supported by the unions. I gave both of them a commitment at that time that I would work with the Board of Regents to try to convince them to do this labor agreement. The labor agreement, I think, was the best thing to do and it was done. What happened to me is that due to the union only labor contract, Daniels Ins. lost six hundred thousand in income from the nonunion contractors we had been insuring. By using the labor agreement, this brought in the governor, it brought in Brian Condit, and of course it brought in the labor unions that supported the project. That's one of the reasons the governor agreed to the cigarette tax. He did it because of the labor agreement we had.

Steve: The other interesting back-story is that there was one member of the Hospital Board of trustees that was not on board with the project labor agreement, but at the end of the day, the way this works is the lease from the county is to the Regents of the University of New Mexico. And so, the Regents are ultimately in control. They have delegated authority to the

Hospital Board, but retain ultimate authority. One of the board members at the hospital put up a very significant resistance to using a project labor agreement and forced the issue at a Board of Regents meeting, of which the Board of Regents voted in favor of it. But it's one of the few times we've actually had differences between the Regents and the Hospital Board. Normally the Regents and Hospital Board work very closely together and are very supportive of each other, but this is one case where there was dissention. But it was only by one member of a nine member board, but when it went to the Regents, the Regents passed it.

Jamie: And the Regents passed it unanimously.

Steve: Right.

Jamie: I am glad we discussed the way the Barbara and Bill Richardson Pavilion got funded. Another reason that I wanted to visit with you Steve, is that people don't realize the relationship the University of New Mexico has with Native American nations, tribes and pueblos.

Steve: One of the other significant things that we had to do to get the project going was be able to get the Indian Health Service to sign off on any change to the lease because they're party to all the transactions, going back to the IHS' donation of land to the county—the nineteen fifty-two contract. So, when we started working with the Indian Health Service, they, under their federal regulations, are required to do consultation with the local tribes. In this case, represented by the All Pueblo, was at that time the All Indian Pueblo Council, it's now the All Pueblo Council of Governors. And there are nineteen governors and they're all sovereigns, and they all have their own opinion. The contract, which the University of New Mexico assumed to be responsible for on behalf of the county, makes a reference to being able to have a hundred beds available *at any and all times* for Native Americans, with preference to Pueblo Native Americans.

So, when we had the go on building the hospital, we had to get a signoff from the Indian Health Service, and then the FHA was very involved because they were gonna issue insurance on the project. They wanted to know who was in control, when they were in control and how are they gonna be in control, because they didn't want to see a default on the bond for which they were insuring. So, we did a lot of work and negotiations and we brought Senator Domenici into the fold. He was extraordinarily supportive. It was a bipartisan effort. There was never any reference to partisanship. It was all about what's good for the state of New Mexico and how do we meet our responsibilities to the Native American community. The building of the hospital, this new wing in the hospital, was going to expand to about a hundred forty to a hundred fifty beds in the hospital. So, that helped the Native, convinced the Native Americans that this was a good project. It wouldn't cost the Native Americans anything, but they still needed to give their permission, and they were interested in the obligations of the nineteen fifty-two contract and that the Regents would be able to uphold those obligations.

So there was a lot of collaboration between different parties: the federal government at the FHA, Department of Health and Human Services (which IHS is involved with). The secretary there had to give his permission. Senator Domenici facilitating that, the All Indian Pueblo Council endorsing that, the Regents being part of it, the governor being part of it, the state Board of Finance being part of it, the legislature being supportive of it and the county being supportive of it. So, it was a real mix of a lot of people working together for the common good. You were very much involved and spearheaded it. I mean you were the one who came in here with Marilyn and looked at the plans and said, "I've been here. You need this hospital." You caught the vision. Then it was a work process to get everybody else on board. And, at least in my career, and you know I think a lot of peoples' career, you don't necessarily run across too many people who when they see the vision, were clear in the vision, work out the details and let's figure out how we can get everybody to agree. Jamie, you really named this book accurately because in the case of this hospital, you really left your ego at the door and you didn't worry about who was gonna get credit for the project. You jumped in and you facilitated this stuff. If we had gotten hung up on egos it would have been very difficult. Jamie, you were a key player, obviously. Marilyn was totally supportive and never wanted any recognition at any time. Senator Domenici was very supportive. Domenici never sought any recognition at any point in time, because he knew it was that important to the state, but he played a big part.

Jamie: That's why we have two Domenici buildings too.

Steve: Right, we got around to some Domenici named buildings.

Jamie: Anyway, that's why I wanted to visit with you, Steve, because people do not know all the things that have been done and how difficult it was to build this hospital. If it hadn't been for you, Steve, leading all the troops

412

necessary to get the facility built, it wouldn't have been accomplished. So thank you Steve.

Steve: That's very kind of you, Jamie to say, but I give you credit. You spearheaded getting the money and without money, nothing happens. Now, if you don't mind, I'd like to talk about two other projects that I think are incredibly important.

Jamie: Absolutely.

Steve: One is the building of SRMC, Sandoval Regional Medical Center.

Jamie: We had a lot of fun with the land on that.

Steve: At a point in time, which was around two thousand nine, two thousand ten, the economy in New Mexico was still doing relatively well, and we saw even with the building of the additional wing (the Barbara and Bill Richardson Pavilion) down here in Albuquerque, that was gonna be insufficient for what the growth in the population in New Mexico would be. And one of the things that was going around the United States was teaching hospitals were building or buying community hospitals, because not everything we do here is high end tertiary. We do a lot of secondary care. And when we strategized with the Hospital Board and the Regents, we made a decision that we ought to go to the west side of the river, because that's where the growth in the metro market is, and probably out to Rio Rancho to Sandoval county. You were involved because there was a lot of controversy going on, and you led a Governor's Summit around two thousand six, two thousand seven, with people in Bernalillo County believing, with merit, that patients were coming from around the state to the University of New Mexico Hospital, and the other counties weren't paying their fair share of the cost of indigent care for patients referred in here. It became very apparent at the Summit that the two biggest counties were Sandoval and Valencia County. And so we had a sub-meeting during this Governors Summit, with the folks from Sandoval County, in a side room, over at the student union. You were there. Paul was there, and I was there. A variety of people were there. And the question was, would folks in Sandoval County implement a tax, a new tax, that you would send to Bernalillo County and to the University of New Mexico to take care of your indigents and they said, "Hell no," and used some other adjectives at the time.

You and Paul came back and said, "Well, what if we build a hospital in Sandoval County? Would you implement a tax in Sandoval County to support us building a hospital in your county? Then you could keep your patients, uninsured patients, in your county?" Remember, this was before the Affordable Care Act, so we're in the two thousand seven and eight timeframe and the Affordable Care Act didn't pass until two thousand nine and ten. And they said "yeah." (Well actually they used some really colorful adjectives saying, "Yeah they'd do that, as long as the University of New Mexico ran it.")

So that got us embarked on a path. Then, because you know how stuff works up in Santa Fe, you visited with Land Commissioner Lyons and said there's some land out in the north part of Rio Rancho. Could we strike a deal because simultaneously to us wanting to build a hospital, main campus at the university was looking at doing a remote campus. So, you visited, I understand, with the land commissioner, struck a deal for about twenty-eight thousand an acre, which was probably one tenth of what the cost of land was running in that part of Rio Rancho at the time. And you were able to acquire over three hundred acres of land and that became the place that we eventually built the Sandoval Regional Medical Center. Then with you at the Regents and stuff, we decided to use the Research Park Corporation to form a new subsidiary corporation and put SRMC in that corporation. We went back to the FHA and asked them to do another insured bond. And we ran this up through the Regents, so this was different than Bernalillo County, different than the University of New Mexico Hospital. But it was totally over at this new corporation and we got funding from the University of New Mexico Medical Group and some from the University of New Mexico. We put it as a down payment and we proceeded along. We didn't need to get any other federal approval on any of those other things. Sandoval County passed a four and quarter mil tax rate. And they built up funds and we got going on that project.

Jamie: Indigent. When I was in the legislature in nineteen seventy-four, I was a co-sponsor of the Santa Fe County Indigent Fund which was designed to help St. Vincent's Hospital.

Steve: So, there's the third thing I'll talk about: Project SEARCH.

Jamie: Project SEARCH.

Steve: Project SEARCH. Jamie, one day, which would have been about five years ago, you went to the president of the university and Dr. Roth and I were called over to his office. And you brought us information about a program, Project SEARCH, that you had been involved with at a personal level and you had been so impressed with it that you asked, "Could the University of New Mexico replicate this program?" And you were very well aware we have a big section at our Health Sciences Center called the Center for Developmental Disabilities. The mission of the Center for Developmental Disabilities is being the center in New Mexico to help build up programs and make sure there's access to care for people in the state with developmental disabilities, principally on the autism spectrum, so you were familiar with this. And when you brought it over, everybody I think, squirmed and put their heads down and wouldn't make eye contact or do any of those things. But I was looking at material and you were explaining the experience you had with your daughter and her friend. You explained how there was a group of people in our community, in every community, everywhere, in all different kinds of families, that may have some developmental disabilities, but they had key attributes about them that potentially could make them exceptional hospital employees.

So, you and I kind of had a side conversation and the request was, "We're gonna need a hundred thousand dollars a year to kick off this program." And we are an educational institution, we're the University of New Mexico, and I said "We'll do it at the hospital." And then everybody perked up and said "Okay we'll do it at the hospital and this is great" and stuff like that. So, then you and I worked together, and everybody else lost track of this, but we worked, went to the Center of Development and Disability and they worked with Adult Protective Services and they started identifying a cohort of folks, I think twelve or thirteen. And three years ago we enrolled them in a program and the CDD brought the folks, matriculating them over from APS to make sure they had certain skills and background. We got the curriculum from Project SEARCH, so it's a license. You pay them to be part of their system.

I think of the thirteen we enrolled, eleven graduated and we hired eight at the hospital. And they had developed very good skillsets that they would be employees in the hospital. And your daughter came and was our commencement speaker at the first graduation. And she did a fabulous job and we had people jumping up and down, standing ovations, yelling and cheering. Because you had families, you had grandparents, you had parents, you had siblings, you had aunts and uncles and all these family members were emotional because they had lived with a family member, who they loved and cared for, but were very concerned that this family member may not ever be able to be independent, get a job, and sustain themselves. And that day we had eleven people graduated, who are now capable of being pretty independent citizens in our community. Those eleven people were going to have self-sustaining employment and would be able to contribute to teams, and would have people in their work environment that would be their friends, their colleagues and supporters. And it's been one of the most marvelous programs. Project SEARCH met a work need because before Project SEARCH, frequently in those positions, we'd get phenomenally unreliable workers. Now we have highly skilled, highly reliable workers who are tremendous colleagues and team members. And that opened something up for me that I was unaware of, didn't know about, couldn't have thought of, would never have thought it would have been a source of new team members for our organization. And Jamie, you brought us to that. And I knew we just had to kick it off.

I think part of it is a trust you build between people. Jamie, you brought it and it had nothing to do for you personally. It wasn't gonna help you and your family per se, but you care about this community of folks and you thought this would benefit the hospital. You thought this would be a great transaction that could bring groups together to work together and make our community better. Boy, you were right. You started it and we're now on our third class that's enrolled right now, that'll graduate in May and we're very excited about it.

Jamie: I agree that Project SEARCH has been a game changer for so many families and for the hospital. So, let's shift gears.

As we think about the future, because you've talked today about three different big projects that you worked on with me, all of them had very important outcomes for the health of individuals and families here in New Mexico. As you think about healthcare and you think about hospitals here in New Mexico, as we look towards the future, what do you think is gonna be important for New Mexico to grow and prosper?

Steve: Well, one thing you see, at least in the business I'm in, is that every major city in the United States has a teaching hospital and the two that don't are getting them right now—Phoenix and Austin. And healthcare is a huge part of our economy, almost eighteen percent, and in knowledge economy research is important and biomedical research is one of the most important of them. None of that stuff is done without having an academic medical center. And academic medical centers don't exist unless they have a flagship teaching hospital. So, this is all very synergistic. What I observe, I think, is New Mexico's trying to convert from government based, energy based economy, to the knowledge economy. It obviously has attributes with weather, location, diversity, friendliness, and a variety of things that make it an ideal place for the evolution of our economy. But I have a pretty firm conviction. It isn't going to happen unless you have an academic medical center. The University of New Mexico has the wherewithal, it has the vision, it has the mission and it has the capability.

So, doing these projects, big, medium and small, we talked about them, all three, are vital to being able to advance that mission. And at least I'm of the conviction, without this academic medical center, the ability for New Mexico to ride the wave of the knowledge economy and convert from government based, energy based, to tech based is not gonna happen. If you have a good academic medical center, a great academic medical center, anchored to a research university that has the engineering school and the business school and the arts and sciences and everything, well it's gonna be a magnet to attract people. It's gonna be the hub that allows for the development of the new technologies and it's gonna serve the people of New Mexico so they get great healthcare and education that otherwise wouldn't be available.

To give you one idea, just as a scope, this rings with me, it may not ring with a whole lot of other people. At the University of New Mexico Hospital on any given day, we have more than six hundred students and trainees. We have, in the hospital, four hundred eighty residents, graduate medical education. These are the people who are going into the community. They'll become the doctors. The hospital with the next biggest resident training program in New Mexico has five residents.

Jamie: People don't know that.

Steve: Nobody knows that. And if you're going to have doctors in New Mexico, you're going to have to support rural New Mexico, because rural New Mexico is still an important part. If you're gonna have doctors, if you're gonna have nurses, if you're gonna have pharmacists, physical therapists, occupational therapists, if you're gonna support developmental disabilities in rural New Mexico, if you're gonna support trauma centers, if you're gonna be able to deliver a cancer center, if you're gonna be able to deliver stroke services through telemedicine, it's gonna be hubbed out of Albuquerque and it's gonna be hubbed out of the University of New Mexico Hospital. Absent the University of New Mexico Hospital, none of this is going to happen.

We know we're going to have to rebuild a significant part of this hospital to be able to fulfill the vision and accomplish the mission. We're not going to have a vibrant academic medical center without a good teaching hospital.

Jamie: Right, because it was absolutely in the media, reported like "well you could just use the Lovelace, it's a great building."

Steve: It's not a teaching hospital. They don't have the faculty practicing at Lovelace. They don't have the residency base at Lovelace. They never will under federal law right now, be able to have the residents over at Lovelace, or at Presbyterian, which hospital is completely filled. The other part of it is location is important. If you have faculty that are simultaneously involved with research, clinical care and teaching, tell them to drive twenty minutes across town to do an hour's worth of work and then drive twenty minutes back across town to do it, they're gonna be miserably inefficient and not capable. The centers for research and clinical care and education are all flagship teaching hospitals, which are based in one place.

And so, I was going to say, in our business, at least I like to talk about, there are three things that are important: place, people and program. You have to have the right place, which includes the buildings, the facilities, the equipment—all that stuff. You have to have great people. You're not going to do anything without great people. And you have to have well defined programs. The Cancer Center is National Cancer Institute-Designated. Comprehensive Cancer Center, is a program run by great people at a great place, great building. The University of New Mexico's children hospital has got a great building. It's got great people in it and it has well defined programs, like its cancer program, and its emergency medicine program, and its pulmonary program, and its hematology program and a variety of things. It's a resource for the whole state of New Mexico and parts of other states, where kids are sent here to receive that care.

One of our great limiting factors at the University of New Mexico right now is the facility constraint. There's a lot more people we could serve and deliver better outcomes for the people of New Mexico, but we are constrained by our facility. For us that becomes a big, important thing. And maybe we can stretch it out for two or three or four more years, but at some point in time a building built as a public hospital in nineteen fifty-four is not going to serve as the basis to advance an academic medical center in the University of New Mexico. It's going to have to be replaced.

Jamie: So when you talk about the importance of the flagship university with an academic medical research center, what I'm hearing is that this new hospital, it's not just about being able to serve more people. Obviously that's great, but it's also about the hospital being a driver for the economy. This knowledge economy is vital for the state to turn the corner economically and get the kind of job growth that we need.

Steve: Well if you look at where economic expansion is happening in the United States and where it's not happening, it's happening in towns that have academic medical centers.

Jamie: It's true. Is there anything else you want to add before we wrap up?

Steve: You are a great guy.

Jamie: Thank you, Steve.

The last person I sat down with to discuss the evolution of the University of New Mexico Health Sciences Center was Dr. Paul Roth. Dr. Roth is currently the chancellor of the University of New Mexico Health Sciences Center. He is known nationally as a pioneer in emergency medicine, and he has been an innovator in medical education. He was among the first to devise a system of "urgent care" and he founded the first private urgent care clinic in New Mexico. He also founded the University of New Mexico Center of Disaster Medicine and coordinated the nation's first civilian Disaster Medical Assistance Team.

Roth graduated from George Washington University School of Medicine in 1976 and completed his family practice residency in 1979 at the University of New Mexico School of Medicine. He completed a BS in 1969 and an MS in biology in 1972, at Fairleigh Dickinson University.

In addition to his duties as chancellor of the University of New Mexico Health Sciences Center, he is also the dean of the School of Medicine, a position that he has held since 1994, making him the longest-serving dean of any medical school in the nation. The University of New Mexico School of Medicine ranks third in the nation for its Rural Medicine Program in the upcoming issue of *U.S. News & World Report's* "America's Best Graduate Schools" for 2016. The University of New Mexico's medical school has maintained this top-five national ranking since 1996. Out of 130 U.S. accredited medical schools, *U.S. News & World Report* ranks the University of New Mexico School of Medicine's Primary Care 18th, tied with University of California.

∿∿∿

Paul Roth, MD, chancellor, the University of New Mexico Health Sciences Center, CEO of the Health System, dean of the School of Medicine / Interviewed January 2017

Jamie: So, can you tell us a little bit about yourself? Where you were born, raised, how you came to New Mexico?

Paul: I wasn't born in New Mexico but I was professionally bred in New Mexico. So, I was born in New Jersey and grew up just outside of Newark, New Jersey in a type of tenement building and my dad was a traveling salesman. He actually sold insurance for a while. He sold everything. He sold welding supplies. He was a used car salesman, a new car salesman, and he sold some real estate. And so, in my early childhood, he would be gone for a very long time because his district was New Jersey and parts of Pennsylvania and a large segment of the North East. He would be gone for a week or two at a time.

When he came back home it was always a great celebration and it was a lot of fun. Then when I was eight years old, my parents saved up enough money to buy an unfinished house in another very agricultural part of New Jersey. So in that part of my life I grew up in a town called Lake Hiawatha in a township called Parsippany. I went to elementary school, junior high and high school there. I went to college at Fairleigh Dickinson University and got a Bachelor's and a Master's in biology. I applied for medical school and went to the University of Nevada for my first two years of medical school. At that time, it was only a two-year medical school. And then I ultimately transferred to George Washington University in DC, where I received my MD degree. I went on to a residency program in family medicine here at the University of New Mexico. That was in nineteen seventy-six. So forty-one years ago I moved to Albuquerque. I finished my residency program in family medicine in nineteen seventy-nine. I joined the faculty in that department but became very much enthralled with emergency medicine and began moonlighting. I created two companies while I was a resident and set up the first urgent care center around this part of the United States while I was a resident. I really enjoyed emergency medicine. At that time, there was not a subspecialty in emergency medicine.

After finishing my training in family medicine, I focused more of my attention in emergency medicine. I moved from a faculty member in family medicine to a faculty member in emergency medicine. I became the director of the division of emergency medicine here in the early eighties. I eventually became, not only boarded in family medicine but also board certified in emergency medicine. We were able to start the very first residency program in emergency medicine. We created our disaster medicine program here. I was involved with disaster medicine on a national level for many years. In the early nineties, I was able to move the division of emergency medicine out of the department of family medicine and set up a freestanding academic department of emergency medicine. I became the first chair of the department of emergency medicine. Leading up to that time, I became the director for ambulatory care here. At that time, it was called the University of New Mexico Medical Center. That was before there was a Health Sciences Center. In nineteen ninety-four, Dean Napolitano retired as the dean of the medical school and the director of the University of New Mexico Medical Center. At that time, we had the University of New Mexico Hospital, Carrie Tingley Hospital, the Children's Psychiatric Hospital, the Bernalillo County Mental Health and Retardation Center. Those facilities made up the University of New Mexico Medical Center.

Dean Napolitano was the dean of the medical school and those hospitals reported to him as the director of the medical center. So, he had both of those positions. President Peck eventually decided that the university needed to consolidate all of its health programs, and the Regents approved the creation of the Health Sciences Center in nineteen ninety-four, and pulled in the colleges of nursing, and pharmacy and dental hygiene program all under the umbrella of the Health Sciences Center. In fact, while I was on a deployment at the North Ridge earthquake commanding our disaster team at the time, I got a call from President Peck asking me to be the interim director of the medical center while they were recruiting for a vice president for the new Health Sciences Center. And so, I took on that role for a while. Jane Haney was recruited and became a vice president. They recruited her from the Food and Drug Administration. I became the interim dean of the medical school in nineteen ninety-four. There was a national search and I threw my hat in the ring and was appointed the permanent dean a year later in ninety-five. After Jane Haney left, Phil Eaton was selected to be her successor and they changed the title to executive vice president. I remained the dean and Phil remained in that role until he retired in late two thousand five. I was then appointed the interim executive vice president for the Health Sciences Center and early in two thousand six, I was appointed to that position permanently. I also remained the dean of the medical school.

When Governor Martinez campaigned, she said there were too many vice presidents. So, that criticism of the University of New Mexico remained for a couple of years. President Schmidly felt that he wanted to respond to that and so he changed all the titles over here from vice president. Instead of me being the executive vice president, he said, "Well, why don't you be a chancellor so that we don't have as many vice presidents?" So my title changed around two thousand twelve. That's the title I've had up to the present day. However, for a brief period, I did serve as the acting president of the University of New Mexico while President Schmidly had a severe illness. He asked me to serve as the acting president while he was being treated and recuperating from his illness.

Jamie: When you became chancellor, what was your budget at that time? It was less than a billion dollars right?

Paul: When I started it was about seven hundred million.

Jamie: And what is it now?

Paul: This year we have an operating budget of slightly over two billion. [About $2.1 billion]

Jamie: So since you've been chancellor, you've increased revenues threefold?

Paul: Yes.

Jamie: A threefold increase, when the rest of the state is still trying to recover from the Great Recession. I am so pleased with what you and the rest of the HSC leadership have been able to accomplish with the Health Sciences Center. It is really phenomenal what you all have built. People just don't realize that. How many people work here?

Paul: We have about eleven thousand people working with us.

Jamie: Financially, how strong are you?

Paul: We're extremely strong. Of course there are challenges we face with the proposed changes to the Affordable Care Act. There are always challenges, but we're well poised to be able to weather that storm. So, we're in a very solid position.

Jamie: We established the Health Sciences Board when Raymond Sanchez was president of the Board of Regents, correct?

Paul: Yes.

Jamie: Tell us about that. Did we have somebody come and study and did we spend some money doing that?

Paul: We did. We had the Chartis Corporation complete a study. President Schmidly wanted to re-examine the governance and the structure of the Health Sciences Center. And we issued an RFP and contracted with an outside consulting firm called Chartis who came in and they actually interviewed all the Regents. They looked at the current structure of the Health Sciences Center and recommended a series of changes. They felt the Regents needed to be better informed about the details of the operations of the Health Sciences Center in order to properly govern a complex organization like an academic health center. That approach has been duplicated in many other academic health centers around the country. We also have one of the smallest number of Regents in the United States with only seven. Usually there's nine or eleven or thirteen members on a governing body for a big university, and so one of the problems was that the Regents not only had to manage the whole university, but they also had to staff all of the committees. That was very time consuming and they felt that if there was a subset of the Regents who, along with community members that would be appointed by the Regents, to dive deeper into the operations of the Health Sciences Center, we would have a more informed and properly governed Health Sciences Center. That body would report to the full Regents but it would be an HSC Board that would have certain authority to act on an array of topics. So we did that in two thousand twelve. We began the task of re-writing all of the Regents' policies to embrace the concepts in that Chartis report. Scott Sauder, our Health Sciences health attorney and I, began drafting changes in the language. Scott and I would travel up to Santa Fe to meet with you and Gene Gallegos to go through some of the wording. You were very instrumental in modifying the language to more appropriately reflect the role of the Regents and to make sure we didn't diminish the authority of the Regents. At the same time, the new wording also allowed for a more expansive role for the HSC Board. And of course, we met with the other Regents too, and with Raymond Sanchez, of course, who was the president of the Regents at the time.

Jamie: But the whole concept, just to summarize, the whole concept of this reorganization was that in an organization this large, a two billion-plus [$2.1 billion] organization with eleven thousand employees, in order for a board to be actually, properly, overseeing it, required more individuals being able to be properly briefed and have the amount of time to be able to attend the various committees because there are a lot of components to oversee. Correct? Just three people couldn't really cover it all. There are just not enough hours in the day. Another problem was with Health Sciences Center committee before was that we had three Regents and they didn't meet regularly.

Paul: Previously, it was a Health Sciences Center committee, and you are correct, it was not well attended.

Jamie: They didn't meet and when you're looking at a two billion-plus organization and you're not meeting, this is a problem. And on the other hand, you have about an eight hundred million organization, with many subcommittees, and they are meeting all the time. So, with only seven Regents, they are spread too thin. That's why the Health Sciences Center Board was set up that way.

Paul: That's right. The whole point of the restructuring was to assure that there was proper governance of a huge and complex organization such as ours. And just as you said, there was a lot of scrutiny over main campus, which was really only about a third of the entire University of New Mexico. The other two thirds of the University of New Mexico is the Health Sciences Center. There was very little discussion, barely any comments about our finances or what we were doing or any of that. The healthcare industry then, and still is, going through huge changes and many universities began spinning out their hospitals because of the risk, the economic risk to the rest of the university. So, if the University of New Mexico was to retain the Health Sciences Center, it probably had to have a more rigorous review of our operations. It was just obvious that in order to assure the public that there was proper oversight of a huge part of the University of New Mexico, that it needed more of a focused governance structure and other community input into what was happening. And so that was all approved after almost a year of writing the new policies and visiting with everyone. I remember bringing drafts to President Schmidly at his home because he was still recuperating, and making sure that he was well informed about what was going on and that he approved all of these things as well. It was a very productive time. The new HSC Board had three Regents and four community members.

Jamie: Yes, there were a total of seven.

Paul: Seven. And then the composition changed over the subsequent few years. Finally in early two thousand sixteen, the Regents felt that it was not proper to have community members serving on that group. The new Regents for the university eliminated the board, modified the policies and returned back to the Health Sciences Center committee structure. And that's where we are today.

Jamie: So as I see it, there are two ways to manage this situation. One scenario is that the Regents all are on the Health Science Board.

Paul: And that was suggested.

Jamie: The Health Science Board would meet once a month. The main Regents board would meet on different days. And you could do that. And I think that's the best model at this time.

Paul: Yeah. We suggested that. That was an option. But I think the reality was, at least at that point, most of the Regents had jobs. And this is all volunteer time. And it was so time consuming. I think while that was an option, I think at least the Regents at the time suggested well maybe we could still keep it at three Regents. Bring in some other people; retain the ultimate authority over what was going to be done. But clearly, there are all kinds of ways that you can exercise that type of oversight. It does require a huge amount of time and effort. And when you only have seven Regents, it would basically be a second full time job. One other option that I had suggested was for the Regents to meet every other month. And so, one month it could be the Regents meeting for the entire university. The alternate months could be all the Regents meeting but just focusing on the Health Sciences Center. So, there's a whole bunch of different ways that you could have done that with the full Regents or with subsets. There's a lot of permeations and variations to that.

Jamie: When the new hospital is finished, that's going to really send your budget way up with the dollars.

Paul: Probably, yes.

Jamie: Don't you think there's a problem, a natural problem, when you have somebody doing two billion-plus and somebody doing eight hundred million and the Health Sciences Center is not having financial problems? It just keeps growing, but main campus is really strapped for cash. Don't you think that's a problem? And pretty soon, you're going to be at three billion or whatever it is and the main campus is not going to grow nearly as fast... don't you think that's going to create even more tension?

Paul: Yeah, I think that that kind of contrast does create a lot of stress and conflict. There is huge growth in the healthcare market. And at the same time, higher education in the United States is facing huge challenges. Actually it's very similar to what happened in healthcare back in the eighties, and in the early nineties. The costs associated with healthcare continued to rise significantly. The percentage of the gross national product that was associated with healthcare began growing almost exponentially. And so, there were a number of initiatives to begin reducing those costs resulting in President Obama's Patient Protection and Affordable Care Act. The whole point was recognizing that the average citizen was paying a lot more than they should for healthcare and there wasn't adequate attention to quality outcomes. The Act was exactly what needed to be done. Not to say that there were parts of it that still needed improvement, but I am hopeful that the replacement the senate is working on will retain a lot of those principles, but also fix those parts of the act that were problematic.

Jamie: We hope.

Paul: But the problem that higher education has now is exactly what we were facing in healthcare a couple of decades ago. Where the cost for a college education has been skyrocketing and the average person in the United States, middle class, certainly lower income brackets, simply can't afford going to college any more. So, the business model for higher education will have to undergo a transformation the same way that healthcare had to. Universities in the country are going to have to re-examine how they provide a higher education for the population in the United States at a lower cost and at a higher quality to allow them to get good jobs and to add more value to our society. What the country really needs is a Student Protection and Affordable Education Act. That's what should probably occur, although probably not under President Trump's time in office.

Jamie: No, I doubt it.

Jamie: But, getting back to the Health Sciences Center, I believe the governance really needs to be addressed more. Don't you think?

Paul: Yes.

Jamie: Not to be critical of the Regents. Not doing that. But as the HSC budget grows, it is going to have so much complex stuff going on and you only have three Regents trying to handle that. It can't be done. All of that is going to have to be looked at real hard.

 I think this really needs to be looked at. I think the legislature needs to form an interim committee to take a look at the governance at the university in regards to Health Science and the main campus.

Paul: I would hope that at some point the Regents would recognize that there needs to be a much greater engagement and review of the manner in which the Health Sciences Center and main campus operates. And as we discussed earlier, that could be done in a number of ways. Now there's only a very cursory review by the current Health Sciences Center committee. Before, we would have much greater detail reviews of the Health Sciences Center. We'd average, between the formal HSC Board meetings and the committee meetings, probably about eight to ten hours a month. And currently, we're down to a two hour meeting where we present in a very cursory fashion some of our finances, some of the other highlights of the Health Sciences Center and that's all. It's my view and I think it's the view of national experts that a more reasonable role for governance in a complex organization like an academic health center is to learn much more of the basic workings and financial issues associated with this type of organization. And as you and I have also talked about, the challenges on main campus will be monumental.

Jamie: I agree one hundred percent. So, switching gears, while I was on the Regents, can you talk about how we also created a new hospital in Rio Rancho?

Paul: Yes. You were very instrumental in securing the land in Rio Rancho. That's a separate story all by itself.

Jamie: Yes. I talk about that process of getting the land earlier in the book.

Paul: Well at this point, we have a campus at the University of New Mexico west campus which is about half of that full parcel of land. President Frank came to me a couple of years ago and said that he thought the original plan for the development of the University of New Mexico west campus was not as viable of an option at that point. The economy changed. The growth rate that had been predicted didn't happen, for all the reasons people know. So the main campus was actually beginning to see student enrollment dropping and the economics of higher ed in general was being challenged. At the same time, the healthcare industry was growing and the demand for more health professionals continued to rise. We were trying to figure out ways to expand our class size and our academic programs and space for that. And so, the president transferred the responsibility for the majority of the University of New Mexico west campus to the Health Sciences Center on that parcel where we currently have our Sandoval Regional Medical Center. There's already an existing education building there and we're talking to the City of Rio Rancho to build a second building that would be dedicated to expansion of student activity. More classrooms, more teaching programs, but oriented around the health professions.

Jamie: So you're in charge of the University of New Mexico Sandoval Regional Center in Rio Rancho too? Am I correct?

Paul: Yes. Currently, I have that responsibility as well.

Jamie: Tell us about the proposed expansion. How that's going to work out? For the new replacement hospital opportunity, can you tell us where we are on that?

Paul: While all of this growth was occurring, we also realized that our current facility at the University of New Mexico Hospital was insufficient to meet the current demands. Two things happened. The facility is a much older facility. Parts of the hospital were built in the late fifties and in the early sixties. The actual building itself is crumbling in some areas. Simultaneously the demand for the types of specialized services that we are uniquely capable of providing in the state of New Mexico has grown dramatically. And so, we were not able to meet the full needs of the patients in the state of New Mexico. We felt we had to replace the old facility and allow for a larger capacity to meet those needs. The kind of building that we're in right now, the older facility, is part of the reason that we're lacking in some capacity. The way hospitals were constructed and the way they were designed initially (while it was state-of-the-art at the time sixty years ago) is no longer consistent with modern medical practice. So about five years ago, we began studying ways in which we could begin replacing the old facility and deal with expanding capacity at the same time. We came up with a proposal for a ninety-six-bed, freestanding hospital, on lands west, which is the area west of University Boulevard, north of Lomas. The new facility would have allowed us to move a lot of our surgical cases to that facility and open up space in the older part of the hospital. That would have not only expanded beds but also would have allowed us to move patients from the worst part of the hospital. It would have accomplished, in a small way, both of those things as a first step to completely rebuilding all of the adult inpatient areas of the hospital. The plan was a three phased project that would begin with ninety-six beds and then over subsequent years, gradually build another wing and move more facilities out. And ultimately, we would have all of the adult beds to a new facility over multiple years. The Regents approved the plan and the master plan that was associated with it, and we received approval by the Higher Ed Department. Sadly, the state Board of Finance did not approve it.

When the Board of Finance refused to vote, even after multiple efforts on our part, we took a hiatus from our planning for several years while we were trying to respond to questions from the governor's office. That effort also fell flat and it was clear that there was not a lot of support to go forward at the governor's level.

Jamie: And of course, by not being approved back four years ago, obviously it's going to be more costly for us.

Paul: Yes. It's more expensive now.

Jamie: I think there was confusion because the media was portraying a story that there was all this other hospital space. Oh, Lovelace had a great big old building right over here. Why didn't you just use that? My understanding is that if the issue is crumbling infrastructure, you are not going to be able to be state-of-the-art. That's what you do need when you're a Level One Trauma Center and an academic medical research center. It doesn't necessarily help you when you're trying to get out of crumbling infrastructure to move into a crumbling infrastructure. Right?

Paul: That's right. It doesn't help to move from one old facility to another old facility.

Jamie: In very layman's terms, I believe it was not well conveyed to the public that the costs to bring the Lovelace building up to snuff did not make that a reasonable alternative. I mean, anybody who's every pondered doing renovations versus buying something new has been faced with this dilemma. Sometimes what it's going to cost you to fix up something old is so costly you might as well just build new. Am I watering it down too much?

Paul: No. I think that accurately summarizes the problem. There was a lot of confusion about the intent of the new hospital at that time. There was push-back from one of the local hospitals that felt threatened by it. I think there was a lot of deliberate misinformation. One argument we had to respond to was, "Why we didn't just use empty beds at Lovelace Hospital." The problem with that is that in order to take care of the high acuity, highly complex patients, you need a nursing team. Facilities like ours require special imaging equipment as well as specialty nurses and doctors—i.e. we require specially designed facilities to manage those patients. So, you can't just take a major trauma patient and put them in any hospital bed. You can't do that and expect that they will live. That concept was ill conceived. But nevertheless, it was very publicly argued: why spend all this money when we could use empty beds in other facilities? There was also the rhetoric that we were building a boutique hospital that was only for rich people because the idea for the ninety-six-bed hospital was that it would be for scheduled surgical cases, not emergent. The emergency department would have remained at the current facility for the first phase and so all the traumas will still need to be there...and those aren't scheduled. And so, if we moved a large volume of surgical cases that could be scheduled like gall bladder operations and other non-emergent surgeries, we would increase our capacity. But the fact that those were scheduled, it was portrayed as well, "We're just wanting to do cosmetic surgery." It was portrayed as just a way to compete with the private sector, which was completely false. There was a lot of rhetoric and messaging going on opposing the facility and a lot of concern and criticism from the governor's office about the rationale for building the facility. We believe at least, that we answered all those questions but to no avail. We weren't able to get approval for the facility.

430

Jamie: We had just passed the mill levy right?

Paul: The mill levy. Yes.

Jamie: You did some surveys on that. Tell us about what the public opinion was.

Paul: A couple of years ago, we began preparing for the mill levy vote. We wanted to get a sense of where the voters were on that issue and it was clear that while the University of New Mexico Hospital was viewed very positively, there was still confusion. A lot of people didn't really understand the full scope of services and the value that the University of New Mexico Hospital brought to the community. As a result, we began a program to better inform the public through print, radio ads and through TV. We engaged in a number of marketing efforts to better inform the public about what their public funds were actually supporting. As a result of that, we were very successful.

Jamie: Do you remember the spread in Bernalillo County? What percentage voted for it?

Paul: It was fifty-eight percent.

Jamie: Did the Sandoval County mill levy pass?

Paul: No, the Sandoval County mill levy did not pass. There was a lot of pushback from the voters in Sandoval County where, by the way, we did not do a major information campaign. They were very much opposed to taxes. What was interesting in Sandoval County is that the mill levy in Sandoval County actually went to two hospitals. It supported the Sandoval Regional Medical Center but it also supported Presbyterian Rust Hospital. Many of the voters, when we surveyed them later, commented that if the tax were only going to the University of New Mexico, they would have voted for it. But they didn't think their tax dollars should go to essentially a private hospital. Presbyterian is a great hospital, but it's not a public hospital. So the voters were clear about not wanting public dollars to support a private entity.

Jamie: On the medical students, how many of the medical students do you send to rural communities when they graduate?

Paul: Well currently about forty percent of all of the practicing doctors in New Mexico graduated from our programs.

Jamie: Don't you have some sort of agreement that we recruit some of the students to go back to their rural areas?

Paul: Well we've got two things. We started something called the BA/MD program. We're celebrating our tenth anniversary this year. Two thousand six was the first year of the BA/MD. The tenth entry class actually began this past fall. The idea was to expand our class size in medical school so that there would be more opportunities for our graduates to stay in the state of New Mexico. Additionally, the data we had showed that for the previous twenty years, the percentage of graduating medical students returning to practice medicine in New Mexico plateaued at about twenty to twenty-five percent. I felt that we needed to do a better job than that. One way to do it, would just be to expand the class size and even if it stayed at twenty percent, there would be more practicing in New Mexico just by that alone. But the other data we had showed that those who did return usually had roots in New Mexico. And there was a higher percentage of under-represented students who not only had roots but felt a commitment to return and practice medicine in their communities. And so, we designed the program based on these facts. We would go out to high schools and recruit students from New Mexico high schools. Mostly from medically underserved areas of the state and we admitted those students into the BA/MD program. We partnered with the College of Art and Sciences on main campus to customize a curriculum that would be purely focused for those students. After successfully completing that curriculum they would automatically be admitted to the medical school.

Jamie: That was under your leadership. Am I correct?

Paul: Yes, I created that program.

Jamie: I remember that.

Paul: It's one of the things that I'm particularly proud of.

Jamie: So as we look to the future of healthcare in New Mexico and how the University of New Mexico Health Sciences Center has an important role to play, what do you think will be important for the future?

Paul: Dramatic reform will have to happen in higher education across the United States—particularly in flagship universities. Those challenges have to involve university-governing bodies to be fully engaged in coming up with solutions. At the same time, the Health Sciences Center here will continue to grow and there will be a dramatic increase in complexity of care. The new growth will require even more time and demand more effort and attention by the Regents. I hope there will be another review of the process of governance that would assure the success of the entire university. We are one university, but we clearly have three different segments of the University of New Mexico—each with its separate set of priorities and business models. We have the main university, which is an incredibly wonderful organization that is a traditional flagship university. We have a health sciences center with a totally different environment competing in a highly competitive marketplace. Additionally the way we go about our teaching and our research is radically different than the operations of a traditional university. And then, we have an athletic department that has a totally separate business model with their own demands, different requirements and different needs. Therefore, the leadership, the management, and the executive roles within the university must be designed to assure the success and advancement of all three pieces of the university. The governing body structure must similarly be designed to advocate and support the advancement of those three parts of a big flagship university like the University of New Mexico.

EPILOGUE

I never gave anybody hell! I just told the truth and they thought it was hell.
—Harry S. Truman

I hope I have accomplished what I set out to do, which was to give credit to the many extraordinary individuals I have had the honor of working with over the years. To those people I didn't mention, I apologize. There were many fellow legislators I worked with throughout the years to get legislation passed, both when I was a legislator and in later years when I led initiatives as a member of the Game and Fish Commission or as a member of the University of New Mexico Board of Regents.

I could not conclude this book without discussing my very close friendship with David Salman. I've mentioned him a few times in this book. He had at one time considered a run for governor. Due to a devastating head-on car accident, which severely limited his mobility, David did not run for governor. But if he had run, I would have supported him. He worked tirelessly and selflessly for the people of New Mexico. He was a terrific storyteller and we always said we would write a book together, so I know David would have been involved in this book if he were still here.

I mentioned in the introduction that I have been a member of Rotary Club, like my father, for fifty-eight years. I have a paperweight on my desk that states "The Four Way Test" that Rotary Club members are encouraged to follow. The International Rotary Club website:

my.rotary.org describes the Four Way Test as follows, "The Four-Way Test is a nonpartisan and nonsectarian ethical guide for Rotarians to use for their personal and professional relationships. The test has been translated into more than 100 languages, and Rotarians recite it at club meetings." The test is:

Of the things we think, say or do:

Is it the TRUTH?
Is it FAIR to all concerned?
Will it build GOOD WILL and BETTER FRIENDSHIPS?
Will it be BENEFICIAL to all concerned?

I have used this test throughout my lifetime to guide my decision-making process. These days, in the era of "fake news" it has become harder than ever it seems to ferret out the truth. But use the tools at your disposal. Hold elected officials accountable. I think the number one theme I strived to reiterate throughout this book is that being open and transparent in your actions is really important for all public servants. For that matter, it is important for everyone all the time. Every position I held I tried to ensure that the public could be involved in resolving problems and building consensus for solutions that everyone could live with.

Anyone can make an Inspection of Public Record Request (IPRA), not just journalists. Start reading the notices published online about what will be discussed at the meetings of public bodies. If you can make the time, start attending those meetings and creating dialogue with your elected representatives. If you don't like what someone had done that supposedly represents you, get out and vote. Most importantly, talk with your neighbors. Get to know them. I wrote this book as a series of conversations because everything I have ever accomplished has happened as a result of the relationships I was able to build upon. We are living through an era of increased polarization at every level of society. It really is important to listen to what everyone has to say and consider thoughtfully where you stand.

When I was on the Game and Fish Commission, I mentioned how Simon Gomez was able to change my opinion. Simon and I became very good friends. Sally Rodgers talked about how she and I didn't always see eye to eye but we've also been very good friends over the years. Billy Sparks complimented me on my ability to speak truth to power, but I never looked at it that way because I speak the truth to everyone I meet. You saw in my interview with interim president of the University of New Mexico, Chaouki Abdallah, that despite the fact that he organized over eight hundred people who were hell bent on my removal from the Regents, I never felt angry with him personally. To the contrary, I was very impressed with his obvious leadership skills.

When I began writing this book, I did not know that President Trump would be elected, although my family and friends can affirm that I predicted he would win. Now it seems, the Trump Administration's policies are on course to undermine some of the most important issues I have worked hard to promote and protect, including Open Meetings and Open Records, and I am especially concerned about the Trump Administration's attacks on the environment.

All I can say is, "If you are unhappy with the situation, change it." I hope this book has shown that every one of us has the ability to effect real changes if we set our minds to it. Finding other people that feel the same way won't happen by simply surfing your phone to read the latest trending news or texting someone. There is no substitute for meeting face-to-face with people. I am very grateful for all the people that contributed to this book.

Lastly, in the last few decades, American culture seems more and more focused on "get rich quick schemes" whether it's the national obsession with winning the lottery or the rise of "reality TV shows," where people become instant celebrities overnight. I hope we can reverse this tide and get our young people focused more on how they can make lasting contributions to their communities. Of all the initiatives I discussed in this book, the one I am the most proud of, is the replication of Project SEARCH here in New Mexico. I love this project because it demonstrates clearly that everyone, and I mean everyone, can make a positive contribution and be a productive member of society if we give him or her the chance.

I have worked hard in my career, but that wouldn't have happened if people hadn't helped me along the way. Jim Snead has helped others and me so many times. I can't even count how many times he has jumped in (without any compensation or the expectation of compensation), and he has helped solve a problem he didn't make. I especially want to thank my wife Nene, and my daughters Amy and Julie, for their love and their support. Help someone achieve his or her dreams and if you take nothing else away from this book, just remember President Truman's extremely wise words: "It's amazing what you can accomplish if you do not care who gets the credit."

BIBLIOGRAPHY

Books

Chapter 3:

McDuff, Leon. *Tererro*. Bloomington, Indiana: Trafford Publishing, 2006
Paulson, Morton. *The Great Land Hustle*. Washington, DC: Regnery
    Publishing, 1974
Wolff, Anthony. *Unreal Estate*, chapter "Showdown at Santa Fe." San
    Francisco, California: Sierra Club Books, 1973

Periodicals

Chapter 1:

James Madison, Federalist Paper #51
Business Wire news release for CNA, 1982

Chapter 2:

New Mexico Legislative Council Service, 1967

Chapter 4:

Haley Wachdorf, *New Mexico Business Weekly*, "The Kingmaker: Jamie
    Koch Telles It Like It is"

Chapter 8:

New Mexico Business Weekly, "Powerbrokers," 2009

Chapter 9:

U.S. News & World Report, 2016

Newspapers

Preface:

Brian Sanderoff, President of Research and Polling, Inc., *Albuquerque Journal*, January 29, 2017

Autumn Gray, *Albuquerque Journal*, 2010

Chapter 1:

Santa Fe Mirror, 1961

Albuquerque Tribune, February 4, 1974

Autumn Gray, *Albuquerque Journal*, April 26, 2010

Chapter 2:

Jack Sitton, *The Santa Fe New Mexican*, 1970 – "Koch Theatrics Aided Martinez"

The Independent

Albuquerque Journal, February 20, 1973

Chapter 3:

Rio Grande Sun, March 31, 1994

Kate McGraw, *The Roswell Daily Record*, March 7, 1993

Cheryl Wittenauer, *The Santa Fe New Mexican*, September 6, 1990

Associated Press, *The Santa Fe New Mexican*, February 17, 1993

Chapter 7:

Editorial, *Albuquerque Journal*, May 17, 2017

Major Ca pital Projects

Chapter 8:

New Facilities – Major Capital Projects 2003 to 2015

ACKNOWLEDGMENTS

I did not interview President Bob Frank because at that time he was in the middle of negotiations with the current Board of Regents to renew his contract when I was originally working on this book. I felt it would not have been appropriate for me to insert myself in the middle of that process. I had a good association with Bob and we were able to accomplish many things together. Bob's contributions include: improving student success in retention and graduation rates; creation of Innovate ABQ and the Innovation Academy which includes raising $6.5M which led to the creation of the Lobo Rainforest Building opening August 2017; creation of the Honors College; creation of the College of Population Health; and record breaking fundraising including a 30% increase in the university's endowment. He made more than $100M in gift requests.

When I served as president of the Board of Regents, and later as chairman of the Finance Committee and Lobo Development Committee, I was able to get a lot done because I had the full support of my fellow Regents. I want to thank the following former Regents for their exceptional professional conduct and their dedication to serving the university. Thank you to: Carolyn Abeyta, Dahlia Dorman, Douglas Brown, Andrea Cook, James Conrad, Jacob Wellman, Emily (Kate) Wisdom, Heidi Overton, Ryan Berryman and Rosalind Nguyen.

There are two outstanding former Regents that I wish to recognize: Sandra Begaye and Maria Griego-Raby.

Sandra Begaye served on the Regents from 2001 until 2006. Her roles with the University of New Mexico include past Board membership: the University of New Mexico Foundation, the University of New Mexico School of Engineering Advisory Council and the University of New Mexico Civil Engineering Committee. Her current roles are STC University of New Mexico Board Chair, the University of New Mexico Alumni Board Executive Committee, Hibbon Foundation Board and NSF University of New Mexico Civil Engineering Water Initiative Advisory Committee. I hope that Sandra will be able to get back onto the Board of Regents in the future.

Maria Griego-Raby was an outstanding Regent appointed in 2003. There are so many important contributions Maria has made to the university, some of which include: currently sitting on the Board of STC, currently on the Lobo Development Board, previous president of the University of New Mexico Alumni Association, previous president of the University of New Mexico Hospital Board, and she sponsored a University of New Mexico Presidential Scholar Student for over 20 years. This is the type of person who should be on the University of New Mexico Regents and I hope that she can eventually get back onto the Board of Regents.

Don Chalmers passed away. If he hadn't, I am sure that he would have become president of the Board of Regents. He was a tremendous supporter of the university and has been greatly missed.

Jack Fortner is the longest serving Regent, appointed in 1999 by Governor Gary Johnson. He retired from the Regents, August 2017. Jack received the Alumni Lobo Award honors as a graduate distinguished by professional achievement or dedication to the betterment of the university.

I intentionally did not interview any of the current Board of Regents at the time I was writing this book. I felt it would not have been appropriate to do so since this book is only about the time of my participation with the Regents.

There is one outstanding former Alumni president that I wish to give recognition to: Steve Ciepiela. He was president of the Alumni Lettermen in 1987 and president of the Alumni Association in 2003. Steve started attending Regents meetings in 2003 when the university signed the first MOU with the Alumni Association. He was first involved with the Alumni Lettermen when Bobby Santiago was president. He served on that board until 1995. He also served on the Alumni Board from 1996 until 2004. He managed the Alumni Association' funds until 2013, growing the account to over $7M. Steve attended the University of New Mexico on a football scholarship and received his master's degree from the University of New Mexico in Public Administration. Steve cofounded Charles Stephen and Company, Inc. in 1983, a multifaceting financial planning service. In his role as president of the University of New Mexico Alumni Association, he was instrumental in getting the University of New Mexico to give Hodgin Hall Alumni Center, the "Heart and Soul" of the University of New Mexico, to the Alumni Association. With Steve's business and university background, I would hope that he would be considered for a Regent in the future.

Similarly on the Game and Fish Commission, I was fortunate to serve with an equally conscientious group of people. I wish to thank those commissioners also for their work. The commissioners I served with included: Robert Forrest, Ed Munoz, Dr. A.H. Gutierrez, Christine Di Gregorio, Robert Jones, David Salman, Bruce Wilson, Jake Alcon and Andrea Maes Chavez.

Finally, there are two individuals that have been part of my political success for decades. Steve Flance and Bill Sisneros have raised funds and organized campaigns. They have been stalwart supporters throughout the years. We've worked together on every campaign I have been involved in.

Steve has a BA in Liberal Arts and an MS degree in Community Development from the University of Missouri and served three years in the U.S. Peace Corps. He spent five years with the City of Santa Fe as Assistant Planning Director, Director of Community Development and Assistant City Manager. In 1975 Steve established The Flance Company and for the past forty-two years has been engaged in planning, development and marketing of high quality resorts and residential communities in the Santa Fe area. Steve worked on political campaigns for Senator Jeff Bingaman, Governor Bruce King and Governor Bill Richardson. Steve is well known for hosting outstanding fundraisers at his home for the candidates he is supporting.

Bill obtained a Master Degree (MPA) in Urban Affairs and Public Administration from the University of Colorado at Boulder in 1972. He is the former CEO and executive director of the New Mexico Finance Authority, an infrastructure financing and development bank. The Finance Authority received a AAA Rating for its bonds 2003 through 2011. Bill is the owner of Jenkeel, Ltd., a New Mexico Corporation doing business as El Gancho Athletic Club. The Club has served Santa Fe for 28 years. It is a full service athletic club offering fitness, swim and racquet sports. Bill was formerly City Manager of Santa Fe and Taos in New Mexico, as well as former Assistant City Manager in Boulder, CO and administrative assistant to the City Manager in Englewood, Colorado. In the early 1980s, Bill founded EnRes, Inc. Consultants, specializing in management and organization development consulting and land development process consulting. He provided services to both public and private sector clients. Bill was elected and served as Santa Fe County Democratic Chairman from 1999 to 2001 and resigned to serve as political director for the Bill Richardson campaign. In 2003 he was elected chairman of the New Mexico Democratic Party by unanimous vote. Bill was responsible for getting 80% of the state democratic votes for the Governor Richardson at the state convention.

As I worked through editing the thirty-nine interviews I conducted to create this book, I realized I needed to streamline the information to create a manageable sized book. I originally had over seven hundred pages to edit. I just couldn't interview everyone I wanted to. About sixty hours of interviews were conducted in this process. I wish to thank Ruth Frank since she did all of the transcribing of the interviews.

Jennifer Sparks is an established and recognized writer, producer and director. She has been successful as a marketing and communications professional with broad agency, governmental and non-profit organizations. Jennifer graduated Cum Laude from the University of Chicago with a degree in European History. She did extensive research for me to compile the data and create a clear impactful draft into a highly readable narrative with a clear beginning, middle and end. She spent over three hundred hours reviewing old newspaper clippings, minutes from state commissions and governor appointed boards I served on throughout my sixty years of public service. Jennifer was the facilitator and editor for each of the persons I interviewed for these conversations.

Barbara Gay has been working off and on for the legislature during the legislative sessions since 1979. I have known her for over forty years. In 2003, Barbara jointed Governor Richardson's staff as part of his management team and also as legislative liaison. In 2006, she joined the New Mexico Supreme Court which also included acting as legislative liaison. In 2015 she started researching all of the legislation I introduced during my time at the legislature, obtaining copies as well as my voting records for me to use in this book.

Sylvia Palmer and I have worked together at Daniels Insurance in Santa Fe for the past thirty-nine years and with her insurance credentials I was able to successfully provide insurance for many, many New Mexico clients. Sylvia and I have spent well over one hundred hours reviewing and editing the contents of this book into a final document.

The author on a pack trip in the Peco wilderness in 2014.

CPSIA information can be obtained
at www.ICGtesting.com
Printed in the USA
FFOW01n1134300418
46395129-48166FF